WORLD LITERATURE IN THE SOVIET UNION

Studies in Comparative Literature and Intellectual History

Series Editor
Galin Tihanov (Queen Mary University of London)

Other Titles in this Series
Fate, Nature, and Literary Form: The Politics of the Tragic in Japanese Literature
Kinya Nishi

Travels from Dostoevsky's Siberia: Encounters with Polish Literary Exiles
Edited and Translated by Elizabeth A. Blake

Inspired by Bakhtin: Dialogic Methods in the Humanities
Edited by Matthias Freise

Dostoevsky as a Translator of Balzac
Julia Titus

Heterotopic World Fiction: Thinking Beyond Biopolitics with Woolf, Foucault, Ondaatje
Lesley Higgins and Marie-Christine Leps

Visions of the Future: Malthusian Thought Experiments in Russian Literature (1840–1960)
Natasha Grigorian

Reading Novels Translingually: Twenty-First-Century Case Studies
Julie Hansen

For more information on this series, please visit:
academicstudiespress.com/studiesincomplit

WORLD LITERATURE IN THE SOVIET UNION

Edited by
Galin Tihanov,
Anne Lounsbery,
and Rossen Djagalov

BOSTON
2023

Library of Congress Control Number: 2023042825

Copyright © 2023, Academic Studies Press
All rights reserved.

ISBN 9798887194158 (hardback)
ISBN 9798887194165 (Adobe PDF)
ISBN 9798887194172 (ePub)

Cover design by Ivan Grave.
On the cover: Maksim Gorky with the staff of Vsemirnaia Literatura, 1919.

Book design by Kryon Publishing Services.

Published by Academic Studies Press
1577 Beacon Street
Brookline, MA 02446, USA
press@academicstudiespress.com
www.academicstudiespress.com

Contents

Acknowledgments	vii
Introduction *Galin Tihanov, Anne Lounsbery, and Rossen Djagalov*	ix

1. World Literature in the Soviet Union: Infrastructure and Ideological Horizons   1
   Galin Tihanov

2. On the Worldliness of Russian Literature   25
   Anne Lounsbery

3. Armenian Literature as World Literature: Phases of Shaping it in the Pre-Soviet and Stalinist Contexts   35
   Susanne Frank

4. The Roles of "Form" and "Content" in World Literature as Discussed by Viktor Shklovsky in His Writings of the Immediately Post-Revolutionary Years   67
   Katerina Clark

5. *"The Treasure Trove of World Literature"*: Shaping the Concept of World Literature in Post-Revolutionary Russia   91
   Maria Khotimsky

6. The Birth of New out of Old: Translation in Early Soviet History   119
   Sergey Tyulenev

7. *International Literature*: A Multi-Language Soviet Journal as a Model of "World Literature" of the Mid-1930s USSR   137
   Elena Ostrovskaya, Elena Zemskova, Evgeniia Belskaia, Georgii Korotkov

8. Translating China into *International Literature*:
   Stalin-Era World Literature Beyond the West   165
   Edward Tyerman

9. World Literature and Ideology: The Case of Socialist Realism   189
   Schamma Schahadat

10. Premature Postcolonialists: The Afro-Asian
    Writers' Association (1958–1991) and Its Literary Field   207
    Rossen Djagalov

11. Can "Worldliness" Be Inscribed into the Literary Text?:
    Russian Diasporic Writing in the Context of World Literature   237
    Maria Rubins

    Contributors   263

    Index   267

Acknowledgments

The volume is based, in part, on the proceedings of workshops on world literature in the Soviet Union held at Queen Mary University of London (QMUL) and at New York University (NYU). The London workshop was organized under the auspices of the Open World Research Initiative (OWRI) funded by the UK Arts and Humanities Research Council (AHRC). The New York workshop was sponsored by the Jordan Center for the Advanced Study of Russia at NYU which also provided a generous subvention that made the publication of the book possible. The editors extend their gratitude to both the UK AHRC and the NYU Jordan Centre for the Advanced Study of Russia. Thanks also to Academic Studies Press (ASP) for accepting this volume in its series on comparative literature and intellectual history, to Alessandra Anzani and Ekaterina Yanduganova for their expert editorial assistance, and to Alana Felton for her excellent work as copyeditor.

Introduction

Russian interest in world literature predates 1917, but it was the October Revolution that gave special impetus to this attention so that it could begin to materialize, not least through generous state support.[1] The contributions to this wide-ranging volume, the first to consistently examine Soviet engagement with world literature from multiple institutional and disciplinary perspectives (intellectual literary; literary history and theory; comparative literature; translation studies; diaspora studies, to name but a few), focus on Soviet Russia, encompassing a period of some seventy years, while not neglecting the post-Soviet space where preoccupations with world literature continue to be relevant in the context of Russophone (often diasporic) writing. Our emphasis is on the lessons one could learn from the Soviet attention to world literature, both institutionally and intellectually; as such, we hope that the present volume would make a significant contribution to current debates on world literature beyond the field of Slavic and East European Studies and would foreground the need to think of world literature pluralistically, in a manner that is not restricted by the agendas of Anglophone academe.

***

The opening chapter of the volume, by Galin Tihanov, seeks to 'multiply' world literature and demonstrate that there is no world literature per se, but rather different world literatures, because at different times different communities produce different constructs that they label as world literature. Foremost amongst the lessons one could draw from the Soviet engagement with world literature is the compelling determination of Soviet intellectuals to conceive of world literature in a systematically non-Occidentocentric manner. With this, the Soviets were pioneering an approach to world literature that foreshadows our current concerns. But there is also another lesson emerging from the Soviet preoccupation with world literature: the conversation on world literature does

---

1 For earlier accounts of the Soviet engagement with world literature, see the literature in Galin Tihanov's contribution to this volume (esp. page 5 footnote 4).

not proceed in a vacuum, it is constantly interacting with, impacting on, and being impacted by, the conversation societies have about national literatures and literary theory. The chapter begins by briefly adumbrating four historically attestable meanings of 'world literature,' some of which can be seen at work in the Soviet discourse on world literature; it then identifies three different cultural and ideological horizons (or frameworks) of thinking about world literature in the Soviet Union and, significantly, locates their common ground—the glue that bound them together—in the master approach of de-Westernizing the very notion of world literature, an attitude consistently enacted by Soviet intellectuals engaging with the history of world literature.

The second chapter, Anne Lounsbery's "On the Worldliness of Russian Literature," opens with an inventory of Russia's omissions from world literature scholarship. Rather than viewing them as a lapse (because it seems implausible to assume that all these scholars simply forget about, say, Tolstoy), Lounsbery asks what has made this sort of erasure possible—or perhaps even necessary? Could serious acknowledgement of Russia throw a wrench into western models of World Literature? *Must* Russian literature be absent from systems like Casanova's? Her answer to this question grows out of nineteenth-century Russian literary texts themselves. These texts reveal an inchoate awareness that a category like World Literature—as it is articulated in the West—will not be able to accommodate them. In effect, classical Russian novels predict the neglect they will suffer at the hands of such systems, which is precisely the neglect that the Soviets' new conceptions of World Literature will aim to redress.

Most of the following chapters in this book are devoted to the Soviet project for World Literature. A consistent theme in some of them, however, are the continuities between Soviet and pre-revolutionary conceptualizations of World Literature and practical efforts to realize them. Thus, focusing on the example of Armenian literature, Susanne Frank's chapter "Armenian Literature as World Literature: Phases of Shaping It in the Pre-Soviet and Stalinist Contexts" reconstructs the modelling of the national canon of Armenian literature from 1915 throughout the twentieth century and demonstrates that already in the late imperial period, Armenian literature was conceptualized as "world literature." The chapter also asks what happened to the canon when Armenian literature was reshaped as part of Soviet multinational literature and its most important contemporary representatives fell victim to Stalinism. It ends by retracing the phases of their re-canonization in later Soviet Union and in post-Soviet times.

By contrast, Katerina Clark's chapter, "The Roles of 'Form' and 'Content' in World Literature as Discussed by Viktor Shklovsky in his Writings of the

Immediately Post-Revolutionary Years," focuses on some of the intellectual breakthroughs of the early Soviet era. Clark opens her chapter with Franco Moretti's conceptualization of the novel's worldwide journey from the Anglo-French core to the periphery "as a compromise between foreign form and local content" and then, using Shklovsky's writings and biography between 1917 and 1923, moves on to reconstruct the evolution in the latter's thinking on the form-content binary. Clark concludes that over this half-decade Shklovsky made a double shift as compared with his pre-revolutionary writings: both a shift from a primary concern with the impact of specific features on the beholder/reader to a concern with overall plot organization and the orchestration of formal techniques, and a shift from relying exclusively on Russian literature to a main focus on West European literature. These shifts, she demonstrates, occurred as a result of Shklovsky's work in the "World Literature" (*Vsemirnaia Literatura*) publishing house.

Appropriately, the next two articles concern that publishing house, which Maxim Gorky spearheaded shortly within months of the October Revolution and which existed for another five years. Conceived as a grandiose enterprise, it could not, under the conditions of the Civil War and post-Civil War institutional fragility, realize its ambition to translate "the treasures" of world literature into Russian. Nevertheless, it not only came to provide subsistence to some of Russia's leading writers and intellectuals during these hungry times but also defined subsequent trends for Soviet translation. More specifically, in her chapter, "'The Treasure Chest of World Literature': Shaping the Concept of World Literature in Post-Revolutionary Russia," Maria Khotimsky examines early Soviet attempts to define the concept of world literature and the publishing house's practical efforts to present world literary heritage to the Soviet readers. She does so by analyzing the programmatic statements in the publishing house's first two catalogues and then the paratextual practices of the actual translations.

In his chapter, "The Birth of New Out of Old: Translation in Early Soviet History," Sergey Tyulenev tempers the novelties introduced by the publishing house with its inevitable reliance on pre-revolutionary traditions. The first generation of translators and members of the editorial board were representatives of the pre-revolutionary literary intelligentsia and as such selected pieces from the old world, which was supposed to be "destroyed to its foundation." Tyulenev sees the overall project as a series of negotiations between continuities and discontinuities, ideological problems and suggested solutions, challenges and compromises, which came to define the new Soviet school of literary translation.

The *Vsemirnaia Literatura* chapters are followed by two others that deal with a slightly later institution that grounded Soviet literary internationalism: the multilingual magazine *International Literature* (1931–1943). In their chapter, entitled "*International Literature*: A Multi-Language Soviet Journal as a Model of 'World Literature' of the Mid-1930s USSR," Elena Ostrovskaya, Elena Zemskova, Evgeniia Belskaia, and Georgii Korotkov offer the first holistic account of this journal across its four main linguistic sections (Russian, English, German, and French), seeing in it a utopian space in construction, premised on total translatability of world literature. The four different editions were, however, never uniform and the authors use the tools of digital humanities to establish their differences.

Edward Tyerman's contribution, "Translating China into *International Literature*: Stalin-Era World Literature Beyond the West," comes to similar conclusions regarding the centrality of translatability to the Soviet project for World Literature by examining the translation of contemporary Chinese literature on the pages of the magazine, and more specifically, the Soviet negotiation of the tensions between difference and commensurability within its literary map of the globe. Focusing on two case studies—Emi Siao's poems and Lu Xun's short stories—he concludes that Soviet translators of the 1930s sought to affirm the principle of translatability of Chinese culture. Texts produced in diverse global spaces reached the Soviet reader as commensurable specimens of "international literature," rendered legible through translation and accompanying paratextual materials (introductions, critical essays, photographs, etc.).

Concluding the interwar history of the Soviet Republic of Letters, Schamma Schahadat's chapter, "World Literature and Ideology: The Case of Socialist Realism," finds the Republic's most explicit articulation in Maxim Gorky's and Karl Radek's famous speeches delivered at the inaugural Writers Congress. The literary histories with which their accounts open culminate in the Soviet-proletarian-socialist realist literature of the 1930s. In this vision, Moscow emerges as a capital of both the worldwide international proletarian literature and Soviet multinational literature.

Taking us to the post-WWII reconfiguration of Soviet literary internationalism, Rossen Djagalov's chapter, "Premature Postcolonialists: The Afro-Asian Writers' Association (1958–1991) and Its Literary Field," traces the rise and fall of this international organization that sought to be the literary equivalent of the Non-Aligned Movement, except that it was aligned: thanks to the writers of Soviet Central Asia and the Caucasus, Soviet literary bureaucracies were able to claim a prominent place on the Afro-Asian table. Relying on the archives of Soviet literary internationalism and the biographies of multiple Association members (now canonical postcolonial writers), this chapter places it in the longer history of Soviet literary internationalism and competing Cold-War literary internationalisms and then describes the main structures through which it sought to forge its own literary field: literary congresses, a Permanent Bureau, a multi-lingual literary quarterly (*Lotus: Afro-Asian Writings*) and an Afro-Asian literary Prize (also Lotus), institutions that remind us of interwar-era Soviet literary internationalism.

The volume ends in the present moment and outside of Russia, with Maria Rubins's chapter "Can 'Worldliness' Be Inscribed into the Literary Text? Russian Diasporic Writing in the Context of World Literature." Focusing on Andrei Makine's novels, the poetry of the Ferghana school, and the transcultural pluralistic practices of contemporary Russian-Israeli writers, she returns to the question of (un)translatability, which concerned early Soviet writers, translators, and critics, too, but which contemporary Russophone diasporic writing tends to resolve completely differently. Their search for the untranslatable becomes a means for inscribing their worldliness into the text. Rubins's analysis, thus, articulates the self-reflexive strategies of authors who depend on the Russian publishing industry yet reject Russian national identity and try to position themselves in a broader, if imprecisely defined, "world."

Galin Tihanov, Anne Lounsbery, and Rossen Djagalov

CHAPTER 1

World Literature in the Soviet Union: Infrastructure and Ideological Horizons

Galin Tihanov

This text wants to pursue a somewhat different direction in the current conversation on world literature; it seeks to 'multiply' world literature and demonstrate that *there is no world literature per se, but rather different world literatures,* because at different times different communities produce different constructs that they label as world literature. In my title, I signal that here we are dealing with answers to the questions what world literature is and how to write its history that come from Soviet Russia, encompassing a period of some seventy years. My emphasis is on the lessons one could learn from the Soviet attention to world literature; foremost amongst these is the compelling determination of Soviet intellectuals to conceive of world literature in a systematically non-Occidentocentric manner. With this, the Soviets were pioneering an approach to world literature that foreshadows our current concerns, as I will try to demonstrate. But there is also another lesson emerging from the Soviet preoccupation with world literature: the conversation on world literature does not proceed in a vacuum, it is constantly interacting with, impacting on, and being impacted by, the conversation societies have about national literatures and literary theory. I begin by briefly adumbrating four historically attestable meanings of 'world literature' that are still at work in the Soviet debates; I then identify three different cultural and ideological horizons (or frameworks) of thinking about world literature in the Soviet Union and, significantly, locate their common ground, the glue that bound them together, in the master approach of de-Westernizing the very notion of world literature, an attitude consistently enacted by Soviet intellectuals engaging with the history of world literature.

Four Meanings of 'World Literature'

I commence with a brief exploration of exactly what is meant by 'world literature,' so that we could fathom the relevance of its various meanings to the debates in Soviet Russia. I will single out four facets of the concept of world literature. Let me begin with the first understanding which continues to be significant: the understanding of world literature as *evidence and embodiment of cultural diversity*. Needless to say, this understanding is today upheld by various cultural institutions that (re)produce the materiality of world literature; literary prizes and international book festivals play a particularly salient part, the latter often operating on an almost quota basis that ensures diversity is honored and championed, sometimes at the expense of overlooking aesthetic preeminence. The roots of this understanding of world literature go back to the end of the eighteenth century, to the work of historians and literati, notably Schlözer and Herder. Coincidentally, Schlözer was a historian of Russia (but also an author in the tradition of what at the time would be referred to as 'universal history') who spent some not inconsiderable time in St. Petersburg before accepting a chair at the University of Göttingen. Schlözer conceives of world literature precisely as evidence and embodiment of the world's cultural diversity. From this point of view, for him, there are no large and small literatures in the evaluative sense we would read into this opposition today. On the contrary, for Schlözer, even the smallest literature can be an object of admiration, of study and of cultivating the ability of recognizing and accepting cultural difference.[1] This attitude is also recognizable in Herder's work; Herder also behaves as a collector of samples of the literatures and oral cultures of various communities. By the second (posthumous) edition of his famous anthology, *Stimmen der Völker in Liedern* (Voices of the Peoples in Songs), which has a complicated editorial history into which I will not go on this occasion, we find examples from Peru, Madagascar, etc. This unrelenting push to absorb the cultural diversity of the world is, of course, related to the philosophical tendency of the time, which tries to imagine an extended humanity and to 'find' signs of rational life far beyond the borders of Europe; at the same time, the Enlightenment begins to work out in earnest the

---

1   On Schlözer, Herder, and world literature, with references to the relevant secondary literature, see G. Tihanov, "Cosmopolitanism in the Discursive Landscape of Modernity: Two Enlightenment Articulations," in *Enlightenment Cosmopolitanism*, ed. David Adams and Galin Tihanov (London: Legenda, 2011), 133–152, esp. 142, and G. Tihanov, "Introduction," in *Vergleichende Weltliteraturen/Comparative World Literatures*, ed. Dieter Lamping and Galin Tihanov (Stuttgart: Metzler, 2020), 283–287.

doctrine of Eurocentrism, according to which European literature and culture are the pinnacle of civilization, while the monuments of culture one locates outside of Europe should serve as little more than intriguing, even praiseworthy, but rarely perfect iterations of universal rationality. In Soviet Russia, as we shall see, this ambivalent drive towards incorporating non-Western literatures and cultures whilst preserving the educational and cultural primacy of the European canon is very much on display.

The second understanding of world literature which is actively present in the debates in Soviet Russia sees world literature as a special *conduit of culture, of knowledge, erudition, and as a mechanism that cultivates the ability to communicate.* The beginning of this understanding of world literature can be attributed to Wieland who briefly wrote at the turn of the nineteenth century about world literature as a source of new knowledge about the world that is bound to enhance one's capacity of communicating with others. This is a slightly different view of world literature, an understanding related to what in Foucauldian language might be called "practices of the self," although Wieland is not at all interested in the intervention of power or the role institutions would play in this essentially humanistic pedagogical project. He seems to envision this process as pure, unencumbered, and unmediated. The individual is alone in the company of good literature: it enriches him/her, s/he learns in the process; as a result, the human within the individual expands, and the valences of communication multiply.

These two possible definitions of world literature begin to converge and intertwine in a visible way in the third understanding of world literature: world literature conceived of as a *canon,* as all the best and most enduring that humanity has succeeded in producing, taken, according to the first understanding, from all possible sources, from all parts of the world, from small and large cultures, from cultures of colonizers and of the colonized. This is a humanistic, often conservative understanding of world literature, which also often forgets to ask the crucial questions about politics, power, and history. This understanding of world literature has proved tenacious and resilient, it continues to shape, in no small measure, current notions and practices of world literature.

The last definition of world literature, the last type of understanding I want to articulate, is historically much more recent; it is related to polemics around world literature which take us into the twenty-first century. David Damrosch's ground-breaking, and later often interrogated and contested, *What is World Literature?*[2] works out an understanding of world literature that is different from

---

2   David Damrosch, *What is World Literature?* (Princeton: Princeton University Press, 2003).

the first three in that it is interested not solely (perhaps not even as much) in literature per se and seeks instead to establish a common denominator between literature and other discourses. Here, literature becomes a *participant in an endless flow of information* which, through translation and intermedial adaptation, transgresses national, linguistic, and discursive boundaries. It is not by chance that Damrosch defines the subject of world literature as the study of the *circulation of texts in translation*. This idea of circulation is not insignificant; it is part and parcel of this new understanding of literature as inclusive and representative of larger information flows and exchanges.

All this seems to me to be verily important because it is an understanding that finds itself in tension with the idea of world literature as a canon. In some ways, Damrosch's approach to world literature is foreshadowed by Goethe's. Of course, the idea of world literature did not begin with Goethe in 1827 (an already old Goethe talking to Eckermann, and Eckermann writing down these conversations years later based on the notes he took, sometimes producing entire sentences or even paragraphs out of a few keywords); in fact, this entire discourse commenced about fifty years earlier, with Schlözer and Wieland. What Goethe did, however, unlike Schlözer and Wieland, was to dynamize the notion of world literature. Schlözer, Wieland, and Herder would imagine world literature as statically available, they were not particularly interested in the dialogue or the communication between different literatures from different cultural zones. The samples of writing that caught their attention would often inhabit the drawers of an imaginary cabinet of curiosities; these samples could always be conveniently pulled out, enjoyed, and put back in their place again, without any stipulation or expectation of interaction between them.

Goethe, however, believed that world literature is an effect of the transborder communication of entire networks of people involved in the production of literature: writers, translators (a no doubt important group), critics, and readers.[3] Without communication between these networks, world literature would not be impossible: in this sense, it is not a given any more (as it was for his predecessors), it is a task (hence his belief that its advent could be accelerated). In a sense, Damrosch retains this pragmatic disposition, but he tends to further de-canonize world literature and really only imagines it as *one* of the ingredients of the information flow that globalization has made possible. To this, he also

---

3   The literature on Goethe and *Weltliteratur* is vast; of the more recent comprehensive accounts, see, e.g. Dieter Lamping, *Die Idee der Weltliteratur. Ein Konzept Goethes und seine Karriere* (Stuttgart: Metzler, 2010).

adds the logic of the market and its mechanisms (something already present in an inchoate manner in Goethe's vision of world literature).

Marx, of course, is also relevant here, partly because we are talking about the Soviet debates, but also because Marx and Engels, in *The Communist Manifesto*, twenty-one years after Goethe, return to his idea, now insisting on the emergence of world literature as inevitable. According to them, this inevitability is grounded in the expansion (but also contraction) of the world that is available to us, which is in turn rooted in technological progress and homogenization as a result of the global spread of the capitalist mode of production that really knows no national boundaries, just like the world literature that they believed, passionately and perhaps somewhat naively, would ineluctably supersede national literatures.

The Soviet Interest in World Literature: Chronology and Infrastructure

Russian interest in world literature predates 1917, but it was the October Revolution that gave special impetus to this attention so that it could begin to materialize, not least through generous state support.[4] The founding father of the Soviet discourse of world literature is an intellectual who cannot be contained within the narrow confines of Marxism; even as he was often a proponent of left-leaning policies and ideology, Maxim Gorky was an *enfant terrible* more than a predictably loyal fellow-traveler. It was Gorky who founded, in the midst of a brutal civil war, an important publishing house with the support of his influential friends in the communist hierarchy; "Vsemirnaia Literatura" ('World Literature',

---

4   For a general account of the Soviet engagement with world literature between the two world wars, see Annie Epelboin, "Littérature mondiale et Révolution," in *Où est la littérature mondiale?* (Saint-Denis: Presses Universitaires de Vincennes, 2005), 39–49; for a more essayistic account see Jérôme David, *Spectres de Goethe: les métamorphoses de la 'littérature mondiale'* (Paris: Les Prairies Ordinaires, 2011) (there the chapter "Petrograd, 1918"). More recently, see, amongst others, Rossen Djagalov, *From Internationalism to Postcolonialism: Literature and Cinema Between the Second and the Third Worlds* (Montreal: McGill-Queen's University Press, 2020); Amelia M. Glaser and Steven S. Lee, eds., *Comintern Aesthetics* (Toronto: University of Toronto Press, 2020); Katerina Clark, *Eurasia Without Borders: The Dream of a Leftist Literary Commons, 1919–1943* (Cambridge, MA: Harvard University Press, 2021). For seminal studies that go beyond the Soviet period and look at Russian literature and culture from a global perspective, see Kevin Platt, ed., *Global Russian Cultures* (Madison: The University of Wisconsin Press, 2018) and Maria Rubins, ed., *Redefining Russian Literary Diaspora, 1920–2020* (London: UCL Press, 2021).

1918–1923) was a focal point of Soviet Russia's efforts to bring to the masses a canon of world literature that would serve an educational purpose with a noble, levelling-up social intent. This was an extremely ambitious, perhaps even megalomaniac undertaking. In its strongest years, the publishing house would employ on its various projects around three hundred-fifty people who would receive honoraria and other payments even when they would not deliver on the contracts they had signed.[5] But that was not all: alongside the publishing house, there was a translation theory studio. We find some of the Petrograd Formalists, notably Shklovsky and Tynianov, amongst the lecturers in that studio,[6] next to recognized translators such as Chukovskii. There was also a studio for young writers who needed to learn the basics of literary theory. As one can appreciate (but this has not happened until now), Gorky's project envisaged and produced an organic connection between creative writing and literary and translation theory. It is vital to recognize that very early on literary and translation theory went hand in hand in Soviet Russia, and that they did so in productive symbiosis with creative writing. (Shklovsky's memoires of the 1920s, especially his *A Sentimental Journey*, is one of the most powerful examples of this symbiosis.) For too long, we have tended to treat literary theory as pure sublimation, a sum total of principles and approaches that are detached from, and hierarchically elevated above, the practice of creative writing. This foundational synergy between theory and creative writing, as well as the effective coexistence of literary and translation theory, are crucial in understanding the genesis of the modern notion of world literature, for which translation, as Damrosch persuasively argues, is as indispensable as is the belief in what, elsewhere, I have termed "the portability of literariness."[7]

Less than a decade after the demise of Gorky's World Literature publishing house, and in the year when Gorky returned to the Soviet Union for good, the Soviet infrastructure of research in, and appropriation of, world literature

---

5   There is a considerable body of research on the "World Literature" publishing house; the details adduced above can be found in the documentation and introduction in "A. M. Gor'kii—organizator izdatel'stva "Vsemirnaia literatura," *Istoricheskii arkhiv*, no. 2 (1958): 67–95. Of the more recent work, see, e.g., Maria Khotimsky, "World Literature, Soviet Style: A Forgotten Episode in the History of an Idea," *Ab Imperio*, no. 3 (2013): 119–154, and Sergey Tyulenev, "*Vsemirnaia Literatura*: Intersections between Translating and Original Literary Writing," *Slavic and East European Journal* 60, no. 1 (2016): 8–21.

6   On Shklovsky and world literature (and on his mixed reactions to Gorky's project), see Galin Tihanov, "World Literature, War, Revolution: The Significance of Viktor Shklovskii's *A Sentimental Journey*," in *Transnational Russian Studies*, ed. Andy Byford, Connor Doak and Stephen Hutchings (Liverpool: Liverpool University Press, 2020), 112–126.

7   See the epilogue in my book *The Birth and Death of Literary Theory: Regimes of Relevance in Russia and Beyond* (Stanford: Stanford University Press, 2019).

underwent expansion through the creation of the Institute of World Literature (IMLI: Institut mirovoi literatury; in Russian, there is a subtle but not insignificant difference between 'vsemirnaia' and 'mirovaia,' which deserves special treatment beyond the scope of this text). Significantly, when IMLI was founded in 1932, the adjective 'world' was absent from the title; named in honor of Gorky, the new institution was called simply The Maxim Gorky Institute of Literature. At the time this would be interpreted as Stalin's reward for Gorky's many contributions (or, by some, as a preemptive bribe that would make it difficult for Gorky to dissent from the Party line). Only in 1938, after the death of Gorky, was the Institute renamed, and from then on to this day it continues to be known as the Institute of World Literature. The question arises as to what exactly had happened in Soviet Russia in the intervening years to make it both possible and necessary to rename this scientific institute and include the descriptor "world" in its title. By the mid-1930s, the USSR had begun changing its cultural policy, actively seeking the support of left-wing democratic intellectuals from the West.[8] By that time, the queue of prominent visitors to the USSR was growing longer; anybody who was somebody would be invited, especially if s/he was of leftist or at least democratic persuasion: Henri Barbusse, Romain Rolland, Lion Feuchtwanger, and even André Gide, a choice the Soviets would later regret, because upon his return he would write his famous book of detraction, *Return from the Soviet Union*, in which he made a number of observations the Soviet authorities would perceive as extremely unpleasant, nay offensive. (Lion Feuchtwanger offered a competing narrative designed to demonstrate solidarity with the Soviet regime: *Moscow 1937: my visit described for my friends.*) This is also the time when the Soviets would send delegations to various international fora taking place in the West, notably to the First International Congress of Writers for the Defense of Culture in Paris in 1935. The Soviet delegation in Paris included prominent Russian-Jewish writers; in Paris, these Soviet intellectuals practiced what could oxymoronically be called licensed dissidence: Pasternak, Babel, and Ehrenburg talked about a humanism that tends to eschew class ideology and veers rather towards a set of universal values.[9]

---

8   Of the literature on this, see especially Katerina Clark, *Moscow, the Fourth Rome: Stalinism, Cosmopolitanism, and the Evolution of Soviet Culture, 1931–1941* (Cambridge, MA: Harvard University Press, 2011), and Michael David-Fox, *Showcasing the Great Experiment: Cultural Diplomacy and Western Visitors to the Soviet Union, 1921–1941* (Oxford: Oxford University Press, 2011).

9   All speeches delivered at the Paris Congress can be found in: Sandra Teroni and Wolfgang Klein, eds., *Pour la défense de la culture: les textes du Congrès international des écrivains. Paris, juin 1935* (Dijon: Éditions universitaires de Dijon, 2005).

Thus, what was taking place in the mid-1930s in Soviet Russia is probably best grasped as a two-way process: the Soviet Union invites the world to see and appreciate it, but it also exports its culture to the world. As a result of these changes in cultural policy in the mid-1930s, a gradual rethinking of world literature took place in the Soviet Union, fostering a view of world literature as the literature of the global left: the class attribute is not removed, but the scope is now global, accommodating various shades of leftism and a whole swathe of legitimate cultural differences. Writers from the USA would also be invited to the Soviet Union at that time (Theodore Dreiser is just one example), as were writers from the Global South. In a very consistent manner, during the 1930s this policy of breaking with cultural isolationism helped the maturation of an idea of world literature in which the world (both in terms of provenance and in terms of the values the process of literary world-making articulates) was largely synonymous with the ideas, aspirations, and symbolic repertoire of the global democratic left.

The last major episode in this enduring Soviet interest in world literature—and a pillar of the institutional infrastructure buttressing this interest—was the multi-volume collective *History of World Literature*, a unique accomplishment of the Soviet humanities and a monument to the Soviet ambition to conceive of world literature as a process rather than a static given. Initially planned as a ten-volume publication, it was eventually completed in eight volumes. The beginning of this project lay back in 1960–1961, when the first conference of Soviet literary scholars on the issues of world literature was convened; even at that early stage, pressing issues and disagreements around methodology would make themselves felt; the crucial question, which fueled prolonged discussion, was how to write the history of world literature so that it is not simply a narrative about individual national literatures that coexist but somehow do not intersect or interact. The Soviet history of world literature wanted to be a decisively non-Occidentocentric history built on the recognition of temporal depth and change rather than an account of the literatures of the world that would follow a static encyclopedic design. In the absence of access to relevant documents, it is difficult to determine what exactly caused the huge gap between 1960 and 1983 (when the first volume saw the light of day), but in a country practicing centralized planning and distribution of resources, a prestige project such as this multi-volume work would have hardly been affected by lack of funding. What held up this project for so long was most likely the substantive and prolonged debate within the authors' collective about the methodology that was to be adopted if this were to be a modern, genuinely non-Occidentocentric history of world literature that offers a narrative grounded in the centrality of process and change, and is guided by a *longue durée* perspective.

Changing Ideological Horizons (And What Ultimately Connects Them?)

Now, I would like to move on to a more important question, which this chronology and the succinct overview of the infrastructure of the Soviet interest in world literature would enable us to discuss; the focus here is on the changing ideological horizons of interpreting world literature after 1917. The first such horizon I wish to single out could be termed the *humanistic horizon* of understanding world literature; the key figure here, right at the start of the Soviet attention to world literature, is once again Gorky. Gorky's ambitious publishing project wanted to deliver to the culturally disenfranchised masses hundreds of titles of world literature, of which, in the end, only a small fraction came to see the light of day. This endeavor very clearly rests on an understanding of world literature as an educational tool supported by a reliable canon of representative works. It was the duty of the new regime, Gorky believed, to make available to the hitherto oppressed classes (peasants, workers, soldiers) the best fruits of world literature in cheap but reliably translated and academically sound editions. Many of the published titles (their number being rather unimpressive when compared to the scale of ambition displayed in Gorky's original design for the Vsemirnaia Literatura project) were indeed translated anew and incorporated extensive introductions and often even a scholarly apparatus. This commitment to world literature in the early years of the Soviet regime was indeed genuinely humanistic. It aimed to lift from ignorance a vast mass of people by opening the door for them to enter the realm of what, at the time, was thought to be universal human culture. In this sense, it was both a class-based project (the cultural elevation of the wronged classes), but also a supra-class undertaking (the reaffirmation of universal cultural values, such as they were conceived of at the time). The organization of this entire project around a presumed canon that should serve unfailingly as a wider educational tool, cultivating civility and expanding one's knowledge of the world (in Wieland's sense of seeing in world literature an instrument of enhancing one's capacity to communicate with others) harks back to Matthew Arnold's understanding of culture which seeks to reconcile elitist (only the best that has been thought and said would do) and truly egalitarian principles (the best education possible should be available to all, including the sons and daughters of the miners in the benighted towns and villages of Britain). A foundational paradox at the heart of Gorky's project should therefore not go unnoticed: radical in its desire to facilitate social mobility for those previously relegated to the "lower depths" of society (as Gorky himself would put it in a play he wrote in 1902), this project was also unabashedly conservative in its reliance on the canon as an instrument of cultural and social amelioration.

This humanistic vision is also sustained in that rather interesting but short-lived magazine that Gorky would publish in Berlin, *Beseda* (Conversation, 1923–1925). It also aimed to be supra-political, a platform from which the voices of both democratic, even pro-reform or activist writers, alongside some on the conservative end of the spectrum, are heard, in short, a universal humanist tool for cultural dialogue. (It is known, for example, that Gorky sought to enlist as contributor Oswald Spengler, an author who could hardly be accused of left-wing sympathies.)

This humanistic horizon of understanding world literature, which is intimately bound up with the idea of world literature as embodying cultural diversity, and just as much with the idea of world literature as a canon and a tool of education, of expanding one's knowledge and inner world, gradually enters into a dialogue and a somewhat fraught coexistence, in the latter 1920s and the 1930s, with a second ideological horizon which could be termed the *global leftist horizon* (and which I discussed at some length when addressing the renaming of the Institute of Literature to IMLI, i.e. Institute of World Literature). This new interpretative framework began to conceive of world literature in a much more overtly political way, reimagining it as the literature of the global left, while retaining some latitude and situational flexibility. This new direction in the Soviet involvement with world literature came to prominence in the pages of two noteworthy journals, *Literatura mirovoi revoliutsii* (The literature of world revolution, 1931–1932), and especially its successor, *Internatsional'naia literatura* (International literature), the latter published in different editions in Russian (1933–1943), English, German, and French, with more short-lived versions also in Spanish and Chinese (the foreign-language versions, except for the Chinese one, survived until the end of World War II). The editorial policies of these journals and the overall cultural and ideological tenor of their work were markedly different from those of their pre-revolutionary predecessors engaged in the dissemination of non-Russophone literature in translation (going back to the mid-1850s, or 1856, to be more precise).[10]

The third, I think extremely important, ideological framework that sustained this continuous Soviet interest in world literature, is what I would call the *anti-colonial horizon*. Although it has its roots back in the 1920s (as we shall see later on), this interpretative framework begins to dominate the intellectual landscape (we can date this moment quite precisely) only from the early 1960s onwards. This is the time, of course, of acceleration and particular intensity of the process of decolonization, with significant social and political consequences for Asia, Africa, and also for France and Great Britain. This profound shift compelled the Soviet Union to seek a proactive response, ensuring its influence would extend to these emerging subjects of politics and international law. In 1960, the famous University of Peoples' Friendship (Universitet druzhby narodov) was founded in Moscow. The following year, 1961, this university was renamed in honor and in memory of Patrice Lumumba, a major figure in the anti-colonial movement in the Congo assassinated earlier in that year. This was the first Soviet institution to be given carte blanche to educate primarily students from Africa, Asia, and Latin America, with a very clear focus of cultural and ideological impact in these parts of the world. (In the 1920s–1930s, there was a similar institution focused on Central Asia, China, and the Far East [KUTV: Communist University of the Toilers of the East, 1921–1938], but its agenda was initially driven more by Comintern dreams of a proletarian revolution than by anti-colonial concerns.) 1961 was also the year when the Non-Aligned Movement was founded in Belgrade, in which India, Indonesia, Egypt, and Yugoslavia played a major role. The Soviet Union, and of course also the United States, now faced a new agenda; amongst its priorities was exerting influence on these numerous, some also demographically formidable, countries that had elected to take a third road between capitalism and socialism. The growing scholarly interest in world literature in the Soviet Union in the early 1960s, including the launch of the multi-volume *History of World Literature* discussed above, is very much part and parcel of this concerted effort to conduct cultural and foreign policy that would ensure these countries are, or continue to be drawn, into the Soviet orbit of influence.

---

10 On the chronology of Russian journals of foreign and "universal" literature prior to the late 1920s, including those originating in the nineteenth century, see Arlen Blium "'Internatsional'naia literatura': podtsenzurnoe proshloe," *Inostrannaia literatura*, no. 10 (2005): https://magazines.gorky.media/inostran/2005/10/internaczionalnaya-literatura-podczenzurnoe-proshloe.html.

It is no coincidence that this is the time when two important literary magazines in the USSR, both established earlier, would come of age and flourish, *Druzhba narodov* (Peoples' friendship, founded in 1939 as an almanac that would at first appear irregularly, and as a magazine in 1955) and *Inostrannaia literatura* (Foreign literature, also established in 1955). They both became visible platforms for translated literature; while *Inostrannaia literatura* featured primarily Western authors and authors from Eastern Europe and Latin America, the pages of *Druzhba narodov* were filled with examples of writing from the decolonizing world, as well as—sometimes putting this decolonizing agenda to the test—numerous works of non-Russophone Soviet literatures that enjoyed official sponsorship but were nonetheless perceived as secondary, mildly exotic, and benignly peripheral.

But what do these three different ideological horizons have in common when it comes to how they shaped the incessant Soviet conversations on what constitutes world literature, how should one conceive of it, and how and to what effect it should be used? It seems to me that the most significant unifying factor here is the continuity that stems from the determination of the Soviet intellectuals involved in these discussions to think about *world literature in a non-Occidentocentric way*. Let me return for a while to the multi-volume *History of World Literature*, whose first volume appeared in 1983, with the last, eighth volume, seeing the light of day in 1994. Even before this publication project was concluded, a Danish scholar went to the trouble of calculating with precision (in percentage terms) the space assigned in its first five volumes to non-European and non-North American literatures, as compared with other similar multi-volume histories of world literature in Western languages. His statistics-based conclusion is that the Soviet multi-volume *History of World Literature* did indeed pay significantly more attention to non-European and non-North American literatures than any other of its Western predecessors.[11]

A brief chronological examination would further highlight this enduring non-Occidentocentric perspective that would direct Soviet interest in world literature. When Gorky founded the "World Literature" publishing house, from the very beginning he was adamant that this should be an undertaking that should include not just the great works of European literature but also those of the literatures in non-Western languages, especially Arabic, Persian, Sanskrit, Chinese, and Japanese. Very little of this actually came to fruition, but Gorky's

---

11 For details, see Peter Ulf Møller, "Writing the History of World Literature in the USSR," *Culture & History*, no. 5 (1989): 19-37.

ambition was nonetheless clearly stated. When he established the editorial committee that would steer the wide-ranging publishing program of "Vsemirnaia Literatura", he also established a board in charge of selecting and preparing book editions from the literatures of the East headed by Sergei Ol'denburg, the most authoritative figure in Russian Indology at the time, an academician elected to the Russian Academy of Sciences before 1917, a superb scholar of Sanskrit who was also visible in the West (and a personal friend of Gorky's from the time before the October Revolution). More viable than the book series proved a journal, *Vostok* (The East, 1922–1925); its five issues carried translations of some of the classics of the literatures of the East and managed to attract the attention of a wider circle of Orientalists in the early 1920s, as is evident from a contemporary overview of Russian Oriental Studies published in 1924.[12]

This non-Occidentocentric framework is at work even in the class-based discourse on world literature as the literature of the global left which complements (and competes with) the humanistic horizon. Here is an example that reveals the enduring relevance of the non-Occidentocentric perspective, not least for a class-based interpretation of world literature. A most interesting periodical would commence publication in Russia in 1922; titled *Novyi Vostok* (The New East), it was the journal of the All-Russian Association of Oriental Studies. The introductory article in the first issue of this journal, written by Mikhail Pavlovich, is truly remarkable in expanding the East far beyond its geographical borders and redefining it in a way that blends the class-based and the non-Occidentocentric approach, while also anticipating the later centrality of the anti-colonial framework: as Pavlovich puts it, "The East—this is the entire colonial world, the world of the oppressed peoples not just of Asia, but also of Africa and South America; in a word, [the East is] the entire world on the exploitation of which the power of capitalist society rests, in Europe and the United States."[13] This is a verily powerful and revealing metaphor of the East as an emblem of globality (long before the 'Global South')—no doubt in unison with the class approach to world literature, but clearly also retaining and foregrounding the non-Occidentocentric perspective. Equally, the chronologically final horizon (framework) we identified, the anti-colonial one, breathes incessantly this pathos of breaking away from the West and looking to other

---

12 Cf. I. Borozdin, "Izuchenie Vostoka v sovremennoi Rossii," in *Kolonial'nyi Vostok: sotsial'no-ekonomicheskie ocherki*, ed. A. Sultan-Zade (Moscow: Novaia Moskva, 1924), 345–353, esp. 352.

13 M. Pavlovich, "Zadachi Vserossiiskoi Nauchnoi Assotsiatsii Vostokovedeniia," *Novyi Vostok*, no. 1 (1922): 3–15 (here 9).

14 | Galin Tihanov

continents and other cultures as evidence of future-shaping vigor and creativity. This was also sustained on the level of institution-based research: in 1958, just before preparations would begin for the writing of the multi-volume *History of World Literature*, IMLI (Institute of World Literature) initiated a collective project on the "correlation of Western and Oriental Literatures."[14] One would thus be justified in reaching the conclusion that it was the non-Occidentocentric perspective that brought together and ran as a red thread through the various changing (also a times overlapping and vying for supremacy) ideological horizons (humanist; global left; anti-colonial) that circumscribed and sustained the Soviet engagement with world literature.

Two Actors: Bakhtin, Konrad

I should like now to dwell in some detail on two major actors in this process of de-Westernization of the notion of world literature that was afoot in the Soviet Union; the two proceed in a very different way but to a similar net effect. Let me begin with Bakhtin. If we look at Russian literary theory during the inter-war decades, we will be struck by the fact that many of its major trends were, obliquely or more directly, relevant to 'world literature' as a framework of understanding and valorizing literature in the regime of its global production and consumption. Bakhtin begins his book on Rabelais with a reference precisely to world literature: "Of all great writers of world literature, Rabelais is the least popular, the least understood and appreciated."[15] Bakhtin, however, pays lip service to the then powerful notion of world literature as a body of canonical writing: he ostensibly compares Rabelais to Cervantes, Shakespeare, and Voltaire. But this entrenched understanding of world literature does not really interest him. Instead, he takes a different route, reconceptualizing the study of world literature as an examination of the processes that shape the novel to become a world genre, a global discursive power that, according to Bakhtin, impacts upon all other genres. Of course, Bakhtin is here indebted to the Russian Formalists: for him, too, the novel is the underdog of world literature, whose discursive

---

14 The formulation is Marián Gálik's; see his article "Comparative Literature in Soviet Oriental Studies," *Neohelicon* 3, nos. 3–4 (1975): 285–301 for a survey of Soviet Oriental Studies and comparative literature in the 1960s–1970s.
15 Mikhail Bakhtin, *Rabelais and His World*, trans. Hélène Iswolsky (Bloomington, IN: Indiana UP, 1984), 1.

energies are at first feeble and scattered, unnamed for a long time, until they begin to coalesce and rise to prominence.

Even more importantly, Bakhtin's engagement with world literature holds a distinctly non-Eurocentric and non-philological charge. He works with the novels he lists mostly in translation, as does Shklovsky before him (as a brief reminder: a lot in the recent rise, or—historically speaking—return, of 'world literature' as a prism through which to spectate and study literature hinges on accepting the legitimacy of reading and analyzing literary texts in translation). At first glance, Bakhtin appears to be relying on a Western canon to validate his theses; but, in truth, he is more interested in the literature and culture of pre-modernity, the time when Europe is not yet a dominant force, long before the continent begins to see itself as the center of the world. Bakhtin is thus actually a thinker much more fascinated by the subterranean cultural deposits of folk-lore, of minor discourses, of ancient genres, of anonymous verbal masses—all of which long predate European culture of the age of modernity (beginning roughly with the Renaissance, but especially since the eighteenth century when the doctrine of cultural Eurocentrism is worked out by the French *philosophes*, only to witness its first major crisis in the years around World War I), which is the only *dominant* (Eurocentric) European culture we know. Even Rabelais's novel interests him above all for its traditional, pre-modern, folklore-based layers. Bakhtin performs a flight away from Eurocentrism not by writing on non-European cultures, but by discussing pre-European cultures, cultures that thrive on the shared property of folklore, rites, rituals and epic narratives, before Europe even begins to emerge as a self-conscious entity on the cultural and political map of the world. His is an anti-Eurocentric journey not in space, but in time. His contemporaries, the semantic paleontologists Nikolai Marr and Olga Freidenberg, whose writings Bakhtin knew, did something similar in their work on myth and pre-literary discourses.[16] All of this casts Bakhtin's work in a new light and allows us to enlist him as an early predecessor of the non-Eurocentric and translation-friendly drive of today's Anglo-Saxon academic programs in world literature.

Nikolai Konrad (1891–1970), the "engine" behind the multi-volume *History of World Literature* in its early stages, made a critical contribution in for-mulating the central question (and offering a tentative answer to it) that the Soviet team of literary historians at IMLI faced: how should one write a history

---

16 For details, see Galin Tihanov, "Semantic Paleontology and Its Impact," in *Central and Eastern European Literary Theory and the West*, ed. Michał Mrugalski, Schamma Schahadat and Irina Wutsdorff (Berlin: De Gruyter, 2023): 787–806, esp. 801–802.

of world literature so that it wouldn't be a mere compilation of the histories of particular national literatures? Konrad, a Japanologist and Sinologist equipped with the *longue durée* perspective which the study of Chinese literature makes more readily available, attempted an interpretation of world literature based on the same premise from which Franco Moretti would work later: that world literature is not the product of late modernity and its globalizing trends, but rather a phenomenon that had been there for centuries before that. Konrad essayed to understand the evolution of world literature by looking at how paradigmatic formations, both aesthetic and ideological in their make-up, resurface across the globe. The Renaissance, for example, which Konrad took to be a recurrent phenomenon of renewal through reconnecting with tradition, had first been in evidence, according to Konrad, not in Italy in the thirteenth century but in China in the eighth century AD, with the so-called *fugu* movement. Konrad has been severely criticized for the methodology that informs this daring reinterpretation of European literary history.[17] It is true that he defines the Renaissance in a deliberately one-sided manner, largely downplaying its socio-economic dimensions, especially the gradual growth of urban bourgeois forms of sociality, production, and culture. For him, another aspect is central—the turn to tradition with the aim of cultural renewal and replenishment; from this he infers that there is a Renaissance whenever and wherever a civilization performs such return to its own traditions, to the resources of its own past. To Konrad, the *fugu* movement was a full and legitimate instantiation of this historically recurring situation of renewal through a reawakening of tradition, in this case a return to traditional Confucianism in order to reinvigorate Chinese culture. Since he held this to be a recurrent pattern that can be observed across different cultures, Konrad preferred to speak not of "the" Renaissance but of a multitude of Renaissances. According to him, after China, Iran becomes the playground of such Renaissance renewal, and only then does a European Renaissance emerge,

---

17 The relevant Soviet polemics are analyzed in M. T. Petrov, *Problema Vozrozhdeniia v sovetskoi nauke. Spornye voprosy regional'nykh renessansov* (Leningrad: Nauka, 1989). Although there are no references to Konrad in their work, two scholars have recently dedicated a book to the question of whether there was a Renaissance in China (cf. Thomas Meissen and Barbara Mittler, *Why China did not have a Renaissance—and why that matters: An interdisciplinary dialogue*, Berlin: De Gruyter, 2018 [the title is somewhat inadequate as it reflects solely Meissen's position; Mittler is in fact in favor of there having been a Chinese Renaissance]). The question arises (so far neither posed nor studied) as to whether Konrad knew similar work by foreign Sinologists, especially Naito Konan's hypothesis according to which the transition from medieval life to early modernity in China occurred precisely in the period in which Konrad situates the Renaissance in China. I am grateful to Professor Martin Powers for directing my attention to Naito's work.

first in Italy and then in Northern Europe. Another important aesthetic and ideological formation, Realism, follows the opposite direction of travel. For Konrad (still very much a Marxist, despite the liberty he took by willfully ignoring the socio-economic aspects of the Renaissance), Realism began in Europe (it was after all in Europe that the contradictions of capitalism were already ripe to capture and analyze in the genre of the novel), then crossed over into the Middle East (but there, the novel had a difficult time asserting itself as the dominant genre of realist prose; the short story played that role for a long time), only to arrive in the Far East as late as the 1920s–1930s.[18] The breath-taking scale of Konrad's vision of the evolution of world literature clearly prepares the ground for Moretti's own exciting exploration of how the European novel journeys to the shores of Brazil and to other corners of the world, and how it changes in the process. Both Konrad and Moretti, in order to sustain this admirable scale, have to make sacrifices. What is sacrificed is the traditional understanding of literary form, relying as it does on the classical (by now irretrievably compromised) notion of literature as a specific and autonomous discourse. While the formal aspects do remain important, form is no longer analyzed, either by Konrad or by Moretti, as the outcome of the micro-workings of language; its analysis is largely pegged to an understanding of the workings of genre that can be ascertained through various procedures of "distant reading."

Thus, for Konrad the history of world literature is only possible if it adopts a truly *longue durée* approach. In this case, the fact that he was a Sinologist is not at all insignificant, for his background was that of a scholar steeped in a culture whose literary tradition is longer than any other in the West (including ancient Greece). For him, a convincing answer to the question of how the history of world literature ought to be written has to rise to the challenge of capturing long-term changes in worldview and mental structures, while at the same time registering and seeking to explain aesthetic innovation. In other words, a history

---

18 Konrad's explorations of world literature can be found in his collection of articles, *Zapad i Vostok: Stat'i* (Moscow: Nauka, 1966). There is an abridged, linguistically rather inadequate and not particularly reliable, English translation (*West-East: Inseparable Twain* [Moscow: Nauka, 1967]; in 1973-1974, attempts were made for the book to appear in English in a new translation (cf. the correspondence preserved in Konrad's archive at the Russian Academy of Sciences between various scholars, including Toynbee, and Konrad's widow). Konrad's book had a significant impact in the Soviet Union, especially with reference to the study of the literatures of the Caucasus and Central Asia (all of this deserves special attention beyond the scope of this article). For a monograph on Konrad's life and work, see Evgenii Badaev, *Formirovanie kul'turno-istoricheskoi kontseptsii N. I. Konrada* (Kemerovo: Kemerovskii gosudarstvennyi universitet, 2010).

of world literature should remain Marxist in spirit, without reducing literature to an imprint of ideological, cultural, or political change.

'World literature'; Literary Theory; Histories of National Literatures

The Soviet debates on world literature created a conceptual force-field that turned out to be seminal not only for discussions related to world literature; they had immediate bearing also on conversations in Russia about Russian literature and literary theory. World literature and national literatures, different as they might be as prisms or units of analysis, are communicating vessels, something we have been too reluctant to acknowledge for too long; just as the opposition cosmopolitanism vs. nationalism is historically untenable, so is the one that casts world literature and national literatures as discrete phenomena that are divorced from one another. Here, I would like to offer just three examples to illustrate how the conceptual force-field generated by debates on world literature was beginning to affect key discussions related to Russian literature and literary theory produced in Russia.

The first example references the fierce controversies surrounding Russian Formalism. To this day, the overwhelming majority of scholars writing on Russian Formalism tend to think that the only serious enemy of Russian Formalism was Marxism, for Marxism would stigmatize Russian Formalism as a way of thinking about literature that is apolitical, running away from history, economics, law, etc. The truth is that the objections to Russian Formalism in the late 1920s and early 1930s were not so dogmatic and unsophisticated, nor would they stem solely from the Marxist intolerance towards the basic belief that literature has its own autonomous life, independent of politics, economics, and various societal factors.

In 1930, Aleksandr Kholodovich, a budding Orientalist, a student of Konrad and Marr, and a friend of Valentin Voloshinov (one of the most prominent members of the Bakhtin Circle),[19] at the time not even twenty-five years old and still a graduate student (later to emerge as the greatest Soviet authority on the Korean language), published an article in a collection uninspiringly titled *In the Struggle for Marxism in Literary Scholarship* (V bor'be za marksizm

---

19 These biographical details can be found in V. M. Alpatov, "Aleksandr Alekseevich Kholodovich," in *Otechestvennye lingvisty XX veka*, vol. 3 (Moscow: RAN INION, 2003), 90–100.

v literaturnoi nauke, 1930). The article is directed against the Formalist school. There, Kholodovich addresses the Formalists with a forceful rhetorical question that is much harder to deflect than the staple accusations levelled by Soviet Marxism. Targeting the Formalists' implicit Occidentocentrism (Eurocentrism, most of the time), Kholodovich rightly cast doubt on their ambition to articulate a literary theory that would hold universal validity: how could such a claim be convincingly staked out given that almost all of the texts analyzed by the Formalists hailed solely from European and American literature? In Kholodovich's own words, the seemingly universal literary theory Formalism had essayed to articulate was the theory of thinkers "brought up on samples of European poetics and poetic schools"; as such, it was bound to "omit the most basic phenomena of the poetic life of the 'East.'"[20] Of course, an Occidentocentric history of world literature would run the risk of internalizing a number of tacit assumptions that reflect Western aesthetic experience, assigning, for example, particular value to originality, creative invention, subversive, at times also antagonistic, imagination, and other characteristics that in cultural zones of non-Western formation may not necessarily enjoy such prominence. Kholodovich's critique of Russian Formalism was thus substantive and much more difficult to handle than the rather more trivial objections raised by the Marxist camp.

The second moment takes us to the late 1960s and is closely related to Konrad's theory of the multiple Renaissances that make their appearance in different parts of the world. The way Dmitry Likhachev (1906–1999), the dean of Russian medieval literary studies at the time and one of Konrad's friends, conceived of Russian literary history was clearly impacted by Konrad's 1966 book. In the wake of Konrad's advocacy for the ubiquity of the Renaissance as a cultural-historical phenomenon, Likhachev would emphasize what he would call the "pre-Renaissance elements" in Russian literature. There is a deeper subtext here going back to the old trauma of Russian culture and Russian literary studies to do with the realization that Russia never had its own Renaissance in the form in which it would be known to cultural historians working on Western Europe. (For this reason, Russian philosophy would tend to conjure up various Russian Renaissances—second, third, etc., all with their different but equally powerful claims to Russian spiritual and cultural superiority.) Likhachev was at pains to demonstrate that, since Konrad had given legitimacy to the Renaissance not only in Europe (and certainly not only in Western Europe), his own quest

---

20 Aleksandr Kholodovich, "K voprosu o lingvisticheskom metode v poetike," in *V bor'be za marksizm v literaturnoi nauke: Sbornik statei*, ed. V. Desnitskii, N. Iakovlev, and L. Tsyrlin (Leningrad: Priboi, 1930), 241–277, here 242.

for a Renaissance in Russian literature was far from pointless. Russian medieval literature, according to Likhachev, could thus be seen as issuing in certain pre-Renaissance phenomena. Likhachev's critics would ask awkward questions: what are these pre-Renaissance phenomena that never actually materialize, never lead to a Renaissance proper; where is this phantom Renaissance literature, whose allegedly pre-Renaissance sprouts are so ardently extolled? To his credit, in his magisterial work on the poetics of Russian medieval literature that endeavors to offer a conclusive account of the period, Likhachev takes seriously this skepticism and proposes a distinction between "proto-Renaissance" (*Protorenessans*, in Russian: Renaissance phenomena that merely precede the Renaissance chronologically but are essentially of the same nature as the Renaissance in Italy) and "pre-Renaissance" (*Predvozrozhdenie*, in Russian: a term he reserves for the Russian case, in which there were some Renaissance elements but they could not mature and yield a Renaissance proper, mostly due to inclement external circumstances).[21] It is, however, largely irrelevant whether Likhachev's interpretation as such could be substantiated or not; what does matter here is grasping its logic and trying to understand the methodological toolkit and resources it draws from Konrad's scenario, in which the Renaissance can no longer be attached solely to the cultures of (Western) Europe.

The last example I wish to discuss briefly foregrounds the work of Irina Neupokoeva (1917–1977), a specialist in English (later, more widely, also European) Romanticism, forgotten for a very long time, but now briefly resuscitated through the inclusion of one of her articles in the Routledge anthology, *World Literature: A Reader* (2012).[22] Here, again, we have a background story one would need to be aware of: for about thirty-five years after the mid-1930s, in the USSR there was hardly any research on Romanticism in literature

---

21 See D. S. Likhachev, *Poetika drevnerusskoi literatury*, 2nd, enlarged ed. (Leningrad: Khudozhestvennaia literatura, 1971), 38. This differentiation is absent in the first edition of the book (1967); the first edition of the book, published only a year after Konrad's *Zapad i Vostok*, does not yet make the case for pre-Renaissance developments in Russian mediaeval literature.

22 Irina Neupokoeva, "Dialectics of Historical Development of National and World Literature," in *World Literature: A Reader*, ed. Theo D'haen, César Domínguez, and Mads Rosendahl Thomsen (London: Routledge, 2012), 103–112 (originally presented as a paper in Budapest in 1971). Neupokoeva was the first head of the newly created IMLI Sector on the History of World Literature which was established in 1963 within the Department of Foreign Literatures (at the time chaired by Roman Samarin); later, this sector became a department in its own right, led by Neupokoeva until 1977, when she was succeeded by Yuri Vipper (for details, see G. Berdnikov, "Institutu mirovoi literatury imeni A. M. Gor'kogo AN SSSR—50 let," *Voprosy literatury*, no. 9 (1982): 102–131, here 122).

World Literature in the Soviet Union | 21

and the arts, except for scant attention to what Gorky would call, before the October Revolution, "Revolutionary Romanticism," itself regarded by Marxist aesthetics as no more than an ally (and a predecessor) of the later and more mature Socialist Realism. Gradually falling out of grace, for a long time to come Romanticism became an undesirable item on the research agenda, with interest in it resuming only in the late 1960s and early 1970s.

The reasons for this particular dynamic take us back to the First Congress of Soviet Writers in 1934, at which Gorky's vision of Revolutionary Romanticism and Socialist Realism as coequal artistic methods suffered a defeat. In the resolution of the congress, Socialist Realism gained the status of the only true creative method of Soviet literature, while Romanticism was relegated to a permissible mode of expression, an acceptable stylistic register, but not a method of conceptualization as such. This non-acceptance of Romanticism in official Soviet literary studies that often saw Romanticism as synonymous with a deeply apolitical (sometimes even counter-revolutionary) attitude, would force the rewriting of Russian literary history of the first half of the nineteenth century, which now had to be reinterpreted as little more than preparatory work for the ascent of Realism. All this changed in the late 1960s and early 1970s when Romanticism slowly began to reenter literary studies as a legitimate subject. This return was made possible by a legitimization that came not so much from historians of Russian literature, but primarily from scholars dealing with comparative and world literature, finding inspiration, not least, in the *Communist Manifesto*.

In 1971, Neupokoeva published a book on the history of the revolutionary poem as a genre.[23] This is a very competent philological study, with knowledge of English, Russian, Polish, Czech, and Hungarian literature. Neupokoeva there quotes the famous passage from the *Communist Manifesto* by Marx and Engels, in which they state that the collapse of national borders is inevitable, as is the concomitant emergence of literatures from their national encapsulation, which would ineluctably ensue in the rise of world literature. Neupokoeva constructs an effective argument that highlights the particular historical moment: the *Communist Manifesto*, having been published in 1848, was written—significantly—at a time when European literature, especially in Central and Eastern Europe, would see the ascent of Romanticism. Reinterpreting Romanticism away from its disturbing nationalist overtones, Neupokoeva believed that Marx and Engels's optimistic vision of the unarrestable growth of *Weltliteratur* was

---

23 Irina Neupokoeva, *Revoliutsionno-romanticheskaia poema pervoi poloviny XIX veka: opyt tipologii zhanra* (Moscow: Nauka, 1971).

sponsored by a whole swathe of contemporary cultural trends, foremost the rise of Romanticism (her emphasis was, of course, on its 'revolutionary' variant that dreamt of a liberated humanity claiming its own right to creativity across borders and/or advocated the overthrow of Empire as an obsolete and oppressive form of political organization). Romanticism thus finally gets its seat at the table, no longer overlooked or vilified, enjoying a new legitimacy bestowed upon it by the founding fathers of Marxism: what stronger legitimation could there be in the land of the Soviets?

This momentous change that saw Romanticism gain a new status in the Soviet Union, no longer the ugly duckling of literary studies but a progressive aesthetic and ideological force worthy of focused attention, was made possible through the resources of the "world literature" discourse in the late 1960s and early 1970s. The moral of the story, in this and in the other two examples, is that thinking about world literature is actually closely related to how the histories of national literatures and literary theory are thought about; what is more, this imbrication is not just intellectual, it is also cultural and ideological. The discourse on world literature, in other words, does not exist in isolation from the conversations societies conduct about national literatures; these two discourses remain entwined in what Oskar Walzel used to call, in a different context, a state of "mutual elucidation" (*wechselseitige Erhellung*).[24]

A lot of this Soviet legacy remains significant today. Ironically, although it is not known in the West, Konrad's hypothesis of the multiple Renaissances informs a good deal of current debates on the permissibility and conceptual risks of deploying terms of Western provenance in global history.[25] The Soviet experience also allows us to appreciate the rather precarious balance between committing to a genuinely non-Occidentocentric vision of literature and

---

24 See Oskar Walzel, *Wechselseitige Erhellung der Künste. Ein Beitrag zur Würdigung kunstgeschichtlicher Begriffe* (Berlin: Reuther & Reichard, 1917).

25 The literature on the so-called "global Renaissance" is growing fast. See, more recently, Peter Burke, Luke Clossey, and Felipe Fernández-Armesto, "The Global Renaissance," *Journal of World History* 28, no. 1 (2017): 1–30, Pablo Ariel Blitstein, "A Global History of the 'Multiple Renaissances'," *The Historical Journal*, no. 1 (2021): 162–184, and Michel Espagne, "The Global Renaissance: Extended Palimpsests and Intercultural Transfers in a Transcontinental Space," in *Global Literary Studies*, ed. Diana Roig-Sanz and Neus Rotger (Berlin: De Gruyter, 2023), 185–198, amongst others. In the West, the foundational text favoring a globalized, multiple Renaissance remains Jack Goody's *Renaissances. The One or the Many* (Cambridge: Cambridge University Press, 2010); see also Bernd Roeck, *Der Morgen der Welt. Geschichte der Renaissance* (Munich: Beck, 2017). With special reference to world literature, see the articles in *Other Renaissances: A New Approach to World Literature*, ed. Brenda Deen Schildgen, Gang Zhou, and Sander L. Gilman (New York: Palgrave, 2006).

culture, while continuing to operate from within an imperial set-up that treats other cultures as dependent, in need of guidance and protection, often "smaller," "younger," and immature (a phenomenon that fuels, at least in part, the Russian aggression in Ukraine today). When all is said and done, one would still need to acknowledge and embrace the epistemic energy behind the Soviet engagement with world literature, especially its determination to see world literature from a non-Occidentocentric perspective, and, as a corollary to this, as a process of uneven interaction between literatures in different times and cultural zones sustained by a logic of deeper *longue durée* transformations.

CHAPTER 2

On the Worldliness of Russian Literature

Anne Lounsbery

It is difficult to imagine a tradition more consistent with a genuinely worldly view of "World Literature" than that of the nineteenth- and twentieth-century Russian novel. The baggy-monster Russian realists can be seen as precursors of Salman Rushdie and the other big, messy, hybrid (and mostly male) geniuses who are typically located at the top of today's World Literature pyramid.

And yet, bizarrely, Russian texts are almost completely absent from the standard contemporary accounts of World Literature that have been developed in the West. The 2012 *Routledge Companion to World Literature*, for instance, makes virtually no mention of either Russia or the Soviet Union.[1] Whole theories of World Literature have been articulated with barely a passing mention of writing in Russian. Pascale Casanova's *World Republic of Letters* (first published in 1999 and still highly influential today) is a case in point, but one might also adduce works by other theorists who helped establish the parameters of the discussion: Fredric Jameson, Aijaz Ahmad, Franco Moretti, Emily Apter, David Damrosch, etc. Occasionally an individual Russian author rates a mention in these discussions; Fredric Jameson's influential essay "Third-World Literature in the Era of Multinational Capitalism," for instance, adduces Dostoevsky as a decontextualized, denationalized example of "great literature," and Casanova cites Nabokov as a laudably "cosmopolitan" writer.[2] But the Russian literary *tradition* has no place in their systems.

---

1   See index of *The Routledge Companion to World Literature*, ed. Theo D'haen, David Damrosch, Djelal Kadir (New York: Routledge, 2012).

2   Fredric Jameson, "Third-World Literature in the Era of Multinational Capitalism," *Social Text*, no. 15 (Autumn, 1986): 65.

Indeed, a common feature of this scholarship is that it simply does not deal with Russia. Rather than viewing the omission as a lapse (because it seems implausible to assume that all these scholars simply forget about, say, Tolstoy), we might ask what has made this sort of erasure possible—or perhaps even necessary? Could serious acknowledgement of Russia throw a wrench into Western models of World Literature? *Must* Russian literature be absent from systems like Casanova's? My answer to this question grows out of nineteenth-century Russian literary texts themselves. These texts, I argue, reveal an inchoate awareness that a category like World Literature—as it is articulated in the West—will not be able to accommodate them. In effect, Russian works predict the neglect they will suffer at the hands of such systems, which is precisely the neglect that the Soviets' new conceptions of World Literature will aim to redress.

Before turning to the Russian texts, let us examine Casanova's *World Republic of Letters*, which did much to set the terms in which World Literature has been analyzed and debated. *The World Republic of Letters* constructs a system that leaves national literary traditions two options: you are either *cosmopolitan* (if you are in the center) or you are *provincial* (if you are on the periphery). And according to this system, to be provincial is to be not just in the wrong place, but also in the wrong *time*. Casanova's Paris is the "Greenwich meridian" of culture, a point both spatial ("the center of all centers") and temporal ("a basis for measuring the time that is peculiar to literature"),[3] making it at once the undisputed "center" of the literary world and the vanguard of a literary "progress" that is essentially linear. Here as in most other Western theories of World Literature, *spatial* peripheries are dependent and sterile because they are *temporally* behind.[4]

Casanova argues that France's preeminence long served to divide the high-culture world into what was French, what was consecrated by the French, and what was neither of these. She marshals a long list of quotations in which writers from the non-center bemoan their peripheralness and genuflect to the power wielded by Paris.[5] In the 1830s, for example, Swiss artist Rodolphe Töpffer wrote that if a man "values being illustrious," "it is therefore wholly necessary . . . that this man bring to the capital his bundle of talent, that he lay it out before the

---

3   Pascale Casanova, *The World Republic of Letters* (Cambridge, MA: Harvard University Press, 2004), 87–88.

4   Casanova is drawing on Immanuel Wallerstein's "world systems theory" as articulated in his works including *The Modern World-System I: Capitalist Agriculture and the Origins of the European World-Economy in the Sixteenth Century* (New York: Academic Press, 1974).

5   Note the selection bias here: Casanova is not quoting all the writers who simply did not care about Paris enough to mention it.

Parisian experts, and that a reputation is then made for him that from the capital is then dispatched to the provinces, where it is eagerly accepted."[6] Serbian writer Danilo Kiš said virtually the same thing a century and a half later: "in order to exist it is necessary to pass through Paris."[7] One might also cite here Milan Kundera's claim that a Polish writer needs to know French literature, but a French writer does not need to know Polish literature: simply because "[a French writer's] own culture *contains* more or less all the aspects, all the possibilities and phases, of the world's evolution."[8] Kundera would love the quotes marshaled by Casanova—like Valery Larbaud's claim that "every French writer is international . . . a writer for all Europe . . . All that which is 'national' is silly, archaic." Or Harold Rosenberg's: "Paris was the opposite of the national in art, [and thus] the art of every nation increased through Paris."[9]

Casanova describes the "decentering" and "disadvantaged remoteness" experienced by those on a periphery who feel stranded in what she describes as "a place outside real time and history."[10] She quotes Octavio Paz's account of his own coming of age in Mexico:

> I felt dislodged from the present. . . . The real present was somewhere else. . . . For us Spanish Americans this present was not in our own countries: it was the time lived by others—by the English, the French, the Germans. It was the time of New York, Paris, London.[11]

This belief, Paz explains, gave rise to his urgent need to find "the gateway to the *present*": "I wanted to belong to my time and to my century. . . . My search for modernity had begun."[12] Paz's alienation is the result of a geographic localization of cultural authority so intense that it forces those on the periphery to judge their own reality by Casanova's "Greenwich meridian of literature." Once

---

6   Casanova, 126.

7   Quoted in Casanova, 129.

8   Milan Kundera, "Die Weltliteratur: How We Read One Another," *New Yorker*, January 8, 2007, 30.

9   Casanova, 31, 87. Statements like these call to mind the deracinated cosmopolitan intellectuals—Nabokov, Brodsky, and T.S. Eliot all come to mind—who most long to be universal, to rise above the merely local and particular. In fact such writers often argue that real art is defined above all by its universalness. This plays well in Casanova's version of France, which is entitled to transcend all particularity on the basis of its centrality.

10   Casanova, 93, emphasis mine.

11   Casanova, 92–93.

12   Casanova, 93, emphasis mine.

spatial decentering (being on the physical periphery) is experienced as temporal decentering (being outside of "modern," "real" time), the quest for modernity in literature can take on a desperate urgency. "To be decreed 'modern,'" Casanova writes, "is one of the most difficult forms of recognition for writers outside the center."[13]

The World Republic of Letters, despite its attention to translation's impact on literature as a world system, does not acknowledge the massive work undertaken in this field by the Soviets. The American experience, too, is underplayed, since Casanova concentrates almost exclusively on examples of US writers for whom Parisian cultural authority played a key role in their canonization (Poe, Whitman, Faulkner). The book's focus, when not on France, is generally on what it calls "small countries," or else on countries so disadvantaged by distance and colonial status that they might as well be small.

Russia, of course, is anything but small. In fact, it is probably in part because the country is so enormous (physically, culturally, historically) that Russians have not tended to see themselves as being simply on a periphery, as might, say, a Serb like Kiš. As one critic has written, the scenario put forth in *The World Republic of Letters* is one of "underdog nations battling for a place in a literary sun blocked by the shadow of tyrant languages and literatures"[14]: again, not a model that works very well for Russia, especially if you ask a Ukrainian. Furthermore, the writers whose work forms the basis of Casanova's system tend to cast the quest for modernness in straightforwardly geographic terms in the way that Paz does, confidently locating the present they seek in real geographic space ("New York, Paris, London"). Russians recognized France's cultural preeminence and made the requisite pilgrimages there, but they were less confident that Paris—or Petersburg or Moscow or anyplace else—could "save [them] from provincialism," as the Peruvian writer Vargas Llosa once expected Sartre (that is, Paris) to do for him and his peers.[15]

---

13 Casanova, 75.

14 Christopher Prendergast, "The World Republic of Letters," in *Debating World Literature*, ed. Christopher Prendergast (Verso, 2004), 17.

15 Casanova, 94. As early as 1778 Fonvizin wrote that "Paris is not a city at all; it must in truth be called an entire world." But Russian travelers also considered French belief in French preeminence to be a bit ludicrous, even once we correct for a good dose of *ressentiment*: as Glinka wrote in 1814, "the residents of Paris consider themselves their city to be the capital of the world and the world to be their provinces. They consider Burgundy, for example, a near province and Russia a far one. A Frenchman coming here from Bourdeaux and a Russian from Petersburg are both called foreigners." Sara Dickinson, *Breaking Ground: Travel and National Culture in Russia from Peter I to the Era of Pushkin* (Amsterdam: Rodopi, 2006), 150.

Russians often felt themselves to be "divorced from *time*," in Pyotr Chaadaev's oft-quoted words, no matter where they were in *space*. Chaadaev's description of Russia from the 1829 First Philosophical Letter is an early articulation of a sentiment that will recur over and over: the sense that Russia's failure to follow normative patterns of progressive time is linked to geography but cannot be remedied by any geographic fix, because all of Russian space and time is insufficiently structured (unmoored, unregulated, unbordered) and thus resistant to coherence. Cast adrift in the world, he writes, "We all resemble travelers. . . . In our own houses we seem to be camping, in our families we look like strangers, in our cities we look like nomads, even more than the nomads who tend their herds on our steppes, for even they are more attached to their wastelands than we are to our cities." Inhabiting "a culture based wholly on borrowing and imitation," in which "new ideas throw out the old ones because they do not arise from the latter, but come among us from Heaven knows where," Chaadaev's Russians "live only in the narrowest of presents, without past and without future, in the midst of a flat calm."[16]

The kind of temporality Chaadaev describes—which recurs over and over in literary texts, as I will discuss—is not exactly "behind." Rather, it is disordered, unstructured, confused. And here we come to another reason why Russia cannot be accommodated by Western ideas of World Literature: in the nineteenth century (and arguably after that as well), Russia was not "modern," but it was not straightforwardly "backward," either. Russia just does not fit comfortably into what Arjun Appadurai calls "Eurochronology," a kind of time that represents itself as a universal standard.[17] Eurochronology is also the normative temporality reflected in Casanova's World Literature, with its binaries like ahead/behind and cosmopolitan/provincial. In order to arrive at such binaries, as we will see, such a picture of the literary "world" must leave out Russia altogether.

Russian literary texts often represent temporality in ways that undermine Eurochronology's totalizing claims. Suspicion of normative chronologies is

---

16 Peter Yakovlevich Chaadaev, *Philosophical Letters and Apology of a Madman,* trans. and intro. Mary-Barbara Zeldin (Knoxville: University of Tennessee Press, 1969), 35–37 (translation adjusted slightly).

17 Arjun Appadurai, *Modernity at Large: Cultural Dimensions of Globalization* (Minneapolis: University of Minnesota Press, 2000), 30, 1. Appadurai explains: "Modernity belongs to that small family of theories that both declares and desires universal applicability for itself. What is new about modernity (or about the idea that its newness is a new kind of newness) follows from this duality. Whatever else the project of the Enlightenment may have created, it aspired to create persons who would, after the fact, have wished to have become modern."

particularly apparent in depictions of the provinces, *provintsiia*—a term that has a much more complicated and ambiguous resonance in the Russian tradition than does "la province" in French, or words like "periphery" in English. Indeed, the complexity of this category—Russia's imaginary *provintsiia*—can help explain not only why it is so difficult to assimilate Russian literature to Casanova's system, but also how Russian texts end up mounting a certain resistance to a Paris-centered map of the literary world. The word *provintsiia* designates the non-exotic, non-borderland, "native" spaces that are outside of and symbolically opposed to Petersburg and Moscow, all the nameless *Gorod N's* that literature most often represents as devoid of coherent meaning. *Provintsiia* is not rural life (which is simply backward, whether that backwardness is seen as bad or good); rural life is *derevnia*. *Provintsial'nyi* (or *gubernskii*) generally refers to provincial cities and towns, and sometimes to gentry estates that fall short of an acceptable level of civilization. Peasants, then, are never provincials, and peasant culture is not provincial culture. Nor is *provintsiia* the exotic periphery of the imperial borderlands, often resonant with mystery and significance. The provinces, by contrast, are *boring*; they are the always already known. From Gogol through Turgenev, Dostoevsky, Chekhov, Sologub, and beyond, we get one nameless city after another, all characterized by overdetermined anonymity and cultural incoherence. The trope is particularly telling because it is counterfactual: there is no evidence that real life in *provintsiia* was terrible. Intellectuals outside the capitals tried over and over to defend their localities against metropolitan slurs, but still the *idea* of the provinces seemed to live its own life, ignoring obvious divergences between reality and literature.

What is the connection between Russian literature's fascination with provincial places and its exclusion from World Literature? A key clue lies in the fact the provinces—like Russia itself—are not simply "behind." Rather, they exist in an ambiguous temporality, one that poses a challenge to totalizing systems like Casanova's. The provinces are consistently represented as a mishmash of objects and styles and words and temporalities, a place where you might encounter virtually anything dating to virtually any period. Think of the estates in Gogol's *Dead Souls*, for example: each landowner's home contains a few vestigial and fragmentary bits of imported "culture." Manilov's garden features an inept attempt at English landscape design (a ramshackle arbor dubbed the "Temple for Solitary Meditation") surrounded by peasants' log huts. Inside his house, "an exceedingly elegant candlestick of darkened bronze, with the three Graces of antiquity and an elegant mother-of-pearl escutcheon" stands

On the Worldliness of Russian Literature | 31

alongside another candlestick, one that is homemade, broken, jerry-built.[18] Similar representations of provincial incoherence recur constantly in texts ranging from the hyper-canonical to the obscure. In a story by Melnikov-Pechersky, we encounter a provincial merchant's house where the décor includes a parrot, a bust of Voltaire, and the letter "Ф" cut out of paper; in the provincial town of Herzen's *Who is to blame?*, an ugly church combines Byzantine, classical, and Gothic elements; in Chekhov's stories and plays, the aesthetic incoherence of provincial ideas and objects signals a culture that is jumbled, inappropriate, at times radically indiscriminate.[19] Objects and ideas are decontextualized; nothing here has what an art historian would call provenance: as the narrator of *Dead Souls* says of the paintings hanging in Pliushkin's house, "there was no way of knowing how or why they had gotten there."[20]

Consider Turgenev's anonymous town ("a city like any other," in Bazarov's dismissive formulation) in *Fathers and Children*. Here the paradigmatic provincial subject is Kukshina, who prattles on incoherently about everything from Bunsen burners and embryology to Ralph Waldo Emerson. Kukshina longs to be known as a "progressive woman" (*peredovaia zhenshchina*), a person who is decidedly modern, moving forward in step with History—but her city regularly burns to the ground and must be built anew ("it is a well-known fact that our provincial towns burn down every five years").[21] How is any standard version of "progress" possible in a town that is periodically reduced to ashes and must be reconstructed? What does it mean to live in a house that has to be rebuilt twice every decade using whatever materials are at hand? It is difficult to imagine a more fitting symbol for the futility of trying to join the linear, progressive temporality that characterizes Western modernity's view of itself.

These examples suggest that the provinces, rather than being behind the times, are not in *any* (single) time—thereby raising the possibility that Russia's disordered temporality might be permanently outside of the normative chronology implied by European history. To be clear, the *provintsiia* trope is not another way of developing the familiar (eventually Trotskian) idea that backwardness will allow Russia to line-jump in or into History; in other words, the provinces are not represented as a place where you go back

---

18 N. V. Gogol', *Polnoe sobranie sochinenii*, vol. 6 (Moscow: Akademiia nauk 1952), 22, 25.

19 P. I. Mel'nikov (Andrei Pecherskii), "Krasil'nikovy," *Sobranie sochinenii v vos'mi tomakh*, vol. 1, ed. M. P. Eremin (Moscow: Pravda, 1976), 56–57; A. I. Herzen, *Sobranie sochinenii v 30-I tomakh*, vol. 4 (Moscow: Izd. Akademii Nauk SSSR, 1954), 115.

20 Gogol', *PSS*, vol. 6, 95.

21 I. S. Turgenev, *Polnoe sobranie sochinenii I pisem v 30-i tomakh*, vol. 7 (Moscow: Nauka, 1978), 64, 61.

32 | Anne Lounsbery

to get ahead. In fact, rarely does *provintsiia's* temporal mode imply the possibility of a "straight line" of historical progress: representations of provincial culture reveal no trajectory of development, no chronological *telos*. Nor is *provintsial'nost'* an idea that locates value in an idealized version of some coherent past (any such ideal would be located in *derevnia*, not *provintsiia*). We should read the *provintsiia* trope not as a way of thinking about backwardness or behind-the-times-ness—not about trying to get in line, as Casanova implies everyone feels compelled to do—but rather as a way of thinking about the relationship between Russian time and cultural syncretism.

We can read such representations of *provintsiia* against the Western theories of World Literature that depict peripheries as sterile and dependent because they are (supposedly) behind. *Provintsiia* highlights the Russian tradition's willingness to borrow and work with ideas that were "chronologically out of sync with European fashion," to "conflate and play off of [them] *simultaneously*."[22] When Gogol's contemporary Nikolai Nadezhdin describes his era's prose as "a confusion of all the European idioms having overgrown in successive layers the wild mass of the undeveloped Russian word," he is identifying precisely those phenomena from which Gogol's art would draw its greatest power.[23] And this is where we should look for the utility of the *provintsiia* trope, with its insistence on all that is ad hoc and syncretic: its hodge-podge draws attention to the possibilities inherent in simultaneity and non-synchronicity, the possibility of a connection between chaotic simultaneity and creative potential. It implies that the jumbled-up quality of Russian time might prove fruitful and modern rather than sterile and behind, something other than the barren "flat calm" of Chaadaev's diagnosis. It signals not just the conflation and out-of-syncness that are characteristic of Russian literature, but also Russians' *awareness* of these phenomena. This is what Andrei Sinyavsky alludes to when he says that all art "has the provinces in its blood" ("art is provincial in principle, preserving for itself a naïve, external, astonished and envious look"), and it is what Platonov hints at when he wonders whether maybe "genuine art and thought can in fact only appear in . . . a backwater."[24] It is the opposite of Casanova's thinking.

---

22 Monika Greenleaf, *Pushkin and Romantic Fashion* (Stanford: Stanford University Press, 1994), 15–16. Greenleaf is referring to the Romantic period, but her insights shed light on the tradition as a whole.

23 Quoted in Donald Fanger, *The Creation of Nikolai Gogol* (Cambridge, MA: Harvard University Press, 1979), 30.

24 Abram Terts [pseud. of Andrei Sinyanvsky], *V teni Gogolia* (Moscow: Agraf, 2003; orig. pub. 1981), 328. Platonov quoted in Thomas Seifrid, *Andrei Platonov: Uncertainties of Spirit* (Cambridge: Cambridge University Press, 1992), 18. Here Thomas Seifrid's remarks on

Provintsiia's mixing of time periods and cultural categories can not only make visible Russia's vexed relationship to European models; it can also hint at the irrelevance of these models in general—an irrelevance that might hold true not just for Russians but for all modern subjects. As Michael Holquist has argued, some Russians aimed to "universalize [the] dilemma" of being off of any heaven-ordained timeline, outside of any "transcendent system for ensuring order," thereby redefining what it meant for *everyone* to be modern.[25] Holquist shows how Lermontov's *Hero of Our Time*, for example, anticipates Lukács's famous diagnosis of the "transcendental homelessness" that defines the modern subject. Russians may have been the first to sense that this kind of homelessness opens up new possibilities, creates new centers and timelines: instead of simply trying to catch up to or get ahead of everyone else ("everyone else" being the West) while moving along the same axis, they might redefine what it meant for *everyone* to be modern.[26] The *provintsiia* trope takes part in this effort by suggesting new ways of imagining time, because provincial chaos points toward a fundamentally modern insight: *all* culture is syncretic, not just that of the provinces, or that of Russia. No temporality can claim to be universally valid. In Edward Said's words, "all cultures are involved in one another; none is simple and pure, all are hybrid, heterogeneous, extraordinarily differentiated and unmonolithic."[27]

The ambiguities of Russia's situation—peripheral but not small, European but also Asian, behind but potentially ahead, Christian but perhaps not exactly Christendom in the sense of "the West," etc.—help explain why the *provintsiia* trope came to play such a complicated and useful role in its literature, and ultimately why this tradition resists assimilation into "World Literature." Russians' strange and often excruciating relationship to "Eurochronology" turned out to be productive, in part because Russian thinkers drew on the sense of being "out of sync" in order to find new ways of thinking about time, history, and modernity.

In other words, there are other ways of imagining the "world" of World Literature. As we are learning from new scholarship, while World Literature

---

Platonov's relationship to modernism are suggestive for trying to understand how a provincial perspective might benefit an artist: Platonov, according to Seifrid, represents "a kind of de facto modernism developed, at a remove from the centers of Russian modernist culture, out of the satirical-grotesque tradition of Gogol, Leskov, and Saltykov-Shchedrin and emphatically preserving the "crude" perspective of the semi-literate provincial masses."

25 Michael Holquist, *Dostoevsky and the Novel* (Evanston: Northwestern University Press, 1986), 15–16, 30–31.

26 Holquist, *Dostoevsky and the Novel*, 15–16, 30–31.

27 Edward Said, introduction to *Culture and Imperialism* (London: Vintage, 1993), xxv.

in the West tends to be conceived as centripetal, remaining tightly focused on centers that represent themselves as the source of all creative energy, Russian and Soviet versions of this world are likely to be centrifugal, attentive to the peripheries, boundaries, and contact zones that they perceive to be more lively and artistically productive than the comparatively rigid centers. Veselovskii, Bakhtin, Tynianov, Lotman—all are examples of this willingness to refocus attention on peripheries of various sorts, so that "the boundary rather than the center" becomes the site of "literary and cultural transformation."[28]

Nineteenth-century writers foretold this development when they learned to make conscious and sophisticated use of Russia's supposed provinciality, and in doing so they provided a basis upon which later thinkers could develop a more nuanced understanding of center/periphery relations than did those who occupy undisputed centers. An example of the world and the canon as seen from such a center can be found in T. S. Eliot's essay "What is a Classic?," which condemns "provincialism" in the following terms: "By 'provincial' I mean here something more than I find in the dictionary definitions. . . . I mean also a distortion of values, the exclusion of some, the exaggeration of others, which springs, not from lack of wide geographical perambulation, but from applying standards acquired within a limited area, to the whole of human experience." The result, Eliot writes, is a sensibility that "confounds the contingent with the essential, the ephemeral with the permanent."[29] Russian writers' legacy belies this claim: even when their work would seem to be doing exactly what Eliot accuses "provincials" of doing—"[confounding] the contingent with the essential, the ephemeral with the permanent"—they themselves are never provincial in Eliot's disparaging sense. Or perhaps more accurately, the tradition nurtured by Gogol reminds us that views like Eliot's are by no means the last word on the phenomenon of provinciality: it can be reimagined and contested, along with Eurochronology, the Greenwich Meridian of Culture of literature, the equation of Europeanness with universality, and the world in World Literature.

---

28 Kate Holland, "Narrative Tradition on the Border: Alexander Veselovsky and Narrative Hybridity in the Age of World Literature," *Poetics Today* 38, no. 3 (September 2017): 429. See also Ilya Kliger, "World Literature Beyond Hegemony in Yuri M. Lotman's Cultural Semiotics," *Comparative Critical Studies* 7, no. 2–3 (2010): 257–74, and "Historical Poetics between Russia and the West: Toward a Nonlinear Model of Literary History and Social Ontology," *Poetics Today* 38, no. 3 (September 2017): 453–83; Galin Tihanov, "The Location of World Literature," *Canadian Review of Comparative Literature* 44, no. 3 (September 2017): 468–81.

29 T. S. Eliot, "What is a Classic?" *Selected Prose of T. S. Eliot*, ed. and intro. Frank Kermode (New York: Farrar, Straus and Giroux), 129.

CHAPTER 3

Armenian Literature as World Literature: Phases of Shaping It in the Pre-Soviet and Stalinist Contexts[1]

Susanne Frank

Preliminary Remarks

This chapter is a case study in the context of a larger project, where I investigate the immediate prehistory of the Soviet and later the Stalinist project of literary nation-building that invented the literatures on the Soviet territory as national units and positioned them on a scale of world literary development among all other literatures of the world that were also understood within a national paradigm. Soviet literature—conceived as multinational and as part of world literature (also understood as multinational)—by means of the norms of Socialist Realism should become the center of an expanding world literary community of socialist literature that was regarded as the only legitimate heir of world literature.[2] For this purpose, national literatures had, firstly, to be

---

1 I am grateful to Sona Mnatsakanian for checking the Armenian sources and finding some valuable supplementary documents.
2 It was Lenin who coined this claim first in his early article "Which inheritance we reject?." Later on it was repeated many times at the First All-Union Congress of Soviet Writers in 1934. Cf. Vladimir I. Lenin, "Ot kakogo nasledstva my otkazyvaemsia?," in *Polnoe sobranie sochinenii v 55 tom.*, vol. 2 (Moscow: Politizdat, 1967), 543–50.

defined and, secondly, to be classified on the teleological scale of world literary development. In some cases, "define" meant to "invent" completely, in other cases it happened through severe re-canonization. This is true for literatures which had been part of a nation-building process before like Ukrainian, Georgian, or Armenian literature that underwent a series of revisions between the years of the October Revolution and the years of Stalinism, when the previous models and the canon were replaced violently. There we can observe a clash of perspectives on national literature and world literature between the point of view of the national peripheries and the Soviet center.

Among those literatures, the Armenian case seems to be especially interesting, but not because it is so typical. On the contrary, it is specific and in a certain sense unique, not only because Armenian literature is many centuries older than Russian or Slavic literatures, but also because the Armenians, after they had become part of the Russian Empire, developed very special strategies to integrate themselves as indispensable partners into the imperial society, and, lastly, because in Armenia an attempt to canonize Armenian literature and position it as a constitutive member of the world literary community preceded the Soviet and Stalinist canonization. On the following pages, I will focus on the history of the famous anthology *Poeziia Armenii* whose official editor is Valerii Briusov. I will demonstrate that despite the fact that there was a parallel imperial project by Maxim Gorky, this anthology was the product of the initiative of some Armenian poets. In their work, the Russian poet Valerii Briusov functioned as a kind of mystification. Using Briusov's renowned name, they intended to position Armenian poetry through translation into Russian in a World literary context. I argue that the anthology *Poeziia Armenii* is symptomatic for the Armenians' older and well-established strategy to integrate and to obtain agency in the very center of the Empire.

The "Lazarian Institute of Oriental Languages" (Lazarevskii institute vostochnykh iazykov) is exemplary of this strategy and a powerful measure in this context. When it was founded in Moscow in 1814,[3] it was intended to be the educational institution for Armenians in the center of the Russian Empire. Secondly, it was intended to become and eventually became the center for the

---

3   According to Hovsep Tadeosian, the Institute was "founded in 1814 not in 1815, as it was known for hundred years." Cf. Hovsep Tadeosian, *Patmutiun Lazarian tohmi yev Lazarian chemarani Arevelian lezvats* (Vienna: Mechitaristen Buchdruckerei, 1953), 6. Cf. Kananov, Georgii I. "Semidesiatipiateletie Lazarevskovo instituta vostochnikh iazykov" (Moscow: Izdatel'stvo Instituta Lazareva, 1891), 3. Georgii I. Kananov was the director of the Institute from 1881–1897.

study of oriental languages in the Russian Empire. And, thirdly, it should open its doors as an educational institution for everybody, and it did. Very quickly the Lazarian Institute was established as an elite school for Russian administration officials who were sent to the Caucasus region.

The first collections of Armenian literature in Russian translation appeared also thanks to the initiative of a graduate of the Lazarian Institute Yurii Veselovskii—son of Aleksei Veselovskii who was already a teacher of literary history at the Lazarian Institute, and nephew of Alexander Veselovskii, the famous pioneer of comparative genre theory. After a journey to Venice to visit the community of Armenian Mekhitarists in 1889, Yurii Veselovskii edited two comprehensive anthologies of *Armianskie belletristy* in Russian translation.[4] In 1902, Veselovskii published the biography of the Armenian poet Smbat Shah-Aziz,[5] *Ocherki armianskoi literatury i zhizni* in 1906, and *Armianskaia muza* in 1907.[6] Yurii Veselovskii can be called one of the first popularizers of Armenian literature in Russia, but because of his untimely death in 1919 he could not complete his mission.

A decade later, the Lazarian Institute again served as the base for projects to mediate Armenian literature to a Russian audience. But this time it was the Armenians themselves who took the initiative and made use of Russian as a "world language" and of renowned Russian poets as editors to give Armenian literature a (stronger) voice in the context of European and world literatures. In 1916, a year before the October Revolution, two Armenian anthologies came out in Russia: The *Sbornik armianskoi literatury*, a collection of Armenian poetry, drama, and prose, edited by Gorky in Petrograd; and the anthology *Poeziia Armenii* initiated by the Armenian committee and edited by Valerii Briusov in Moscow. Until today, this anthology, which in the course of the decades and even after 1991 has seen many new editions, is considered to be the work of Briusov both in Russia—where Briusov's numerous translations as well as his extensive introduction to this anthology had been included into volume seven of Briusov's Collected Works in 1973–1975—and in Armenia— where the Pedagogical Institute was named after Briusov in 1962 (Valerii Briusov State University of Languages and Humanities of Yerevan—Erevanskii

---

4   Veselovskii, *Armianskie belletristy*, vol. 1, (Moscow: Kushnerev, 1893). A second volume that, in addition to poetry, included some articles on Armenian literary history came out in 1894.
5   Yu. Veselovskii, "Armianskii poet Smbat Shahaziz," *Russkoe Bogatstvo* 4 (1902).
6   Veselovskii published also on Armenian political history: In 1895 a study on "Polozhenie tureckich armjan do vmeshatel'stva derzhav," and in 1915 a study titled "Tragediia turetskoi Armenii." Yurii Veselovskii, *Tragediia turetskoi Armenii* (Moscow: Zvezda, 1916)

gosudarstvenii universitet iazykov i sotsial'nykh nauk imeni V. Ia. Briusova). The anthology itself was republished in Yerevan in 1966, and fifty years later in Moscow by Novoe Literaturnoe Obozrenie.[7]

In order to demonstrate the shift in the concept of the edition, I will compare the first 1916 edition of *Poeziia Armenii* with its second edition under the title *Antologiia armianskoi poezii s drevneishikh vremen do nashikh dnei* that was commissioned by Gorky in 1935 with the instruction to modify the face of Armenian literature, significantly adapting it to the Soviet norm. It came out in 1940 long after Gorky's death and after Karen Mikayelian, one of the two main editors of the first edition and co-responsible for the second edition, had been exposed to repressions ending his days in a Soviet labor camp in the Far North.

Short Remarks on the Genre of Anthology

Recent studies have focused on anthology as a genre which, in the context of modernism, repeatedly served as a powerful instrument of literary politics. It is an instrument which—often by an act of mystification—programmatically set a new aesthetic position, an instrument of literary nation-building, an instrument to invent and to position a modern national literature/poetry in a world literary context.

Think of Macpherson, who, with his Ossian, can be regarded as the founding father of this genre-tradition; or Koz'ma Prutkov, invented by Aleksei Tolstoi and the brothers Zhemchuzhnikov as the incarnation of an epigonal, naïve poet; or, think of Valerii Briusov, who by his two small volumes, the "fictitious" anthology *Russkie simvolisty*, created Russian symbolism as a "literary fact."[8] Or, think of the Bulgarian modernist Pencho Slaveikov, who by his fictitious anthology *Na ostrova na blazhenite* (1910) conjured up nineteen poets (including women), their biographies and work, which included examples of all the important genres of modern poetry (songs, ballads, sonnets, philosophical

---

7   M. D. Amirkhanian, *Poeziia Armenii s dreveneishikh vremen do nashikh dnei: k 100-letiiu Pervogo izdaniia*, 5th ed., ed. Valerii Briusov (Yerevan: Airapet, 2016). (Three earlier editions in 1966, 1973, 1986); Valerii Briusov, *Poeziia Armenii* (Moscow: Novoe Literaturnoe Obozrenie, 2016).

8   Cf. Yurii Tynianov's term "literaturnyi fakt." Tynianov, *Literaturnyi fakt* (Moscow: Vysshaia Shkola, 1993), 121–37.

aphorisms), and thereby invented modern Bulgarian literature as an "imaginary world literature."[9]

Slaveikov's example illustrates the anthology's function as an important instrument of literary nation-building—especially for minor literatures—which recently has been demonstrated through the examples of Bulgarian (Schmidt) and Ukrainian literature (Haleta)—and, simultaneously, of intercultural communication. Conveying self-images and images of "others," they are the media of world literary communication.[10]

From the very beginning of the 1930s, anthologies of Soviet national literatures served as an effective instrument of centralized Soviet literary politics to shape and control national canonization and to build up a canon of multinational literature. In some cases, Soviet anthologies invented a national canon that had never existed before. In other cases, they re-canonized what had been previously canonized, often severely changing the face of it, as demonstrated by the Armenian example below.

In this context, the Armenian case seems to be particularly interesting because it was the Armenians themselves, who, on the eve of the October Revolution, first took the initiative to launch their literature as a national canon and heritage, their tools at hand being translation into Russian and the genre of anthology. But what they invented was not so much the literature itself as a frame for its presentation.

Who were "these Armenians?": the poets and translators Vahan Terian (1885–1920) and Poghos Mkrtychevich (Pavel Nikitich) Makintsian (1884–1938),[11] both graduates from the Lazarian Institute, and the prose writer and journalist Karen Mikayelian (1883–1941), who studied at Moscow University

---

9 Galin Tihanov, "Revisiting, minor literatures,'" in *Die bulgarische Literatur der Moderne im europäischen Kontext. Zwischen Emanzipation und Selbststigmatisierung?*, ed. Bisera Dakova et al. (München: Sagner, 2013), 103–122; Galin Tihanov, "Beyond Minor Literatures: Reflections on world literature (and on Bulgarian)," in *Bulgarian literature as World Literature*, ed. Mihaela P. Harper and Dimitar Kambourov (New York: Bloomsbury, 2020).

10 Helga Essmann, *Übersetzungsanthologien. Eine Typologie und eine Untersuchung am Beispiel der amerikanischen Versdichtung in deutschsprachigen Anthologien, 1920–1960* (Frankfurt a.M.: Lang, 1992). H. Essmann and U. Schönig, eds., *Weltliteratur in deutschen Versanthologien des 19. Jahrhunderts* (Berlin: Schmidt, 1996); Monika Schmitz-Emans, "Mapping poetry: poem anthologies and the modelling of world literature," *Journal of Romance Studies* 11, no. 1 (2011): 37–50.

11 Cf. Vahan Terian, *Sobranie stikhotvorenij* (Moscow: Sovetskii pisatel'. Biblioteka poèta, bol'shaja serija, 1980). Vahan Terian, *Yerkeri zhoghovatsu* (Yerevan: Hayastan, 1975). On Terian's work in general cf. Robert A. Bagdasarian, "Vahan Terian: 'Ia s iunosheskikh let liubil,'" 2012, https://www.proza.ru/2012/02/06/890.

in the first years of the twentieth century.[12] None of them survived the Stalin era. Vahan Terian died very early in 1920 after contracting tuberculosis, whereas the other two, Makintsian and Mikayelian, both of whom were important agents of official Soviet cultural and foreign policy, fell victim to the Stalinist persecutions. To understand how decisive their initiative actually was for the anthology that came out under Valerii Briusov's name, it is important to take a look at their activities in the preceding years.

Vahan Terian, one of the most famous poets of Armenian modernism and symbolism, was born in an Armenian village in the south of Georgia. He came to Moscow in 1899 as a student. After he finished his studies at the Lazarian Institute, he continued his education in Moscow and, eventually, at Petersburg University, where he enthusiastically attended Nikolai Marr's lectures in Caucasiology. In 1902–1903, while studying at the Lazarian Institute, together with his friends Tsolak Khanzadian, Poghos Makintsian, Onik Ohanjanian, and Melkon Karamian, Terian founded and co-edited a samizdat (handwritten) school newspaper *Huys* (Hope), where he published programmatic essays and editor's notes, and also poetry, mostly under his pseudonym Shvin or Volo.[13] When his first collection of poetry, *Mtnshaghi anurjner* (Dreams of the Dawn), came out in 1908, it was perceived by his contemporaries as an epochal event. In memoirs, the period is characterized as the beginning of the "Terian era," "the air was filled with Terian."[14] Having read Terian's collection of poems, Hovhannes Tumanian wrote to him: "You are a poet, above all. You are not playing with words. I greet your literary debut with great joy, congratulations."[15] While studying at Moscow University in 1910, Terian edited a literary almanac *Garun* (Spring). It was in these days that he met Karen Mikayelian—who had been studying at Moscow University since 1905 (and for a while in Germany)— and invited him to become a co-editor. One of the aims of this almanac was to

---

12 On Mikayelian's work in general and on his relations to Briusov cf. a whole number of studies by Robert Bagdasarian: *Karen Mikayelian: Tvorchestvo i vklad v russko-armianskie literaturno-kul'turnye vzaimosviazi* (Yerevan: Lingua, 2010); "Karen Mikayelian i vidnye deiateli armianskoi literatury," *Lraber hasarakakan gitutyunneri* 2 (1996): 123–33. "Publicistika Karena Mikayeliana," *Lraber hasarakakan gitutyunneri* 1 (2003): 169–81.

13 Cf.: "В газете Терьян в основном выступает с редакционными статьями и передовицами. Он возглавлял в газете также отдел поэзии, где помещал свои стихи,"–писал в своих воспоминаниях М. Карамян.

14 Cf. the memoirs of Stepan Zorian: Stepan Zorian, *Yerkeri zhoghovatsu*, vol. 11 (Yerevan: Sovetakan grogh, 1985), 172.

15 In a letter to Tsolak Khanzadian (May 4–8, 1908), Terian tells his meeting with Tumanian, during which the latter welcomed his entrance into the world of literature. Cf. Vahan Terian, *Yerkeri zhoghovatsu*, vol. 3 (Yerevan: Hayastan, 1975), 257.

model a national canon of modern Armenian literature. Apart from editing, the young students also organized literary events such as an evening on the occasion of the thirtieth jubilee of Tumanian's first publication. In 1910, even before the first book-length publication of Terian's poems appeared, a biographical portrait of Terian by Arsen Terterian was published in Tbilisi: "Vahan Terian. Tsnorki, ts'aravi yev hashtutyan yergichy" (Vahan Terian: The singer of dream, thirst and reconciliation). Not until 1912 did a first edition of Terian's *Poems* come out in Moscow with illustrations by Martiros Sarian.

There are some very explicit statements from the early 1910s where Terian defines the relationship between Armenia and Russia as very close and where he characterizes it as an important precondition for the survival and further development of Armenian literature as a modern national literature in the context of European modern literatures. For example, Terian argues that "The Armenians proved their solidarity and aspiration towards Russia long before," that "It is already a historical tradition for us."[16] In the talk "Hay grakanutian galiq ory" (The future of Armenian literature), that Terian gave in Tbilisi in the Hall of Musical Association on April 30, 1914, Terian writes "Our homeland is Russia, and we are willing to promote and preserve our culture in her bosom—if we are able to grasp all the cultural heritage of Europe, then we can live, if not, we will die as a nation."[17] With this attitude, Terian follows the tradition of Khachatur Abovian, who in 1840 in his novel *Verk Hayastani: Voghb Hayrenasiri* (Wounds of Armenia: Lamentation of a Patriot) envisioned Russia as Armenia's patron and mediator on its path to becoming a modern nation.

In order to intensify communication between modern Armenian literature and European literatures, Terian himself translated (or facilitated translations of) important contemporary authors from different European countries such as Arthur Schnitzler or Charles Baudelaire. He promoted the translation of all Russian classics into Armenian. Together with Mikayelian, who was a reliable

---

16 Նոր չէ, որ հայույթյունը պետք է վկայե իր համակրությունը և ձգտումը դեպի Ռուսաստանը։ Դա մի պատմական ավանդություն է արդեն մեզ համար։ Մեր ժողովուրդը բնագրով միշտ զգացել է իր փրկության ուղիղ ճանապարհը, և մեր մտավորականության ներկայացուցիչները արտահայտել են այդ զգացմունքը շատ պարզ ու ցայտուն կերպով։ Gevorg Emin-Terian, *Vahan Terian. Antip yev anhayt ejer* (Yerevan: Tigran Mets, 2014), 341. Cf. Gevorg Emin-Terian, *Vahan Terian. Antip yev anhayt ejer* (Yerevan: Tigran Mets, 2014).

17 Մեր հայրենիքը Ռուսիան է և նրա ծոցում է, որ կամենում ենք մենք առաջ տանել ու պահպանել մեր կուլտուրան—եթե կարող ենք մենք յուրացնել ժամանակակից Եվրոպայի ամբողջ կուլտուրական ժառանգությունը, ուրեմն կարող ենք ապրել, եթե ոչ, մենք կմեռնենք իբր ազգ: Vahan Terian, *Yerkeri zhoghovatsu*, vol. 3 (Yerevan: Hayastan, 1975), 99.

assistant, supporter, and sometimes even sponsor at his side, Terian tirelessly collected money for translations and convinced other authors of the importance of translations for the "modernization" of Armenian literature. Terian himself was probably the most diligent translator of Russian symbolist poetry into Armenian.

Karen Mikayelian, who during his studies in Jena had joined the social democrat movement back in Moscow, became one of the most important Armenian journalists of his time. Beginning in the early 1900s, Mikayelian published critical essays not only on provincial life, social discrimination and literary history with the intention to spread knowledge about the national canon, but also about the Russian classics. While he co-edited the almanac *Garun* (Spring) with Vahan Terian, he developed the idea to compile a comprehensive anthology including Armenian poetry from all periods and from all parts of the dispersed nation.

The question of who had the idea to publish Gorky's anthology, whether it was Mikayelian and Terian or Gorky himself, is not conclusively resolved, but researchers agree that it was Mikayelian and Terian's initiative to edit the comprehensive anthology *Poeziia Armenii* in Russian, and that it was Gorky who recommended them to ask Briusov to be the editor.[18]

In any case, it is a remarkable fact that the first two anthologies of Armenian literature in the twentieth century both came out in 1916 in the metropolises of the Russian Empire, Moscow and Petrograd. And both of them were produced and edited by Moscow-based Armenian authors of the first rank.

In the following, I will focus on the outcome of both anthologies.

1. Sbornik armianskoi literatury (1916)

When the anthology *Sbornik armianskoi literatury* was released in 1916 by the publishing house "Parus," it was the first of a whole series of anthologies Gorky

---

18 In D. Semenovskii's book *A. M. Gorky. Pisma i vstrechi*, the author describes his visit to Gorky's summer house in Musta Miaki. There he met Vahan Terian and Tikhonov who were guests of Gorky at that time: "Referring to Tikhonov and Terian, Aleksei Maksimovich opened a conversation about publishing the new anthology of Armenian literature. Terian gave the names of Armenian literary critics and Russian poet-translators, who could be involved in the works of anthology. Gorky wrote their names down." Quoted in Vahan Terian, *Yerkeri zhoghovastu*, vol. 4 (Yerevan: Sovetakan grogh, 1979), 425. Cf. also R. A. Bagdasarian, "Velikii drug armianskoi kul'tury: K 150-letiiu so dnia rozhdeniia Maksima Gorkogo," *Golos Armenii*, March 3, 2018, https://golosarmenii.am/article/64477/velikij-drug-armyanskoj-kultury.

had been planning for almost fifteen years. Referring to the correspondence between Briusov and A. N. Tikhonov Ol'ga Avdeeva states that the foundation of the publishing house Parus in 1915 in Petrograd was only the last preparatory step on the way to implement Gorky's idea to edit a series of "Anthologies of the literatures of the peoples of the Russian Empire,"[19] and thereby to give a survey of these literatures as they existed now under the rule of Russia. In Gorky's preface to "Ot izdaltel'stva," he wrote:

> The *Anthology of Armenian Literature* is meant to be the first in a series of anthologies dedicated to the literatures of peoples living together with us, the Russians. In the near future, the publishing house "Parus" will bring out anthologies of Latvian, Finnish, Tatar, Jewish, Ukrainian and other literatures as well. Each of these anthologies would include an introductory article on the history of the people's cultural production and the determinants of its emergence.[20]

The Armenian sbornik (collection) came out first, but already in early 1917 two other anthologies of Latvian and Finnish literature were published. A two-volume anthology of Jewish literature was announced in the publishing program for 1918 but could not be realized because of the October Revolution. Instead, the Moscow publishing house "Safrut," which Leib Iaffe had just founded, released the *Evreiskaia antologiia: Sbornik molodoi evreiskoi poėzii pod redakciei V.F. Khodasevicha i L.B. Iaffe* (Jewish anthology: Collected volume of young Jewish poetry edited by V.F. Khodasevich and L.B. Iaffe) with an introduction by M. Gershenzon in 1918.[21]

---

19 Avdeeva refers to the memoire of K. P. Piatnitskii stating that Gorky already in 1901 started to make plans for a series of national anthologies with the publishing house "Znanie." Cf. Ol'ga Avdeeva, *Iz istorii podgotovki sbornika latyshskoi literatury v izdatel'stva "Parus,"* in *K 125-iubileiu so dnia rozhdeniia Iurgisa Baltrushaitisa,* ed. Nikolaj Kotrelev (Moscow: Nasledie, 1999), 34.

20 "Сборник Арманской литературы является первым, по очереди, в ряду сборников, посвященных обзору литературного творчества племен, живущих с нами, русскими. В ближайшем будущем книгоиздательство "Парус" выпустит сборники по литературам латышской, финской, татарской, еврейской, украинской и пр. Каждый из этих сборников включает статью по истории художественного творчества народности и очерк общих условий ее бытия." Gorky, *Sbornik armianskoi literatury* (Petrograd: Parus 1916), III.

21 Cf. Aleksandr Lavrov, "Lejb Jaffe i 'Evrejskaja antologiia': k istorii izdaniia," in *Simvolisty i drugie* (Moscow: NLO, 2015).

Susanne Frank

The plan for this series gives us an idea of how Gorky imagined canonizing the literatures of the Empire from the point of view of the center, and we may guess how closely his political strategy of designing a multinational literature was related to his simultaneously developing ideas for the publishing program of World Literature (*Vsemirnaia literatura*). The fact that only literatures that already had a "history" (and thereby a stabilized canon) were chosen for the anthologies indicates the gap between this program and the later project of multinational Soviet literature which was also designed by Gorky in the early 1930s. The way these early anthologies were edited also very much differed from the policy of the 1930s. The former were conceptualized and edited by representatives of the respective literatures who had taken on—as was the case with Leib Iaffe, with Viktors Eglītis, editor in chief of the Latvian Anthology,[22] and also with the Armenian editors—the mission of literary nation-building.[23] And it was in their interest to engage and cooperate as closely as possible with the most famous Russian poets of the day as their translators.[24]

---

22 In the case of the Latvian anthology only one person, A.N. Tikhonov, served as mediator between the Russian poets-translators such as Valerii Briusov and the Latvian editorial board. On the one hand, Briusov strongly supported the "national" poets—defended them against numerous Russian chauvinist accusations such as V. Rozanov's Essay "Tsentrobezhnye sily Rossii (k voprosu ob inorodchine"), who suggested that in the context of such insignificant small cultures there couldn't emerge a new Schiller (cf. Avdeeva 1999, 37)—because he was convinced in the aesthetic potential of small cultures; on the other hand, Briusov would always prefer to include into the anthologies the aesthetically most advanced young poets whose works were aesthetically strong enough to earn them a voice in transnational context of world literature. But in more than one case, the national editors were more conservative than the Russian poets-translators and refused to include more modernist authors in the anthologies. Cf. Avdeeva, *Iz istorii podgotovki sbornika.*

23 Cf. Iaffe in his preface to the "Jewish Collection" who underlines the programmatic task of the volume as a combination of strong awareness of national traditions and expression of a common modernist state of mind. Cf. *Evreiskaia antologiia. Sbornik molodoi evreiskoi poèzii*, ed. Vladislav Khodasevich and Leib Iaffe, (Moscow: Safrut', 1918), XII.

24 Interesting to compare these anthologies with a scholarly collective volume edited by Baudouin de Courtenay and others also in 1916: I.A. Baudouin de Courtenay, N. A. Gredeskul, and Boris Gurevich, eds., *Otechestvo. Puti i dostizheniia natsional'nykh literatur Rossii. Nacional'nyi vopros* (Petrograd: Izdatel'stvo Popova 1916). The contributions to this volume include articles on Finnish, Estonian, Lithuanian, Latvian, Ukrainian, Jewish, Polish, and Georgian literatures. In his opening article "Rossiia—tvorimaia naciia," Boris Gurevich describes the required integration in the terminology of possession and property: All languages/literatures on the territory of Russia are property of Russia. Accordingly, he underlines the importance to strengthen the leading role of Russian as the lingua franca of a multinational nation and the importance of Russian (literature) as the only possible member of world literature among the numerous literatures and languages on the territory of Russia. This scholarly volume is not only explicitly imperialist–concluding his article, Gurevich speaks of an „imperial national self-consciousness"–, but also anticipates the role Stalin and

Armenian Literature as World Literature | 45

In the case of the *Sbornik armianskoi literatury* it becomes clear from the documents how closely Gorky collaborated with Terian and what a crucial role Terian played in the composition of the volume. Thus, he writes in a letter to Gorky from July 21, 1915:

> Dear Aleksei Maksimovich! In a few days, the interlinear translation of Sundukian's "Pepo" will be finished. Please, tell me how to proceed. Should I send the translation or come myself (as you asked me before)? If you intend to deal with it immediately and if you deem my presence necessary, I could come by on Saturday and bring the manuscript. Among the poets there are left only a couple of works that were not included in their collected works editions and came out in dispersed journals. I will choose from these works and present them to the translators. About the rest, regarding the volume, I will tell you in person. Let me know if I should come, or wait and transmit through Aleksandr Nikolaevich [Tikhonov, director of the publishing house "Parus" and Gorky's closest consultant] Sincerely yours, loving and honoring you Vahan Terian"[25]

In this sense, it is perfectly logical that Gorky did not raise his own voice anywhere in the book. Two framing essays are written (and authorized) by Armenians: Davit Ananun is indicated as the author of an essay on Armenian history told as a story of persecution, dispersion, and prevented nation-building. Armenia is portrayed as a victim of the East, of the two Muslim powers, of the Ottoman and the Persian Empires, a victim that was finally able to find protection under Russian rule. Formulations like "mnogostradal'nyi pasynok istorii" (long-suffering step-child of history) or "siryi i odinokii narod" (raw and lonesome people), whose "tvorcheskii dukh" (creative genius) never had the chance to evolve, pave the way for the image of Russia as a savior that guarantees shelter and brings European enlightenment to the East.[26]

---

under his aegis the late Gorky of the mid-1930s ascribe Russian language and literature—without, of course, using the word "imperial" any more. (ibid., 11)

25 Vahan Terian, *Yerkeri zhoghovatsu*, vol. 4 (Yerevan: Sovetakan grogh, 1979), 223.

26 But as we know from Davit Ananun's other works, first of all "Social development of Russian Armenians" (consisting of 3 volumes), he thought that the Armenians' orientation to Russia and Russian rule should be temporary, as one necessary step on the way to "conquer the homeland and state." Cf.: "Promoting the Russian domination in the East and [bringing] the Armenians under the Russian state, was not [only] really a great deed, but was a way to

In the second introductory essay on the history of Armenian literature the already mentioned Poghos Makintsian paves the way and lays the ground for the narrower focus of the anthology of modern Armenian literature. Telling the story of Armenian literature from the very beginning with all its peripeteias and splits, he compensates for what the reader cannot find in this anthology. As the introduction admits: this anthology offers an insight only into "the least significant part of Armenian literature so far."

A glance at the table of contents shows that on the one hand the editors had no problem to diligently exclude Turkish Armenian literature—because, according to the concept of the anthology, it did not belong to the Armenian people living on the territory of Russia.[27] On the other hand, it obviously was the intention of the editors to compile a comprehensive anthology of Armenian literature and therefore to represent a whole specter of genres: besides poetry and pieces of prose the volume contains also two dramas.

This kind of composition involved the Armenian authors to a very high extent, much higher than in Briusov's collection—which I will discuss next: It was them (mostly Terian and Makintsian) who translated the prose and the dramas, whereas poetry was mostly translated into Russian on the basis of interlinear cribs by Russian poets, all of whom were renowned representatives of symbolism (Valerii Briusov, Ivan Bunin, Konstantin Bal'mont, Vladislav Khodasevich, Aleksandr Blok).

Terian's letters demonstrate the extent to which the Armenians conceptualized the anthology on their own, and to which Terian and Mikayelian worked as a team to implement their ideas. For instance, in a letter to Karen

---

serve a great purpose. Armenians took that path at the beginning of the century, and here their collective will was strengthened. But after the implementation of the Russian conquest program, another principle did not strain the Armenian forces and thought" (from volume 2, Ejmiatsin, 1922, digilib.aua.am/am/ԴԱԻՒՒԹ-%20ԱՆԱՆՈՒՆ/library/1650). Davit Ananun was arrested and exiled in 1927.

27 Obviously, there was yet another reason for this omission: In a letter to the poet Aleksandr Tsaturian, which is dated 1915, June 29–July 15, Terian writes: "... there will be two anthologies—one dedicated to Turkish Armenian and one to Russian Armenian (at least there are plans for that), but for now the Russian Armenian anthology will be released." (Vahan Terian, *Collected works*, vol. 4 [Yerevan: Sovetakan grogh, 1979], 209). In later letters, Terian comes back to the above mentioned anthology of Turkish Armenian literature, and also mentions a third one, which should be called "Armenian library," again with Gorky. Cf. a letter (written in second half of July 1915) to Nvart Tumanian [Hovhannes Tumanian's daughter]: "Another anthology will be published by Gorky (again, he will be the editor and I will compile it), dedicated to Turkish Armenian Literature. And then he will publish a series of books under the title of "Armenian library" that will include translations of extensive works which because of their size were not included in the anthology."

Mikayelian dated April 2, 1915, Petrograd,[28] Terian explains that due to Gorky's and Briusov's interest he understood how important the publication of not only one, but even two anthologies of Armenian literatures in Russian translation would be and that this task would need his and Mikayelian's expertise to be fulfilled:

To Karen Mikayelian, April 2, 1915, Petrograd[29]

> I cannot say anything bad about a Russian anthology, and I am not against it. But will it come true and can *those* people make it? I think both Veselovskii and Totomian are not capable, and it could be better if me and Paolo [Poghos Makintsian] were there to counterbalance the "older ones." I think you can do your best as our representative to help us participate actively in that work.
>
> I have some news for you. Maxim Gorky called me to his place (I will go the day after tomorrow) for a similar work. He also intends to publish a collection of Armenian literature (he will publish several "national" and "provincial" [*oblastnoi*] anthologies, including Armenian as well). For now, do not tell anything about this to anyone (especially as it may get in the way of your initiative. Though I think the one should not get in the way of the other. What harm could there be? Let there be two anthologies). I will visit Gorky and whatever happens, I will write to you in detail, solving this issue as soon as possible."
>
> I was told that Boris Lazarevskii (whom you definitely know) is looking for my address, I think, with a similar issue. Though I do not feel comfortable to show myself earlier, maybe I will learn from him soon.
>
> Dear Karen, with a bitter heart I notice how these foreigners are much more interested in us, than we ourselves, our intelligentsia, and our bourgeoisie, who as you can see are ready to pay for Russian anthology the kind of money they would never

---

28 Կ. Միքայելյանին (To Karen Mikaelian /2 April 1915/) Վահան Տերյան, երկերի ժողովածու, հատոր չորրորդ, Երևան, Սովետական գրող, 1979, էջ 199–201: Vahan Terian, *Yerkeri zhoghovatsu*, vol. 4 (Yerevan: Sovetakan grogh, 1979), 199–201, here: 200–201.

29 Նվ. Թումանյանին
Վահան Տերյան, երկերի ժողովածու, հատոր չորրորդ, Երևան, Սովետական գրող. Vahan Terian, *Yerkeri zhoghovatsu*, vol. 4, (Yerevan: Sovetakan grogh, 1979), 220–23, here: 220–21.

give to Armenian [literature]. They want to boast with our literature and show it to the foreigners, they are ready to give everything to a Russian writer, only if he deigns to edit and participate, but they refuse to give some money to Armenian writers, and by now they did not want to do anything for developing that same literature and they will not want it in the future either.

Believe me, now we need to think more about developing our literature, than about presenting it to the foreigners. Karen, we must gather, unite our youth and work."[30]

With this sentence Terian indicates that a programmatic structure of the anthologies should and would help to shape the ground for the further development of Armenian literature in the direction of European modernism. He was more explicitly schematic in how he envisioned the anthology in a letter to Nvard Tumanian writing (from Petrograd, in the second half of July, 1915) that:

In our anthology, only 50 pages (from 320) are preserved for poetry. I chose the following works from Ivan Fadeich:[31]

1. "Parvana" (maybe we will arrange a new translation and probably Bunin will translate it. Gorky has already sent him the interlinear translations done by me, and now if Bunin needs help, he will contact me. I am waiting, let us see what he will write.

2. "Monastery of the Doves."

3. "Paul and Peter" (this work is not appreciated very much among us. Frankly speaking, previously I did not pay attention to it either, but when I read it again and *closely*, I liked it and advised it to Gorky, who read my *literal* translation and liked it *very much*. I am afraid Bunin will not be able to translate it *well*, though in general Bunin is a good [translator], and I think he will translate Ivan Fadeich better than any Russian poet, since he is also an *epic* [writer].

4. The first of the "Psalms of Sorrow," i.e. "God." This one also sounds well in Russian and is quite *typical for our*

---

30 Vahan Terian, *Yerkeri zhoghovatsu*, vol. 4 (Yerevan: Sovetakan grogh, 1979), 223.
31 He is alluding here to Hovhannes Tumanian.

literature, for life and for Ivan Fadeich. If it is translated well, it will have a great impact.

5. "Descending." These days I will do the literal translation and will send it to Bunin.
6. "Armenian grief" (I have not sent this one yet. I will send it with the previous one).
7. "Aghtamar." (We will probably put Bal'mont's translation of it. He is good, isn't he?)

Maybe "Gikor" will be included too. As you notice, I tried to choose *typical* works from Ivan Fadeich, that is, from his 1. Epic works 2. Lyric works a. personal, b. national 3. Prose works.

I wanted to include "David of Sassoun" as well, but it is too large, and, besides that, you should know that there is going to be published another anthology in Moscow, and they decided (Paolo is working in the editorial board) to have "David of Sassoun" there. They can include more, because they will publish only poetry, while "our" anthology (i.e., Gorky's) will be dedicated both to prose and poetry. Also, Gorky does not want increase the size so that it would be reasonably priced and accessible to a wide range of people."[32]

The selection of poems in Gorky's anthology widely differs from the selection in Briusov's *Poeziia Armenii*. Even though the composition of the authors (poets) is more or less the same in both volumes, there is little overlap in the selection of poems. In both anthology Rafael Patakanian, Smbat Shakh-Aziz, Ioannes Ioannisian, Aleksandr Tsaturian, Hovhannes Tumanian, Avetik Isahakian, Derenik Demirchian and Vahan Terian are represented with five to ten poems, but only in five cases there is an overlap of one poem (Patakanian, Shakh-Aziz, Ioannisian, Tsaturian, Hovhannes Tumanian, Isahakian). And the fact that the archival documents related to *Poeziia Armenii* contain, for the most part, exactly those poems (in Briusov's translation) that have been included in Gorky's anthology may serve as additional proof that the Armenians—as secret editors—coordinated both anthologies.[33]

---

32 Ibid, 220–21.

33 Cf. in his letters to P. Makintsian (June–July 1915), Vahan Terian expresses his concerns about the problem of choosing works for translation for two different, but equally representative anthologies at once: "Now a question arises—would it be good if the same things were in our collection and yours? . . . and wouldn't it be possible to coordinate the

2. Poeziia Armenii (1916)

When the "Moskovskii armianskii komitet" was founded in October 1914 with the aim to support Russia against Turkey during what became World War I and to provide help for its victims and fugitives from Armenia, Mikayelian had the idea that it should be a concern of this committee also to promote the image of Armenia on the international scene by means of a magnificent anthology of Armenian poetry of all periods in Russian translation. And indeed, when Mikayelian came up with his proposal in early 1915, the committee agreed to support the project. As the documents show, Mikayelian and Terian confidentially approached Gorky with the question of who could be the editor of an anthology of Armenian poetry. And it was Gorky who recommended Briusov to them. When Mikayelian and Terian first met Briusov on June 26, the Russian poet agreed more or less on the spot and professed readiness to start working on this project immediately. Thus, a period of quite intensive collaboration with the two Armenians started in July 1915 and finished at the end of August 1916 with the presentation of the anthology to the public. Briusov frankly admitted that he did not have any knowledge of Armenian literature before, but that the collaboration with the Armenians allowed him to read a lecture on the history of Armenian poetry from the ancient times to the beginning of the twentieth century already in mid-October 1915.[34] In his (self-)presentation, he oscillated between seeing himself as a pioneer explorer of this rare "treasure" of world literature and admitting to be a complete newcomer: "Only now—says the poet—when I am able to read Narekatsi, Akhtamartsi, Kuchak Nahapet, Sayat-Nova, Tumanian, Isahakian, Tsaturian, Hovhannisyan, Terian and other Armenian poets in the original version—only now do I understand what a precious treasure had been hidden from the eyes of the Russian society for such a

---

content of the collections so that each would be a little different (prose). If you could agree and manage this issue on your own with me, it will be very good." (Vahan Terian, Collected works, vol. 4 (Yerevan: Sovetakan grogh, 1979), 211.) Or cf. a letter from summer 1915 or 1916: "I hope you will not give preference to "your" collection [*Poeziia Armenii*] over "ours" [*Sbornik Armianskoi literatury*], because you are as much, if not [even] more "ours," as "yours," since the introductory article in "ours" [means "anthology"] is yours." (ibid, 212.)

34 15.10. organized by the "Общество свободной эстетики" [Society of free aesthetics] in the restaurant "Альпийская роща" [Alpine grove]. E. Zh. Mnatsakanyan, "Puteshestvie Valerii Briusova na Kavkaz. Antologiia Poèziia Armenii i Hovhannes Tumanian," in *Gumanitarnye i iuridicheskie issledovaniia SKFU* 4 (2017), 203–209, here: 204.

long time," and in a flowery image he continues that it seems to him "as if until now the door to a paradise of which we did not know had been locked."[35]

It was Briusov who in the course of the following year—during the months before the anthology was released—won the fame of an explorer, protector, and promoter of Armenian poetry not only in Russia but also and especially in the Transcaucasian region. After his lecture in Moscow, where he declared Armenian poetry a "rich treasury" and a "wonderful paradise," Briusov was invited to visit Baku at the very beginning of 1916. His journey turned out to be a triumph. When he arrived, he was welcomed with honors.[36] After giving an extensive lecture at the Theater of the Mayilian Brothers in Baku, Briusov was invited by The Caucasian Society of Armenian Writers (Kavkazskoe obshchestvo armianskikh pisatelei) to visit Tbilisi. Introduced by the then already famous poet Hovhannes Tumanian, Briusov read his lecture at the Artist's Theater to an audience of two thousand people. During Briusov's stay in Tbilisi, the Armenian poets Makintsian and Terian prepared his invitation to Yerevan. And so, on January 15, Briusov left Tbilisi for Yerevan, the third stop of his two-week trip. His Yerevan lecture gave him the opportunity to present Terian to the Armenian public as one of the most promising Armenian poets. Back from *Zakavkaz'e* (Transcaucasia), Briusov continued to deliver lectures on the Armenian topic in Moscow and Petrograd—January 28 at the Polytechnical Museum in Moscow; March 25 at a meeting of The Society of the Aficionados of Russian Language (Obshchestvo liubitelei Rossiskoi slovesnosti) headed by its president, Professor Aleksei Gruzinskii, at Moscow State University; and on May 14 at the prestigeous Tenishev School in Petrograd—until the anthology finally came out in mid-August 1916 and became a great success.[37]

There can be no doubt that Briusov's authority was most important in this context—without a renowned poet like him, the anthology of Armenian poetry in Russian translation could not have been that successful and would not have

---

35 ". . . Нарекаци, Ахтамарци, Кучаком Наапетом, Саят-Нова, Туманяном, Исаакяном, Цатуряном, Ованнисяном, Терьяном и др. армянскими поэтами,–только теперь я понял, какой драгоценный клад был скрыт от русского общества. Мне кажется, что перед нами была закрыта дверь, ведущая в дивный рай, о существовании которого мы были в полном неведении". Mnatsakanyan, Puteshestvie, 204.

36 Cf. R. A. Bagdasarian, *Armianskoe literaturnoe okruzhenie V. Briusova*, in *Briusovskie chteniia 2018* (Yerevan: Airapet, 2019), 440–55.

37 Cf. Anushavan Zakarian, "Lekcii V. Briusova ob armianskoi poėzii. K 100-letiiu izdaniia sbornika *Poėziia Armenii*," in: *Istoriko-filologicheskii zhurnal*, 2 (2016): 48–73. See also Anushavan Zakarian, *Armeniia v literaturno-obshchestvennoi dejatel'nosti Briusova*, (Yerevan: Izdatel'stvo "Gitutiun" NAN RA, 2016).

become canonical—even in Armenia! But, as we can see, for example, from the fact that the only time during his journey when Briusov presented a different lecture, a lecture written on his own—on the interdependence between the political history of Armenia and the history of Armenian literature—he failed. This second lecture in Tbilisi was not appreciated at all, and Briusov did not try to deliver it anywhere again. Owing to his popularity as a Russian author and intellectual, Briusov could serve as an influential promoter of Armenian poetry in and especially beyond the boundaries of Armenia, but his all too hastily acquired expertise had no solid foundation and did not allow him to be recognized as a real expert. Thus, when Briusov tried to promote his idea for a second volume of the anthology in 1918 that would contain prose, this idea was appreciated neither by the Armenian Committee nor by Mikayelian to whom Briusov sent the proposal personally: "I send you a notice on the idea for the anthology *Aiastan*. [. . .]. I am very excited about it. The second edition of *Poeziia* is more or less ready for print. [. . .] Yours, Valerii Briusov."

For me, these traces of the negotiations between Briusov and the Armenian poets-editors demonstrate that it was the Armenians' strategy to instrumentalize Briusov's authority for their purpose. Even though they had, in fact, composed and compiled it themselves, they decided to launch the anthology as Briusov's work to suggest the recognition and canonization of Armenian poetry as world literature by a famous Russian poet, representative of a major literature who was able to introduce and affirm the position of a small literature among the members of world literary community.[38] It seems to me that the strategy to launch a national canon by means of an anthology in (Russian) translation and to consolidate it by means of the editor, a famous Russian poet closely resembles a mystification—an aesthetic device Briusov himself made use of extensively at the outset of his career when he established his fame as a poet by launching a fictitious anthology under the title *Russian symbolists*. In the case of the Armenian anthology, the mystification of the editor served the purpose of sustainable and wide-reaching (literary) nation-building.

As we now turn to the composition of the anthology and its conceptualization in the editor's introduction, we can see how thoroughly it differs from

---

38 Cf. in his memoirs about Hovhannes Tumanian, Derenik Demirchian, pointing on "Vernatun," says, "The views of Tumanian and Briusov were coinciding in many points. These were views of our "Vernatun." The fact that the eternal stars of our literature can be only those writers, be from ancient or modern times, who gave universal ideas and struggled for the higher literary quality." (Derenik Demirchian, Tumaniani het [Yerevan: Hayastan, 1969], 30). That is, Demirchian also suggests that the canon of the anthologies was kind of composed in the circle of Armenian writers and intellectuals.

Gorky's approach to his anthology. The introduction to *Poeziia Armenii* does not put Armenian poetry in the context of a multinational empire. Instead, it foregrounds the unique specificity of Armenian poetry that results from its age and its geocultural position. As the volume's title indicates, the task is to define Armenian poetry as one single entity across all boundaries of history and geographical dispersion: *Armenian Poetry and its unity in the course of the ages: An outline of literary history* (*Poeziia Armenii i ee edinstvo v protiazhenii vekov. Istoriko-literaturnyi ocherk*) This aim is also the reason for focusing exclusively on poetry, because only poetry has developed continuously from the very beginning of medieval Armenian up to the twentieth century. In addition, the introduction defines three aspects of this unity: First, Armenian literature (poetry) is conceptualized as an equal member of the European and world literary community. The obvious aim of the introduction is to define the canon of Armenian literature (with poetry as its core) in its full scope as an extraordinary, rich national heritage that bridges the diasporic divide and defines it in total in a world literary horizon as equal to other European literatures. Therefore, according to the criterion of poetic quality, only the best poems of each period should be selected and included, and the anthology in toto should represent the best of Armenian poetry as a kind of treasure chest. Second, within the frames of canon-building procedure West Armenian (Turkish Armenian) and East Armenian poetry figure as two complementary halves of one national unit that both contribute, in their respective way, to the common development of national literature. From this point of view, West Armenian poetry, which preserves the rhetorical/figurative memory of European poetry, assumes the role of a partner in a poetic dialogue that normally foreign literatures have. In the author's opinion, the contribution of West Armenian poetry to the national development in toto is not that significant, and, compared to East Armenian poetry, rather modest because West Armenian poetry could not claim any originality in relation to other Western European literatures.

A third aspect concerns the role of Armenian poetry in the context of the Russian Empire: the introduction defines Armenian poetry as *the* mediator between West and East, between the European West and the Orient, but not in the, at that time, usual sense of "Armenia as the spearhead of Christianity in the East," but rather in the sense of a synthesis, the sense that Nikolai Marr—at that time professor at the University of Petrograd whom both Briusov and Terian admired—had brought up. Marr understood the Armenian culture as the product of a merger of the Indo-European people of Phrygia who had migrated to the East and the Japhetite people from Urartia (Nairi).

Accordingly, the introduction sets out a plan for the future development of Armenian poetry/literature: to recognize and preserve it as a precious heritage and to productively use it for further developments (even though the term "heritage" is not used explicitly by the author, its meaning is implicitly present in the argumentation); to open up new perspectives for a fruitful dialogue between the East and the West. And, finally, to bring forward the "national spirit"—as the author puts it—in order to let Armenian poetry resonate in harmony with other national literatures as "one of the strings on the harp of world poetry."

While East Armenian poetry is the more important one, its West Armenian counterpart is included in Briusov's anthology and is defined as a constitutive part of the national corpus of Armenian poetry. At this point, it becomes obvious how significantly the concepts of *Poeziia Armenii* and Gorky's *Sbornik* differ: Whereas Gorky aimed at representing the literatures "of Russia"—literatures on the territory of Russia—in a series of anthologies, *Poeziia Armenii* does not define Armenian poetry as a poetry of Russia, neither does it understand it from a territorial perspective. It rather constructs it as a unit in the sense of a "cultural nation" and clearly places it not only into the context of the Russian Empire, but rather into the global context of world literature. [39]

From this point of view, Russian language is understood as a tool of mediation to the arena of world literature. In this respect, I find most interesting what has been uttered by Armenian authors during Briusov's lecture-journey to the centers of Armenian culture in Zakavkaz'e: It was T. Hovhanisian, chair of the "Association of Friends of the Armenian literature," who at the reception after Briusov's lecture made his vision and mission concerning Armenian literature clear: Hovhanisian spoke of a "small culture" for which literature serves as one of the most important if not the only indicator of its significance in a broader international context and the only way to legitimate the claim for its independent existence. But the only feasible way to raise this claim can be through the

---

39 "Cultural nation" refers to Otto Bauer, one of the most influential founding fathers of European social democracy whose book *Die Nationalitätenfrage und die Sozialdemokratie* (Vienna: Vorwärts, 1907) may have inspired Karen Mikayelian. The latter could have met Bauer during his studies in Germany at the Congress of the II International in Stuttgart in 1907, where Bauer's just released thesis was the object of a lively discussion. In the first decade of the twentieth century, Bauer's concept of "cultural nation" inspired also a new generation of political thinkers in Georgia like Akaki Čxenkeli who opposed territorial thinking of the founding father of the Georgian national idea, Ilya Čavčavadze. Cf. Zaal Andronikashvili, "*Politische Nationen- und Staatskonzepte im Kaukasus um 1900*," in *Landna(h)me Georgien. Studien zur kulturellen Semantik*, ed. Zaal Andronikashvili et al. (Berlin: Kadmos, 2018), 205.

recognition of a "major culture/literature" that helps to mediate its significance to the other members of the world literary community:

> "If for great peoples literature is an important achievement, then for minor peoples it not only serves as a cultural, entrance certificate, but mostly the only justification, the only meaning of its independent existence. It is for this reason that these people highly appreciate those foreigners who show interest and study their literatures.
>
> But your [his text is addressed to Briusov] merit is even more important, because you directed the attention of intellectual Russia to the beauty of Armenian poetry at the most tragic moment of the deplorable history of the Armenian people [...]."[40]

Reading these lines, today's readers will find it hard to avoid the association with Kafka's use of the term "minor" in relation to German-language Jewish literature of Prague—probably more so owing to Deleuze and Guattari's reflection on it than to Kafka himself. Hovhanisian's argument and his conceptualization of the strategy a minor literature could have vis-à-vis a major one are remarkable. Hovhannes Tumanian reiterated it later in his introduction to Briusov's lecture in Tbilisi. And there it can be seen that it significantly differs from Kafka's reflection because it does not deal with a "minor literature" in Kafka's sense: a minor literature written in a major language. Hovhanisian and Tumanian speak of a small literature that gains recognition by means of translation into a major language and, thanks to this translation, gets a chance to be recognized as a full member of world literature. In this spirit, Tumanian writes: "Without any doubt, this recognition on the part of a large literature ingratiates the self-esteem of our people."[41] "As for us, we have been devoted to Russian

---

40 "Если для великих народов литература является лучшим национальным достоянием, для мелких народностей она служит не только аттестатом культурной зрелости, но и чуть ли не единственным оправданием, единственною целью их самостоятельного существования. Отсюда–то глубоко благодарное, скажу, любовное отношение, которое эти народности проявляют к чужеземцам, изучающим их литературы. Но значение Вашей заслуги перед армянским народом усугубляется тем, что Вы обратили внимание мыслящей России на красоты армянской поэзии в самый трагический момент его горемычной истории [...]" Published in the Russian newspaper *Baku*, January 10, 1916.

41 Cf. the Armenian newspaper *Horizon*, published in Tbilisi during 1909–1918: *Horizon* 7 (January 1916): 1.

literature for a long time and appreciate the relation, established by you, becoming now reciprocal."[42]

It seems to me remarkable that this strategy of translation into a "major language" in order to introduce the "small literature" to a wider, world literary public was the strategy the Armenians pursued themselves—all the more so because it anticipated the strategy of Soviet policy of literary nationalization plus integration into the large Russian language literature (then under the auspices of Socialist Realism), but here in 1916 from the point of view of a "small literature." But let us take the opportunity of this comparison to jump across the decades and take a look at what happened when the anthology *Poeziia Armenii* was re-edited in the context of the program of "multinational Soviet literature" in 1940.

3. *Antologiia armianskoi poezii s drevneishikh vremen do nashikh dnei (1940)*

When in 1934 Gorky engaged Mikayelian to compile a new anthology of Armenian poetry with the focus on the program of "peoples' friendship" and "multinational Soviet literature,"[43] Mikayelian started immediately to prepare the new edition. He tried to respect Gorky's recommendation not to follow Briusov's anthology too closely. When the volume was ready for print in 1936, Gorky was the designated editor-in-chief, even though Mikayelian—as his letters show—had done the whole work completely alone.[44]

Not only in the framing parts of the anthology but also in a newspaper article in *Literaturnaia Gazeta*, which intended to promote the anthology, Mikayelian—wherever he can—tried to adapt to the new canonization. Referring to *Poeziia Armenii*, Mikayelian modified the terminology in a way that develops a completely different image of Armenia adjusting it to the Soviet perspective on so called "small nations" (*malen'kie narodnosti*). When he calls the Armenians *inorodtsy* (of another race) and speaks of one of the "small nations," the category "small" here acquires a completely different, much more colonial

---

42 "несомненно ласкает национальное самолюбие нашего народа и утешает его омраченное сердце–это полное уважения и любви отношение со стороны большой литературы. . . . Сами мы давно уже связаны с русской литературой и теперь очень рады, что связь эта становится взаимной." *Horizon* 11 (January 1916): 4.

43 Gorky: "в момент замечательного роста национальных литератур"

44 Robert Bagdasarian, *Karen Mikayelian* (Yerevan: Lingua 2010), 160–81.; On the close connection between Mikayelian and Charents in their work on the anthology, see 166 ff.

meaning than in the speech of the Armenian author on the occasion of Briusov's lecture:

> "Briusov's anthology with all its deficiencies was an extraordinary event on the literary scene of the so called "aliens" [*inorodtsy*] not only because representatives of Russian poetry were involved, but due to the enormous engagement of all participants, first of all its editor Valerii Briusov. It is this anthology that could break the ice of disinterest towards the literatures of the small peoples that inhabit the immeasurable Russian lands. For the first time Russian poets descended from their tower of arrogance to focus on the poetry of one of these small peoples, and unveiled unexpected treasures presenting them to the public not in a dilettante way but applying all their arts of translation."[45]

But still, in the same article Mikayelian dares to dispute one important part of the Soviet program and thus indicates that he has retained a last vestige of free intellectual reflection. He contradicts the new Soviet norms of *vol'nyi perevod* (free translation)[46] when he states that as "each poetic work is a synthesis of its semantic content and the formal element such as strophes, meter, rhymes, onomatopoeia, phonetical parallelisms, and, finally, inner breath of the verse" to by means of translation pour the content "in an arbitrary form" would "produce a beautiful result but would not be adequate, especially in the case of Armenian poetry, which in the course of its thousand-year development brought forward an amazing variety and an exuberant richness of form."[47]

---

45 "Брюсовский сборник со всеми его недостатками был из ряда вон выходящим событием в литературной жизни так называемых "инородцев" не только потому, что в нем участвовали лучшие представители русской поэзии, но и по тому необычному для того времени отношению, которое было проявлено к делу участниками сборника и в первую очередь его редактором В. Брюсовым. Этим сборником как будто ломался непроницаемый лед безразличия к литературным ценностям живущих в пределах необъятной России малых народностей. Впервые русские поэты, отбросив свое полупренебрежительное отношение, снизошли со своей поэтической башни и обратили свой взор на литературу одной из малых народностей, выявляя до того неведомые им литературные ценности и представляя их русской общественности не с дилетантской небрежностью, а применив требовательные методы переводческого искусства."

46 Witt, Susanna [Witt, Susanna]. "'Sovetskaia shkola perevoda'—k probleme istorii kontsepta," in *Perevodcheskie strategii i gosudarstvennyi control,'* ed. Lea Pild (Tartu: Tartu University Press, 2017), 36–51, here 46ff.

47 "... Каждое поэтическое произведение является синтезом его смыслового содержания и присущей произведению формы, т.е. строфики, размера, чередования рифм, звукописи,

58 | Susanne Frank

When Gorky died in 1936, the anthology was ready for publication, but not yet printed. The new version came out only in 1940 under the title *Antologiia armianskoi poezii* with S.S. Harutiunian and V. Ia. Kirpotin as the editors.[48] Gorky is mentioned there as the initiator who produced the idea of a series of anthologies of the poetry of the peoples of the USSR. *Briusovskaia antologiia* along with *Armianskaia muza*, edited by Yu. Veselovskii and Khalatiants, are mentioned in a by-the-way fashion as among other sources. The name of Mikayelian as well as the names and texts of many of the most important poets of Armenian modernism and avant-garde—such as Yeghishe Charents—were deleted. All in all, in the attempt to transform Briusov's anthology into an utmost representative and contemporary collection of Armenian poetry very few was left from the composition of the anthology as Mikayelian had conceptualized it.[49]

At least three features distinguish the profile of Armenian literature as it is given here from the earlier anthologies: First, the new Soviet anthology emphasizes the role of the Persian and the Ottoman Empires as oppressors even more. It presents the history of Armenia as a series of suppression attacks and defense attempts which continued until Armenia sought the protection of Russian rule.[50] Russia is presented then as the liberator and the Soviet Union as opening the door to Europe and for national consolidation:

словесной инструментовки и, наконец, внутреннего дыхания стиха. Дать перевод смыслового содержания какого-нибудь произведения в форме, произвольно избранной переводчиком, без соблюдения отличительных особенностей подлинника, которыми оперировал автор, в наших условиях стихотворного мастерства может каждый, если он одарен поэтическим даром. Такой перевод может быть очень красивым, но он не будет верным, или, как мы говорим, адекватным. Применить этот принцип перевода в отношении армянской поэзии, отличающейся на протяжении своей тысячелетней истории изумительным разнообразием и пышным богатством форм,—значит не дать верного изображения." This is a quotation from Mikayelian's article "O perevodakh s armianskogo" that remains unpublished.

48 S. S. Harutiunian and V. Ia. Kirpotin, *Antologiia armianskoi poèzii s drevneishikh vremen do nashikh dnei* (Moscow: Khudozhestvennaia literatura, 1940).

49 Cf. Bagdasarian, 181–82.

50 Cf.: "At the dawn of its history the Armenian people was oppressed by Achaemenid Persia. Liberating themselves from despotic Persia and defending their autonomy, the Armenian people entered a period of flourishing statehood. [. . .] Before the nineteenth century, Armenia remained under the Turkish-Persian sword." (На заре своей истории армянский народ был угнетен ахеменидской Персией. Освободясь от ига персидской деспотии и отстояв свою самостоятельность, армянский народ вступил в пору расцвета своей государственности. [. . .] До XIX в. над Арменией висел турецко-персидский меч.) S. S. Harutiunian and V. Ia. Kirpotin. *Antologiia armianskoi poèzii s drevneishikh vremen do nashikh dnei* (Moscow: Khudozhestvennaia literatura, 1940), 7.

Before the union with the Russian Empire, Armenia was under the Turkish-Persian yoke. When in the 1820s Armenia joined Russia, a new era started in the life of the country. Armenia became a member of the Russian and world market.

New Russian and European culture and most advanced socio-political ideas stimulated the Armenian intelligentsia. Via Russia, Eastern Armenians entered the orbit of European influence. Due to the union with Russia, the Armenian economy grew rapidly."[51] But only in 1920 did "Armenia—[. . .], which always had been betrayed by its friends, achieved its liberation by declaring itself a Soviet republic [. . .]. Only the idea of Soviet power could bring Armenia peace and the chance of a national renaissance." (I. Stalin, *Pravda*, December 4, 1920).[52]

The second distinguishing feature is that the new version of the anthology constructs an overarching national unity that even includes the so called "Armenian cultural colonies" (*kul'turnye kolonii*), which arose as an effect of migration and flight from oppression:

Huge are the merits of Armenian cultural colonies that are dispersed around the globe. These colonies contributed to the spread of European influence and national literature among the Armenians. As a center of gravity of Armenian culture, they concentrated historical-literary investigation. The intellectual

---

51 Harutiunian and Kirpotin, *Antologiia armianskoi poèzii*, 22.
52 Harutiunian and Kirpotin, *Antologiia armianskoi poèzii*, 8. "До присоединения к Российской империи Армения находилась под турецко-персидским игом. В 20-х годах XIX в. Армения вошла в состав России. Тем самым началась новая эпоха в жизни страны. Армения приобщилась к русскому и мировому товарообороту. [. . .] Новая русская и европейская культура и передовые общественные идеи проникли в среду армянской интеллигенции. Через Россию восточные армяне вошли в орбиту европейского влияния. С присоединением к России армянский торговый и промышленный капитал стал быстро развиваться. [. . .]." Лишь в 1920 году "Армения, измученная и многострадальная, отданная милостью Антанты и дашнаков на голод, разорение и беженство—эта обманутая всеми "друзьями" Армения, приобрела свое избавление в том, что объявила себя советской страной. . . Только идея советской власти принесла Армении мир и возможность национального обновления." Iosif Stalin, *Pravda*, December 4, 1920.

60 | Susanne Frank

work of the colonies promoted the formation of national consciousness."[53]

It also includes West Armenian literature, although the introduction underlines a clear asymmetry between the literature of East Armenia—that is seen as the core of Armenian national literature—and its Western counterpart, the literature of the Armenians in Turkey that has developed in much closer connection with West European literatures. West Armenian poets are portrayed as victims of Turkey's gruesome policy of extinction, whose works should not be blamed for bourgeois aesthetic tendencies, but valued for the depiction of political injustice and social suffering:[54]

> The group of West Armenian poets—Metsarents, Siamanto, Varuzhan and Ruben Sevak—to a different degree reflected the influence of West European symbolism. But also in the case of this group, symbolism did not completely determine their work: Siamanto created dark pictures of national suffering—the barbarian mass extinction under Sultan Hamid. Even during his reign of terror Armenian poetry did not lose its political relevance."[55]

---

53 Велики заслуги армянских культурных колоний, разбросанных по свету. Колонии эти были распространителями европейского влияния и национальной литературы среди армян. Являясь центром притяжения армянских культурных сил, они сосредоточили у себя в тот период историко-литературную исследовательскую работу. Деятельность культурных колоний способствовала пробуждению национального самосознания. Harutiunian and Kirpotin, *Antologiia armianskoi poèzii*, 20.

54 "The regime of the sultans and the adventurous policy of the nationalist parties brought the Turkish Armenian mass extinction. The most important representatives of West Armenian literature—Varuzhan, Siamanto, Sevak, and others—were cruelly murdered." (Султанский режим и авантюристическая политика националистических партий обрекли турецких армян на массовое истребление. Крупнейшие деятели западноармянской литературы— Варужан, Сиаманто Севак и другие были зверски убиты.) Harutiunian and Kirpotin, *Antologiia armianskoi poèzii*, 31.

55 Группа западноармянских поэтов—*Мецаренц, Сиаманто, Варужан* и *Рубен Севак*—в разной мере отразила влияние западноевропейского символизма. Но и для этой группы поэтов символизм не определил полностью их творчества, Сиаманто отобразил мрачные картины национальных бедствий—варварское уничтожение народных масс султаном Гамидом. Армянская поэзия не теряет своей политической актуальности даже в годы террора султана Гамида и беспощадного истребления народа. Harutiunian and Kirpotin, *Antologiia armianskoi poèzii*, 30.

The literary career of Vahan Terian is described in similar terms. The symbolism, which he strove for, is excused as a deviation on Terian's way to becoming a revolutionary poet:

> In the works of Terian germinated the self-negation of symbolism because the poet actively reflected socio-political problems. Terian's masterfully conceived "Poems from Nairi" are dedicated to the fate of his homeland and people. Political developments in Russia lead Terian to take the revolutionary stance. Then he wrote his famous poem "The Return" [Veradardz], where he firmly rejected symbolism.[56]

The third distinguishing moment is the way the 1940s anthology reshapes the role of Armenian literature as a mediator between the traditions of Oriental poetry and Western traditions. On the one hand, there can be found even direct quotations from Briusov's introduction such as: "In all its passionateness, Armenian poetry is chaste; in all its ardency, it is reserved in its expression. This is poetry which at the same time blossoms in an Oriental manner and is sage in a Western way, which is able to mourn without despair and to be passionate without crossing the line."[57]

On the other hand, it accentuates completely different points. The permanence of its in-between status is understood neither as determining the role of the spearhead of Christian culture in the East nor as a productive synthesis of East and West. Instead, the continuity of poetry and folklore appears to be a continuity of the parallel between East as "folklore" and West as literature in the modern Western sense of the word, whereby folklore as the element of the East maintains its strong position throughout the epochs.

Distinguishing between 1. Narodnaia poeziia (folklore epic etc.), 2. Poëziia srednevekov'ia i pesni ashugov (poetry of the Medieval ages), and

---

56 Однако в творчестве Теряна было заложено самоотрицание символизма. Это было обусловлено тем, что поэт нашел путь к активному восприятию социально-политвческих вопросов. Терян создал цикл "Наиреских стихотворении"; замечательных по мастерству, посвященных судьбам родины и народа. Политический подъем в России приводит Теряна в лагерь революции. Он пишет знаменитое стихотворение "Возвращение," в котором решительно порывает с символизмом. Harutiunian and Kirpotin, *Antologiia armianskoi poëzii*, 30.

57 При всей своей страстности, армянская песня—целомудренна; при всей пламенности,—сдержанна в выражениях. Это—поэзия, по-восточному цветистая, по-западному мудрая, знающая скорбь без отчаяния, страсть без исступления, восторг, чуждый безудержности. Harutiunian and Kirpotin, *Antologiia armianskoi poëzii*, 38.

3. Novaia poèziia (new poetry), consisting of "Poeziia russkikh Armian" (Russian Armenians) and "Poeziia turetskikh Armian" (Turkish Armenians), Briusov's *Poeziia Armenii*, in its composition, told the story of a linear development towards modernity: from archaic folklore via medieval contemplative poetry and Oriental tendencies in the *ashug* singer tradition towards European modernity.

By contrast, a glance at the table of contents indicates that the 1940 anthology suggests another, dialectical story: from archaic folklore to modernism to modern Soviet "folklore" based on traditional Oriental *ashug art*[58]:

1. Folklore (*Narodnaia poeziia*)
2. Ancient poetry and poetry of the Middle Ages (*Drevniaia and srednevekovaia poeziia*)
3. Poetry of the ashugs (*Poeziia ashugov*)
4. Modern poetry (*Poeziia novogo vremeni*)
5. Soviet poetry (*Sovetskaia poeziia*)

Symptomatically, the last part of the new anthology concludes with a collection of new "Pesni ashugov."

The attempt to reinterpret the history of Armenian poetry, to make it national in form in a new Soviet way ends up underlining a continuity of oriental folkloric traditions. This becomes even more explicit in the course of the introduction, where new Soviet developments in Armenian poetry are accentuated as an oriental revival and the art of the ashug is folklorized:

> The poetry of the folk singers, traditional in its manner and by inheritance related to folklore, has undergone a renewal thanks to new content. Our time has brought forward a new generation of ashugs. Armenian readers are familiar with names like Ashkhuzh, Grigor, At, Grkez, Yesaian, Sazai, Sheram. Some of them are represented in the anthology. Their songs reflect the

---

58 "Ashug" art is known in Armenia and the whole Transcaucasian region as well as Persia and Turkey since the sixteenth century. "Ashug" or "ashik" (etymologically going back to Arabic. "ishq"—"love" and "ashikun"—ardently loving) is the name for a singer poet or bard who accompanies his poetry/songs (a variety of genres, love poetry as well as epic) on a string instrument called "saz." tradition is common for the whole Transcaucasian region including Persia and Turkey. The most famous ashug in the history of Armenian poetry was Sayat Nova (1712–1795). Some researchers see the roots of this art of musical performance of poetry in Sufi mysticism, others in Shamanism.

pathos of socialist work, the joy of victory, the heroism of our days. Ashugs are the singers of Stalin's friendship of the peoples. [. . .] In our days, the poetry of the ashugs in its turn affects the poets in their work. Some of the typical devices of the songs of the ashugs come into general use in contemporary Armenian poetry.[59]

Besides these three distinguishing moments of the 1940s edition of the anthology, there should be mentioned a moment severe distortion, which is the result of a significant omission: an important part of the poetry that was written and published during the period in-between the two anthologies, between 1917 and 1940, was not included in the 1940 anthology: primarily the Soviet-Armenian avant-garde, including Yeghishe Charents, the most important avant-garde poet of Armenia. Born in 1897 in Kars, Charents came to Moscow in 1915 and studied at The People's University named after A. L. Shaniavskii (the predecessor of today's Russian State Humanitarian University (RGGU), which opened its doors to the students in 1908) where among others Valerii Briusov held a chair. But Charents was still a young student when Terian and Mikayelian prepared the anthologies. Charents met Terian for the first time in Tbilisi in 1917. Like Terian, Charents actively supported the October Revolution. He joined the Red Army and later became a schoolteacher in Yerevan. In 1918, Charents established his reputation as a poet of transregional significance by publishing his poem "Ambokhnery khelagarvats" (Frantic crowds) in Tbilisi. Inspired by Mayakovsky and *LEF*, Charents published a series of radio-poems in Yerevan in 1920. In 1922, after a two-volume edition of his works came out in the Armenian original in Moscow, Charents was exposed to persecutions for the first time. It was in these days that Briusov prepared a new edition of the anthology *Poeziia Armenii* and obviously intended to include a collection of Charents's poems.[60]

---

59 Поэзия сказителей но своим приемам—традиционна, и в этой традиционности обнаруживается ее преемственная связь с фольклором, обогатившимся новым содержанием. В наше время выросло новое поколение ашугов. Армянскому читателю хорошо известны имена *Ашхужа, Грисора, Ата, Грнеза, Есаяна, Хазаи, Шерама*. Часть названных ашугов представлена в антологии. В ашугских песнях отразился пафос социалистического труда. В них—ликование и радость победы, героика наших дней. Ашуги—певцы сталинской дружбы народов [. . .] Ашугская поэзия в наши дни заметно влияет и на творчество поэтов. Некоторые формы ашугской песни используются ими. Harutiunian and Kirpotin, *Antologiia armianskoi poèzii*, 35.

60 It would be interesting to see if Charents himself decided to contact Briusov and offer some of his works to be included in the anthology. I am grateful to Sona Mnatsakanian for the hint

Amidst the archival documents related to these plans for a new edition, there is one autograph: Briusov's translation of Charents's poem "Amenapoem" (Allpoem).[61] But this edition has never been published.

Until 1935, Charents's career developed impressively, though always balancing on a knife's edge between a leading cadre and persecution. Already in 1920, Charents became the head of the Narkompros art department, and in 1924, he had to renounce futurism. In 1928, he became the director of the most important state publishing house in Armenia, "Haypethrat," and, despite the repressions of 1932, Charents held this position until 1935. In 1934, he was invited to participate in the First All-Union Congress of Soviet Writers, where he gave a talk on August 29. Charents openly defended Nikolai Bukharin's plea for the acceptance of sophisticated ways of modernist writing as an option for Soviet literature and maintained a position of decentered multinational exchange and transnational unity:[62]

> Important is the role of national cultures in the general system of Soviet culture-building. Having in mind not only the present, but also their past. But, comrades, let us not forget that this role can be fruitful only if we don't look through the lens of self-contained "national cultures." As an Armenian writer, I belong to a "small" nation and I am aware that if I limit myself psychologically to the self-contained frames of the national, the intellectual horizon of my poetry will be ridiculous and its zone of influence all the more. I am happy to feel myself as part of the most advanced movement of mankind owing to the fact that the October Revolution moved the preposterous chimera of self-contained nation out of the field of view.
>
> Speaking of the past, we often have in mind only European literatures and the national literature the given author is representing. But to what extent would it enrich our creative experience if we, the writers of multilingual Soviet Union, would learn from each other. However small a nation and its literature might

that in the context of the publishing story of the novel "Yerkir Nayiri," there are letters to Al. Myasnikian and Ashot Hovhannisian, trying to convince them to publish his novel first in the US, and then in Vienna or Paris. It never happened.

61 Briusov, *Poèziia Armenii*, 570–99.

62 *Pervyi vsesoiuznyi s'ezd sovetskikh pisatelei 1934. Stenograficheskii Otchet* (Moscow: Khudozhestvennaia literatura, 1934; reprint Moscow 1990), 562.

be, the literature will be characterized by a distinctive feature which is exclusive and unique [. . .].”[63]

It was probably there, in Moscow, that Gorky asked Charents to edit the medieval section of the new Soviet anthology of Armenian poetry, and Charents accepted. And, even when Charents was accused of nationalism and terrorism in 1935 and was banned from the Writers' Union, he was still able to continue his work and was mandated to prepare the Pushkin jubilee in 1937. However, after Gorky's death in 1936, Charents, like Mikayelian, finally fell victim to the repressions. In summer 1937, Charents was arrested and when he died in November 1937 at the Yerevan hospital, it was probably not only from a disease.

Conclusion

In this chapter by means of a case study, I reflect on the role of the genre "anthology in translation" as an instrument of literary nation-building and of (self-) positioning of a "minor" literature on the scene of world literature. Focusing on the famous Russian language anthology *Poeziia Armenii*, which, since its first appearance in 1916, has been received as the work of Valerii Briusov and has also been canonized accordingly in Armenian literature, I have tried to uncover its real genesis, its shaping and reception. Retelling the story of its production in Moscow in the context of Gorky's anthology-project and of its presentation

---

63 Yegishe Charents, "Speech," in *Pervyi vsesoiuznyi s"ezd sovetskikh pisatelei 1934* (Moscow: n.p., 1934): 561. "Велика роль национальных культур в общей системе советского культурного строительства—национальных культур, имея в виду не только настоящее, но и прошлое их. Но не забудем, товарищи, что роль эта может оказаться приемлемой и плодотворной лишь тогда, если мы рассмотрим их не сквозь призму замкнутых "национальных культур." Я тоже как армянский писатель принадлежу к "малой" народности и знаю, что если я свою творческую деятельность психологически ограничу рамками национальной замкнутости, сколь будет жалок ее диапазон и сфера ее влияния. Я счастлив и чувствую себя частью наипередового потока человечества благодаря тому, что Октябрьская революция изъяла из духовного поля моего зрения эту жалкую химеру национальных самоограниченностей. Говоря о прошлом, мы часто имеем в виду лишь прошлое европейских литератур и литературу народа, на языке которого говорит данный писатель. Но насколько обогатился бы наш творческий опыт, если бы мы, писатели многоязычного Советского союза, учились также друг у друга. Сколь бы мал ни был народ и его литература, последняя не может не иметь своеобразного оттенка, единственного и неповторимого,—то, что свойственно лишь этой литературе и ее лучшим представителям." It is quite fascinating how from today's point of view Charents' statement in 1934 maintains a position of "diversity" that sounds so familiar to our ears in 2020.

in the Russian and in the Transcaucasian capitals has shown that its real editors were the young Armenian authors Vahan Terian and Karen Mikayelian, who had the idea and designed the compilation of the volume. From this new perspective, the editorship of Briusov, the famous Russian poet, becomes recognizable as a kind of mystification: In fact, it was a self-determined act of Armenian authors who made use of the name of the famous Russian poet and the Russian language as a vehicle in order to position Armenian literature as a small, but valuable literature on the stage of world literature.

Focusing on later editions of this anthology I demonstrated how they changed the image of Armenian poetry significantly. In their plan for a new edition in the 1920s Karen Mikayelian and Valerii Briusov tried to include Armenian modernism and, first of all, its most important representative, Yegishe Charents. But it could not be realized. The second edition of the *Antologiia* was prepared by Gorky and Mikayelian in the 1930s, but came out only in 1940. Even though both editions pursued a strategy to present Armenian poetry in the perspective of national literary history, and even though both included East and West Armenian poetry as two parts of one whole, the underlying teleology of the historical formation of the Armenian national corpus significantly differed. Whereas the original composition of *Poeziia Armenii* told the history of a development towards European modernity, the *Antologiia* revised this picture decisively by means of orientalizing folklorization. Of course, there was no place for a modernist poet like Yegishe Charents in this context either because in those years he was heavily criticized as formalist and therefore bourgeois. Furthermore, if we could analyze *Poeziia Armenii* as the act of self-positioning of Armenian literature as "small literature" in a global (if global European) context, the same is not possible to say about the 1940 edition. Even though it was no longer Briusov, but Armenian poets whose names served as editors, the selection and the concept were now completely in line with the strategies of the Stalinist project of Soviet multinational literature after 1934, strategies to homogenize non-Russian Soviet literatures, to deprive them of their historical specificity, and subordinate them to the asymmetric, Russia-dominated concept of multinationalism. The way to homogenize Armenian literature was to make it seem younger, more Oriental and folklore-bound and more dependent on Russian leadership than it actually was. In this way, it completely contradicted the ideas of horizontal, a-hierarchical dialogue between national literatures as part of a multinational socialist whole that Yegishe Charents himself had formulated in his speech at the First All-Union Congress of Soviet Writers in 1934.

CHAPTER 4

The Roles of "Form" and "Content" in World Literature as Discussed by Viktor Shklovsky in His Writings of the Immediately Post-Revolutionary Years

Katerina Clark

In the early 2000s, when interest in world literature was at its height in American academia, Franco Moretti attempted to present a model for the dynamic of its evolution. In two seminal articles, "Conjectures on World Literature" published in the *New Left Review* in 2000 and "More Conjectures" published there in 2003, he proposes a binary pattern for how literary "forms" move from a metropolitan "core" to the "periphery" (largely in Asia and Latin America), where they are appropriated and reworked. But Moretti struggles as he tries to pin down the precise dynamic. He comes up with several slightly different formulations, including "when a culture starts moving toward the modern novel, . . . it's always a compromise between foreign form and local materials." At other points he posits an antagonistic relationship between the literatures of the core and the periphery, a story of "struggle," and of the resistance of "materials" on the periphery to being subsumed under some metropolitan "form." The "viewpoint that 'receives' it in the periphery" often leads to an ironic re-inflection of the "form" from the core, he contends, and "the pressure from the Anglo-French core *tried* to [make the literature of the center and that of the periphery meld] but it could never fully erase the reality of difference." At another point Moretti

68 | Katerina Clark

enlarges the dyad (form from the core/materials in the periphery) to a triad "foreign form, local material—and local form. Simplifying somewhat: foreign plot; local characters; and then, local narrative voice."[1]

Moretti's struggle to codify the process whereby literary "forms" from the "core" are assimilated in a "periphery" exemplifies a fundamental question: how can you disaggregate form and content–or (Moretti's extremely vague term) "materials"? In order for "forms" to be truly portable, the texts from the "core" have to be very bare bones, somewhat abstract, stripped of vernacular particularity. A further problem in trying to disaggregate them-are tropes and conventional motifs part of a work's form or of its content? Moreover, "forms" are no empty, neutral vessels into which one can pour "content." As Michael Holquist has pointed out in explicating Bakhtin, "features are never *purely* formal, for each has associated with it a set of distinctive values and presuppositions."[2] Context plays a critical role in determining their import, which is in consequence not stable.

Moretti in his formulations for a world literature could well have taken as an unacknowledged point of departure the controversial theories of Russia's most bombastic literary theoretician, the Formalist Viktor Shklovsky. In some of his most infamous statements Shklovsky insisted on privileging form and dismissing content as mere motivation for pyrotechnics. Moretti actually only acknowledges his indebtedness to another Formalist theoretician Boris Tomashevsky and his essay on "Thematics" that appeared in 1925, and was probably the source of his emphasis on "materials." But two key essays by Shklovsky are in the same collection of translated texts as the Tomashevsky essay that Moretti refers to, *Russian Formalist Criticism*.[3] In what follows, I will discuss a much broader range of Shklovsky's theoretical writings on the relationship between form and content in a literary work than were available to Moretti, but will focus on Shklovsky's writings from the time when he gave that relationship his most radical formulation, during the years 1918–1922, in other words the immediately post-revolutionary period. These years also happen to be the time when Shklovsky was most concerned with world literature, or more specifically when he most drew examples for his theoretical investigations from

---

1 Franco Moretti, "Conjectures on World Literature," *New Left Review*, 2000, no. 1 (January-February), 60, 64, 65.

2 Michael Holquist, *Dialogism: Bakhtin and his World*, 2nd edition (London and New York: Routledge, 2002, 69.

3 *Russian Formalist Criticism: Four Essays*, edited by Marion J. Rice and Lee T. Lemon (University of Nebraska Press, 1965). The volume also contains Shklovsky's "Art as Technique" and his "Sterne's *Tristram Shandy*: Stylistic Commentary."

non-Russian texts, albeit they were primarily texts from English literature and to a lesser extent other European literatures such as the French, German and Spanish. As I will argue, that he was focused on both questions of form and on world literature was no coincidence.

Here I will be analyzing Shklovsky's ideas from those years as expressed in numerous public lectures, disputes, and small articles that were incorporated in later anthologies of his writings such as *The Knight's Move* (Khod konia, 1921), or *The Theory of Prose* (O teorii prozy, 1925). But I will be looking at them in the context of two autobiographical books he wrote at the time that provide test cases in the relationship between form and content. The first of these is *Revolution and the Front* (Revoliutsiia i front, 1919), which covers his life during a time of great upheavals during the Great War, the February Revolution of 1917, and in the second half of the book his time while stationed in Persia later that year with the army of the Russian Provisional Government. The second, *Sentimental Journey* (Sentimental'noe puteshestvie, 1923), continues his auto-biography after his time in Persia and chronicles his adventures and misadventures in the aftermath of the October Revolution and during the civil war. The two texts are not entirely separate in that *Sentimental Journey* incorporates as its first part *Revolution and the Front* (previously published separately) and also closes with the "Epilogue" that Shklovsky wrote for *Revolution and the Front* in February 1921 and published in 1922.[4]

I want to argue that Shklovsky's writings of this period, 1918–1922, differ in key respects from those of the pre-revolutionary years. The most famous essay from the earlier time is "Art as Technique" (Iskusstvo kak priem), first published in early 1917. The main concept Shklovsky advances in this essay is "estrangement" (*ostranenie*). "Estrangement" involves making objects or verbal utterances "strange" to the beholder with, for example, unexpected juxtapositions of verbal or visual elements, thus helping the reader or beholder overcome epistemological habituation, what he calls "automatization." Since this technique involves the unfamiliar, it "impedes" the reader/viewer's apprehension of what is being conveyed and forces them to pay closer attention to the text, that will consequently take longer to comprehend. This challenge jolts them out of their mental ruts to a new appreciation of reality that comes from not merely

---

4   A. Galushkin, "Primechaniia," and A. Chudakov, "Dva pervykh desiatiletiia," in Viktor Shklovskii, *Gamburgskii shchët. Stat'i–vospominaniia–ésse (1914–1933)* (Moscow: Sovetskii pisatel', 1990), 504, 15.

"recognizing" (a word, an object), but truly "seeing" it as a creative act.[5] "The purpose of art, then," Shklovsky writes, "is to lead us to a knowledge of a thing through the organ of sight instead of recognition." But, he adds, "art is a means of reliving the making of something (*delan'e veshchi*), but in art what has been made (*sdelannoe*) is not important."[6]

In Shklovsky's literary career there was a short hiatus between his writing "Art as Technique" and his subsequent, post-revolutionary writings and it marks a shift in his central formulations. Though he continued to use some of the same terms as in "Art as Technique" and was still outlining a project for revivification through art, the center of gravity shifted. Where, before, he had been particularly concerned with the impact of "estrangement" on the reader or viewer, now he was more concerned with what he earlier deemed less important, "what has been made" (*sdelannoe*), or more specifically with the relationship within a work between its form and its content, which was not a preoccupation of "Art as Technique."

Some of the shifts one detects in Shklovsky's writings from 1918–22 can be ascribed to the fact that the February and October Revolutions had occurred in the interim. As befits a time of revolution, Shklovsky's writings changed from, in his prerevolutionary essays, rambling excursions into literary theory and displays of erudition, to short, hyperbolic and manifesto-like pieces. They were his interventions into the intense polemics of the post-revolutionary years about the way forward for literature and art. Between 1919 and 1922 he was a ubiquitous figure in the heated debates on this in the Petrograd literary world. Many of his polemical contributions to these debates were published in the Petrograd periodical *Zhizn' iskusstva* (Life of Art) where he placed about 50 articles between May 1919 and August 1921 and one can sense the change in them. In "Art as Technique" estrangement had been promoted as a means of overcoming the habituation of everyday life (*byt*), a favorite bugbear of the avant-garde, now Shklovsky defines "*byt*" differently, as extra-literary factors which he dismisses as irrelevant for texts.[7] Among them, he often singled out the political and chastised such erstwhile Futurist allies as Vladimir Mayakovsky and Osip Brik for putting their writings at the service of the Bolshevik Revolution.

---

5   Viktor Shklovskii, "Iskusstvo kak priëm," *Poëtika. Sborniki poëticheskogo iazyka* II (Petrograd: 18-ia Gosudarstvennaia Tipografiia, Letushkov. 13, 1919), 108.

6   Viktor Shklovskii, "Iskusstvo kak priëm," *Poëtika. Sborniki poëticheskogo iazyka* II (Petrograd: 18-ia Gosudarstvennaia Tipografiia, Letushkov. 13, 1919), 105.

7   See, e.g., "Formy iskusstva ob"iasniaiutsia svoei khudozhestvennoiu zakonomernost'iu, a ne bytovoi motivirovkoi," in *"Tristram Shendi" Sterna i teoriia romana* (Petrograd, OPOIaZ, 1921), 39.

The Roles of "Form" and "Content" in World Literature | 71

Shklovsky presents a strong statement against the relevance of "*byt*" in a literary work what I regard as the most paradigmatic of his various utterances of this time, his "On Art and Revolution" (Ob iskusstve i revoliutsii). In various iterations this was the text he delivered most often, both orally and in print form. It first appeared in print in the periodical *Iskusstvo kommuny* (Art of the Commune) on 30 March 1919 with the subtitle (derived from H.G. Wells) "Ullia, Ullia, [we are] the Martians! (from the Horn of the Martians)." Under this suitably militant sub-title, which implicitly likens Shklovsky's assault on conventional aesthetics to the Martians advancing on a terrorized London in *War of the Worlds*, he declares: "But after all we, the Futurists, entered [the revolution] with a new banner: 'A NEW FORM GIVES BIRTH TO NEW CONTENT' [caps his]." Appropriating the discourse of revolutionary liberation Shklovsky proceeds to say: "After all we liberated art from *byt*, which plays a role in a work of art [*tvorchestvo*] only as form is amplified [*zapolnenie*] and, perhaps, is even banished as Khlebnikov and Kruchenykh did [with their trans-sense poetry]."[8]

Shklovsky's most dramatic formulation of the insignificance of content is, however, in his essay "On 'King Lear'" (Po povodu 'korolia Lira,' 1920), in which he states that, emphatically, "The content of 'King Lear,' in my view, I repeat, is not the tragedy of the father, but a series of postures, [*polozheniia*], a series of witticisms, a series of devices [*priemy*], which are organized in such a way as to create in their interrelationships new stylistic techniques. Simply put: 'King Lear' is a phenomenon of style." The tragedy of Lear he sees as a mere motivation for a display of formal pyrotechnics, and for the stringing along of one stylistic high point after another.[9] A corollary to the rejection of the notion that *Lear* is about the king's tragedy is the idea (expressed in this essay and elsewhere) that psychology and sociology have no role to play in a work of art.[10] The heroic in a text should come from the virtuouso orchestration of techniques rather than the deeds of the protagonists.

The time when Shklovsky presented his most radical formulations about the relationship of form to content was also when he was most concerned with texts from what we would call "world literature" (such as "King Lear"). This was

---

8   Viktor Shklovskii, "Ob iskusstve i revoliutsii," *Iskusstvo kommuny* 17 (30 March 1919): 1.

9   Viktor Shklovskii, "Po povodu 'Korolia Lira,'" *Zhizn' iskusstva*, 1920, no 562–3 (21–22 September), republished in Viktor Shklovskii, *Khod konia. Sbornik statei* (Moscow-Berlin: Knigoizdatel'stvo Gelikon, 1923, 1474–8.

10 See, e.g., Viktor Shklovskii, "O psikhologicheskoi rampe," *Zhizn' iskusstva* no. 445 (May 7, 1920).

Katerina Clark

not a permanent shift, however. After 1918–22 he reverted to drawing most of the examples he used in his theoretical writings from Russian literature.

In his writings of 1918–22, then, Shklovsky made a double shift as compared with his pre-revolutionary writings: both a shift from a primary concern with the impact of specific features on the beholder/reader to a concern with overall plot organization and the orchestration of formal techniques, and a shift from a primary focus on Russian literature to a primary focus on West European literature.

Why this double shift? Commentators often explain Shklovsky's turn to using examples from West European literature in terms of the founding of the publishing house World Literature (*Vsemirnaia literatura*) in the summer of 1918. A fellow Formalist, Boris Eikhenbaum, was on its editorial board for Western literature.[11] Actually, Shklovsky was not involved in Vsemirnaia literatura's translation project, but in February 1919 the publishing house founded a Translation Studio as a place where translation theory and practice could be pursued.[12] The Studio was initially for translators but soon enlarged its scope, incorporating a literary studio, and Shklovsky began to teach there in the fall of 1919, running courses on plot theory; on 19 December, he moved his classes to the House of Arts (DISK) after it opened a new home for the Translation Studio, which was rebranded as the Literary Studio at DISK.[13] In his classes, as he reports in *The Sentimental Journey*, "They worked on the theory of the novel. Together with my pupils I wrote my book on "Don Quixote" and on Sterne."[14] As this account indicates, his seminal essays on plot in fiction that began to appear in a series of pieces he placed in *Zhizn' iskusstva* that fall were based on ideas worked out there.

---

11 Maria Khotimsky, "World Literature, Soviet Style: A Forgotten Episode in the History of the Idea," *Ab Imperio*, 3/2013119–54.

12 "Studiia 'Vsemirinoi literatury,'" *Zhizn' iskusstva*, –21919, no. 217–218, p. 2; "V dome iskusstv," *Zhizn' iskusstva* 1919, no. 316–317 (December 13–14), 4; *Literaturnaia zhizn' Rossii 1920-kh godov.Moskva i Petrograd*, tom I, 1917–1920 gg. Sobytiia. Otzyvy sovremennikov. Bibliografiia, ed. A. Iu. Galushkin (Moscow: IMLI RAN, 2005). 479.

13 "Khronika iskusstv," *Zhizn' iskusstva*, February 6, 1919; Emily Finer, *Turning into Sterne: Viktor Shklovskii and Literary Reception* (London: Studies in Comparative Literature 18: Modern Humanities Research Center and Maney Publishing, 2010), 21–22; [n.a.], "V dome iskusstv," *Zhizn' iskusstva*, 1919 no. 316–317 (December 13–14, 1919), 4.

14 Viktor Shklovskii, *Sentimental'noe puteshestvie. Vospominaniia 1917–1922* (Moscow-Berlin: Knigoizdatel'stvo Gelikon, 1923), 263. In all probability the book referred to was *Razvertyvanie siuzheta* ("the unfolding of plot") which appeared with the Formalist publisher OPOIaZ in 1921.

The problem with this narrative, however, is that the shift in Shklovsky's literary interests to plot construction in West European literature occurred *before* the Studio was founded in February 1919 let alone when Shklovsky joined it during that fall (though admittedly the establishment of World Literature publishing house was first approved in the summer of 1918).[15] Two sources—both his own remarks in *Sentimental Journey* and the annotations to that book by Aleksandr Galushkin, who served as Shklovsky's literary secretary during the last years of his life-suggest that he composed an entire book on "Plot as a Phenomenon of Style" (Siuzhet kak iavlenie stilia) while working that year undercover for the Socialist Revolutionaries in Saratov and Atkarsk.[16] This text was actually never published in book form but some parts of it appeared in *Zhizn' iskusstva* in 1919-1921 and then as OPOIaZ booklets. One of these booklets, *Rozanov* (1921) has the subtitle "Plot as a Phenomenon of Style."

Rozanov makes similar points to those Shklovsky made in his pre-revolutionary theoretical writings but in the middle of the text, during a discussion of a work by Tolstoy, his favorite source of literary examples, Shklovsky remarks that Laurence Sterne's *Tristram Shandy* is hard to classify as a novel just because it "breaks all the laws [*narushaet*] precisely the laws of the novel [construction]," adding "the canon of the novel as a genre, perhaps more than any other genre is capable of being reborn [*perenarodirovat'sia*]."[17] He continues: "I will permit myself, following the canon of the eighteenth-century novel, a digression" and proceeds to analyze digressions and the use of "retardation" in three classics of European literature, *Tristram Shandy*, Miguel de Cervantes's *Don Quixote* and Henry Fielding's *Tom Jones*.[18] These are the texts and some of the key concepts Shklovsky will focus on in his subsequent classes at the Translation Studio and then at the House of the Arts, in his many public lectures, and in his theoretical essays.

I would like to argue here that there was another important, and earlier factor—earlier than the founding of Vsemirnaia Literatura and its translator's studio—that might bear on Shklovsky's shift to writing about texts from "world

---

15 Viktor Shklovskii, "Ob iskusstve i revoliutsii," *Iskusstvo kommuny*, 1920 no. 17 (30 March).
16 "Literaturnye memuary. Kommentarii" in Viktor Shklovskii, *"Eshchë nichego ne konchilos'"* (Moscow: "Propaganda," 2002), 156, 422; Viktor Shklovskii, *Sentimental'noe puteshestvie. Vospominaniia 1917–1922* (Moscow-Berlin: Knigoizdatel'stvo Gelikon, 1923), 213.
17 This unexpected word for "reborn" used here, "perenarodirovat'sia," also has possible connotations of changing ethnic allegiance or transforming the self into something different, both germane to Shklovsky's interest at this time in the picaresque.
18 Viktor Shklovskii, *Rozanov. Iz knigi "Siuzhet kak iavlenie stilia"* (Petrograd: OPOIaZ, 1921), 13–16. The quotations are on page 13.

literature" and also to arguing for the primacy of "form" in a literary text, and that is what one might call the internationalist moment in the earliest years of post-revolutionary culture, a moment that was at its height in 1918–1919. The particular events I will point to actually occurred a little after Shklovsky wrote his first booklet on plot orchestration (*siuzhet*) but before the founding of the translator's studio. But they are symptomatic of this "moment."

On January 1, 1919, leading members of the Soviet avant-garde organized under the auspices of the Department of the Fine Arts an International Bureau, whose main task was to establish links with writers and artists in other countries, so that they might "unite in the name of constructing a new, universal artistic culture," which would serve as a "mighty weapon for realizing world socialism." The leadership of the Bureau included some of the most aesthetically radical members of the avant-garde: Wassily Kandinsky, Kazimir Malevich, Vladimir Tatlin, the leading Formalist theoretician Osip Brik, and the poet Shklovsky particularly admired, Velimir Khlebnikov.

Some members of the International Bureau, and Khlebnikov in particular, engaged the topic of how to establish a common language that would enable intercourse between the world's different linguistic, ethnic and cultural groups. Already in the pre-revolutionary period he had worked up several highly eccentric schemes for attaching meanings to letters or sounds, thus by-passing conventional semantic systems, which were a bar to mutual comprehension by people speaking different languages. He had also begun to write poetry using the very "trans-sense"language that, as mentioned earlier, Shklovsky praised in "On Art and Revolution" as banishing "*byt*." Khlebnikov wrote again about the possibility of a trans-national language in articles he submitted for the group's projected journal, *Internatsional iskusstv* (International of the Arts), where he presented proposals for a "common written language" for the entire world.[19]

For the verbal arts a single, mutually comprehensible language might seem a utopian project. At this time, however, some leading Soviet officials, similarly caught up in this internationalist moment, were also exploring the possibility of an international language. In January 1919, the very month the International Bureau was announced, a movement for a version of Esperanto (often called the "International Language" in Soviet publications) was growing in Moscow where a series of public lectures and courses for propagating it were set up. The ambitious proponents planned to have the "international language" taught in

---

19 See, e.g., V. Khlebnikov, "*Khudozhniki mira!*" and "Ritmy chelovechestva." See https:// lit-ra.pro/na-rubezhe-dvuh-stoletij/bagno-vsevolod-evgenjevich/read/46, accessed 10/26/2020.

The Roles of "Form" and "Content" in World Literature | 75

the schools and even to launch publishing ventures throughout the world where the (politically) most important texts would be published in it; only lesser texts should appear in the vernacular.[20] As if to confirm that both initiatives for an international language were part of the same internationalist moment, Nikolai Punin's contribution to the projected issue of *International iskusstv* was called "Art as Esperanto."

Shklovsky was arguably also seeking at this time to derive an "international language," in his case by adducing an inventory of literary forms that could apply trans-nationally. To this end, in effect, he now declared plots "homeless" (*bezdomnye*); no longer were they seen as embedded in a particular literary tradition.[21] But in order to present plots as so unmoored, in order for his forms and techniques to apply beyond Russian literature, in his analyses of them he had to prune away much of their particularity, leaving them highly abstract. Analogously, as one can see in his account of the significance of Lear in Shakespeare's play, he gave an extremely deindividualized and depersonalized account of the role of a protagonist in a literary work.

In his discussions of Sterne, Cervantes and other writers he was promoting in articles of 1918–1921, Shklovsky derives, as it were, a morphology of techniques he sees as the essence of the novel. His analyses might be compared with what Vladimir Propp did in his *Morphology of the Tale* (1928). In fact, Shklovsky had discussed common features of folktales in an article of 1918 that appeared as a companion to "Art As Technique" when an expanded version of the second anthology of Formalist writings *Poétika* was published in 1919, "The Connection of Techniques of Plot Contruction with General Stylistic Technigues" (*Sviaz' priëmov stikhoslozheniia s obshchimi priëmami stilia*), though that essay contains only gestures in the direction of adducing a morphology.[22]

---

20 V. Kerzhentsev [a pseudonym for Platon Kerzhentsev, which was itself a pseudonym for Lebedev], "Mezhdunarodnyi iazyk," *Izvestiia*, January 14, 1919, 1. See also three notes published in *Izvestiia* by the head of the Soviet Esperanto movement ("Mezhdunarodnyi iazyk i proletariat," January 5, 1919; "Internatsional i mezhdunarodnyi iazyk," February 2, 1919, 6 and "Intelligentsia i mezhdunarodnyi iazyk," January 11, 1919, 4).

21 Viktor Shklovskii, "Ob iskusstve i revoliutsii," *Iskusstvo kommuny*, 30 March 1919, 1; V. Shklovskii, "Sviaz' priëmov siuzhetoslozheniia s obshchimi priëmami stilia," *Poétika. Sborniki po teorii poéticheskogo iazyka II* (Petrograd: 18-ia Gosudarstvennaia Tipografiia, Letushkov. 13, 1919), 120.

22 Viktor Shklovskii, *Sentimental'noe puteshestvie. Vospominaniia 1917–1922* (Moscow-Berlin: Knigoizdatel'stvo Gelikon, 1923), 20620-7; Viktor Shklovskii, "Sviaz priëmov siuzhetoslozheniia s obshchimi priëmami stilia," 115–50. Note: the main difference between the version of "Art as Technique" in the published 1919 version of 1919 and that of 1917 is an inserted section (pp. 1091–12) in which Shklovskii further elaborates on "making strange" in a number of texts, but including Boccaccio's *Decameron*, symptomatic of his increasing interest in world literature.

76 | Katerina Clark

A major difference between the two theorists, however, would be that Shklovsky was not primarily concerned with paradigmatic plot functions, as was Propp, but rather with particular techniques that exemplify deviation from the systematic unfolding of the plot. Unlike Propp, Shklovsky wanted to systematize the non systematic. His, in other words, was a morphology of errancy (or aberrancy). Earlier, in "Art as Technique," he had called for "systematizing deviations" in meter, but his new project, to systematize plot techniques, was more ambitious.[23] For the purposes of this endeavor, new, or newly prominent, terms assumed a central place in his theoretical vocabulary, largely replacing "making strange": "displacement" (*sdvig*), "digression" (*otstuplenie*) and the term he had already used for deviations from a work's metrical system, "violation" (*narushenie*).

The text from which in this period Shklovsky adduced his most worked out account of how these techniques operate in a novel was not a Shakespeare play but Laurence Sterne's *Tristram Shandy*. The sort of virtuoso formal play Shklovsky found in Sterne was central, he contended, to any project for revolutionary regeneration. In his article "Displacement in Plot" (*Siuzhetnyi sdvig*) of 1919 Shklovsky wrote "The first impressions of Sterne will be of chaos. The action is constantly interrupted. Everything is shifted and displaced, transposed (*vse vzdvinuto, vse perestanovleno*). But when you start to look at the structure of the book you will see, above all, that this lack of order is deliberate, here [the text] has its own poetics, its own rules (*zakonomerno*), like a picture by Picasso."[24] What endeared Sterne to Shklovsky was obviously his adeptness at parody and his mockery of conventional narrative schemes in such moves as placing the preface in the middle of the book or the playful "omission" of several chapters, all to Shklovsky eloquent testimony to Sterne's keen awareness of literary form and its essential conventionality. "It is taking this cognizance of form through violating (*narushenie*) it that constitutes the content of the novel," he insists,[25] arguing further that by parodying novelistic conventions, Sterne's novel makes visible what ordinarily remains concealed; *Tristram Shandy* does overtly what other novels do covertly. Shklovsky pronounces this text "the most typical novel of world (*vsemirnoi*) literature," clearly not a statistical but a valorized category. He also declares unpredictability essential in a novel and singles out the

---

Also, in the 1917 version but not in the 1919, he promises a future book on prosody that never materialized. Presumably the two revolutions of 1917 intervened.

23 Viktor Shklovskii, "Iskusstvo kak priëm," *Poètika. Sborniki poèticheskogo iazyka* II (Petrograd: 18-ia Gosudarstvennaia Tipografiia, Letushkov. 13, 1919), 114.

24 "Siuzhetnyi sdvig," *Zhizn' iskusstva*, 1919, no. 327 (26 December), 1.

25 See, e.g., *"Tristram Shendi" Sterna i teoriia romana* (Petrograd, OPOIaZ, 1921), 12.

digression as the creative act, something which "impedes" the systematic unfolding of the plot and is all the more glorious for this.[26]

The digression was to become a hallmark of Shklovsky's writings. In fact, as we saw before, in *Rozanov* he introduced his discussion of the digression in Sterne, Fielding and Cervantes as a digression. But Shklovsky was not only producing theoretical arguments in these years. He was also writing autobiographical texts, and he used them as sandboxes where he could play around with the compositional ploys he had identified in his theoretical writings. More correctly, you can see this "play" in the second half of *Sentimental Journey*, the "Writing Desk" (*Pis'mennyi stol*), which was written in 1922, *after* Shklovsky had worked out his main theories of the relationship between form and content. Digressions, transpositions, shuffling the time sequence, etc. are all techniques that Shklovsky deployed liberally in this memoir. No wonder, as has become a commonplace of the scholarship, Shklovsky's presentation of his autobiographical material in this text was influenced by his own take on Sterne's *Tristram Shandy*–and after all *Sentimental Journey*, the book's overall title, comes from another novel by Sterne. However, "Revolution and the Front," the first half of *Sentimental Journey*, provides a contrast in this respect with the second half, "The Writing Desk" which is ostensibly its sequel. "Revolution and the Front" is unexpectedly staid in literary style, yet allegedly Shklovsky wrote it between June and August 1919, in other words *after* he wrote about Sterne, Fielding and Cervantes in "Plot as a Phenomenon of Style" (if we are to accept Galushkin's chronology).[27]

Though Shklovsky used "The Writing Desk" to flaunt his favorite compositional techniques, one cannot assume he intended that readers should disregard its content as they had been enjoined to disregard the content of "King Lear." According to Shklovsky himself, after he finished *Revolution and the Front* he had not intended to write a sequel but changed his mind after the appearance in February, 1922 in Berlin of a book by G. Semenov (Vasiliev) *Voennaia i boevaia rabota partii sotsialistov-revoliutsionerov v 1918–1919 gg.* (The War-Time and Military Work of the Party of Socialist Revolutionaries during 1918–1919), which includes an account of Shklovsky's clandestine work for that party. At the time, Socialist Revolutionaries were being rounded up for their show trial (that took place from June 8 to August 7, 1922), so the Semenov book rendered his situation in the Soviet Union even more precarious than it had been earlier

---

26 See, e.g., *"Tristram Shendi" Sterna i teoriia romana* (Petrograd, OPOIaZ, 1921), 39.

27 Aleksandr Galushkin and Vladimir Nekhotin, "Kommentarii" in Viktor Shklovskii, *"Eshchë nichego ne konchilos "Literaturnye memuary* (Moscow: Vagrius, 2002), 397.

that year when he realized he needed to flee the country. Shklovsky decided to write a sequel to *Revolution and the Front* to clear his name. He started it in Finland after he escaped there and finished it in Berlin after he arrived in June 1922.[28] In other words, in this text, compositionally his most Sternian, "content" is critical. One could justify this potential lapse of aesthetic principle by pointing to the fact that autobiography is a different genre than the novel, but in this text he uses the very devices he identifies in Sterne's work as the essence of novel form. In fact Galin Tihanov has called *Sentimental Journey*: "a valuable piece of engagement with literary theory *through fiction* [emphasis mine]: an early–and at the time pioneering–attempt to practice theory without a theoretical meta-language."[29]

In essays such as "On 'King Lear'" Shklovsky dismisses the importance of any work's "hero," and yet this egomaniacal theorist could not resist writing a long series of autobiographical vignettes (most of them published in *Zhizn' iskusstva*) and longer autobiographical texts (several of them after the time frame of this article). The theorist who advocated an expreme degree of depersonalization in his analyses of what counts in a literary work himself opted for the most personalized of literary forms, the autobiography. So we have the paradox of a writer who denied the importance of "content" but penned a series of texts in which not just a fictitious protagonist (such as "King Lear") but the purportedly actual writer himself, played the leading role. This paradox gets at the heart of the problem of trying to disaggregate form and content. The rest of this article will focus on this paradox.

I want to argue that in "The Writing Desk" the two–form and content–are intertwined. In fact the one suffuses the other to the point where they cannot be differentiated. Limitations of space do not permit me to discuss all the aspects of this interrelationship so I will confine myself to two topics, that I see as exemplifying it in *Sentimental Journey*. One, ostensibly an example of "form," is the picaresque. The other, ostensibly having to do with "content," is war. As I shall show, the treatment by Shklovsky of both in this text illustrates how both "form" and "content" are imbricated in eachother. Nevertheless, I will cover these two topics in sequence.

---

28 Aleksandr Galushkin and Vladimir Nekhotin, "Kommentarii" in Viktor Shklovskii, *"Eshchë nichego ne konchilos'. . ."Literaturnye memuary* (Moscow: Vagrius, 2002), 397.

29 Galin Tihanov, "World Literature, War, Revolution. The Significance of Viktor Shklovskii's *A Sentimental Journey*" in Andy Byford, Connor Doak, and Stephen Hutchings, eds., *Transnational Russian* Studies (Liverpool: Liverpool University Press, 2020), 123.

The Roles of "Form" and "Content" in World Literature | 79

The Picaresque

Shklovsky in his essays of 1918–21 discusses several genres which feature formal play with plot sequence, such as the adventure tale.[30] In Sterne, he contends for example, the adventure story is parodied as a precondition for the emergence of new novelistic forms.[31] But, arguably, the most Shklovskian among the genres he covers is its generic cousin, the picaresque.

Discussion of the picaresque was a development in Shklovsky's writings. This genre is not featured in "Art as Technique." But in his writings from 1918–1922 he recurrently presents examples of the points he is making from among the classic picaresque novels: *Lazarillo de Tormes* (1554) and *Guzman de Alfarache* (1599) from Spain's Golden Age, *Gil Blas* by the French author Alain Lesage (1715, 1724, 1735), the German author Johann Grimmelshausen's *Simplicius Simplicissimus* (1668), and Daniel Defoe's *Moll Flanders* (1722).[32] Even in discussing *Tristram Shandy* and *Don Quixote* Shklovsky singles out interpolated picaresque sections.[33]

This is not entirely surprising given that Shklovsky was far from alone in enthusiasm for the picaresque at this time. In the post-war years motifs of the picaro became a marked feature of literature and film. Ehrenburg (who like Shklovsky was frequently in a precarious situation for political reasons) produced five picaresque novels between 1922 and 1928, the most famous being his *Julio Jurenito* of 1922 (Neobychainye prikliucheniia Khulio Khurenito i ego uchenikov…), though in the sense that *Julio Jurenito* was conceived as early as 1916, i.e. during the Great War, the vogue for the picaresque could not be seen as a totally post-revolutionary phenomen, but rather as a phenomenon of a time of great upheavals.

In the Soviet Union the vogue for the picaresque was at its height during the civil war when so many became "picaros" because of the exigencies of their situations at a time of constant movement and the need to constantly adapt. The

---

30 "Razvertyvanie siuzheta (roman-drama)," II, *Zhizn' iskusstva*, 1920no 355 (27 January), 1; reprinted in *O teorii prozy*, section IV.

31 "Siuzhetnyi sdvig," *Zhizn' iskusstva*, 1919, no. 327 (26 December), 1; see also "Parodiinyi roman: 'Tristram Shendi' Sterna" in *O teorii prozy*, pp. 177–204.

32 See, e.g., Viktor Shklovskii, "Kak sdelan 'Don Kikhot'," *Zhizn' iskusstva*, no 373 (17 February1920); Viktor Shklovskii, "Siuzhetnyi sdvig," *Zhizn' isusstva* 1919, no. 327 (26 December), 1; *O teorii prozy* (Moscow:Federatsiia, 1929), 85, 88, 116, 142, 249.

33 "Razvertyvanie siuzheta (roman-drama)," *Zhizn' iskusstva*, no 355 (27 January), 1; "Kak sdelan Don Kikhot," *Zhizn' iskusstva*, no 373 (17 February), *Zhizn' iskusstva*, 1920, no. 343 (21 January 1920), *O teorii prozy*, section III, 1.

80 | Katerina Clark

Revolution with its overturning of values and institutions rendered everyone existentially homeless, cut adrift and coping with whatever came up, like the picaro. Actually, in literature and film the vogue for the picaresque was at its height in 1922–1924, probably due to the inevitable time lag in getting texts prepared and printed, exacerbated then by the dire situation of writers during War Communism and the paper shortage which meant that few substantial works could be committed to paper, let alone published.

We have to be clear on what is meant by the picaresque here, and by its hero, the picaro. As several writers on the picaresque have remarked, "there is no such thing as an ideal picaresque hero or a pure picaresque novel." "[P] icaresque fiction is a mixed form" and hence "the term 'picaresque novel' is a synthetic, somewhat arbitrary label."[34] In proposing the centrality of the picaresque in Shklovsky's work of this period I am not trying to be literalistic, to look mechanically for one to one correspondences between typical features of the picaresque and those of Shklovsky's "Writing Desk." This identification is intended to be suggestive rather than watertight. But a typical working definition of the picaresque, this one by Richard Bjornson in his book *The Picaresque Hero in European Fiction*, runs: "episodic, open-ended narratives in which lower-class protagonists sustain themselves by means of their cleverness and adaptability during an extended journey through space, time, and various predominantly corrupt social milieux."[35] These protagonists have become picaros as itinerants, *uprooted outsiders*, sent by circumstances out into the world to roam where fate takes them and who, in Bjornson's terms, "sustain themselves by cleverness and adaptability." In other words, they are homeless" "(*bezdomnye*)" a figure Shklovsky liked to use to characterize the portability of plots; "content" and "form" cannot be disaggregated.

The principle of the picaro is that he keeps moving but that at each location he encounters new people and new situations. In consequence, a feature of the genre is a "stringing along" of episodes (*nanizovanie*, a favored Shklovskian term); closure is somewhat arbitrary.[36] Though sometimes characters may suddenly reappear in a different setting, this recurrence is haphazard. Critics have noted the consequent "infinite possibilities of the picaresque plot," which imposes "no

---

34 Richard Bjornson, *The Picaresque Hero in European Fiction* (Madison: University of Wisconsin Press, 1977), p. 6, p. 4.

35 Richard Bjornson, *The Picaresque Hero in European Fiction* (Madison: University of Wisconsin Press, 1977).

36 Viktor Shklovskii, "Stroenie rasskaza i romana" *O teorii prozy*, 88.

The Roles of "Form" and "Content" in World Literature | 81

limitations of probability" leading to "total openness."[37] This a-causal aspect of the picaresque fits in with Shklovsky's stance in his theoretical writings where he played down such factors as might have accounted for a protagonists actions as their psychology. The plot celebrates errancy in resisting Bildung and closure, two important features of conventional novels.

In the "Writing Desk" Shklovsky effectively casts himself (or more accurately the narrator) as a picaro in several respects other than his haphazard journeying. For a start, he displays the "elemental rootlessness" that many critics see as a central feature of twentieth century versions of the picaresque.[38] Another aspect of the picaresque that is analogous to a feature of Shklovsky's autobiography is the way picaros are represented as misplaced and having to operate in an alien, conformist world, a world of what Shklovsky calls in "Art as Technique" "things, furniture, wives...." As Robert Alter put it in his study of the twentieth century picaresque, in which he claims that the rogue picaro has morphed into a roguish artist, " ... the activity in which [the artist] engages remains profoundly suspect in the eyes of the respectable world ... nothing could undermine comfortable habit, convention, propriety, tradition more than an honest modern art."[39] This reads almost like a Shklovskian manifesto.

Shklovsky uses the features of the picaresque heavily in presenting auto-biographical material in "The Writing Desk." He effectively casts himself as a picaro in several respects other than his haphazard journeying. One of these is the ways he multiply has to extricate himself from political scrapes. Shklovsky as a member of an underground anti-Bolshevik groups of Socialist Revolutionaries was on several occasions about to be arrested when he learned about the impending danger by chance and fled the scene, sometimes using such subterfuges as false passports and dyed hair, sometimes hiding out in some safe house.[40]

The picaresque has two other feature that doubtless made it particularly attractive to Shklovsky as a genre. The first of these is the centrality of the contingent. "*Sluchaino*" (by chance) is one of Shklovsky's key words in "The Writing

---

37 Stuart Miller, *The Picaresque Novel* (Cleveland and London: The Press of Case Western Reserve University, 1967), 10.

38 See, e.g., Alexander Blackburn, *The Myth of the Picaro: Certainty and Transformation in the Picaresque Novel, 1554–1954* (Chapel Hill: University of North Carolina Press, 1979), 12, 14, 20.

39 Robert Alter, *Rogue's Progress: Studies in the Picaresque Novel* (Cambridge,Mass.: Harvard University Press, 1964), 129.

40 Viktor Shklovskii, *Sentimental'noe puteshestvie. Vospominaniia 1917–1922* (Moscow-Berlin,: Knigoizdatel'stvo Gelikon, 1923), 213, 216, 341, 376.

Desk." The arbitrary is the stuff of the picaresque–the chance encounter that threatens the picaro with exposure and forces them to extricate himself and flee to another locale. He is constantly staving off disaster or starvation by use of cunning or by a fortuitous encounter. Many picaresques feature serial complete reversals of fortune (best exemplified in *Gil Blas*, one of the picaresque novels Shklovsky discusses), as the protagonist now has great wealth, now is reduced to dire poverty and starvation, with little in between and no overall causal explanation. These arbitrary bouleversements undermine any possibility of Bildung or learning from experience.

In discussing the picaresque, Shklovsky emphasizes its playful and parodic aspects, its gratuitous "stringing along" of episodes and so forth: "Zhil Blaz is in no way a person, it is a *thread* that stitches episodes in the novel together."[41] But most picaresques also have a serious side. For a start, the classic picaro was typically a marginalized figure. His lower-class status was exacerbated by a dubious parentage (perhaps of uncertain lineage, perhaps the son of a prostitute or criminals). In classic Spanish picaresques, he was also often a converso, a convert to Christianity but in origin a Muslim or Jew, a setback for societal acceptance at the time of the Inquisition. The picaro's lack of a socially acceptable identity was often what thrust him on his journey, but his predicament was one with which Shklovsky could identify as an assimilated (half) Jew, discriminated against in the imperial army (as he relates in *Sentimental Journey*).

In the classic picaresque, the adventures of the picaro often function as entertaining motivations for social satire (as in *Gil Blas* where first this aspect of society is satirized, then that). Many of those set in Spain contain critiques of the Inquisition. Also, the classic picaros are represented as pitted against the hypocrites of the establishment who are, underneath it all, venal. The picaros might be outsiders to society but their group has its own code of honor. As Stuart Miller remarks of Guzman de Alfarache, "he not only becomes a gratuitous trickster, but, like Lazarillo … he joins an underworld that preys on the world." In Miller's account, this underworld implicitly "criticizes the overworld by exhibiting an order within disorder, a stability within instability, that the overworld can never attain." Among the tricksters or beggars that Guzman joins "All is carefully regulated–dress, membership, defense, government, entertainment, seniority, working hours, and so on."[42] In other words, those

---

41 "Razvertyvanie siuzheta (roman-drama)," *Zhizn' iskusstva*, 1920, no. 343 (21 January); *O teorii prozy*, section III, 1

42 Stuart Miller, *The Picaresque Novel* (Cleveland and London: The Press of Case Western Reserve University, 1967), 65.

The Roles of "Form" and "Content" in World Literature | 83

in this underworld observe a code of non-conventional conventions and as such can be compared with Shklovsky's proclivity for systematizing the non-systematic, for the way, as he sees it, in *Shandy* the rogue plot rides roughshod over time sequence, mixing up chronological order. While masquerading as a conventional plot it subversively creates an alternative system for literary narrative. To him, art has its own creative laws, that pay no heed to everyday causality or the mores of the conventional world.

But in Shklovsky's "Writing Desk" not all is joyously iconoclastic. The gratuitous gesture, a favorite of Dada and the Surrealists, rubs up against gratuitous slaughter. The most poignant example he provides–in a digression-is the needless death of his older brother, Evgenii Shklovsky, a talented doctor, who was mortally wounded while trying to defend wounded soldiers from being killed in a train. Some other soldiers who objected to this act of mercy set on him and beat him savagely. Later, under the care of relatives he died, fully conscious, so much so that he was able to keep monitoring his own weakening pulse, and he cried copiously as he recognized the inevitability of his senseless death. Shklovsky adds in an offhand manner the observation that his brother was killed either by the Whites or the Reds. This narrative of an unending series of such tragedies is delivered with panache, in the spirit of Sterne. Death is a digression.

In Shklovsky's narrative with its sudden transitions, then, "art" keeps banging into "life." But nowhere is this confluence more apparent than in his treatment of war.

War:

As Galin Tihanov has observed, Shklovsky's autobiographical writings of the early 1920s are not as concerned with revolution as with war.[43] This is understandable given that he missed the October Revolution because he was still stationed with the Russia army in Persia and saw only the chaos of its aftermath and the civil war. But war and violence are themes that hover over all his writings of the 1910s and early 1920s. The first half of *Sentimental Journey*, "Revolution and the Front" is largely about his time in first the imperial army and then the army of the Provisional Government, while the post-revolutionary moment that he covers in "The Writing Desk" blends in with the war-time moment in a tale of unending horror. There is as it were a clue to this preoccupation in a central formulation of "Art as Technique": "Automatization eats away at things, at clothes, at furniture, at our wives"–in other words at the every

---

43 Galin Thanov, "The Politics of Estrangement: The Case of the Early Shklovsky," *Poetics Today* vol. 26 (2005), no 4, 6707-1.

day (*byt*)–but Shklovsky then adds a phrase that does not appear to belong in this sequence "and at our fear of war."

The subject of war does not in itself preclude the picaresque. War is in some senses the ideal subject for an exemplary narrative (in Shklovsky's terms) because of the element of the arbitrary, especially marked when it is described from within the experience of war, rather than in ex post facto narratives which are structured by some understanding of the inevitability of the outcome. The experience of war is full of the unexpected that comes in a rush of events, a sort of accelerated picaresque. But dark material storms into the narrative from the stark extra-textual realities that the narrator is attempting to convey and it is hard to write them off as "stylistic," as mere technique-fodder.

One can sense this duality in Sterne's *Tristram Shandy*, which also engages the theme of war. The narrator is obssessed with the siege of Namur and the Seven Years' War of 1756 to 1763 and his coverage has tendency to irony, a common feature in representations of war, as Paul Fussell points out. But this novel is also punctuated by periodic meditations on mortality. It is haunted by the specter of the narrator's impending death, a theme of extra-textual relevance in that both Sterne, like his narrator, was at the time contemplating the certainty of his own demise from tuberculosis. In Shklovsy's account of war in "The Writing Desk," to a greater extent than in Sterne, play with Sternian formal techniques bleeds into what Henry James has characterized as "The plunge of civilization into the abyss of blood and darkness."[44] War is after all when "time is out of joint," when humans are placed in extremis, providing an abundance of human trauma ("tragedy," a sentiment Shklovsky dismissed in "On 'King Lear'").

Shklovsky as the author of "The Writing Desk" is both the narrator-picaro as the merry rogue, playing with the conventions of narrative even as in his account he extricates himself from a series of scrapes and in that sense conforms to the plot trajectory of a picaresque, and the the realities he describes in Sentimental Journey challenge his Formalist credo. Though in his theoretical writings of this time he downplays the importance of content in a work of literature to an extreme degree, yet the realities he describes in *Sentimental Journey* challenge his Formalist credo. Paradoxically, at the same time as he was preaching the independence of literature from life, "life" in its most stark form–hunger, cold, disease, slaughter-was impacting both author and text. In war there is no

---

44 Cited in Paul Fussell, *The Great War and Modern Memory* (Newc York: Oxfoird University Press, 1975), 8.

everyday life to be transcended as he urges in "Art as Technique." On the contrary, greater normalcy would have been appreciated. In Shklovsky's memoir event follows event in a haphazard manner but there is no sudden relief. In this sense, it might be seen as a devolution of the rollicking picaresque which so attracted him in his theoretical writings.

"The Writing Desk" could, then, be seen as providing an end case for any doctrine that wants to diminish the significance of content in a text. Several of Shklovsky's favorite terms from his Formalist vocabulary acquire ironic resonance and do double duty as, on the one hand, characterising formal literary devices and, on the other, characterizing some aspect of war, and in that sense belonging to the category of content. One of them is "displacement" (*sdvig*)-veering off at tangents to avoid predictable plot development.[45] During the years of war, revolution and civil war in Russia "displacement" was an all-too common reality with refugees, imprisonments, and forced migrations. Wherever Shklovsky travels he comes across displaced persons of all sorts wandering around, desperately seeking viable shelter, or crammed into perilously overcrowded and marginally functioning trains.

Revolution and the Front, compositionally the most "straight" of Shklovsky's early autobiographies, might seem to have avoided this paradoxical feature. In it, as mentioned, we see few examples of the verbal and compositional pyrotechnics that Shklovsky was to display both in his articles of 1919–1921, and in "The Writing Desk." Yet some of the key concepts from his theoretical writings potentially underpin this text. Two that I will discuss here are "*narushenie*" (breach, violation) and "*bezdomnyi*" (homeless). Firstly, *narushenie*. In his theoretical essays Shklovsky exults in all manner of "*narusheniia*," breaches of plot convention, the way expectations of plot are undermined in an ideal novel by such techniques as digressions, authorial asides and jumping around chronologically. In discussing *Tristram Shandy*, for example, he declares that the novel's "conscious form achieved by breaches" is its very content.[46] But in his account of the inter-ethnic strife in Persia, his main preoccupation in *Revolution and the Front*, what particularly offends him is the constant breaches of, effectively, what had been codified by international legal experts as the "laws and customs of war." These conflicts erupted in marauding, laying villages waste, mass migrations

---

45 In *"Tristram Shendi" Sterna i teoriia romana* (Petrograd, OPOIaZ, 1921), for example, Shklovsky says "The forms of the Sternian novel are displacement (*sdvig*) and breach (*narushenie*) of the customary forms" (17).

46 Viktor Shklovskii, *"Tristram Shendi" Sterna i teoriia romana* (Petrograd, OPOIaZ, 1921), 7.

86 | Katerina Clark

and brutal carnage, practices to which even the Russian army was not immune, though for an occupying army such actions were proscribed by those laws.[47]

If one follows over time both Shklovsky's theoretical texts and and the autobiographical one can see how a particular concept migrates from one text type to another and is in that sense homeless. But in the back and forth process the concept goes through serial metamorphoses: now, in a theoretical work, it is used as a technical term having to do with plot construction, now in an autobiographical context it characterizes some situation in the "real world," but now again incidents occur that are effectively realizations of the metaphorical potential in one of Shklovsky's favorite technical terms. As concepts migrate back and forth from text to text they cross boundaries of generic category and are recurrently translated.

One can see this "migratory" pattern in a cluster of themes and motifs that have to do with what Shklovsky contends is a defining feature of plot forms, that they are "homeless," not tied to any national tradition. His preoccupation with "homelessness" is reflected in his attraction to the picaresque where this quality is exemplied both by the plot structure with its emphasis on non-fixity of location, a-causality and open-endedness, and the rootless picaro. But in *Revolution and the Front* the concept of "homelessness," is treated largely on the level of thematics. It particulatly underpins Shklovsky's sympathetic account of the diasporic Aissors (Nestorian Syrians), who are identified as a "wandering people" (*brodiachii narod*). The Aissors are forced in the period after Shklovsky leaves Persia to uproot themselves yet again and undertake a tragic forced march through the desert that leads to massive losses, especially among their children. Shklovsky was sympathetic to their lot, even though he recognized that they were no less guilty of atrocities than the other ethnic groups he encountered in Persia. Clearly this sympathy is partly derived from an unacknowledged identification on his part with his own "wandering people," the Jews. A version of the "wandering people" is a recurrent in Shklovsky's subsequent writings and can be found in transmogrified form, for example, in *Zoo, or Letters Not About Love* (Zoo. Pis'ma ne o liubvi, ili Tret'ia Éloiza, 1923), Shklovsky's next

---

47 Peter Holquist, "Forms of Violence during the Russian Occupation of Ottoman Territory and in Northern Persia (Urmia and Astrabad), October 1914-December, 1917," in Omer Bartov and Eric Weitz, eds., *Shatterzone of Empires: Coexistence and Violence in the German, Habsburg, Russian, and Ottoman Borderlands* (Bloomington: Indiana University Press, 2013), 334–61; Peter Holquist, "The Laws of War. From the Lieber Code to the Brussels Conference," *The Berlin Journal* 32 (Fall 2018): 69–70.

autobiographical book after *Sentimental Journey*, where he identifies himself as a writer as a "nomad."

The assertion that Shklovsky, as a writer, is a "nomad" draws on the metaphorical potential of the term "homeless" that he foregrounds in his theoretical texts of the immediately post-revolutionary years. But the line beween the literal and the figurative is always blurred in his texts, even in the seemingly straightforward recounting of "actual" events in *Revolution and the Front*. Towards the end of that autobiography he suddenly and unexpectedly introduces a series of short parabolic tales. Considerations of space do not permit me to discuss them here, but defying or undermining conventional sysems of classification is an underlying theme in several of them.[48] In a sense, this unmotivated-seeming shift away from "realism" to parable is a clue pointing the reader to the allegorical resonances of many passages in the book.

Here I will provide just one example. Towards the end of *Revolution and the Front* Shklovsky relates a shockingly gruesome story, allegedly told him by another soldier who had returned from Persia. There had been an explosion, he said, which ripped through a crowd of soldiers, sending body parts flying everywhere. Their comrades set about collecting the parts (*kuski*) but "of course they mixed up the parts of many of them." One body was particularly egregiously reconstituted and comprised a large man's trunk to which a small head had been attached. Across the chest had been placed two non-matching arms, both of them left arms. At the sight of this incongruity the commanding officer just "laughed and laughed."[49]

Several scholars have commented on this striking story and its relevance for Shklovsky's literary theories. The most shocking aspect of the story, and the one with the most relevance for a metacommentary on literary theory, is not the starkly naturalistic detail, the violence as human beings are reduced to severed body parts, but the arbitrary reassemblage of these parts, the botching of an attempt to restore to the dead the dignity of individual personhood. The cobbling together of body parts, ostensibly a grimly naturalistic undertaking, has, then, potential as an allegorical realization of Shklovsky's injunction in "On King Lear'" that in a literary work the "tragedy" of any human protagonist is of no consequence compared with virtuouso, but non-systematic techniques for combining disparate plot "parts."

---

48 One sees this particularly in Shklovsky's account of how a platypus was captured by European colonists in Australia and imprisoned in a beaker of spirit.

49 Viktor Shklovskii, Revoliutsiia i front (Petrograd: R. V. Ts, 1921), 130.

Shklovsky in his theoretical articles of 1918-1922 was particularly interested in the "motivation" for linking disparate parts of a story. In his account of Sterne, for instance, he pointed to "the technique of stitching together a novel from separate novellas," adding that in Sterne this technique was parodied.[50] Versions of an incongruous "stitching together" of "parts" are a recurrent in Shklovsky's writings. Over a decade after the internationalist moment, and after Shklovsky had ostensibly repudiated his Formalist past,[51] one finds one version in an unexpected source, an article he published in the journal *Istoriia zavodov* (History of the Factories) in 1934. In the article Shklovsky discusses how he tackled the task of ghostwriting "autobiographies" for the infamous book *Belomor Canal* (Belomorsko-Baltiiskii kanal imeni Stalina, 1934), that appeared in the Istoriia zavodov book series. This book contains multiple mini-autobiographies of convicts in which they ostensibly recount their own reconstruction through labor on the Canal project under the supervision of officialdom. Most of these autobiographies are based on texts that individual convicts had been required to produce, some of them written down, others dictated to a transcriber. Shklovsky had been put in charge of the "technical" aspects to guide his team in their ghostwriting. In this article he describes how he adopted an approach that bears comparison with the story of how the human bodies were put together after the explosion: his team would take "*kuski*" (pieces) from the autobiography of one convict and then other "*kuski*" from other autobiographies, and combine them to stitch together a composite "biography" which they would attribute to a specific "author." The slogan of his group, tacked on the wall, was "He who does not use montage [*ne montiruet*] does not eat," a parody of the Soviet slogan "He who does not work does not eat."[52]

Shklovsky's cavalier disregard for the particular features of individual convicts' lives in processing their autobiographies can be related to the fact that earlier, in the initial post-revolutionary years, in adducing a transnational morphology of "forms" (compositional techniques), he chose to disregard much of the specificity of the texts he analysed. In particular, in his account of

---

50 Viktor Shklovskii, "*Tristram Shendi*" Sterna i teoriia romana (Petrograd, OPOIaZ, 1921), 7. See also "Paralleli u Tolstogo," *Zhizn' iskusstva*, 1919, no 299–300 (22–23 November): 1.

51 Viktor Shklovskii, "Pamiatnik nachnoi oshibke,"*Literaturnaia gazeta* 1930, no 4 (27 January)1.

52 G. Gauzner, 'Kollektivnaia rabota pisatelei 'Belomorstroi'" and Viktor Shklovskii, "O svoei rabote nad knigoi *Belomorstroi*," *Istoriia zavodov*, 1934, no. 3-4, 111, 113, 1141-7. The collectively written items by Shklovsky in this book are listed in Richard Sheldon, compiler, *Viktor Shklovsky: An International Bibliography of Works by and about Him* (Ann Arbor, Michigan: Ardis, 1977), 35;

The Roles of "Form" and "Content" in World Literature | 89

plot in fiction he chose not to take into consideration the reality that the non-Russian texts, which provided the prime examples for his theoretical writings in these years, were all read by him in translation.[53] As David Damrosch points out "literary language is particularly hard to translate since so much of the meaning depends on culture-specific patterns of connotation and nuance."[54] In his earlier *Poètika* essay, "The Connection of Techniques of Plot Contruction with General Stylistic Technigues," Shklovsky had acknowledged how much in a literary work comes from its "environment" (*stikhiia*), from the national literary tradition in which it had been produced, so that someone not steeped in that environment could not appreciate all the text's nuances (though admittedly Shklovsky made this point in a discussion of poetry).[55] But in his analyses of texts from world literature Shklovsky chose to ignore what Emily Apter has called in her account of translation the "speed bumps" of "untranslatability."[56] Together with his disciples in the Studio of World Literature, he had no patience with the Studio's founding mandate to investigate the nature of translation, and they peeled off and forged ahead, positing universally applicable rules for literary composition without taking into consideration the fact that they were reading their subject texts in translation.[57] Shklovsky himself knew no foreign languages and read in translation all the non-Russian texts that he mined for prime examples of his theories.[58]

To return to the discussion of the theories of Moretti with which I began this article and the idea that "forms" are portable from culture system to culture system: if writers in a "periphery" do not take into account the embeddedness of a text from the "core" in the culture of its country of origin, they can just rework its formal components as "parts" (*kuski*), ignoring the fact that they are organically integral to another, living tradition. Both Moretti, and more egregiously

---

53 Shklovsky, for instance, says explicitly in his book on Sterne that his analyses are based on the translation that came out in the Petersburg journal *Panteon kul'tury* in 1892 (*"Tristram Shendi" Sterna i teoriia romana* [Petrograd, OPOIaZ, 1921], 22).

54 David Damrosch, *What Is World Literature?* (Princeton Princeton University Press, 2003), 292.

55 V. Shklovskii, "Sviaz' priëmov siuzhetoslozheniia s obshchimi priëmami stilia," *Poètika. Sborniki po teorii poèticheskogo iazyka II* (Petrograd:18-ia Gosudarstvennaia Tipografiia, Letushkov. 13, 1919), 1202–1.

56 Emily Apter, *Against World Literature: On the Politics of Untranslatability* (New York: Verso, 2013), 3.

57 "Literaturnaia studiia Doma iskusstv," *Zhizn' iskusstva*, 1920, no 1.

58 Emily Finer, *Turning into Sterne: Viktor Shklovskii and Literary Reception* (London: Studies in Comparative Literature 18: Modern Humanities Research Center and Maney Publishing, 2010), especially 10, 39.

and extravagantly Shklovsky, minimize the problems that arise in trying to import a form or plot from what Moretti calls the "core" to a "periphery," across cultural and linguistic boundaries. Moretti in his struggles to provide a formula for the way "forms" are appropriated in the "periphery" effectively illustrates the utopian nature of Shklovsky's project.

CHAPTER 5

"The Treasure Trove of World Literature": Shaping the Concept of World Literature in Post-Revolutionary Russia
Maria Khotimsky

Founded shortly after the October Revolution of 1917 in Petersburg, the Vsemirnaia Literatura (World Literature) publishing house aimed at creating an innovative, state-supported canon of world literature addressed to the new reading public. The publishing house set forth an ambitious program to publish classics of European, and, subsequently, Eastern literary traditions in new or updated translations. Among more than three hundred fifty employees of the publishing house, there were leading writers, scholars, and translators. The publishing house released a detailed catalog with a visionary preface by Maxim Gorky and presented a program of publishing two book series, with the Main Series (*Osnovnaia seriia*) dedicated to thorough editions, and the People's Series (*Narodnaia seriia*) to brochures and shorter books for general reading public. Although actual publication plans were hindered by the dire economic situation of the early Soviet years, both the publisher's vision of world literature and the established approaches to translating and publishing foreign literary works had long-lasting impacts on this field in the Soviet Union.

Despite its innovative approach to international book canon, the legacy of this publishing house is often overlooked in Western studies on world literature as a concept and an institutional practice.[1] The reasons for this lack are manifold. First of all, there is the inaccessibility of many texts released by Vsemirnaia Literatura in English. Secondly, given the multiplicity of cultural actors involved in this publishing house, it did not feature a coherent program or theory: various statements are dispersed across book introductions, journal articles, and correspondence between the publishing house members and Soviet authorities. Yet, taken together, these excerpts create a particular picture of world literature that echoes several similar developments in the West and in prerevolutionary Russia, while also advancing innovative trends in world literature as an institutional and cultural practice. They certainly merit more attention and complicate the picture of "socialist-realist desiderata under the guise of a Goethean *Verständnis* (understanding) between Europe's—and, later the world's—various peoples,"[2] as defined in *The Routledge Concise History of World Literature*.

Building on earlier studies of the historical[3] and socio-cultural[4] contexts of Vsemirnaia Literatura, this essay analyzes several key statements on world literature that appeared between 1919 and 1924 in paratextual materials of the publishing house (primarily, the program statements in the introductory catalog articles, book introductions, and commentaries). Given the period when Vsemirnaia

---

1 For example, the "Origins" chapter in the anthology *World Literature in Theory* includes Rabindranath Tagore and the New Cultural Movement of China but does not incorporate any Russian or Soviet materials (see David Damrosch, ed., Part 1, "Origins," in *World Literature in Theory* [Hoboken: John Wiley and Sons, 2013], 15–69.) *The Cambridge Companion to World Literature* refers to Vsemirnaia Literatura in the chronological table in the introduction, but does not include further discussions of this enterprise (Ben Etherington and Jarad Zimbler, eds., *The Cambridge Companion to World Literature* (Cambridge: Cambridge University Press), 2018. Theo D'haen offers a two-page discussion of this enterprise in his *Routledge Concise History of World Literature* (London: Taylor & Francis, 2012), 22–23.

2 Theo D'haen, ibid.

3 Earlier studies of Vsemirnaia Literatura history include: L. M. Khlebnikov, "Iz istorii gor'kovskikh izdatel'stv 'Vsemirnaia literatura' i 'Izdatel'stvo Z. I. Grzhebina,'" *Literaturnoe nasledstvo*, 80 (1971): 668–703; I. A. Shomrakova, "A. M. Gor'kii—organizator izdatel'stva 'Vsemirnaia literatura,'" *Istoricheskii arkhiv*, vol. 2 (1957): 69–95. For more recent analyses, see: Tatiana Bedson and Maxim Schulz, "Translation strategies in the Soviet Union in the 1920s and 1930s," in *Going East: Discovering New and Alternative Traditions in Translation Studies*, ed. Larisa Schippel and Cornelia Zwischenberger (Berlin: Frank&Timme GmbH, 2017), 269–92; Maria Khotimsky, "World Literature, Soviet Style: A Forgotten Episode in the History of the Idea," *Ab Imperio*, no. 3 (2013): 119–54; Francesca Lazzarin, *Il libro e il chaos. La casa editrice Vsemirnaja Literatura (1918–1924) tra le luci e le ombre di Pietrogrado* (PhD diss., University of Padua, 2013).

4 See: Sergei Tyulenev, "Vsemirnaia Literatura: Intersections between Translation and Original Writing," *Slavic and East European Journal* 60, no. 1 (2016): 8–21.

"*The Treasure Trove of World Literature*" 93

Literatura was founded, institutional theoretical frameworks are most applicable for this case study. As Venkat Mani notes, "What is identified as world literature undergoes transformations in different historical times and in different geographical locations and linguistic traditions. World literature is historically conditioned, culturally determined, and politically charged."[5] Scholars have proposed a variety of different frameworks for reading world literature (see, for example, David Damrosch's discussion of "the global, the regional, the national, and the individual, with temporal being the fifth dimension").[6] However, these frameworks can overlap, especially in moments of cultural transition, such as postrevolutionary Russia. Here, Galin Tihanov's proposal of "self-reflexivity" as another definitive principle is particularly helpful: "One needs to be aware of at least four major reference points: time, space, language, and, crucially, what one could term self-reflexivity—how literature itself reflects on, and creates images of, 'world literature,' thus opening up spaces for interrogation and dissent from the currently prevalent notions of world literature."[7] While Tihanov's analysis addressed the self-reflexive paradigm of world literature "on the level of individual literary texts that examine artistically *the idea of world literature* and construct images of it,"[8] the self-reflexivity framework can be applied in the institutional context as well. A close reading of materials from Vsemirnaia Literatura shows that, while the founding members inherited earlier models of conceptualizing world literature, they sought to advance their own definitions of world literature in order to accommodate many conflicting agendas at a historical moment fraught with power struggles, where, as Sheila Fitzpatrick put it, "culture was one of the primary spheres of revolutionary contestation, like politics and economics."[9]

To explore how world literature was defined theoretically and envisioned practically through the canon of literary texts and through paratextual materials, I will first discuss the two book catalogs released by the publisher, drawing comparisons with analogous prerevolutionary publishing initiatives. Then I will turn to several examples of book introductions, which sought to present world

---

5   Venkat Mani, *Recoding World Literature: Libraries, Print Culture, and Germany's Pact with Books* (New York: Fordham University Press, 2016), 13.
6   David Damrosch, "Frames for World Literature," in *Grenzen der Literatur: Zu Begriff und Phänomen des Literarischen*, ed. Simone Winko, Fotis Jannidis, and Gerhard Lauer (Berlin: Walter de Gruyter, 2009), 496.
7   Galin Tihanov, "The Locations of World Literature," *Canadian Review of Comparative Literature* 44, no. 3 (2017): 468.
8   Ibid., 475.
9   Sheila Fitzpatrick, *The Cultural Front. Power and Culture in Revolutionary Russia* (Ithaca: Cornell University Press, 1992), 2.

literature to the Soviet readers. My analysis is informed by Gérard Genette's view of the paratext as "a zone of not only transition but also of *transaction*: a privileged place of pragmatics and strategy."[10] In analyzing the paratextual elements of translations, I will explore different "transactions," to use Genette's term, which reveal the early Soviet views on world literature and humanist universalism vis-à-vis national literatures, and attempt "to influence how the text is received,"[11] through addressing different categories of readers.

Defining the Subjects and the Scope of World Literature

Maxim Gorky's introductory article in the catalog contains several metaphors for world literature, and two stand out in particular. The first image depicts the "treasure trove" of humanistic knowledge, which the new publishing house aspires to bring to its readers: "all the treasures of poetry and artistic prose, all that has been created during a century and a half by the efforts of European spirit."[12] The second metaphor presents world literature as a "monument"—a grandiose cultural undertaking by the newly formed state: "By creating such an immense and responsible culture work on the very first year of their active life, under inexpressibly difficult circumstances—the Russian people are justified in saying they are erecting a monument worthy of them."[13] In this quote, the unusual word collocation "culture work" corresponds to "kul'turnoe delo" in the Russian version of the text; it is rendered as "grande oeuvre de civilisation" (great work of civilization) in French, and "Kulturarbeit" (cultural work) in the German version of the article. Taken together, these notions emphasize culture creation and perpetuation of humanistic values. Likewise, two metaphors for world literature reveal the tangle of conflicting agendas: participating in culture building, realizing a grandiose vision of culture that lines up with new sociopolitical context, while also preserving the cultural heritage and supporting the lives of the prerevolutionary intelligentsia.

Indeed, a series of compromises characterize the history of Vsemirnaia Literatura as both the new Soviet print culture and culture in general were

---

10 Gérard Genette, *Paratexts: Thresholds of Interpretation*, trans. Jane E. Lewing (Cambridge: Cambridge University Press, 1997), 2.

11 Kathryn Batchelor, *Translation and Paratexts* (London: Routledge, 2018), 142.

12 Maksim Gorky, introduction to *Katalog izdatel'stva "Vsemirnaia Literatura" pri Narodnom Komissariate po Prosveshcheniiu* (Petersburg: Vsemirnaia literatura, 1919), 20.

13 Ibid., 21.

being contested after the revolution.[14] On the one hand, the publishing house founders appealed to enlightenment ideals and cultural power, and both supporting and expanding the literary canon was a sign of the progressive cultural politics. For example, Aleksandr Tikhonov, one of the founding members of Vsemirnaia Literatura editorial board, commented in his 1920 report to the State Publishing House that Vsemirnaia Literatura "was supposed to serve as a link between the Soviet government and the literary intelligentsia. Besides, the existence of a book publisher with such a wide cultural agenda and a brilliant staff that includes almost all the prominent representatives of Russian literature could be used abroad as a prime example of Soviet cultural policy."[15] The notion of cultural heritage, as Sheila Fitzpatrick explains, was shared by the new government and the intelligentsia: "The Bolshevik Party and the intelligentsia shared an idea of culture as something that (like revolution) an enlightened minority brought to the masses in order to uplift them. There was not sense on either side that the culture that was best for the masses was the culture that the masses liked."[16]

On the other hand, there were many social and economic reasons for the establishment of Vsemirnaia Literatura, which, along with such organizations as Dom Iskusstv (House of the Arts) created enclaves of safety for writers, poets, and artists whose lives were uprooted by the revolution.[17] Between 1918 and 1921, Vsemirnaia Literatura served as one of the few available income sources to sustain the livelihood of prerevolutionary literary intelligentsia members, as most private publishing venues and newspapers were closed. Food rationing was based on professional categories, with members of non-proletarian professions, such as lawyers, doctors, and writers belonging to the third category and having limited access to food rations.[18] Working at Vsemirnaia Literatura enabled writers and poets to receive honoraria for literary work (some payment came in the form of food and firewood) and to maintain a sense of community

---

14 Sergei Tyulenev offers a compelling analysis of the compromise nature of Vsemirnaia Literatura in his essay included in this volume.

15 Aleksandr Tikhonov, quoted in Inga Shomrakova, "A. M. Gor'kii—organizator izdatel'stva "Vsemirnaia literatura," 93.

16 Fitzpatrick, Cultural Front, 5.

17 As Martha Weitzel Hickey explains in her thorough study of House of the Arts, both Gorky and Chukovskii were actively involved in these two cultural institutions. Martha Weitzel Hickey, The Writer in Petrograd and the House of the Arts (Evanston: Northwestern University Press, 2009), 4–5.

18 Tatiana Kukushkina offers a detailed analysis of drastic inflation and changes in food rationing policy, which disadvantaged the intelligentsia members. See Kukushkina, "Iz literaturnogo byta Petrograda," 343–48.

as authors and intellectuals. As Francesca Lazzarin points out in her compelling analysis of the unofficial parodic almanac created by the members of the publishing house, this institution created an informal community of "sharing daily life in the literary sphere," merging translation work, research, creativity, and camaraderie in a difficult time.[19] Due to these complex circumstances, the vision of world literature cannot be defined solely as realizing the Marxist paradigm of culture construction, but rather, as a reframing of earlier models of world literature as a confluence of different agendas and ideas that different stakeholders brought to this organization.

The initial approach articulated in the catalog of the publishing house follows the "humanist" or "philological" genealogy of world literature, to use Jérôme David's terminology.[20] In this context, world literature is represented as "the more or less difficult passage of texts from one language to another, from one nation to another, from one culture to another."[21] The very name of the newly established Soviet publishing house is the Russian word *vsemirnaia* (literally, "whole-world") represented world literature as a pan-humanistic vision, and echoed Goethean ideas by ushering in the imagined era of universal literature. Gorky's introductory article to the catalog, which set the tone for the publisher's cultural and political agenda, is steeped in the Romantic rhetoric of "universal" literature as a cultural aspiration yet to be achieved (with a special emphasis added by spelling Literature with the capital letter):

> There is no universal Literature because—as yet—there never was any universal language common to all mankind; but all Literature, both prose and poetry, is saturated with sentiments, thoughts, [and] ideas that belong to the whole human race, and express the one sacred longing of Man for the joys of spiritual freedom.[22]

This ecumenical vision of world literature makes bold comparisons between cultural traditions and emphasizes the notion of shared humanity. Literary

---

19 Francesca Lazzarin, "'Poka sud'ba ne privela nas na Mokhovuiu, 36': neofitsial'nyi ezhegodnik izdatel'stva' 'Vsemirnaia literatura kak letopis' petrogradskogo literaturnogo byta 1920kh godov,'" in *Tekstologiia i istoriko-literaturnyi protsess*, 1st edition, ed. L. A. Novitskas (Moscow: Filologicheskii Fakul'tet MGU im. M. V. Lomonosova, 2013), 144.

20 Jérôme David, "The Four Genealogies of World Literature," in *Approaches to World Literature*, ed. Joachim Küpper (Berlin: Academie Verlag, 2013), 13–26.

21 Ibid., 18.

22 Gorky, introduction to *Katalog izdatel'stva "Vsemirnaia Literatura,"* 17.

works are drawn together in the "melting pot" of universal literature, which can serve as a repository of humanistic values, and can have the power to educate the reader: "A murderer in Asia is as horrible as he is in Europe; Pliushkine, the Russian miser, is as wretched as Grandet, the French one; the Tartufes of all countries are alike, misanthropes are to be pitied everywhere, and everybody in every country loves the touching image of Don Quixote, the knight of human soul."[23] It is worth noting that this approach to world literature as an accumulation of great masterpiece (mainly, of European lineage, though the publishing house would soon turn to Oriental traditions as well) combines both the philological and pedagogical genealogies of this concept, which, according to Jérôme David, serves "at once as an apprenticeship and an inculcation, an education of taste and a discipline of values."[24] Gorky and other founding members of Vsemirnaia Literatura proposed the task of making a broad array of great literary works available to the Russian readers, and thus enriching their worldview through contact with other cultures, as a path to universal human values.

This approach to world literature, emphasizing a rich dialogue with prior literary epochs, was not new to early twentieth-century Russian culture. It was a significant feature of modernist aesthetics, with its renewed interest in classical antiquity, multifaceted conversations with European literature, and blossoming of translation culture. The confluence of philological and pedagogical genealogies of world literature was shared by prerevolutionary Russian book series that foreshadow Vsemirnaia Literatura, such as Zinovii Grzhebin's Panteon (Pantheon), established in 1907, and Mikhail Sabashnikov's Pamiatniki Mirovoi Literatury (Monuments of World Literature), launched in 1911. For example, in his draft statement, Zinovii Grzhebin described the goal of Panteon as "to collect the masterpieces of world literature and to make them a treasure for Russian readers."[25] Panteon book series encompassed titles ranging from antiquity, the medieval period, and the Renaissance to the works of "recent centuries and our days"; its proposed approach to translations was founded on "strict historical impartiality," with the hope to represent "everything characteristic of each epoch and literature."[26] Sabashnikov's book series also emphasized the notion of timeless cultural heritage: the initial title of this translation series

---

23 Ibid., 19.
24 David, "Four Genealogies," 20.
25 E. A. Gollerbakh, "'Germanskii sled v russkom 'Panteone': peterburgskoe izdatel'stvo 'Panteon' (1907–1912) kak agent nemetskoi kul'tury," in *Vestnik Russkoi khristianskoi gumanitarnoi akademii* 11, no. 3 (2010): 177–86.
26 N. V. Kotrelev, "Materialy k istorii serii pamiatnikov 'Mirovoi literatury' izdatel'stva Sabashnikovykh (perevody Vyacheslava Ivanova iz drevnegrecheskikh lirikov, Eskhila,

was *Vechnye Knigi* (Eternal Books), and one of the goals of his publishing enterprise was to make classical literature accessible to Russian readers.

As Evgenii Gollerbakh has noted, these trends were influenced by similar developments in the European publishing market, such as the demand for republishing the classics of the eighteenth and nineteenth centuries and the popularity of translations, as evident in the successful Universal-Bibliothek series by Reclam Verlag in Leipzig.[27] The mission of Reclam's Universal-Bibliothek was quite similar to Vsemirnaia Literatura's mission: to create world literature "a library of established national canons," with the goal of "educating the public through national and world literatures."[28] Another contemporary European analogy is Joseph Dent's Everyman's Library, established in 1907 to publish affordable editions of British and European classics. Dent, like Gorky, was an autodidact, with an admiration for "the good genuine books of mankind."[29] A venerating attitude to literature, and a belief in the equalizing nature of knowledge, where "great books were an engine for equality,"[30] is evident in Gorky's introduction to the Vsemirnaia Literatura catalog, as is his reverence and adoration of literature:

> Rising from the mysteries of Birth, we sink into the mysteries of Death. Together with our Planet we are flung into incomprehensible space. We call it Universe, but our conception of it is not clear. [...] The loneliness of man in the universe [...] the deadly weariness peculiar to all ages and people alike and which is felt as acutely by Byron, an Englishman, as by Leopardi, an Italian, or by the writer of the "Ecclesiastes" and by the great Sage of Asia, Lao-Tze."[31]

While the emotional appeal to battle the "loneliness of man in the Universe" may be unique to Gorky, the broader intellectual framework points to many predecessors in Russian and European culture. The functions of humanistic

---

Petrarki)," in *Kniga v sisteme mezhdunarodnykh kul'turnykh sviazei*, ed. N. V. Kotrelev (Moscow: Vsesoiuznaia gosudarstvennaia biblioteka inostrannoi literatury, 1990), 133.

27   Gollerbakh, "Germanskii sled v russkom 'Panteone,'" 180.

28   Mani, *Recoding World Literature*, 126.

29   J. M. Dent, quoted in Jonathan Rose, "'Everyman': An Experiment in Culture for the Masses," *Victorian Periodicals Review* 26, no. 2 (1993): 79–87, 80.

30   Jonathan Rose, *The Intellectual Life of the British Working Class* (New Haven: Yale University Press, 2008), 132.

31   Gorky, introduction to *Katalog izdatel'stva "Vsemirnaia Literatura,"* 18.

accumulation of knowledge and enlightenment appeal were part of shaping the national through the "universal" through combining the idea of "treasure" with the notion of *Gemeingut*, or shared intellectual assets. This conflation of Goethean and Marxist approaches to world literature, as Venkat Mani has shown, is closely linked with the idea of constructing the idea of national culture with the help of world literature, and critiquing "the worldwide rise in a "cosmopolitan consumption" through a worldwide circulation of books and literature that depends on transnational trade."[32] Gorky's vision for the publishing house combined the ideas of universal humanistic asset as a shared spiritual possession, however his envisioned the mode of circulation was different since he called on the new government to support this mass publishing initiative.

Gorky's metaphor of world literature as a monumental task was first realized in the grandiose scope of the proposed publication plan that distinguish this enterprise from other analogous prerevolutionary book series. The monumental proportions were evident in the extremely detailed, historically based book lists of the catalog, which, at least in the planning stages, far transcend the world literature canons in pre-1917 publishing venues, in Russia and in the West. Secondly and unsurprisingly, there were greater political overtones and clear appeal to new power structures. In addition to glorifying the young Soviet government as its source of support, Vsemirnaia Literatura mission statement set clear time range for its initial vision of world literature: "from the great French Revolution to the Great Russian Revolution," and presented a teleological view of culture:

> The WORLD'S LITERATURE PUBLISHING COMPANY [VSEMIRNAIA LITERATURA–*M.K.*] has started its activity by choosing—as the appended list shows—books which have been published in different countries from the end of the eighteenth century down to the present day: from the Beginning of the Great French Revolution until the Great Russian Revolution. Thanks to this [selection], the citizens of Russia will have at their disposal all the treasures of poetry and artistic prose, all that has been created during a century and a half by the efforts of European spirit.[33]

---

32   Mani, *Recoding World Literature*, 23.
33   Ibid., 20.

What distinguished its proposed publication plan from earlier enterprises (which developed under different book market conditions) was the perceived opportunity of creating this cultural enterprise from the ground up: establishing the canon, outlining a chronological program, proposing updated editions representative of different countries and cultural epochs, and addressing different groups of readers in Soviet Russia.

This "monumental" appeal was evident in the innovative catalog of the publishing house: the introduction was printed in four languages (Russian, French, German, and English). With its range of books and impressive organization, the catalog and the proposed book canon itself served as tools of political negotiation. To quote just one example, in Gorky's correspondence with Vatslav Vorovsky, head of the State Publishing House, Vsemirnaia Literatura was described as a prime example of a great culture building initiative, which can be used as pro-Soviet propaganda:

> This is a huge undertaking, and, of course, it will position the Soviet government well in the eyes of Western European intelligentsia. But even more important is the propaganda potential of Vsemirnaia Literatura, which, in accordance with our plan, encompasses everything that was created by the European thought from Voltaire to Anatole France, from Swift to Wells, from Goethe to Richard Dehmel, etc. Shortly, our catalog will be ready, printed in English, German, and French. We will send it to all the countries: Germany, France, America, Italy, England, to the Scandinavians, and others. As you see, this is a grandiose task, and no one has attempted it yet, no one in Europe. The government should actively help this enterprise, since this is the largest, and indeed the most cultural undertaking that it can accomplish at this moment in time.[34]

With its proposed plan to publish one thousand five hundred books in the Main series, and from three thousand to five thousand brochures in the People's series,[35] Vsemirnaia Literatura stood apart from its predecessors in its aspiration for a more thorough version of the literary canon. It was precisely the range of the proposed book canon that allowed the publisher to continue to

---

34 A. Tikhonov, quoted in Khleblikov, "Iz istorii Gor'kovskikh izdatel'stv," 74–75.
35 Gorky, introduction to *Katalog izdatel'stva "Vsemirnaia Literatura,"* 8–9.

bring in additional specialists beyond its core editorial group, and to advocate for the participation of leading writers and scholars who were not openly pro-Soviet. The mission to create a new canon of world literature and enhanced approaches to translation (including translation editing, developing a reference library, translation workshops, and literary studios),[36] created ample grounds for self-expression and resistance in translation, as Brian Baer and other scholars have persuasively shown.[37]

The publishing house did enjoy considerable financial and logistical support from the government, especially during the early years of its work. Its books were featured prominently in the Russian materials of the First International Book Exhibition in Florence, which took place in 1922. Vsemirnaia Literatura publications were allotted their own catalog entry in the fiction section of the exhibition's catalog, which included fifty-two volumes out of approximately two thousand total exhibition items (catalog entries 468–520). The book entries were presented in chronological order, and the second entry was a collection of stories by an Italian author: Gabriele D'Annunzio's *Le Novelle della Pescara*, or *Peskarskie rasskazy* (*Pescara Stories*).[38] In his speech at the opening ceremony, Ilya Ionov, the head of the Soviet delegation, also emphasized the Russian readers' interest in world literature,[39] and described the role of the book in Soviet culture "not only as a friend and teacher, but also as a great fighter for the idea of love and brotherhood among people."[40]

The synthesis of political and humanist rhetoric enabled Vsemirnaia Literatura to advocate effectively for the expansion of the world literature canon beyond the temporal markers of the French and the Russian Revolution. Already in the catalog, Gorky mentioned a few ideas for new editions: "the Literature of the Middle Ages, with the Literature of Russia and other Slavonic countries and likewise with the picturesque thought and word painting of the East, with the Literature of India, Persia, China, Japan, [and] Arabia."[41] The creation of the Eastern book series made a significant step forward in expanding

---

36 See Bedson and Shulz, "Translation Strategies in the Soviet Union in the 1920s and 1930s," 271–73.

37 Brian Baer, "Literary Translation and the Construction of a Soviet Intelligentsia," *The Massachusetts Review* 47, no. 3 (2006): 537–60.

38 *Katalog russkogo otdela mezhdunarodnoi knizhnoi vystavki vo Florentsii* (Moscow: Gosudarstvennoe izdatel'stvo, 1922), 468–500.

39 Ilya Ionov, "Russkaia kniga na mezhdunarodnoi vystavke vo Florentsii," in *Katalog russkogo otdela*, xi.

40 Ibid., xii.

41 Gorky, introduction to *Katalog izdatel'stva "Vsemirnaia Literatura,"* 21.

Vsemirnaia Literatura's vision of world literature, compared to pre-1917 publishing initiatives in Russia and in Europe since it offered a range of literary traditions that was rather groundbreaking for its time. Established shortly after the launch of Vsemirnaia Literatura, the Eastern section (*Vostochnyi otdel*) brought together leading scholars of Oriental studies. They leveraged their expertise to create an innovative, remarkably broad list of literary sources that commenced with ancient Sumerian and Egyptian texts, and included the literatures of the Caucasus, the Middle East, China, Japan, India, and more. As the introduction to the Eastern series catalog stated: "... if we are able to fulfil the entire program, we will have the right to say that Russian literature has a series of masterpieces of Eastern literature unlike any other people."[42] The inclusion of the Eastern series was an innovative step compared with pre-revolutionary attempts to create world literature book series, which mainly focused on the Judeo-Greco-Roman paradigm of European culture.

In sum, while the general notions of world literature as an accumulation of treasures or as introduction and assimilation were not new in the European and Russian publishing contexts of the early twentieth century, the scope of the canon and the approaches to book editing brought many new tendencies to the sphere of literary translation. They included not only the tension between national and global frameworks but also the input from particular cultural actors. Their individual perspectives ranged from Gorky's visionary statements (and his genuine desire to protect members of the intelligentsia) to informed contributions by leading scholars and translators who were specialists in their own fields. All of these factors informed the approaches to the formation of the book canon and its presentation in Vsemirnaia Literatura publications.

The New Literary Canon: An Overview of the Eastern and Western Catalogs of the World Literature Publishing House

Compared to European publishing initiatives that appeared in existing book markets, Vsemirnaia Literatura was in a unique position to propose and fulfill a book publishing agenda according with its vision, drawing on the expertise of many prerevolutionary specialists. Among scholars and writers who

---

42 *Katalog izdatel'stva Vsemirnaia Literatura pri Narodnom Komissariate po Prosveshcheniiu. Literatura Vostoka* (Petersburg: Vsemirnaia Literatura, 1919), 5.

oversaw the work of the Western series and contributed to the catalog were Kornei Chukovskii and Evgenii Zamiatin for English literature; Aleksandr Blok, Fyodor Batiushkov, and Fyodor Braun for German literature; Nikolai Gumilev, Mikhail Lozinsky, and Andrei Levinson for French literature; Akim Volynskii for Italian literature; Georgii Lozinsky for Spanish and Portuguese. The addition of the Eastern series was truly innovative compared to earlier developments in Europe and Russia, and brought a group of internationally known scholars, such as Nikolai Marr, Sergei Ol'denburg, Ignaty Krachkovsky, and others, who collaborated on the catalog of the Eastern Series, as well as the two-volume edition *Literatura Vostoka* (*Literature of the Orient*).

The Western series catalog commenced with Gorky's article, which was published in four languages. It included the lists of authors and book titles proposed for publications in different languages, in the following order: French, English, American, German, Italian, Spanish and Spanish American,[43] Portuguese and Brazilian, Swedish, and Danish literatures. The authors' names and the book titles were printed in two columns on each page, with Russian on the left and the language of the respective country on the right.

As the organizing principle of the catalog suggests, it very much followed the tendency of constructing "world" literature through the prism of national literature. At the same time, the catalog sought to bring a greater degree of regional representation into defining the national literary traditions. For example, it included Provençal and Belgian literature in the French section; Brazilian writers were part of the "Portuguese literature" section. The English literature section included "Literature of the Colonies," represented by two authors from Australia, two from South Africa, five from Canada, and two from contemporary India (later, ancient Indian literature would also be included in the catalog of the Eastern series). Swedish literature, in turn, included "Swedish Writers in Finland," while Danish literature featured "Danish Icelandic writers." As Gorky himself noted, the emerging canon, was decidedly Eurocentric; already in the introductory article, he expressed his aspirations to publish "literature of the Slavic countries" and to expand the Eastern section. The very range and level of detail in the descriptions of the works and authors listed in the catalog give the sense of the founder's aspirations: creating an impressive, broad literary canon (albeit, arguably, not feasible, given the scarcity of resources in postrevolutionary Petersburg). Each of the participating writers and scholars brought their own knowledge and aesthetic preferences, resulting in varying levels of

---

43 Gorky, introduction to *Katalog izdatel'stva "Vsemirnaia Literatura,"* 9.

detail provided in the sections of the catalog. For example, the English literature section featured birth and death dates of all the authors, while all other sections only included the names of writers and literary works.

In terms of the books proposed for publication, the catalog mainly included single-author entries, although several anthologies based on period, genre, and occasionally, a literary group were proposed for publication as well. Canonical European traditions dominated the selection of texts: French literature, featuring 179 proposed titles, English literature with 144 titles, German literature comprising 143 titles, and Italian literature with 134 titles. (The Spanish, Portuguese, American, Swedish, and Danish literature sections included fewer titles). Multivolume editions and collected works were proposed for several leading writers: to give a few examples, Voltaire, Hugo, Goethe, Heine, Kleist, Dickens, and others. Along with anthologies of poetry and plays, the publishing agenda of Vsemirnaia Literatura included nonfiction anthologies. For example, there were several edited volumes centering on the French Revolution (*Journalists and Pamphletists of the Revolutionary Epoch* and *Theater of the Revolutionary Epoch*);[44] several proposed anthologies of literary criticism from different countries, without specifying which writers would be included in these anthologies; and anthologies of letters by notable individuals, such as the *Anthology of Letters by Artists* for France and the *Anthology of Letters by Scientists, Composers, and Artists* for Germany. In some instances, gender became a category for literary works: for example, in the section dedicated to German literature, one finds separate anthologies for male and female poets of the late nineteenth and early twentieth centuries. The catalog itself could serve an educational purpose, providing a detailed overview of several European literary traditions. Its meticulously composed list and the inclusion of both key names and lesser-known representatives of different literary epochs distinguished it from earlier Russian book series such as Panteon and Pamiatniki Mirovoi Literatury (Monuments of World Literature).

Vsemirnaia Literatura took a particularly significant step forward by creating its Eastern (or Oriental) series: while the publishing house had made a claim to be a broadening, universalizing initiative, the series was another step towards fulfilling this program. Among the scholars who collaborated on the Eastern series were internationally renowned specialists: Ignaty Krachkovsky, Nikolai Marr, Sergei Ol'denburg, Vasily Bartold, Evgenii Bertels, Vladimir Bogoraz, Boris Turaev, and others. Relying on the expertise of the leading scholars, the publishing house took pride in

---

44 *Katalog izdatel'stva "Vsemirnaia Literatura,"* 37.

expanding the world literature canon. As the introduction to the scholarly volume *Literatura vostoka (Literature of the Orient)* stated, "Now, for the first time [and] with the help of Russian Orientologists, Vsemirnaia Literatura is making an attempt to bring the monuments of the East (the Orient) to the attention of the Russian readers, connecting [these monuments] with the cultural landmarks of the West and incorporating them into world literature."[45] Neither the definition nor the introductory materials of the new approach to world literature were free of the exoticizing tendencies of the Occident-Orient divide. In their statements, editors often expressed regret about their scant knowledge of Eastern tradition: "In the eyes of the Russian reader, world literature has exclusively been seen as literature of the West; occasionally, some vague images of the East appeared on his horizon, and only some chance translations reached his reading circle—most often, however, not as translations from the Eastern originals but as versions of Western translations."[46]

The catalog of the Eastern series proposed to fill in this lacuna in a radical way, by publishing a hitherto inaccessible range of literary, historical, and religious documents. These plans ranged from featuring the oldest extant literatures of Egypt, Assyria, and Babylon to an updated translation of the Bible; from literature of the Christian Orient to literature of the Caucasus; and from ancient Persian writing to the literary heritage of India, Japan, and China. Arab literature was to be brought to the Russian readership in its many manifestations "across Asia, considerable parts of Africa, and medieval Europe."[47] The initial structure of the catalog was based on both regional and temporal categories: it started with the ancient civilizations (Egypt and Assyria) and incorporated vast geographical ranges, from the Caucasus to the Far East, including the folk heritage of nationalities and tribes of Siberia and Central Asia. The Eastern series catalog was printed in Russian and French; its cover, font, and typographic embellishments resembled the Western series catalog, but its pages were slightly smaller in size. The Eastern series catalog was also less uniform, with entries varying considerably in organization and length; one can presume that this depended on the input of the contributing editors.

Compared to the list of books for the Western series, the Eastern series catalog included a broader range of source languages and cultures (eighteen sections total, several of them comprising more than one literary tradition).

---

45 *Katalog izdatel'stva "Vsemirnaia Literatura,"* 5.
46 Ibid., 5.
47 Ibid., 5.

The most striking difference from the Western catalog was the choice of section titles: instead of "literature" as a categorizing title, the sections were titled by ethnicities or nationalities, with some exceptions. Most of the catalog sections were based on names for ethnicities: "the Egyptians," "the Babylonians and Assyrians," "the Jews," "peoples of the Caucasus," "peoples of Iran," "the Turks," "peoples of India," "the Indonesians," "the Tibetans," "the Mongols," "the Chinese," and "the Japanese," concluding with "Paleo-Asian Tribes of the Siberian Northeast." Entries that stood out with their titles were "Khristianskii Vostok (Christian Orient)" (which, in turn, included "the Syrians," "the Copts," and "the Abyssinians"), and "Arabskaia Literatura" ("Arabic literature," which included subsections for the "classical" and "new" periods).

The most detailed section of the catalog was "Narody Kavkaza" ("the Peoples of the Caucasus"), which included "Georgian National Literature," "Armenian National Literature," and "folklore."[48] This section's entries on Georgian and Armenian literature incorporated ancient, medieval, and Renaissance periods (which include epics, religious and folklore texts, and historical texts), and they featured a detailed periodization and literary groups of the nineteenth and early twentieth centuries. In addition, Armenian literature was separated into a larger section of "Armenia of the Caucasus" and the smaller section "Literature of Turkish Armenians." A separate subsection was devoted to the folklore of the Caucasus (epic poems, fairy tales, and songs), which, in a matter of a decade, would become a prominent field in the Soviet editions.

By contrast, several catalog entries were very minimal, serving as placeholders for certain regions on the world literature map. For instance, Indonesia and Indo-China include two entries each, marked as "Antologiia" ("Anthology") and "Narodnaia Slovesnost'" ("Folk Literature"). The rich heritage of Chinese, Japanese, Indian, and Arabic literatures was represented by longer collections; however, the editors focused mainly on the ancient and medieval periods. Arabic literature did incorporate several newer titles, such as the proposed anthology *Arab Emigré Writers in America*. Book titles for Chinese literature were presented in a general list (totaling forty-five entries) whereas Japanese literature included detailed periodization by era and genre, with the total of forty-two entries. Differing from other sections of the catalog, many entries in the Chinese and Japanese sections included translations of book titles, plus parenthetical notes on the pronunciation of the original (transcriptions appeared

---

48 The section of Georgian national literature spanned pages 17–20 of the catalog, while Armenian national literature was allotted pages 20–25.

both in Russian and French). Thus, the catalog itself held educational value, introducing the readers into the world of distant literary traditions and the sounds of unfamiliar languages. What stands out across different sections of the catalog is the variety of sources: inscriptions from ancient monuments, historical chronicles, religious texts, and hagiographical literature, as well as many works of folklore.

Both the broad list of sources and the key message in the introduction to the catalog convey the urgency of knowing more about the non-Western literary traditions:

> It is difficult to say how soon we will be able to realize this program because there are many obstacles to fulfilling it. However, the very fact that we are proposing the program and beginning to fulfill it is—we are truly convinced of this—an enormous step towards getting to know the soul of the East, so ineptly understood by the Western men who are fond of achievements of their own civilization and therefore blind to the great and amazing culture of the East.[49]

Echoing Gorky's introduction, which hailed world literature as a way to expand the spiritual horizons of the Russian readers, the publications of the Eastern series emphasized the difficulty and the importance of appreciating unfamiliar aesthetic forms. For example, Sergei Eliseev wrote in his introductory article on Japanese literature: "Getting to know the literature of Japan, which features rich and beautiful forms, should help us raise—gently and carefully—the veil over a foreign soul; [this effort] should open its beauty and its various expressions of human thought, help us better understand the Far East, and thus increase the multifaceted nature of our own soul."[50] Similar sentiment is expressed by Vasilii Alekseev: "An encounter with the man of the Orient always implies a moment of rebirth, which demands great patience [from us]."[51]

In introducing the heritage of Eastern literary traditions, scholars also invoked the metaphor of the "spiritual treasure," or the image of world literature as a storehouse of riches, which is incomplete without the contributions from

---

49 Katalog izdatel'stva "Vsemirnaia Literatura," 6.

50 Sergei Eliseev, "Literatura Iaponii," Literatura Vostoka 2 (1920): 89.

51 V. M. Alekseev, "Godovoi otchet o deiatel'nosti Kollegii ekspertov Vostochnogo Otdela 'Vsemirnoi Literatury' (28 aprelia 1919–1928 aprelia 1920 g.)" in Nauka o Vostoke. Stat'i i dokumenty, ed. M. V. Ban'kovskaia et. al. (Moscow: Nauka, 1982), 250.

Oriental literatures. This theme is echoed by scholars working on different national traditions. For example, Sergei Ol'denburg called for the inclusion of India in the canon of world literature: "What India has brought to the spiritual treasure-trove of mankind thus far is timeless, and it allows us to talk about the remarkable place India holds in world literature. The more literary monuments of India's creative activity enter the canon of world literature, the richer it will become."[52] Ignaty Krachkovsky uses a similar metaphor of *obshchecheloveches-kaia sokrovishchnitsa* (universal treasure trove) in his discussion of Arabic literature. He also posits "the growth of the human soul," which can be inspired by familiarizing oneself with the history of Arabic literature: "One of the noblest tasks for a thinking human being is to observe the ceaseless growth of the human soul, which happens before us, across the entirety of Arabic literature from the sixth to the twentieth centuries."[53]

In addition to these general humanistic metaphors, which were part of the philological genealogy of world literature, some publications offered new definitions of world literature. For example, Vasilii Alekseev described Chinese literature as world literature, given its ability to influence and shape other literary traditions: "Thus, we can base our definition of world literature not on its history or its volume but on its ability to bring other elements of world literature (now understood as a collective term) under its powerful influence. And indeed, Chinese literature can be described as one of the dominant literatures of this type."[54] Alekseev's framing of the dynamics of world literature as a system taps into the critical genealogy of world literature in Jérôme David's definition and anticipates contemporary discussions on systems of influence in world literature. Questions of comparisons and cross-influences of different national traditions within world literature were central to book introductions in Vsemirnaia Literatura editions.

World Literature in the Introductions to the Main and People's Series

According to Kathryn Batchelor, in the analysis of translation practices the study of paratexts can offer additional insights into the social and cultural contexts of translations: "Paratexts, like the texts to which they give access, are

---

52 Sergei Ol'denburg, "Indiiskaia literatura," *Literatura Vostoka* 2 (1920):38.
53 Ignatii Krachkovskii, "Arabskaia literatura," *Literatura Vostoka* 1 (1919): 33.
54 V. Alekseev, "Kitaiskaia literatura," *Literatura Vostoka*, 2 (1920): 82.

"The Treasure Trove of World Literature" 109

created by people, and to examine them is to examine the activities of people: how people try and persuade, educate, share opinions for reasons of self-interest or benevolence, sell products, demonstrate allegiance, and so on."[55] Among the many roles paratexts can play, establishing a new framework for understanding literary works which could be used as a means of influencing the readers was particularly important for the editors of Vsemirnaia Literatura publishing house. While the proposed book canon was innovative in its thoroughness, book editions allowed republication of earlier translations, supplied with new critical frameworks, which made paratexts a particularly important feature of translation editions. In Gérard Genette's terms, paratexts are "more flexible, more versatile, always transitory because transitive," and these qualities often help them become "an instrument of adaptation."[56] Vsemirnaia Literatura editors relied on this function of paratexts, using the space of the introductions and commentaries to position literary works within the context of world literature, while also addressing two different categories of readers in the Main Series and People's Series. Adaptation, a key function of the paratext in Genette's analysis, went both ways here: scholars and writers adapted to postrevolutionary cultural conditions, and the texts were contextualized for different reader audiences.

Arguably, the very setup of the publishing house emphasized the role of the paratext. The compensation for translation editing and writing of introductory articles was more lucrative than for translations: per the initial publishing house agreement, editorial work paid from seven to eight hundred rubles per printer's signature (twenty to twenty-four pages) and the compilation of anthologies was ranked at five hundred rubles, while prose translations were valued at two hundred to two hundred and fifty rubles (translating poems was priced differently, with compensation per line).[57] As spaces that allows to convey "what texts do not tell,"[58] paratexts served multiple purposes in Vsemirnaia Literatura editions. In addition to fulfilling the prescribed editorial guidelines for introductory articles, they often allowed poets and writers to offer their own subtle commentary on the work of the translated author, to share their aesthetic and philosophical views, and to reflect on the challenges of translation.

---

55 Kathryn Batchelor, *Translation and Paratexts* (London: Routledge, 2018), 195.
56 Genette, *Paratexts*, 408.
57 "Usloviia raboty v izdatel'stve Vsemirnaia Literatura," TsGALI. f. 46, op. 1, d. 58, l. 538. Original. Typewritten.
58 Şehnaz Tahir Gürçağlar, *"What texts don't tell*: The uses of paratexts in translation research," in *Crosscultural Transgressions. Research Models in Translation Studies II. Historical and Ideological Issues*, ed. Theo Hermans (Manchester: St. Jerome's Publishing, 2002), 44.

110 | Maria Khotimsky

The founders of the publishing house adhered to an encyclopedic approach both in creating the book canon and in proposing the guidelines for book introductions. According to the guidelines, the purpose of the introductory articles was "to explain to the reader everything that is necessary for a comprehensive understanding of the text (*dlia vsestoronnego ponimaniia teksta*)," that is, to offer certain important details of the writer's biography, emphasize significant stylistic traits typical for this writer and the literary epoch, and, where possible, "point out connections with Russian literature."[59] As an editorial memorandum explains, the group of editors sought "to introduce a certain degree of planning and uniformity into the collective work of the publishing house, but not to create a rigid template for the 'fabrication' of the introductory articles."[60] As a closer look at book introduction suggests, rarely were these requirements followed to the letter, and paratexts often became the space of negotiation.

The Main Series was supposed to publish "works of the most significant European writers, selected to comprise a library of European literary classics— small but systematically organized."[61] Functioning as "mini-monographs" devoted to a given author, the introductory articles in this series were written by key specialists in the field, and ranged from twenty to thirty pages. Often drawing on ongoing scholarly research, they rarely followed all the editorial recommendations on an exhaustive historical and biographical summary; instead, they presented reflections on the works, along with relevant literary analysis. The interpretation of world literature in these articles is rather open-ended, and it mirrors their authors' scholarly and literary range of vocabulary and available tools for analysis. For example, in his introduction to Heinrich Heine's *Reisebilder* [Travel Pictures], Aleksandr Blok emphasizes the motif of a spiritual journey, and highlights the free flight of imagination as the principle of Heine's poetics: "In a work filled with ethnographic, personal, and novelistic elements, one would be hard-pressed to find a clear architectonic structure. Here, lawlessness is made into law, and the energy that the poet retained until his

---

59   "Ot redaktsionnoi kollegii izdatel'stva 'Vsemirnaia Literatura.'" Instruktsia, RO IRLI, f. 256, op. 2, ed. chr. 30, l. 11, quoted in Francesca Lazzarin, *Il libro e il caos*, 65, http://paduaresearch.cab.unipd.it/5648/1/Lazzarin_Francesca_tesi.pdf, accessed June 10, 2020.

60   A. Tikhonov, Circular from December 17, 1919. PF ARAN, f. 1026, op. 2, ed. khr. 233, l. 54, quoted in Lazzarin, *Tesi*, 65.

61   Draft of the editorial program, GARF. 2306, op. 1, d. 3, l. 73, quoted in L. M. Khlebnikov, "Iz istorii Gor'kovskikh izdatel'stv," 699–700.

death, is not limited by years or experience."[62] Rather than a detailed historical background or textual commentary, Blok's introduction presents an aesthetic reflection, consonant with his own thinking on Heine's reception in Russia. In one of his letters to Vladimir Zorgenfrei, who prepared the translation for this volume, Blok noted the need for new translations as a way of understanding Heine's legacy in the postrevolutionary cultural context: "We need to give Heine for our epoch—a job that demands effort and responsibility."[63] Rather than offering a detailed biographical commentary, Blok's introductory article to the translation dwells on his own interpretation of Heine's role in European intellectual history, and the ongoing intellectual debates on the role of artist in the society.[64]

For writers and scholars who had few opportunities to publish their own work, book introductions offered a way to reflect on literature and on their own turbulent epoch. Gorky's Romantic, humanistic impulse is characteristic of many book introductions. To give another example, in her analysis of Victor Hugo's novel *Ninety-Three* (translated as *Devianosto Tretii God* in Russian), Maria Loewberg writes about the key theme of Hugo's poetics as "overwhelming tenderness towards the world, in the world."[65] In her commentary on a historical novel, Loewberg chooses to emphasize the humanistic, personal connection of the writer's persona, rather than his reflection on the revolution. In fact, some of the introductions argue against a narrow politicizing reading of literary masterpieces. Viktor Zhirmunsky's introduction to Byron's work (which was later published as a monograph), proposes to free Byron's heritage from narrow political readings: "If we were to read Byron's work without our biases of established psychological and historical patterns, we will not find any indication of social motifs of disillusionment, the French Revolution, social idealism, or

---

62 Aleksandr Blok, introduction to Genrikh Geine, *Putevye kartiny* (Petersburg: Vsemirnaia Literatura, 1920), 19.

63 Aleksandr Blok, quoted in Aleksandr Lavrov, "Blok perevodit prozu Geine. Soobshchenie A. Lavrova i V. Toporova," in *Literaturnoe nasledstvo. T. 92. Aleksandr Blok. Novye materialy i issledovaniia*, ed. I. Zil'bershtein (Moscow: Nauka, 1987), 659.

64 In 1919, while editing the volumes of Heine's prose, Blok wrote an article "Geine v Rossii" ("Heine in Russia") and presented it at one of the public lecture events at Vsemirnaia Literatura. Blok's diary entry from March 26, 1919, chronicles the event and the arguments during the discussion. See P. N. Medvedev, ed., *Dnevnik Aleksandra Bloka 1917–1921* (Leningrad: Izdatel'stvo pisatelei v Leningrade, 1928), 150–52.

65 M. E. Loewberg, introduction to Victor Hugo, *Devianosto tretii god* (Petersburg: Vsemirnaia Literatura, 1922), 8–9.

the collapse of political ideals."[66] In analyzing the Byronic woe, instead of the Romantic rebellion (which was often cast in political terms in later Soviet criticism), Zhirmunsky insists on philosophical parallels "between different centuries and different nations:

> We can turn to different centuries and different peoples to look for equivalents of Byronic woe: Petrarch's "taedium vitae" [and] Pascal's religious pessimism represent somewhat similar phenomena in different ways; in earlier epochs—[there are] Job's pessimism and the "vanity of vanities" in the Ecclesiastes, the religious negation of Buddhism and pessimistic refusal of earthy life in early Christianity. All these examples, despite their clear differences, present much closer similarities to the pessimists of the early nineteenth century than any examples of disappointment in social ideals (e.g., after the 1848 Revolution).[67]

As Zhirmunsky's analysis shows, introductions to the Main Series address the questions of world literature through the lens of cultural typology and potential cross-influences.

Compared to the variety of approaches in the introductory articles to Western literary works, introductions to books published in the Eastern Series had a greater emphasis on filling the lacunae in the knowledge of the literary and cultural traditions, and often reflected on the challenges of translation and reception. For example, Vasilii Alekseev's introduction to Pu Songling's *Strange Stories from a Chinese Studio* included notes on Chinese folk beliefs, a discussion of cultural and social context, a brief biography of the writer, and commentary on his style. The introduction also addressed the differences in perception, and cautioned the reader about the difficulty of understanding Eastern aesthetics.[68] Commenting on the whimsical style of Chinese classical tale, Alekseev explains: "The translator and author of this introduction thinks that this fantasy, this mixture of the fantastical and the realistic, may appeal to a Russian reader if he is prone to disengaging from daily life at least for a short while, and [it can] give him several experiences which are unusual and very interesting for Russian and

---

66 Zhirmunsky, "Zhizn' i tvorchestvo Bairona," in Dzh. G. Byron, *Dramy* (Petersburg: Vsemirnaia literatura, 1920), 12.

67 Ibid.

68 Vasilii Alekseev, "Predislovie perevodchika," in Liao Zhai, *Lis'i chary* (Petersburg: Vsemirnaia literatura, 1922).

European literature."[69] Meta-literary reflections are more common among the introductions in the Eastern book series. When introducing unfamiliar literary forms and traditions, translators sought to propose reading guidelines, such as the following: "The translator ought to warn the reader that it is dangerous for a layman to think himself the absolute judge of any foreign work of art (or [foreign] creative expression)."[70] The ideal readers of world literature should be receptive to new aesthetic patterns: "those who, with their whole soul, want to reach a new world of human feelings, experiences, images, and words."[71] When Orientalist scholars acted as the authors of paratexts and translations, they often addressed their readers from the position of guides and arbiters. They cautioned against quick judgement, and they attempted to convey the background historical and cultural knowledge which is necessary for the reception of Oriental literary traditions.

Speaking from a position of authority was even more typical for book introductions in the People's Series, where one finds many examples of negotiating the notion of world literature. As part of this series, Vsemirnaia Literatura aimed to produce short brochures with explanatory introductions for "the broadest circulation among the masses" in order to "instill the habit of reading in uneducated people."[72] Both in the Western and the Eastern editions, this series favored stories with exciting content: "works with an interesting plot, entertaining works, historical and adventure novels, etc."[73] A unique canon of world literature for the masses was being established—a category that was actively shaped in the cultural practices of the 1920s and 1930s, as Evgeny Dobrenko has shown in *The Making of the State Reader*.[74] Nikolai Konrad recounts his editorial experience: "We had to consider the introductions both from the scientific perspective and the emotional aspect, which would attract the reader to the book. Along with that, we had to judge introductions on the basis of being understood by an average reader, especially in the People's series"[75] The notion of an "average reader" played a key role here, creating a certain power dynamic between the critics or translators and their presumed audience.

---

69 Ibid., 11.
70 Ibid.
71 Ibid.
72 Gorky, *Katalog izdatel'stva "Vsemirnaia Literatura,"* 9.
73 Ibid.
74 Evgeny Dobrenko, *The Making of the State Reader: Social and Aesthetic Contexts of the Reception of Soviet Literature* (Stanford: Stanford University Press, 1997).
75 V. M. Alekseev, "Godovoi otchet," 250–51.

Several rhetorical devices that appeared in Gorky's introduction to the Vsemirnaia Literatura catalog are quite prominent here. They include characterizations of historical periods and literary currents, frequent parallels with Russian literature, and appealing to broad humanistic values. However, these introductions deviated drastically from the Main series in their content as well as their style. Addressed to mass readers, introductions to the People's series books were written in a simpler language and relied on shorter sentences and paragraphs. In presenting brief biographies of the writers and definitions for various literary terms, the introductory article authors frequently employed rhetorical questions and short explanations of historical and cultural facts.

For example, the introduction to Sir Walter Scott's historical novel *The Black Dwarf* defines him as a "prominent member of the world literature canon," the "progenitor of the historical novel," and a "brilliant representative of Romanticism."[76] The introduction creates a humanizing portrayal of the writer, with picturesque detail of his ancestral lands on the Tweed River: "He was a sickly, limp child, who could not participate in games with other children. On bright summer days, he would lie on juicy, green grass for hours, along with his friends—sheep and dogs. His eyes looked on the landscape that one often sees in Scotland: below are the silvery bends of the river; on the mountain, gray ruins of an ancient castle; and on the horizon, the majestic peaks of purple mountains."[77] This quote is just one example of how critics and writers of introductory articles sought to bring the reality of world literature to their readers. Short, evocative portrayals, story-like descriptions, and emotional, vivid representations of the writer's lives served to convey the details of life in other countries and foreground the interest in literary works.

In addition to giving biographical and historical details, the introductory articles served an educational purpose, and sought to explain cultural, religious, and philosophical concepts. For example, Izmalkova's introduction explains the contrast between Romanticism and Classicism in very simple terms; it outlines the history of Scotland, and it even offers an "snapshot" view of Christianity: "There is one Christian faith, but it is divided into so-called confessions; so, Russians and Greeks are Orthodox, the French are Catholic, [and] the Germans are Protestant."[78] Appealing to the mass reader had a clear pedagogical purpose:

---

76 V. Izmalkova, introduction to Val'ter Skott, *Chernyi karlik* (Petersburg: Vsemirnaia Literatura, 1922), 9–11.

77 Ibid., 12.

78 Ibid., 14.

critics sought to define historical facts and abstract concepts,[79] while also finding fitting examples in the Russian literary context. Given that target audience just recently became literate, even the Russian cultural references often had to be explained. For example, Fyodor Batiushkov's introduction to Voltaire's *Candide* (which was, in fact, a reprint of the earlier translation Fyodor Sologub had completed for the Panteon edition),[80] concisely explains the meaning of "optimism" and "pessimism," and then goes on to illustrate Voltaire's quote with an allusion to Chekhov's play:

> Voltaire expressed precisely that in the conclusion, saying that we must "cultivate our garden." And what is "our garden"? In his play *The Cherry Orchard*, the Russian writer Chekhov explains that our garden is Russia. Chekhov is right. And next to Russia, we can add the entire world, the entire humanity whose interests are being followed by every man who dutifully works at his plot, because everyone in this world is connected in an unending chain linked by the results of labor.[81]

This quote is highly representative of the style of People's Series introductions: it contains retelling of passages from literary works in simple terms, with broad generalizations and comparisons between foreign and Russian literary works, as well as emphasis on a moral lesson to be learned from the literary work at hand.

As these examples suggest, in terms of ideological framing of world literature, People's Series editions certainly contained more interference from the critics and scholars who penned the introductory articles. Many of these "top-down" explanations sound almost ironic, given the sophisticated educational

---

79 Both the introductory articles and the translated texts in the People's Series often included commentary on vocabulary. They also offer an interesting reflection on the "presumed" intellectual horizon of the reader. For example, glosses to the story collection by Spanish prose writer Gregorio Martinez-Sierra include idioms such as *bashnia iz slonovoi kosti* (ivory tower), described as "an expression used to show impenetrability and seclusion"; abstract words such as *mif* ("myth"), "an ancient Greek story about gods and heroes," *dialektika* ("dialectic"), "the art of arguing and proving"; and simpler terms: *plyazh* ("beach"), "a sandy seaside area that is convenient for swimming." G. Martinez-Sierra, *Blagoslovennaia vesna* (Berlin: Vsemirnaia Literatura; Gosudarstvennoe izdatel'stvo, 1922), 24, 33.

80 For more details on the history of this translation, see E. Gollerbakh, "Chernyi peredel: Vol'ter v izdaniiakh peterburgskogo izdatel'stva "Panteon" (1907–1912)," in *Chetvertye Vol'terovskie Chteniia, Sbornik nauchnykh trudov*, 4th edition, ed. N. Speranskaia (Saint Petersburg: Izdatel'stvo Rossiiskoi Natsional'noi Biblioteki, 2017), 167–210.

81 F. Batiushkov, introduction to Vol'ter, *Kandid, ili optimism* (Petersburg: Vsemirnaia Literatura, 1919), 12.

background of the editors and translators. Since one of the key tasks was to make the world literary heritage pertinent and accessible to the mass Russian reader, the authors of the introductory articles often created quick sketches of different national and cultural traditions. The category of *narod* (the people), as well as the category of *prostoi chelovek* (the common man) were common reference points in these introductions. Painted in broad strokes, these national definitions were saturated with stereotypes, and oftentimes, they used the notions of political and cultural hegemony to define different national groups. For example, in his introductions to the works of Oscar Wilde and Bernard Shaw, Chukovskii often contrasted the Irish and the English. In one instance, he writes: "Bernard Shaw has an Irish background. He was born in Dublin. This explains, in part, his interest in comedy, farce, grotesque, and—sometimes—buffoonery. The Anglo-Saxon mind is too heavy-handed and clumsy for this. There is a reason that many of the funniest English comedies were written by the Irish."[82]

Book introductions in the People's Series editions combined these national descriptions with an insistence on general commonalities among people all over the world. In his account of Saadi's biography, Sergei Ol'denburg recounts how the poet wandered around different countries: "Saadi was greatly interested in learning the hearts of people, he was always interested in humans, their actions and their motivations . . . Judging by his works, he made comparisons and came to the conclusion that humans of all nationalities and countries are not all that different: they love and hate in the same way."[83] The tension between the national and the universal is a recurring theme in many introductory articles in the Peoples' Series. This "productive tension between binaries" can often reveal the socio-political and institutional aspects of world literature,[84] and it offers insights into the early Soviet approach to world literature. From 1919 to 1924, that approach still allowed for pluralism in the book canon and featured an open-ended approach to book introductions. The founders of Vsemirnaia Literatura harnessed this tension between the universalist notion of "treasure trove" and the national aspiration to building a monumental canon of world literature for Soviet readers.

---

82 Kornei Chukovsky, introduction to Bernard Shaw, *P'esy* (Petersburg: Vsemirnaia Literatura, 1922), 8.
83 Sergei Ol'denburg, introduction to Saadi, *Gulistan* (Petersburg: Vsemirnaia literatura, 1922), 12.
84 Mani, *Recoding World Literature*, 33.

Conclusion

The unique position of *Vsemirnaia Literatura* publishing house made it one of the first steps in shaping the Soviet literary field of the 1920s, which, as Harsha Ram aptly describes it, was "the first state-sponsored multilingual and multi-ethnic literature of the twentieth century, anticipating by half a century the re-emergence of world literature in the west as an expression first of postwar liberal multiculturalism and then of neoliberal globalization."[85] The multiplicity of questions, motifs, agendas, and the unintended outcomes that make the Petersburg *Vsemirnaia Literatura* publishing house a fitting example for studying world literature as inextricably linked with socio-cultural contexts. In the short years of its existence, this publishing house established several key precedents for later Soviet-era approaches to world literature defining theoretical and practical principles of the "cultural capital of translation,"[86] which would be instrumental in building the internationalist trends of the 1930s and for subsequent decades. The recurrent metaphors of "treasure trove" and "monument" are reflective both of the many competing agendas of the publishing house members, and more broadly, the overlapping frameworks of the national and the individual approaches to world literature. As the analysis of *Vsemirnaia Literatura* programmatic statements suggests, the "self-reflective" function of world literature, when seen in the institutional context, encompasses the search for a new evaluative system, adaptation to shifting socio-cultural norms, and reassessment of the roles of the readers, the critics, and the endeavor of translation.

---

85 Harsha Ram, "World Literature as World Revolution: Velimir Khlebnikov's Zangezi and the Utopian Geopoetics of the Russian Avant-garde," in *Comintern Aesthetics*, ed. Amelia Glaser and Steven Lee (Toronto: Toronto University Press, 2020), 32.

86 Katerina Clark, *Moscow, the Fourth Rome. Stalinism, Cosmopolitanism, and the Evolution of Soviet Culture, 1931–1941* (Cambridge, MA: Harvard University Press, 2011), 20.

CHAPTER 6

The Birth of New out of Old: Translation in Early Soviet History

Sergey Tyulenev

The Compromised New

No new is completely new. To be completely new, the new should be created out of nothing. But this is impossible, at least in the known universe. Therefore, in every new there must be a ratio of the new and the old. Creating a new is a more or less challenging negotiation of the ratio. This is the main challenge of every social movement or group that claims to be new. Where does one get the new while being surrounded by the old and being part of the old (as well as almost certainly its product, to boot)? This philosophical problem has a number of practical, mundane manifestations which create a great deal of minor hitches and insurmountable hurdles when the new tries to escape the tenacious clutch of the old.

The 1917 Russian October (socialist) revolution was no exception. On the banner of the brave new world, the mottow was writ large: *Ves' mir nasil'ia my razrushim do osnovan'ia, a zatem my svoi, my novy mir postroim...* [We'll destroy the entire world of oppression and then we'll build our own new world...]. These were lines in the Russian version of "The International." The Russian text was a translation (allegedly by Arkadii Kots) of the French *L'Internationale* by Eugène Pottier: "Du passé faisons table rase [...] Le monde va changer de base." Here we can see a kind of miniscule model of the role translation may play in a revolutionary process of molding the new out of the old: it brings inevitably the past into the new.

In the young Soviet state created as a result of the October revolution, the negotiation between the old and the new was anything but easy. The complicated tortuous process of negotiations can be observed in the case of the Vsemirnaia Literatura translation project headed by Maxim Gorky and in the debates in the First Soviet Writers' Congress which also grappled with the problem of translation of works of the old world into the new world. These materials will serve as a corpus of the present discussion.

Molding the new turned out to be a compromise from the very outset. As far as the art of the new world was concerned, a range of problems were to be tackled and resolving them time and again demanded a compromise. Even the most radical revolutionary thinkers and ideologists, such as one of the Proletkul't leaders Aleksei Gastev, admitted the inevitability of trade-offs.

Gastev argued that the new proletarian culture would target a new audience, the proletariat that would be living and working as a collectivity, rather than individuals.[1] New themes and characters would be introduced that would depict complex psychological experiences determined by the new collective coordinated work. Gastev imagined a novel and combined (*kombinirovannoe*) type of art which will overcome purely human manifestations (*chelovecheskie demonstratsii*), pathetic modern clowning (*zhalkie sovremennye litsedeistva*) and chamber music. Rather, there will be unprecedented objective demonstrations of phenomena, mechanized crowds (*mekhanizirovannye tolpy*) "with nothing intimate or lyrical."

This was a daring image of the proletarian culture. Although it was never endorsed by the government, Gastev definitely captured the degree of newness envisaged for the revolutionary proletarian culture. Yet even Gastev, while describing the highly innovative nature of the new culture, disagreed with champions of naïve simple, if not downright simplistic, proletarian art modeled on the unsophisticated Russian folk art of lubok:

> Usually, when speaking about the proletarian art, its ideologues [...] consider deliberate simplicity (*narochitaia prostota*) as its principal property. Such an approach to the greatest problem of modernity seems to us a grave misunderstanding. Even

---

1   Aleksei Gastev, "O tendentsiiakh proletarskoi kul'tury," *Proletarskaia kul'tura. Ezhemesiachnyi zhurnal* 9–10 (June–July, 1919), 44–45; https://viewer.rusneb.ru/ru/000200_000018_ RU_NLR_BIBL_A_012164478?page=48&rotate=0&theme=white.

The Birth of New out of Old | 121

when one speaks not of proletariat, but more inclusively of the present-day people (*narod*), who had gone through the crucible of technological transformations, the war, the revolution, one will realize that the people (*narod*) cannot be described with the same pristine simplicity (*netronutoi prostotoi*) characteristic of our classic folk artists. When it comes to proletarians, to approach them simplistically is tantamount to preaching hypocrisy. Of course, there's no need to act the ape or to imitate styles (*krivliat'sia i zanimat'sia stilizatsiei*), but one should not get carried away with [the primitivism of] lubok.[2] (All translations in this chapter are mine—*S.T.*)

Gastev here advocated a search for a medium ground between the conception of the proletarian art conceived in a lubok-like fashion and what he, somewhat condescendingly, referred to as acting the ape or imitating styles implying the bourgeois artforms. While being quite radical, he, however, called for a more balanced approach than any of the extremes was able to offer. Interestingly, the models, the lubok or the bourgeois arts, were summoned from the past. The new could not do without the past: what else could it draw upon?

This shows how tricky creating the new with the old, always still in view, can be. There would be more give-and-takes in the history of the Soviet state. In the present chapter those of them that involved translation will be examined.

Inveterate Translation

Translation has always to do with a precedent. A text, which was created elsewhere and in the past (it must have been created before it was translated), reappears as a translation now and here. Translation, as was the case of the above-cited Russian version of the *L'Internationale*, may link the new, struggling to free itself from its old, to another "new" which fought against its respective old but that new came from the past and was, therefore, itself already something belonging to the old. Translation inevitably adulterates the professed radicality of the new, in the case at hand the radicality of revolutionary social processes. In the ideal world, theoretically, the new socialist state being molded in Russia in the beginning of the twentieth century should have been created from scratch,

---

2 Gastev, "O tendentsiiakh proletarskoi kul'tury," 45.

from everything new but that was simply impossible. The new was emerging inveterately from the old (it will be recalled that the Latin root of the English word is *vetus* meaning *old*): the agents of the new were products of the old, the new contents could not get rid of the old semantics and old *expressives*, the old languages, their graphic systems, their vocabularies, their symbolism. A tension between the old and the new was inescapable, and the tension was of the onto-logical nature. The only way to tackle the tension was to condone compromise. To give just one example, after an attempt to negotiate between international-ism and nationalism, the new state had to settle for a new version of the old Romantic nationalism.[3]

The focus of this chapter is not on the relationship between the new and the old in the young Soviet state in general but only on one dimension of the early Soviet history. That dimension had to do with one of the culprits respon-sible for the old's lingering in the new project—interlingual translation.[4]

Translation in Early Soviet History

The Soviet translation project "Vsemirnaia Literatura" (henceforth VL, trans-lated literally—'world literature') (1918–1937) was initiated in the early days of the young Soviet Russia. The goal was to translate or retranslate foreign literary classics. The project was led by Maxim Gorky and several prominent literary figures of the time. The project was initially carried out on the basis of the specially created eponymous publishing house "Vsemirnaia Literatura" (1918–1925). Starting from 1922 another publishing house, "Academia" took over the publishing plan of "Vsemirnaia Literatura."[5] The project ended in the late 1930s. But the Soviet translation project conceived more broadly was not abandoned.[6] On the contrary, with the formation of the multinational Union

---

3 Brian James Baer, "From International to Foreign: Packaging Translated Literature in Soviet Russia," in *Slavic & East European Journal* 60, no. 1 (Spring 2016): 49–67.

4 Interlingual translation is a transfer between languages as opposed to intralingual transla-tion (a transfer within one and the same language) and intersemiotic translation (a trans-fer between different semiotic systems). See Roman Jakobson, "On Linguistic Aspects of Translation," in *On Translation*, ed. Reuben A. Brower (Cambridge, MA: Harvard University Press, 1959), 233.

5 Kornei Chukovskii, *Sovremenniki: Portrety i liudi* (Moscow: Molodaia Gvardiia, 1967), 136; Viacheslav Krylov and Ekaterina Kichatova, *Izdatel'stvo "Academia": liudi i knigi: 1921–1938–1991* (Moscow: Academia, 2004), 41.

6 See a detailed discussion of Gorky's World Literature project with an emphasis on how it influenced the field of literary translation in the Soviet Union in Maria Khotimsky, "World

of Soviet Socialist republics (1922), it acquired another dimension: in addition to appropriating the foreign literature, the Soviet translators had to mediate between the languages and literatures within their own state. Arguably, it is logical to examine the ideas about translation within the VL project and the later discussions as documented in the minutes of the First All-Union Congress of Soviet Writers (1934) together, the latter being viewed as the continuation of the former.

The scale of the operation of the VL testified to the young state's ambition and demonstrated the importance ascribed to integrating the world literary culture into its socio-political project by means of translation.[7] The VL involved as many as 350 translators and editors. According to the VL commercial director Aleksandr Tikhonov's report as of 19 April 1923, the plan was to prepare translations of up to 2500–3000 printer's sheets (*pechatnyi list*) which would amount to more than 100 million characters and 300 volumes to be put out yearly.[8] Unsurprisingly, the scale of operation challenged everybody involved. One of the most active contributors to the project, Kornei Chukovskii, a prominent Russian/Soviet literary figure, poet and translator, wrote in his diary: "It was hard work: we had to plan translating and publishing several thousand books in different languages; we had to find skilful translators; we had to assess prosaic and poetic translations of the past in a detailed fashion and based on rigorous criteria."[9]

The First All-Union Congress of Soviet Writers took place from 17 August to 1 September 1934 in Moscow. The Congress was opened by Gorky. Next, Andrei Zhdanov, the member of the Central Committee of the All-Union Communist Party responsible for the ideology in the realm of culture, took the

---

Literature, Soviet Style: A Forgotten Episode in the History of the Idea," in *Ab Imperio*, no. 3 (2013), 119–54. A different view of world literature (as a global network of literary exchanges) and the place Soviet literature and translation aspired to occupy in it is discussed in Katerina Clark, "Translation and Transnationalism: Non-European Writers and Soviet Power in the 1920s and 1930s," in *Translation in Russian Contexts: Culture, Politics, Identity*, ed. Brian James Baer and Susanna Witt (New York: Routledge, 2018), 139–58 and in Elena Ostrovskaya and Elena Zemskova, "From *International Literature* to world literature: English translators in 1930s Moscow," *Translation and Interpreting Studies* 14, no. 3 (2019), 351–71.

7   On the role culture played in legitimating the Soviet state, see Katerina Clark and Evgenii Dobrenko, eds., *Soviet Culture and Power. A History in Documents. 1917–1953* (New Haven: Yale University Press, 2007).

8   Maksim Gor'kii, *Arkhiv A.M. Gor'kogo: M. Gor'kii i sovetskaia pechat*,' vol. x, book 1 (Moscow: Nauka, 1964), 20.

9   Kornei Chukovskii, *Dnevnik, 1901–1929* (Moscow: Sovetskii pisatel', 1991), 130.

floor.[10] The first session of the Congress was followed by twenty-five sessions in which representatives of fifty-two Soviet republics and nations and of different organisations as well as different foreign writers took part. The Congress assumed a grand scale; the republics reported about on the state of their literary affairs; special addresses were pronounced in honour of Stalin, the Defense Commissar Voroshilov and the entire Central Committee and the Soviet of People's Commissars of the USSR, for good measure; the participants greeted the leading foreign writers who were seen as the main ideological sympathizers or 'fellow-travellers'.

The World Literature and the New Socialist State

The unprecedented proletarian state that had been seen during all its history to its last days as having no "analogues in history or in the modern world"[11], would not settle for anything shorter than a universe-challenging translation project. Initially, in the VL, the idea was to transfer the world literature written in many (potentially all/any) languages into the language of the state of workers and peasants who will be the new appreciators of the best of what the entire world could offer—Russian. This megalomania did not escape criticism for interpreting the world literature purely in terms of space and reducing the Russian literature to a provincial tradition within the canonical corpus of the world literature.[12] But a handful of dissenting voices could do little to dishearten the ambitious VL leaders who intended to embrace the classics of the Western European literary traditions as well as the masterpieces of the other parts of the world, notably the 'Orient' and the Americas. There was a method in that madness. The VL project was conceived along the lines of the Leninist version of Marxism which argued that the newly created socialist state would serve as a springboard for the world revolution.[13] The expanse of the corpus echoed the

---

10 On the role ideology played in the realm of Soviet translation, see Susanna Witt, "Arts of Accommodation: The First All-Union Conference of Translators, Moscow, 1936, and the Ideologization of Norms," in *The Art of Accommodation: Literary Translation in Russia*, ed. Leon Burnett and Emily Lygo (Bern: Peter Lang, 2013), 141–84.

11 Mikhail Gorbachev, *Perestroika: New Thinking for Our Country and the World* (New York: Harper & Row, 1987), 18.

12 Galin Tihanov, "World Literature, War, Revolution: The significance of Viktor Shklovskii's *A Sentimental Journey*," in *Transnational Russian Studies*, ed. Andy Byford, Connor Doak, and Stephen Hutchings (Liverpool: Liverpool University Press, 2020), 122–23.

13 Vladimir Lenin, *Polnoe sobranie sochinenii*, vol. 38 (Moscow: Izdatel'stvo politicheskoi literatury, 1969), 303.

The Birth of New out of Old | 125

scale of the envisaged revolution and, in its own way, even contributed to setting the scene for it. Interestingly, the new Soviet literature saw itself growing not so much out of its own "local" tradition, i.e. the Russian literature. Rather, it saw itself as inheriting the best from the entire world literature.

In 1848 Marx and Engels wrote briefly in their *Manifesto of the Communist Party* about the world literature which was part and parcel of the bourgeois global and cosmopolitan universe. Both in material and intellectual production individual nations' creations became common property: "National one-sidedness and narrowmindedness become more and more impossible, and from the numerous national and local literatures, there arises a world literature."[14] This was interpreted as the bourgeoisie's objectively preparing the historical scene for the proletariat. The venerated classics of Marxism sanctioned the concept of world literature. This must have set up the frame of reference for the Soviet Kulturträger and also their attitude to the world literature of the bourgeois period of the evolution of human society: there was a positive aspect about the cultural heritage of the otherwise rejected class. On the one hand, following the dialectic principle of the new growing out of the old by negating the negation, the new had to engage with the old, albeit in a critical fashion. The interaction of the new with the old was to be conducted from the point of view the world revolution. In the First All-Union Congress of Soviet Writers in which discussions of the translation of world classics would figure most prominently, a leading Soviet poet Dem'ian Bednyi formulated the rule of thumb: "I belong to the group of proletarian poets who look at the world literature from the viewpoint of the world revolution"[15].

On the other hand, the bourgeois literature, it was believed, reflected not only what the bourgeoisie wanted it to reflect but the entirety of the social reality around it.[16] This conceptualization of the literature of the bourgeois past (and, according to the same logic, of the previous periods) was another aspect of the endorsement of the Soviet world literature project. This view concurs with what Gorky reported in the First All-Union Congress of Soviet Writers: "The proletariat [...] is the only heir of all the best that is in the treasury of the

---

14 Karl Marx and Friedrich Engels, *Selected Works*, vol. 1 (Moscow: Progress, 1969), 16.

15 *Pervyi vsesoiuznyi s'ezd sovietskiikh pisatelei. Stenograficheskii otchet.* (Moscow: Khudozhestvennaia literatura, 1934), 558.

16 Vladimir Lenin, "Lev Tolstoi kak zerkalo russkoi revolutsii," in Lenin, Vladimir. *Polnoe sobranie sochinenii*, vol. 17 (Moscow: Izdatel'stvo politicheskoi literatury, 1968), 206–13.

literary world. The bourgeoisie has squandered its literary legacy, but we must collect it, study it and, critically assimilating it, move forward."[17]

Yet a crucial question was bound to arise: how to separate the useful from the useless? Here another aspect of the overall translation project is to be considered. Gorky's VL project and the translation in the early Soviet history as documented in the minutes of the First All-Union Congress of Soviet Writers echoed another world literary project—the German concept *Weltliteratur* as a treasure house of all literary chef-d'oeuvres which were to be gathered, among other things, for educational purposes which, arguably, inspired Marx and Engels' concept of the bourgeois world literature. Gorky insisted that creating the corpus of world classics would be "a source of cultural strength" of the new state.[18] This, however, presented a paradox: how was this educational goal to be achieved if the new was to rely on the old? The project was supposed to support the radical revolutionary transformation but it was compromised by the conservative nature of the corpus to be translated—the "notion of world literature as a canon of texts and a tool for inculcating the virtues of civility and erudition."[19]

The Soviet translation project also attempted to formulate and develop principles of literary translation as a literary activity in its own right (in the sense in which Kornei Chukovskii would refer to it later as a high art—*vysokoe iskusstvo*).[20] If such an ambitious project as the VL was to be realized, there was a bevy of questions to be answered and problems to be resolved. Which works were to be translated? Who was to select the works for translation? According to what criteria? Who was to translate and how? What strategies were to be employed? In the new society these questions gained additional acuteness— out of the old the new was being created. The new could not afford to retain from the old more than was absolutely necessary.

A Megapolysystem

In Itamar Even-Zohar's theory, dubbed "the polysystem theory," translation is viewed as part of a complex national literary system. A polysystem is defined as a multiplex and multitiered system composed of literary subsystems formed by prosaic or poetic or dramaturgical genres. There are elements, that is, individual

---

17 *Pervyi vsesoiuznyi s"ezd*, 5.
18 Gor'kii, *Arkhiv*, 5.
19 Tihanov, "World Literature, War, Revolution," 117–18.
20 Kornei Chukovskii, *Vysokoe iskusstvo* (Moscow: Sovetskii pisatel', 1964).

The Birth of New out of Old | 127

works, and their properties that make up hierarchies within the subsystems to which they belong. The elements within the subsystems and the subsystems themselves manifest different dynamics of interrelations.[21]

The literary system of the early Soviet state when the VL project was conceived and realized can be described as any other polysystem in Even-Zohar's theory: one literary network within one nation-state. When the Union of Soviet Socialist Republics was formed in 1922, a new type of literary polysystem emerged. It was a polysystem that contained not only a variety of genres and their subsystems, but also a number of languages and entire literatures, each being a polysystem in its own right. As a consequence, translation began to play a completely new role, different from any of its roles described in Even-Zohar's theory. Translation was no longer mediating between a multitude of foreign languages and the polysystem's language(s). The new polysystem included not only a variety of literary genres but also a variety of languages and cultures, each in dialogue with all the other languages and cultures. Translation became a complex hub of interconnections between a great deal of languages and cultures (it will be recalled that as many as fifty-two nationalities were represented in the First All-Union Congress of Soviet Writers). All in all, the literary system that was created in the USSR should be described as a supranational polysystem linked by translation. The USSR literary system might, therefore, be called a megapolysystem.

In the First All-Union Congress of Soviet Writers, Ivan Kulik said that it was impossible to require from anybody to know the languages of all the peoples of the USSR. Translation was called upon to assist:

> Those of us who cannot read in German, can still discuss Goethe; those who cannot read English, can nevertheless talk about Byron; those who does not know French, are able to speak about Molière or Balzac. Obviously, translation can help. Translating literary works of the peoples of the USSR into Russian and the rest of the languages of the peoples of the USSR is a paramount and urgent task.[22]

Translation became an indispensable element of the entire megapolysystem and, by the same token, of each polysystems, because all the polysystems

---

21 Itamar Even-Zohar, "Polysystem studies," *Poetics Today* 11, no. 1 (Spring 1990): 9–26.
22 *Pervyi vsesoiuznyi s"ezd*, 44.

existed within the overall megapolysystem. Translation was no longer an optional element, sometimes marginal, sometimes vying for centrally located positions. Now it became an obligatory means on which the megapolysystem's existence was predicated.

To describe the role of translation in the Soviet literary megapolysystem as proposed by Kulik, one has to go beyond the polysystem theory. For instance, Even-Zohar observed the following three scenarios when translation moves centre stage in a national literary polysystem:

(1) A literary polysystem may be *in statu nascendi* without a fully formed literary tradition and with a certain number of free genre "slots" which are to be filled up and which cannot be developed within the literary polysystem itself; in this case, translation introduces the lacking genres into the polysystem.

(2) A literary polysystem may occupy a 'peripheral' position among other national literatures or be considered 'weak,' or a combination of the two of these states of affairs may be observed; in such cases, translation makes up for what the literary polysystem lacks; by introducing literary masterpieces from 'stronger' literary traditions, translation confers a lacking prestige to its home polysystem.

(3) A national literature may be experiencing a crisis or it may find itself at a 'turning point' in its evolution; then translation infuses 'new blood' and brings in new inspiration to its polysystem.[23]

The Soviet megapolysystem translated actively not because its own shelves were empty or because it needed inspiration from foreign literatures—on the contrary, it claimed its independence. Also, the Soviet megapolysystem inherited from more or less mature national literatures, each with its more or less rich literary traditions, and that heritage was taken on board (albeit not indiscriminately!). Yet, initially the Soviet megapolysystem started also culling 'the best' (that is, ideologically the most suitable) from the entire world literature. The new megapolysystem translated because it aspired to create a new proletarian literary tradition that would absorb all what was considered signs of the dreams that have finally come true.[24]

A key role in this assimilation process was naturally assigned to translation. According to Chukovskii, translation was no longer merely a concern of a couple of literati or a subject of discussion in a philological dissertation; rather

---

23 Even-Zohar, "Polysystem studies," 47.

24 On the Soviet 'local' criteria of forming the world literature see Maria Khotimsky, "'The Treasure Trove of World Literature': Shaping the Concept of World Literature in Post-Revolutionary Russia" (in the present volume).

The Birth of New out of Old | 129

it became "a matter of the highest state importance which is of vital concern to millions [...] who needed a constant exchange of multifarious cultural goods, including literary works [...]"[25]

But as we have seen translation always renders something already existing. It is a locus of intercultural and intertemporal negotiations, a compromise between the old and the new, and as such, it inevitably contradicted the proletarian radicalism. A new world built on translation that mediated not only between the national literatures of the Soviet present but also brought in works of the literary past (both from within the Soviet Union and from without) was inevitably compromised. In the period of the VL project and the deliberations of the Soviet writers' First Congress, discussing the new Soviet style of translation, Chukovskii rejected dilettantism, amateurism and blind inspiration of "yesterday's literary day."[26] The past had to be refuted exactly because it was still haunting the present. This was only natural seeing that the medium of expression was still the Russian language or the languages of the Soviet nations. Literary experts inevitably had to come from the pre-revolutionary past. The challenge was to forge a new tradition recycling 'old materials'. The questions discussed in the VL and the Congress were about what of the world literature (the literature of the past) was to be translated; who could/had to translate; how translation practices were to be modified in order to appeal to a new, proletarian-cum-peasantry, audience; what literary criticism had to be like for assessing 'new' translations.

Translation in the megapolysystem was from the beginning an activity that was controlled by the state. In Chukovskii's diary, under 15 October, 1918, we read that Lunacharsky reported to the Narkompros (The People's Commissariat of Enlightenment/Education) that Comrade Gorky had pointed out that the situation in the book market was abnormal. In Moscow a certain Polianskii was publishing Zola, Hugo, Thackeray; in St Petersburg Ionov put out Romain Rolland's *Jean-Christophe*. All those publishers worked without any system. It was decided that everything had to be concentrated in one person's hand—in Gorky's. This is how all translated books had to be published only in Gorky's VL series.[27] The VL became an exclusive professional project

---

25 *Pervyi vsesoiuznyi s"ezd*, 566.
26 Ibid., 567.
27 Chukovskii, *Dnevnik*, 106.

sanctioned by none other than the political government—Lenin, Lunacharsky and Narkompros.[28]

Like the VL project, the destiny of the Soviet literary translation at a later stage as reflected in the minutes of the First Congress was also considered strictly as an integral part of a social, political and ideological, programme designed by the Soviet Communist Party leadership. In the Soviet writers' First Congress, the then main ideologue of the Soviet culture Zhdanov's presence was a sign of the Party leadership's supervisory role. Zhdanov described the Party's vision of the Soviet literature (and translation as implied by the materials of the Congress) as follows:

> Our literature is the youngest among the literatures of all peoples and nations. It is also the most ideologically advanced and the most revolutionary of literatures. There is no other literature, except ours, that would organize workers and the oppressed people to fight for the final destruction of all and every kind of exploitation and the yoke of hired slavery. There has never been a literature that is based on the theme of the working class and the peasantry and their struggle for socialism. [...] The Soviet literature is flesh of flesh and bone of bone of our building of socialism (*sotsialisticheskogo stroitel'stva*).[29]

It is noteworthy that the Soviet literary megapolysystem is seen in Zhdanov's speech as new rather than an heir of the fifty-two national cultures represented in the Congress. He also circumscribed it fully in the socialist project: it depicted the life of proletariat and peasantry and at the same time it inspired these classes for the revolutionary struggle.

It will also be noted that there was a translated biblical citation in Zhdanov's speech. It is a good illustration of how in a revolutionary discourse there is inescapably an element of the past. In this case it was used to express the closest relationship between the political project and the literature that served it. The insertion was undoubtedly to signify the high level of education of the speaker and it was meant to appeal to the gathered literary pandits. Moreover, the inserted quotation is a translation from an iconic cultural text of the past. Translation found itself in a new type of literary polysystem—a megapolysystem,

---

28 Sergey Tyulenev, "Vsemirnaia Literatura: Intersections between Translating and Original Literary Writing," in *Slavic & East European Journal* 60, no. 1 (Spring 2016): 8–21.

29 *Pervyi vsesoiuznyi s'ezd*, 3.

and at the same time in a radical social project—the building of socialism. Yet translation implied in Zhdanov's speech was its usual self—it brought the old into all things new, even in the discourse of a revolutionary ideologue.

The Nitty-Gritty of Translation in the Soviet Megapolysystem

In the new landscape and the new social project, translation can be discussed in terms of what was (to be) translated. First, world classics and Soviet nations' classics worthy of translating into the languages of the Soviet state were to be identified. What were the selection criteria?

The old literature was viewed mostly as expressing primarily (although not exclusively) the values of the leading classes of the preceding periods. The bourgeois literature was, therefore, found unacceptable. Yet, as Gorky explained in his plenary speech,[30] there were progressive literary works which expressed what was referred to as critical realism, that is, works that depicted bourgeoisie critically. Also, translation-worthy were those works of the past that testified to the budding materialist worldview; they had to be selected and the works that showed low-class or people's (*narodnye*) heroes.

Another criterion was educational value of the works of the past, especially when it came to the literature intended for children. In his Congress speech, Samuil Marshak said that historical poems, ballads and novels that would allow children to understand the long-gone past also deserved being translated. He gave examples, such as *The Song of Roland*, Skaldic poetry, *Iliad* and *Odyssey*, Titus Livy's, Tacitus', Benvenuto Cellini's writings and *Decameron*, although only fragments from the latter were recommended to be translated. Marshak also suggested the possibility of translating the best among the contemporary historical belles-lettres works for adult readers, reworded if necessary. Here Marshak gave an example of Charles Lamb's simplified Shakespeare.[31]

While introducing the literature of the past it was necessary to engage with it critically, the goal being "to overcome the classical heritage" (Kulik).[32] An example of what was seen as a result of the socialist recycling of the classical masterpieces was mentioned by Nikolai Bukharin—a "socialist *Faust*" that

---

30 *Pervyi vsesoiuznyi s"ezd*, 6–18.
31 *Pervyi vsesoiuznyi s"ezd*, 35.
32 Ibid., 39.

would reflect the heroism of the people living in the Soviet era.[33] While Marshak mentioned Charles (and Mary) Lamb's simplified versions of Shakespeare's plays as an example of literary adaptation, Bukharin gave Goethe's *Faust* as an example of the type of literary work that would be needed to do justice to the scale of the heroism of the Soviet people. Obviously, in order to create adaptations of the highest quality (like Lamb's) or the long poems of Goethe's calibre, the model texts had to be translated and translated so that their true literary worth would be rendered appreciable.

This means that translation itself had to be of the highest quality. How could that be achieved? Kornei Chukovskii reported to the Congress that a new style of translation was being worked out and established (*vyrabatyvaetsia i utverzhdaetsia*). He continued explaining that it was "the Soviet style of translation, the style that I would call scientific-artistic (*nauchno-khudozhestvennym*)."[34] He described that translation style apophatically, i.e. in terms of what it would be not.[35] It would have nothing to do with dilettantism, amateurism, blind inspiration and other features of the literature's yesterday. The only positive characteristic of the Soviet translation style was that it was to be scientific, but that characteristic was used, it seems, as a pretext to bow to the important people— Bukharin, an influential Soviet functionary, and Gorky, both present in the Congress. Chukovskii also reminded the participants that back in 1919, when Gorky had initiated the VL project, he "steeply headed (*kruto vzial kurs*) for maximum scientific accuracy of translation and fighting against dilettantism."[36] Chukovskii's speech, thus, was another evidence of the Party's regulation of the Soviet literary translation.

However all Chukovskii's wishful thinking was easier said than done. There were still unsatisfactory translations and there were reports in the Soviet writers' Congress about such cases. For instance, Ivan Kulik described the situation with translating works of Ukrainian authors as follows:

> We would like to praise the work of the Ukrainian section of the All-Union organizational committee headed by Comrade Stetskii. This work is very significant and useful for us. It aims at making the achievements of the Ukrainian Soviet literature

---

33 Ibid., 575.
34 Ibid., 567.
35 Later this apophatic style would be the hallmark of his discussing literary translation (see Chukovskii, *Vysokoe iskusstvo*).
36 *Pervyi vsesoiuznyi s"ezd*, 567.

The Birth of New out of Old | 133

known and at translating the best books of the Ukrainian literature into Russian. It must at the same time be reported that the situation with translation is not always good. Several books of the Soviet Ukrainian writers, among them those published by GIKhL [*Gosudarstvennoe izdatel'stvo khudozhestvennoi literatury*, the State Publishing House of Artistic Literature] for this Congress, turned out to be unsuccessful, and this is another proof how complicated the problem of translating artistic works into the languages of the USSR. [...I]t is not enough that we are translated; it is equally important that we are translated culturally (*kul'turno*), without blunders (*liapsusy*), which happen very often.[37]

Kulik added that translation should be "thorough and professional" (*tshchatel'nymi i gramotnymi*).[38] Obviously even in the central state publishing houses, such as GIKhL, the quality of published translations was far from desired. Translations were riddled with blunders and lacked professional thoroughness. This flew in the face of Chukovskii's pronouncements. The translation in the Soviet state needed the 'old' expertise, the old 'culture' of literary translation.

Another vital question was who was to translate. There was a group of experts who took upon themselves to guide the activities of the VL. Originally, it consisted of nine people: the experts in the Indian literature were represented by Academician Ol'denburg, the Arabs—by Academician Krachkovsky, the Chinese—by Academician Alekseev, the Mongols—by Academician Vladimirtsov. Together with two professors of Germanic Studies, Aleksandr Blok was responsible for the literature in the Germanic languages. Nikolai Gumilev and Andrei Levinson were responsible for the literature in French. Evgenii Zamiatin and Chukovksii coordinated translations of the British and American literatures. Akim Volynskii supervised the Italian literature.[39] Thus, the revolutionary project had to rely on the old-school experts. Once again, the new could not do without the old.

With actual translators the situation was even more challenging. Chukovskii recollected that at the initial stage of the VL project in Petersburg, many representatives of the former Petersburg nobility, princes and princesses, Fräuleins, pages, lyceum students, Kammerherren, senators, who imagined themselves

---

37 *Pervyi vsesoiuznyi s''ezd*, 44.
38 Ibid., 45.
39 Chukovskii, *Sovremenniki*, 126.

as capable translators, came and offered their services. They tried to convince the VL committee they were the right people to whom translations of Molière, Voltaire, Stendhal, Balzac, Anatole France, Victor Hugo could be entrusted because they could chat fluently in French. Gorky patiently explained to them that knowing a foreign language was not sufficient to be a translator because an excellent knowledge of the target language was a must. But there were few other candidates and since the would-be translators insisted, they were given an opportunity to try and translate several pages of a French author but the results were mostly deplorable.[40]

Only later the VL administration was able to add a translator training studio. In the studio, the theory of literary translation was taught and workshops were organized by such experts as Blok, Gumilev, Chukovskii, Gorky, Zamiatin, Lozinsky, Shklovskii and others. As the VL director Tikhonov reported in 1923, the theoretical findings of the studio were compiled in two editions of *Principles of Literary Translation* published within the VL project and "the practical result was a considerable number of experienced translators who graduated from the Studio and who became a great help to the VL publishing house."[41] It took some time to raise a new generation of translators but even that new would have been impossible without the old: the new generation was trained by the 'old' experts.

Translation was initially planned into each and from each language within the Soviet Union.[42] And an attempt to realize that plan was made according to the reports from republics. Ivan Kulik, the representative from the Ukrainian Soviet Socialist Republic, reported that a growing number of translations was made from national languages into Russian and from Russian into national languages.[43] According to D.A. Simonian, the representative of Armenia, the state publishing house, literary journals and newspapers in the republic did a great deal to translate the best works of the writers of the brotherly republics into Armenian from Russian, Georgian, Ukrainian and other languages.[44] I. Dzhansugurov, the Kazakh representative, told that the Kazakh organization of the Union of the Soviet writers and the publishing houses in Kazakhstan undertook translations of the best contemporary works from the Ukranian, Belorussian, Georgian, Uzbek, Tatar and other literatures of the Soviet Union.[45]

---

40 Ibid., 136–7.
41 Gor'kii, *Arkhiv*, 20–21.
42 Brian James Baer, "From International to Foreign," 56.
43 *Pervyi vsesoiuznyi s"ezd*, 44–45.
44 Ibid., 112.
45 Ibid., 241.

Both in the VL and later, the most numerous readership, however, was supposed to be Russian speakers (not necessarily native). Moreover, the Russian language acquired the status of the pivotal language from and into which the majority of translations in the Soviet Union were made because it was a kind of supranational or transnational language. World classics were appropriated by the Soviet literary canon mostly via translations into Russian and only then they were rendered into the other languages. Chukovskii emphasized the increasing importance of translation in such circumstances: Shakespeare was first translated into Russian and from those Russian translations, translations into the national, i.e. the languages other than Russian, were attempted. The Mordovians and the Erzya and the Kazak[h]s and the Tatars read Shakespeare translated from Russian.[46]

The Russian language in the Soviet era inherited its pivotal role from the Russian Empire.[47] In other words, in this aspect the pivotal role of Russian and, consequently, of translating from/into Russian as a preferable channel was inherited from the old, although the official explanation was different:

> Russian was certainly not to be seen as the language of the former imperial hegemons; it was instead cast as the language of the first proletarian state, and as such the bearer of the most progressive universal values. More importantly still, Russian needed to be constructed differently from all the other, "national" language of the USSR [...].[48]

Conclusion

The Soviet state was born as a revolutionary effort of the 1917 October Socialist Revolution. It was yet another attempt of humanity to create something

---

46 *Pervyi vsesoiuznyi s''ezd*, 565.
47 Sergey Tyulenev, "Through the Eye of the Needle of the Most Proletarian Language," in *mTm (Minor Translating Major, Major Translating Minor, Minor Translating Minor)* 2 (2010), 70–89; Sergey Tyulenev and Vitaly Nuriev, "'Sewing up' the Soviet Politico-cultural System: Translation in the Multilingual USSR," in in *Transnational Russian Studies*, ed. Andy Byford, Connor Doak, and Stephen Hutchings (Liverpool: Liverpool University Press, 2020), 155–68.
48 Tyulenev and Nuriev, "'Sewing up' the Soviet Politico-cultural System," 165–66.

radically new. And predictably, this attempt turned out a complicated negotiation between the old/past and the new.

The negotiation unfolded on several levels. Translation became one of the focal means of the negotiation. In the Vsemirnaia Literatura project, translation was the principal and in fact the only available means of forming the literary treasury for the new ruling class—proletariat and peasantry, the citizens of the new, Soviet state. Later, in the Soviet Union, an unprecedented type of literary polysystem emerged—a multicultural, multinational and multilingual megapolysystem made up of the ideologically united individual polysystems of the Soviet peoples.

It was impossible to create such a megapolysystem from scratch. Translation was called upon to constitute the new megapolysystem and also serve as a mediating agent between the different polysystems, on the one hand, and the outer world, on the other hand. Translation was supplying the newly created megapolysystem with the native and foreign 'old' literary masterpieces found suitable for the new kind of readership. Translation also helped overcome the seclusion of individual polysystems. A typical example which can be seen as a succinct summary of the discussion above was M. S. Dzhavakhishvili's speech in the First All-Union Congress of Soviet Writers. When he talked about the new "Soviet [literary] style" (*stil' sovetik*, the term was modelled on the French 'le style soviétique', yet another implied translation from another 'old' into the Soviet 'new'), he admitted that at that point in time there were no Soviet Pushkin, Tolstoy, Rustaveli, Balzac, Shakespeare.[49] The standards were set by translations, only Rustaveli was a national poet for a Georgian, the other ones were all foreign, and even if a Georgian, like Dzhavakhishvili, was able to read Pushkin and Tolstoy in Russian, it was less likely that any Georgian could appreciate Balzac or Shakespeare without the mediation of translation. Thus translation made it possible to read foreign classics and set standards for the Soviet writers. Yet translation inevitably adulterated the newness of the new society, the new Soviet people and their literature. Translation inescapably brought the old into the new.

---

49 *Pervyi vsesoiuznyi s"ezd*, 146.

CHAPTER 7

International Literature: A Multi-language Soviet Journal as a Model of "World Literature" of the Mid-1930s USSR

Elena Ostrovskaya, Elena Zemskova, Evgeniia Belskaia, Georgii Korotkov

Introduction

From the moment Goethe supposedly heralded the advent of *Weltliteratur*, it was projected as a utopia on the brink of becoming reality, hence the future tense used by both Goethe and then Marx and Engels—the communist prophets of the concept. It came as no surprise thus that the notion was gladly accepted and employed by the young Soviet state—another utopia on the brink of becoming reality. The emergence of the eponymous publishing house "Vsemirnaia literatura"—the most prominent Soviet cultural project of the early Soviet Union—as early as 1919 is the most conspicuous and widely discussed example of the trend.[1] The next 15 years brought important changes to the way the concept was explored and applied. Throughout the late 1910s and 1920s it was this utopian

---

1   Maria Khotimsky, "World Literature, Soviet Style: A Forgotten Episode in the History of the Idea," *Ab Imperio* 3 (2013): 119–54, accessed August 12, 2020, doi:10.1353/imp.2013.0075.

sense of the future about to come true that was the foundation of the Soviet ideology, suggestively, reflected in the cultural policy. The 1930s, however, saw an important change in attitude; if the West and East were still approaching the beautiful utopian future, the USSR was the country yet to achieve communism, but already living in this future utopia. Such an approach brought to life a rather straightforward, yet complicated, system of organizing the space of foreign culture that was to accommodate the emerging cultural center of this new world system.

Theorizing world literature in the communist and then Soviet terms, which had famously begun in Marx and Engels's *Manifesto*, was an important part of the Soviet theory of literature and engaged a whole set of different terms.[2] However, in the mid-1930s it was the term "world literature" (*mirovaia literatura*) that came to the surface. As literary critic Aleksei Selivanovskii said in 1936, "We live in Moscow, the capital of world literature [. . .] Soviet literature is the brain and the heart of world literature."[3] Anticipating the world-system model of world literature with the center and periphery[4] Selivanovskii's metaphor reflected both the distorted vision of a narcissist culture and a utopian future yet to come. Apparently, the beautiful new world of literature was anything but a *fait accomplit*. (Re)imagining and (re)constructing the space of world literature in the communist vein required an immense effort on the part of the USSR. The ideological basis was provided by Karl Radek in his speech at the the plenary meeting of the Soviet Writers' Union in 1932.[5] But making utopia come true, or, to translate it into the language of world literature, turning Moscow into a "sub-center" of world

---

2   Larissa Polubojarinova, "Vsemirnaja—Internacional'Naja—Mirovaja: Transformationen Des Weltliteratur Begriffs in Sowjetrussland 1918–1983," in *Vergleichende Weltliteraturen*, ed. Dieter Lamping and Galin Tihanov (Stuttgart: J.B. Metzler, 2019), 305–322, accessed August 12, 2020, doi:10.1007/978-3-476-04925-4_21.

3   Nailya Safiullina, "The Canonization of Western Writers in the Soviet Union in the 1930s," *The Modern Language Review* 107 (2012): 563, accessed August 12, 2020, doi:10.5699/modelangrevi.107.2.0559.

4   Franco Moretti, "Conjectures on World Literature." *New Left Review*, no. 1 (2000): 54–68; Pascale Casanova, *The World Republic of Letters*. (Cambridge, MA: Harvard University Press, 2004); Mads Rosendahl Thomsen, *Mapping World Literature: International Canonization and Transnational Literatures*. (London: Bloomsbury Academic, 2008).

5   Safiullina, "The Canonization of Western Writers in the Soviet Union in the 1930s": 563.

literature[6] required an elaborate system of institutions that was efficiently put into place as part of the Soviet cultural policy.[7]

The cosmopolitan Moscow of the 1930s, claiming to be a new world capital,[8] was a multilingual city, where newspapers, magazines and books were printed, and radio broadcasting was provided in different European languages. Among several media printed in foreign languages such as the journal *USSR in Construction* and *The Moscow Times* newspaper, there were two literary journals. Both were changing the very notion of "literature" in the interwar years, as well as the established "literary geography." The literary journal of the German communist emigration *Das Wort* (1936–39) was an example of local displacement in the imaginary literary geography, aimed at a German-speaking audience dispersed over several countries. *International literature* was conceived as a much more global project.

The journal appeared as an official mouthpiece of IURW (International Union of Revolutionary Writers), the literary subsidiary of the Comintern, which was seeking ideological foundations of the new proletarian literature, so in 1930 at the Congress in Kharkiv it was decided to launch a four-language journal *Literature of the World Revolution*, which was first published in 1931. Already in 1932, the title shifted its radical focus to "internationalism" for non-Russian editions, and from 1933 the Russian journal also got the same title *International Literature* (*International'naia literatura*). In this form of a multilingual project, the journal existed until the end of 1942, when the Russian edition was cancelled; at the end of 1935, when the IURW was dissolved and the International Association of the Writers for the Defense of Culture was established at the Congress in Paris, its status changed from the mouthpiece of a "literary group," the IURW, edited by a small circle of Communist political emigrants, to the official organ of the Union of Soviet Writers. Also in 1935, two issues of the Chinese edition were published, and from 1942 the Spanish journal started, so that from 1943 to 1945 there were four journals again, but no Russian edition.

---

6   Mads Rosendahl Thomsen, *Mapping World Literature: International Canonization and Transnational Literatures* (London: Bloomsbury Academic, 2008).

7   Michael David-Fox, *Showcasing the Great Experiment: Cultural Diplomacy and Western Visitors to the Soviet Union, 1921–1941* (Oxford: Oxford University Press, 2012).

8   Katerina Clark, *Moscow, the Fourth Rome* (Cambridge, Massachusetts; London: Harvard University Press, 2011).

We claim that *International Literature* as a multilingual journal project became an ideal space of a utopia in construction, a project that was partly in place, in a form to showcase Soviet achievements, yet anticipating the real communist utopia to come true and meanwhile focusing on the process of construction as a means of establishing the Soviet hegemony in the field.[9] Therefore, all four journals in different languages—and the editorial board did insist that each language version is a separate periodical—are considered a whole, a coherent unit, a multilingual and multifaceted publishing project meant to reflect the processes going on in world literature and to construct a new model of it. Up to the present moment, *International Literature* has not been described through such a holistic perspective. Although it has been frequently discussed recently and many of its scholars emphasize its multilingual nature, they usually focus on one or another journal of the four in only one language (including our own previous publications), thus limiting a scope and context of the project and its expected impact. Both Nailya Safiullina and Samantha Sherry exclusively address the Russian edition,[10] while Angela Huss-Michel and other scholars working on German anti-fascist exile deal with the German *Internationale Literatur* (from 1937 on—*Internationale Literatur. Deutsche Blätter*).[11] The English journal is discussed as a separate periodical,[12] in relation to the Anglo-Saxon reception of Georg Lukács's literary theory and works of Bertolt Brecht and Isaac Babel,[13] and the French journal *La littérature internationale* almost has yet to attract

---

9 The same concept was reflected in the title of another multilingual journal project, *USSR in Construction*.

10 Nailya Safiullina, "Window to the West: From the Collection of Readers' Letters to the Journal Internatsional'naia Literatura," *Slavonica* 15 (2009): 128–61, accessed August 12, 2020, doi:10.1179/136174209x12507596634856; Nailya Safiullina and Rachel Platonov, "Literary Translation and Soviet Cultural Politics in the 1930s: The Role of the Journal Internacional'naja Literatura," *Russian Literature* 72 (2012): 239–69, accessed August 12, 2020, doi:10.1016/j.ruslit.2012.08.005; Samantha Sherry, *Discourses of Regulation and Resistance: Censoring Translation in the Stalin and Khrushchev Era Soviet Union* (Edinburgh: Edinburgh University Press, 2015).

11 Angela Huss-Michel, *Die Moskauer Zeitschriften "Internationale Literatur" Und "Das Wort" Während Der Exil-Volksfront (1936–1939): Eine Vergleichende Analyse* (Bern: P. Lang, 1987).

12 Elena Ostrovskaya and Elena Zemskova, "Between the Battlefield and the Marketplace: International Literature Magazine in Britain," *Russian Journal of Communication* 8 (2016): 217–29, accessed August 12, 2020, doi:10.1080/19409419.2016.1213614.

13 Glyn Salton-Cox, "Polemics pertinent at the time of publication": Georg Lukács, International literature, and the Popular front, *Twentieth Century Communism* 12, no. 12 (2017): 143–16; Elena Ostrovskaya and Elena Zemskova, "From International Literature to World Literature: English Translators in 1930s Moscow," *Translation and Interpreting Studies* 14 (2019): 351–71, accessed August 12, 2020, doi:10.1075/tis.18025.ost.

scholars as it is mainly used by historians and literary critics as a source rather than an independent object of study.[14]

The proposed "holistic" approach goes in line with the perspective of the field of periodical studies, which considers its object of research as "media rather than as depositories for texts",[15] thus avoiding the temptation to focus on the most prominent names and works and ignore the rest. In the case of *International Literature*, the phenomenon is even more complicated as the unity includes not only the journal as a whole, but all four editions as parts of the project. The original impetus seems to have been towards creating a medium that would actually realize the utopian model of world literature premised on total translatability: that is the most valuable content, one and the same, simultaneously translated into different languages.[16] The multilingual journal as it came into being, however, did not reproduce one and the same content and the four language editions were never uniform. Each of them was autonomous, and the potential reader did not even have to be aware of existence of the other three eponymous periodicals, let alone read them all, in all four languages. To address this unity in diversity functioning as a utopian space of world literature, we will attempt to approach it from different perspectives, emphasizing the unity and juxtaposing the language editions (different journals). Our approach suggests different kinds of material, which, in turn, involves different research methods. So we opted for digital humanities to complement the traditional literary historical approach, as this combination seems to be the most appropriate for our goal.

The intersection of world literature studies and digital humanities was originally introduced in a seminal work by Franco Moretti *Distant Reading*.[17] The common interest of these disciplines in "an orientation towards the large

---

14 Sophie Cœuré, *La Grande Lueur à l'Est. Les Français et l'Union soviétique* (Paris: Éd. du Seuil, 1999); Pascal Ory. *Nizan: Destin d'un révolté* (Paris: éditions Complexe, 2005); Danielle Risterucci-Roudnicky, *France-RDA: anatomie d'un transfert littéraire 1949–1990* (Bern: P. Lang, 1999).

15 J. Stephen Murphy, Introduction: "Visualizing Periodical Networks" in "Visualizing Periodical Networks," ed. J. Stephen Murphy, Special issue, *The Journal of Modern Periodical Studies* 5, no. 1 (2014): iv.

16 Cf. Martin Puchner's claim that the Marx and Engels's Manifesto "no longer has an original language but only a first language" and "insists on a 'simultaneous' publication in many languages." Martin Puchner, "The Geography of the Communist Manifesto," in *Poetry of the Revolution: Marx, Manifestos, and the Avant-Gardes* (Princeton: Princeton University Press, 2006), 54, accessed August 12, 2020, https://doi.org/10.2307/j.ctt5hhpz1.9.

17 Franco Moretti, *Distant Reading* (London, New York: Verso, 2013).

scale" in computational methods is rather self-evident as they "enabl[e] quantitative studies of large corpuses in the case of digital humanities, and literary systems on a global scale in the case of world literature."[18] Periodical studies discovered these methods even earlier. The Modernist Journal Project started as early as 1995, and in 1996 digitalization was complemented by research.[19] For the purposes of the present study digital humanities with their "democratic", or "non-hierarchical"[20] approach towards data seems the obvious pair for the traditional literary-historical analysis.

To approach the journal from the digital perspective, we rely on the dataset amassed within the framework of our collective project "InterLit."[21] One of the main objectives of the project was to compile a database of bibliographical data (metadata) for all the five language editions (the two Chinese issues excluded) for all of the 17 years it was published under different titles and in different versions. As analysis of all the data is a gigantic task whose scope is far beyond that of an article, for this research, we focused on the data for just two years of the mid-1930s, 1934–1935. These were the years commonly recognized as the most noticeable in the journal's history, and it is during them that the concept of world literature had the leading position in the Soviet theory of literature as well as cultural policy.

The years 1934 and 1935 were a time of bustling literary life. In politics it was the time of hectic attempts to create a wide political coalition of the left, the Popular Front. The literary capitals of the time were Moscow, which in the summer of 1934 hosted a large international delegation at the Congress of the Soviet Writers, and Paris, which in the summer of 1935 held the writers' Congress in Defense of Culture, unofficially sponsored by Moscow. Fueled by the political motives and the quest for a wider coalition, the journal's model of world literature seems to be as significant and representative as ever. Its editors took an active part in the preparation for both congresses, corresponded with many people, and covered some events in the journal. Apart from that, these years were special for

---

18 Jenny Bergenmar and Katarina Leppänen, "Gender and Vernaculars in Digital Humanities and World Literature," NORA—Nordic Journal of Feminist and Gender Research 25, no. 4 (2017): 232.

19 Modernist journals project is the most significant and elaborated project of the digital humanities in periodical studies for today: https://modjourn.org.

20 Philip Gleissner, "Soviet Union on the Seine: Kontinent, Sintaksis, and the Social Life of Émigré Journals," The Russian Review 77 (2018): 446–69, accessed August 12, 2020, doi:10.1111/russ.12189.

21 The preliminary version of the project is temporarily located at http://interlit.000webhostapp.com, accessed April 10, 2023.

the Russian edition as it was in this short period that it published James Joyce, Aldous Huxley, Alfred Döblin, and a number of other authors, important actors of world literature, even in its narrowest sense, that of the canon, previously and later ignored or ostracized by the Soviet critics.[22] Thus, it was during these two years that the journal reproduced the most elaborate model of world literature.

This chapter will attempt to describe the work of the journal as a utopian space of world literature in 1934–1935. It will start with a brief outline of the project as a whole and the mechanics of its works, discuss its structure, common features of all the four journals as well as their specific facets, and then move on to more specifically theoretical readings of the journal as world literature, that is, geography of world literature and networks.

A Multilingual Journal Project: Four in One

The "leading theoretical journal" as *International Literature* was conceived by the IURW, even in 1934 it promoted itself on the back cover of each issue as "[a]n organ of revolutionary militant thought" and promised "Marxist analysis" of cultural phenomena in "all countries."

> The only international publication devoted to the proletarian and revolutionary literature of all countries. An organ of revolutionary militant thought. The magazine will provide a comprehensive Marxist analysis of the cultural life of all countries, including the Soviet Union, the land of the proletarian dictatorship. Special attention devoted to questions of Marxist literary criticism.
>
> Stories, poems, sketches, feuilletons, articles, workers' correspondence, international chronicle, book reviews and biography.... Cartoons and drawings by revolutionary artists. ....Photos and reproductions.

To see how this unity in diversity worked one could compare and contrast the four editions. Even the appearance of the printed issues reflects this controversy: three journals had identical cover design, while the German version had

---

22 Safiullina and Platonov, "Literary Translation and Soviet Cultural Politics in the 1930s: The Role of the Journal Internacional'naja Literatura," 253–54.

a different font and a bleak monochrome cover; the Russian version usually had more pages than the others. The English edition had the most illustrations, while in the German journal there were rather few pictures. It might be assumed that the German version had specific funding conditions as it was linked to the German sub-section of the Union of Soviet Writers.

In accordance with the announcement above, all four journals had a similar structure comprising three regular sections: [Fiction and Poetry] (the versions varied in whether they chose to use a title for it), Literary Criticism, and International Chronicle. In addition to these, each issue could have some occasional headings, under which it published materials on writers' biographies or anniversaries, reportage, letters to editors, and so on. The *belle-lettres* section was given from a third to two thirds of space in the journal. First and foremost was prose, but they also published poetry and drama. In this section, the content of the non-Russian editions differed significantly from that of the Russian versions, namely, by the presence of translations of Soviet authors, who were published in the originals in other Soviet literary journals.

Conceptualizing the new format of the journal in late 1932 as the Russian edition was to assume the same title as its "foreign" sisters, the announcement put forward the texts published as works of "foreign revolutionary writers" as well as those of *poputchiki* of outstanding artistic value and even those of the "enemies." "The concept of the German, French and English editions was to publish first and foremost the works of revolutionary authors of that nationality that could not find their way to print back home due to censorship, along with outstanding works of revolutionary authors of other nationalities."[23] However, with the numbers of revolutionary authors suppressed by censorship scarce,[24] the foreign versions soon switched to a model similar to that of the Russian edition that favored a foreign, translated text over the original.

Thus, translation became the main constructive principle, the core of the whole project. And it is translation that best demonstrates how this model of world literature worked. If the original IURW model emphasized simultaneity: the outstanding revolutionary authors were to achieve the world at the same time, as if transmitted by radio waves, the reality proved this model not very

---

23 L. R. Lanskii, "Periodicheskie izdaniia MBRL i MORPa," in *Iz istorii Mezhdunarodnogo ob"edineniia revoliutsionnykh pisatelei (MORP)*, ed. A.N. Dubrovikov and L.R. Lanskii, Literaturnoe nasledstvo 81 (1969): 583.

24 Since 1933, when the Nazi took over Germany, the status of the German journal was very different from that of its sisters.

feasible, and even the works that were published in all the four language editions–and these were scarce–very rarely made it into the same issue of their respective journal. When at work, the principle was more common in the "foreign" versions, which promoted outstanding works of Soviet literature, but a number of authors from other countries were also published in all or some of "foreign" editions. For example, the German author Anna Seghers was translated into Russian, English and French, without being published in the German edition.

However, the supposed universal value of works published in the journal in the ideal Marxist model was counterbalanced by the editorial policies of specific journals: the differences in design went beyond the cover and involved the choice of texts, authors, and even countries, defined by the target audience as well as many other circumstances. Thus, the *Internatsional'naia Literatura* of the two years in question is famous for its publications of outstanding Western modernists, previously and afterwards banished from Russian books and periodicals. The most conspicuous case was the serial publication of the first ten chapters of Joyce's *Ulysses* in 1935-1936.[25] The other language versions of the project did not translate it for the obvious reason: it had long been translated into both German and French. The same year saw the partial translations from *A Brave New World* by Aldous Huxley, *Berlin, Alexanderplatz* by Alfred Döblin and Heinrich Mann's *Young Henry of Navarre* to name just a few. All these publications were relevant to the Soviet discussion on modernism rather than to the political and cultural agenda of the IURW as a whole or specific agendas of other language versions.

The choice of specific authors for specific versions can be self-explanatory or reflect a number of heterogenous circumstances. For instance, the German writer Friedrich Wolf was published in the German and English editions a lot (four times in each version), while neither the French nor the Russian journal printed a single piece from him, and it is hard to say what is more interesting in the context of the functioning of this world literature, the way in which the German journal willingly published German authors (the editorial board apparently did follow the principles of the diaspora periodicals in exile) or the reasoning of the English *International Literature* (these seem to be personal as well as ideological).[26] On the other hand, both Jean Giono and Heinrich Mann

---

25 Neil Cornwell, *James Joyce and the Russians* (London: Palgrave Macmillan, 1992).
    Emily Tall, "The Reception of James Joyce in Russia," in *The Reception of James Joyce in Europe*, ed. Geert Lernout and Wim Van Mierlo (London: Continuum, 2009), 244–57.
26 Ostrovskaya and Zemskova, "From International Literature to World Literature: English Translators in 1930s Moscow," 351–71.

were published in all the journals but the English version, including those that did not require translation, that is the French and the German respectively.

The section of literary criticism promised programmatic works on art by the classical communist theoreticians, such as the recently deceased Lunacharsky, Lenin and even occasionally Stalin, and "Marxist analysis" of literary phenomena in "all countries," including rather extensive critical articles, mainly by Soviet critics, such as Dinamov, Dmitrievskii, Tretyakov and others, but also by prominent figures from other countries, like Jean-Richard Bloch, and members of the editorial staff, like Johannes Becher, Walt Carmon, Klemens Ludkiewicz, and Paul Nizan. Each issue published several such articles. This section kept closer to the original ideal model of world literature as it kept to the principle of simultaneous translation: these texts were most often translated into the other three languages. It also emphasized the leading role of Moscow as a capital, or center, of world literature as leading Soviet critics predominated. Moreover, it featured critical essays by the Moscow-based German-speaking exiles, such as the Hungarian Georg Lukács (in Russian he was published in the journal *Literaturnyi kritik*) and the German Trude Richter, which worked to the same effect.

"International Chronicle" also contributed to the journal's construction of world literature from yet another perspective as it reported on the recent literary and cultural events around the globe, expanding the geographic scope of the journal. It mainly consisted of short reports, but their form and genre conventions could vary importantly. Sometimes there were other sections–biographies (a very popular genre with the journal, especially when written by other writers), autobiographies (for instance, Theodore Dreiser's was published throughout 1935 [No 2-12]), literary portraits, letters to the journal (mainly, from prominent writers) and questionnaires sent out by the journal and filled out by the writers. Quite a few of those were also translated and published in some or all the journals.

Another way to address how this unity in diversity, this republic of letters functioned is to compare how different journals of the project responded to major literary events of the period. As the literary life of 1934 rotated around its most prominent literary occasion, the First Congress of the Soviet Writers, which brought some of *International Literature's* regular contributors to Moscow, the journal could not help but cover it in its pages. However, the versions differ importantly in the scope of their response to the Congress. The Russian double issue of Nos. 3-4 was built around the event with the writers' addresses towards the Congress scattered throughout the volume and a structure devised specifically for this special issue. The addresses came from everywhere, from literary organizations to revolutionary journals to household names—Romain Rolland, Henri Barbusse, Theodore Dreiser, and Andersen Nexø—the journal introduced the topic to never let it go. The congress became the backbone for the whole issue: the editorial board had sent out questionnaires and methodically went through the answers from different correspondents. These were organized in sections from different countries along with the same countries' fiction and poetry and critical reviews. The showcased countries were France, Germany, the USA, Spain, Poland, and China and the issue included 91 different materials.

The geography of the addresses and the number of authors who signed them is much wider, of course. The first cluster of addresses includes not only the major countries of the IURW, such as France and Germany and the usual suspects Vaillant-Couturier, Moussinac, Aragon, Nizan, Becher, etc., but also the Union of revolutionary writers of Austria, the Union of proletarian writers and artists of Valencia, and even revolutionary writers of Iceland. Among the country sections of the IURW the French one was the largest. Interestingly, it opens not in the usual way, with fiction and poetry, but with long biographic essays on the main French revolutionary writers—Barbusse, Gide and Vaillant-Couturier followed by more addresses from less prominent or less obvious figures, such as the famous pointillist artist Paul Signiac and a teacher Célestin Freinet. The fiction section is rather small this time and includes excerpts from Andre Gide's drama *OEdip* and Paul Nizan's book followed by two more clusters of addresses interrupted, in turn, by two articles on French literature by the Soviet critics Ivan Anisimov and N. Pavlov.

Other countries may have a smaller selection and thus a more straightforward structure, like Germany, Poland and China, or also a rather big and complicated in structure as "America" (the USA) and Spain, but the main elements in all the sections are basically the same: addresses, literature *per se* (fiction and poetry), critical reviews, and overviews.

The German version followed suit as its fifth issue of 1934 opened with a big section from the Congress's materials comprising a twenty-two-page full text of Radek's speech entitled "Modern World Literature and the Objectives of Proletarian art" (*"Die moderne Weltliteratur und die Aufgaben der proletarischen Kunst"*) and a separate subsection of thirteen other speeches by the "foreign guests" of the forum, including for some reason another speech by Radek. All in all, the section takes seventy pages, i.e., over a third of the whole 188-page issue. The rest is structured in the usual way: a big section of fiction and poetry and three much shorter sections, "Illegal Voices," "Literary Portraits," and "Visual Arts."

Surprisingly, the English and French journals virtually ignored the Congress: each had a three-page article on the Congress, and the French also published the statute of the Union.

The difference in the journals' responses to the Congress is defined by a number of factors, one of which will be the expected response of the audience. It may seem counter-intuitive, but the main goal of the journal's work with the Congress seems to have been not informing the foreign readers of the seminal event in world literature but constructing the space of such literature for each country. Thus, the Russian reader, already informed of the paramount importance of the Congress would have been acquainted with foreign authors' vivid response to it. The German audience was the only of the four to be informed about the world literature project put forward by Radek at the Congress, while the English- and French-speaking audiences seem excluded from the field, even though the utopian space of world literature as projected into the Russian double issue is mainly populated by French writers and artists.

To return to the project as a whole, it is important to outline the main principles of its work in constructing the utopian space of world literature. Originally based on the Marxist notion of world literature, "a generalized, atemporal and transregionally valid literature resulting from the development of the world literary process"[27] that relies on simultaneous translation to achieve its world audiences, by the mid-1930s it kept its original utopian quality, but had importantly adjusted to reality and the new objectives. As the egalitarian communist world was yet to come, becoming a center of world literature meant a claim at world hegemony. To translate it into the terms of the journal project, Moscow had to become such a center both geographically and ideologically. Being centered on Moscow suggested an asymmetry of Russian and "foreign" journals in the project. In both Soviet literature was to become the core of world literature,[28] but as the Russian edition published only foreign authors, the leading positions were given to theoretical and critical articles. Foreign authors were not only translated, but also packaged properly for the Soviet readers. Another way of promoting it was "letters to the editor" from the foreign authors and questionnaires: both were an excellent vehicle of admiration with Soviet

---

27 John Pizer, "Johann Wolfgang von Goethe: Origins and Relevance of Weltliteratur," in *The Routledge Companion to World Literature*, ed. Theo D'haen, David Damrosch and Djelal Kadir (London Routledge, 2012), 3–11, accessed August 12, 2020, doi:10.4324/9780203806494:ch1.

28 Nailya Safiullina, "The Canonization of Western Writers in the Soviet Union in the 1930s," 559–84.

literature and the recognition of its leading positions. The mission and structure of the foreign versions was more straightforward as they were honored to bring the light of Soviet literature into the masses of foreign readers. So, the central place was given to Soviet literature and its interpretation; however, another important part of creating this utopian space was establishing the real diversity and connection with the call of the day. Interestingly, this asymmetry suggested that ideological center in these two models was different.

Geography of World Literature

An impressive number of people from all over the world were linked to this project in one way or another during this two-year period, a fact that was constantly emphasized by the journal itself on its covers. Most issues contained an extensive list of up to two hundred names of permanent contributors by country, even if many of them were immigrants and their identification with only one country would be problematic. The list varied slightly from issue to issue: for instance issue four of 1934 mentioned writers from Germany, France, England, Austria, Spain, Czechoslovakia, Poland, Hungary, Latvia, Lithuania, Finland, Holland, Bulgaria, Romania, USA, Brazil, China, Japan, Indonesia, Surinam and Persia. The last two countries were included on questionable grounds: Anton de Kom from Surinam had emigrated to Holland more than ten years before, and the Persian poet Lahouti had long been a Soviet citizen and lived in Moscow. Soviet writers were linked to their national republics, the list included the RSFSR, Ukraine, "White Russia" for Belarus, Georgia, Armenia and the Tatar Republic. The diversity of nationalities referred to the communist thesis of the right to national self-determination, at the same time it drew a map of the world literature, on which even small nations were marked. However, not all the writers mentioned in this list actually published their works in the journal.

Each issue contained another two lists of names, which reflected the multi-level hierarchy of the whole project. The international editorial board of the journal, with a very wide geography of participants, included representatives of various national sections of the IURW, already known left-wing writers or journalists. The United States had the largest number of representatives in the Board: Michael Gold, Upton Sinclair, John Dos Passos and the journalist Abraham Magil. Soviet, German and Chinese literatures had two representatives each: Gorky and Serafimovich, Erich Weinert and Johannes Becher, Guo Moruo and Lu Xun. Martin Andersen Nexø (Denmark), Henri Barbusse (France) and Naoshi Tokunawa (Japan) were the sole representatives of their countries.

Obviously, this structure of the board reflected not so much the contribution of each participant to the development of the journal as the symbolic capital of the countries within the IURW and on the literary world map. The two symbolic figures of Gorky and Serafimovich for the USSR look surprisingly few in contrast to the American five–in accordance with the high standing of the John Reed clubs within the IURW.

The editorial committee, the people more closely related to the production of the journal, as opposed to the board, mostly included the writers who lived in or frequently visited Moscow. Along with the Soviet writers Aleksandr Fadeev, Sergei Tretyakov, Vladimir Ognev and Ivan Mikitenko and the academic Ivan Anisimov, it also included political exiles: the Hungarians Béla Illés and Antal Hidas, who were among the initiators of the IURW and the journal, the Italian Giovanni Germanetto, and the Chinese writer Emi Siao, who produced two issues of the journal's edition in Chinese in 1935. The only foreigner who could not be called an exile was the French communist writer Paul Vaillant-Couturier, who left Moscow in 1933 and was an active member of the IURW in Paris.

The whole enterprise was headed by the editor-in-chief Sergei Dinamov, a graduate and then professor of the Institute of Red Professors, deputy editor-in-chief of the *Literaturnaia Gazeta* in 1929–31, a Marxist literary critic and Shakespearean scholar who had been working in the IURW since 1933. Dinamov had an assistant editor, the Polish communist Klemens Ludkiewicz, who had emigrated to the USSR in 1930. Three members of the council and the board were editors of the journals. Sergei Tretyakov, the editor of the Russian journal, was a former *LEF* member with a wide range of international contacts, especially German, and Mikhail Koltsov's deputy in the Foreign Commission of the Union of Soviet Writers. The German edition was headed by Johannes Becher, an expressionist poet and a member of Communist Party of Germany since 1917, who emigrated to the USSR in 1933. In this journal the whole editorial staff consisted of communist immigrants: Becher was assisted by Hans Günther and his wife Trude Richter, and then by Karl Schmückle. While Vaillant-Couturier was in Paris, other writers edited the French version out of Moscow. In 1932 and the first half of 1933 it was Louis Aragon; until January 1934, Louis Moussinac; and from the second issue of 1934 until mid-1935, Paul Nizan. The last French editor to work on this version was Pierre Herbart, as his name is to be found in nos. 1–7/8 for 1936, but he probably started his work earlier as he arrived in the late autumn 1935. After his departure, no further indication appeared that the issue was produced under the supervision of any French writer present in Moscow. Finally, the English version was edited by Dinamov himself, with the American communist Walt Carmon as an assistant editor (until the latter's departure from the USSR in 1936).

Thus, the editorial staff was mainly located in Moscow. Employees who came to the USSR temporarily or permanently, native speakers of the languages of the journals were directly involved in the production of non-Russian versions. Also, native speakers were required for translation, so the project's translators were often just temporary "guests of the USSR," many of them did not know Russian and translated from other languages, and those who knew Russian often used it as a mediating language for indirect translation.[29]

Let us see how this wide geography of writers from all over the world, as demonstrated on the covers of the journals, correlates with their actual content published by the international editorial office associated with the IURW and headed by a senior Soviet literary official. We will rely on information available on the pages of the journal itself, which did not indicate the country the author was from, but in most cases provided information on the language from which the text was translated. Obviously, the list of countries does not fully coincide with the list of languages, for example, translations from Spanish could indicate both European and Latin American authors, but the data allows us to easily distinguish between the British and the US authors, as the editors marked "English" and "American" as separate languages.[30]

As a preliminary way of visualizing the data, we produced a diagram of the source languages of translation for all the four journals published in 1934–1935 (Fig. 1). The texts marked as translations with no indication of a source language were categorized as "unspecified". The overall geographic span of the journal project is still quite impressive: apart from the four main languages of separate journals, 1934 and 1935 saw translations from major Southern European languages (Spanish, Italian, and Portuguese), Northern European (Dutch, Danish), Eastern European (Czech, Polish, Croatian, and Hungarian) and Central and Far Eastern (Chinese, Japanese, and Turkish) (Fig. 1). Seventeen countries is a rather impressive scope for the world literature of the time.

However, each of the journals presented its own version of world literature. The Russian edition accounted for fourteen out of seventeen source languages, by far the largest number among all. One will find there all the Western European languages present in the journal, some Eastern European (Polish and Czech) and eastern (Chinese, Japanese and Turkish). As for the other editions, their geography is half as varied (eight countries for the English and German versions and seven for the French).

---

29 For more details about translators to English see: Ostrovskaya and Zemskova, "From International Literature to World Literature: English Translators in 1930s Moscow," 351–71.

30 In fact, Latin American authors were few: according to our data, throughout 1934–1935 there were only four.

Elena Ostrovskaya, Elena Zemskova, Evgeniia Belskaia, Georgii Korotkov

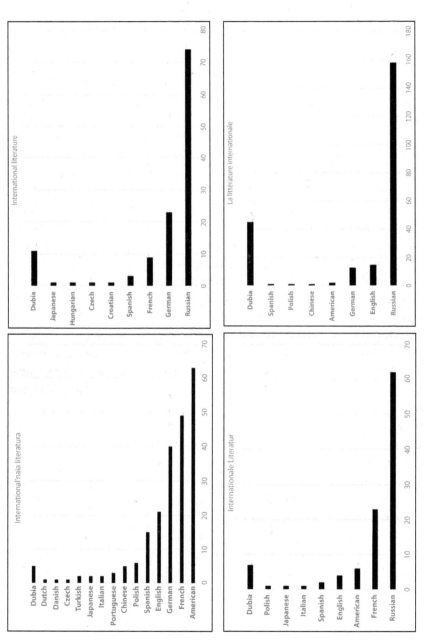

Fig. 1. Languages of translation in *International Literature* in 1934–1935.

The Russian edition also demonstrates a distinct inclination towards American literature that reflects the prominent position of the John Reed clubs within the IURW, the personal tastes of Sergei Dinamov and the aesthetic priorities of the time. In terms of publication numbers, French texts come next and only then German ones. The whole picture may seem counter-intuitive as it was the German and not French or American communist writers who had had to flee their home land and were admitted to the USSR as refugees and thus were handy and really needed all the support the journal could provide. The fact could be interpreted as the journal's participation in the Soviet cultural policy of the time aimed at attracting as many allies as possible, and that would involve focusing on Paris as a major center of world literature, as described by Pascale Casanova.[31] Another fact worth noting is the high number of Spanish texts, which is not to be found in any of the other journals and which anticipates the place of Spain in the journal's agenda of 1937–1938.

As opposed to the Russian, the foreign editions look rather uniform in that Russian (that is, Soviet) literature by far dominates them all. If the Russian version has priorities, they have a distinct center, Moscow, anticipating the system in the late USSR, where the Russian journal morphed back into *Inostrannaia literatura (Foreign Literature)*, while all the other versions became *Soviet Literature* with the respective change in content. At the time, however, it was not the case and each of the three "foreign" editions presented their own version of world literature. The German edition prefers French texts, the English–German texts, while the French journal is virtually devoted to the Soviet literature: the sum total of translations from Russian is twice as big in the French version as in the other two, so that English and German texts occupy an equally small place in it, and other translations seem virtually nonexistent.

Although the diversity of the source languages in the project turned out to be far less than could be expected from the list of permanent contributors, the Russian version appeared to be the closest to world literature in terms of the number of languages and their proportion to each other. In both the English and German journals, the center of world literature shifted significantly to the USSR, but a diversity of languages and authors remained. The French journal can be seen as a model of the world literature to the least extent, as it was almost entirely dedicated to Soviet literature and contained a maximum of one translation from such languages as Chinese, Polish and Spanish.

---

31 Pascale Casanova, *The World Republic of Letters* (Cambridge, MA: Harvard University Press, 2004).

In its utopian dimension, the whole project of *International Literature* turned out to be an implementation of the new world literature, potentially involving writers from all countries in all languages and translating all texts into all languages. In the reality of the 1930s, the results of the project depended on the political circumstances, the financial resources, and communication skills of the editorial office in Moscow. The real geography and language diversity of the project reflected the ability and willingness of the Soviet and in general, pro-communist agents of the world literary field to discover and utilize new opportunities for world literary communications.

World Literature as a Network

While the analysis of the data according to such a parameter as the source language of translation allowed us to generalize the data, working with a different parameter, the names of the authors of published materials, or entries in the database, will produce a more differentiated picture. The author's name appears in the dataset if it signed one or more texts in one or more language versions of the journal.[32] The resulting corpus, which is rather extensive, even for the two-year span under consideration, will be visualized in two different ways. First, we will use the most basic options of the Digital Humanities as a search engine, calculating and ranging device. At this stage, we will arrange the authors according to the number of texts they published and present this list as a table that shows the number of texts of every author in each journal and the sum of the entries in the whole project. Then we will switch to network analysis, "a new tool for literary historians," which "provides a new way to reveal the social constructedness of literary history and literary value."[33] With all these steps, we will organize the data in a network graph that will show the journal as a whole and the standing of each author within this system.

One of the most impressive facts about the list of contributors is the immensity of its span: the total number of contributors to all the four journals over the two years is near five hundred (479), while each of the journals published about two hundred (220 for Russian, 177 for English, 186 for German and 174 for French). Almost two thirds (345) of contributors appear to be the

---

32 What matters is the appearance of the name as such, not the length of the text. After the data was collected, the names were associated with the people, if recognizable, so that initials and full name that stood for one author were counted as one entity.

33 Murphy, "Visualizing Periodical Networks," vi.

authors of one or two texts, in either one or two journals. Some of these authors are hard to identify today, while others are still part of the canon. Particularly diverse is the list of the Soviet authors translated one or two times in the foreign editions: from Bagritsky and Mayakovsky to a historian Nechkina and film directors Eisenstein and Pudovkin. As examples of foreign authors, we can mention Mark Twain, John Galsworthy and Hans Fallada in the Russian journal or French communist writers Pierre Drieu la Rochelle and Georgette Gueguen-Dreyfus in the French one, as well as a film director Piscator in the German journal. On the opposite end of the range there is an impressive number of anonymous texts, which makes up a quarter to a third of all the texts in all the four journals (the total figure is 309; 20 percent). Most of these are short informative texts to be found in the "Chronicle."

Author	International'naia literatura	International Literature	Internationale Literatur	La Littérature internationale	Total
Anonymous	109	161	19	20	309
Dinamov, Sergei	9	7	4	7	27
Lunacharsky, Anatoly		5	4	9	18
Dreiser, Theodore	14		1	1	16
Leschnitzer, Adolf	3	2	6	4	15
Kel'in, Fedor	7	1	2	5	15
Nizan, Paul	4	3	5	3	15
Durus, Alfred	5	3	6	1	15
Carmon, Walt	4	3	4	3	14
Becher, Johannes	2	1	9		12
Dmitrievskii	3	1	3	5	12
Babel, Isaac		5	1	5	11
Feuchtwanger, Lion	7		4		11
Tretyakov, Sergei	2	3	2	4	11
Ludkiewicz, Klemens	3	2	2	3	10
Ottwald, Ernst	2	2	4	2	10
Hughes, Langston	6	1	1	2	10
Rolland, Romain	2	1	5	2	10
Gide, André	6	1	2		9
Bredel, Willi	2	2	4	1	9
Sender, Ramon	5		2	2	9
Chernyshevsky, Nikolay		5	4		9
Bloch, Jean-Richard	4	1	2	2	9
Richter, Trude	3	2	1	2	8

Caldwell, Erskine	5			3	8
Siao, Emi	3		3	2	8
Mann, Heinrich	4		2	2	8
Wolf, Friedrich		4	4		8
Seghers, Anna	4	2		1	7
Gergely, Sándor		4	1	2	7
Schmückle, Karl	3	1	3		7
Alberti, Rafael	4	2		1	7
Nikulin, Lev		2	2	3	7
Olesha, Yury		2	1	4	7
Malraux, André	4		3		7
Joyce, James	6	1			7
Svyatopolk-Mirsky, Dmitry	2	2		2	6
Gsell, Paul	4			2	6
Lukács, Georg		1	3	2	6
Mao Dun	3	1	1	1	6
Benavides, Manuel Dominguez	4	1	1		6
Metallov, Yakov	4		1	1	6
Plievier, Theodor	3	1	2		6
Gorky, Maxim		1	2	3	6
Kassil, Lev		1	3	2	6
Weinert, Erich	1		4	1	6
Radek, Karl	1		3	1	5
Strachey, John	3	1		1	5
Kisch, Egon	1	1	1	2	5
Giono, Jean	2		2	1	5
Pilnyak, Boris		2	1	2	5
Margueritte, Victor	5				5
Scharrer, Adam	1	1	2	1	5
Günther, Hans	2		3		5
Seifullina, Lidia		3	1	1	5
Hemingway, Ernest	5				5
Toller, Ernst	2		3		5
Arcos, René	3		1	1	5
Last, Jef	2	1	2		5
Bukharin, Nikolai				4	4
Gladkov, Fedor		2	1	1	4
Smedley, Agnes	1	1	1	1	4
Aksionov, Ivan	4				4

Masereel, Franz		2	2		4
Pesis, Boris	2	1		1	4
Zech, Paul	1	1	1	1	4
Aragon, Louis	3		1		4
Levidov, Mikhail	2		1	1	4
Pla y Beltrán, Pascual José	3			1	4
Elistratova, Anna	3	1			4
Lardner, Ring	4				4
Kensaku, Shimaki	1	1	1	1	4
Galperina, Eugenia	1			3	4
Anisimov, Yulian	1			3	4
Queens, Peter	2	2			4
Vildrac, Charles	2	1	1		4
Stalin, Joseph	1	1	1	1	4
Razumovskaya, Sofia		2		2	4
Rein, Boris		2		2	4
Ostrovsky, Nikolai		1	2	1	4
Kataev, Ivan		2	1	1	4
Calmer, Alan	2	2			4
Pogodin, Nikolai		1	2	1	4
Kurella, Alfred	1	1	2		4
Zoshchenko, Mikhail		2	1	1	4
Koltsov, Mikhail		1		3	4
Inber, Vera		1	1	1	3
Serveze, Gérard	2			1	3
Kalar, Joseph	1	1		1	3
Fedin, Konstantin		1	1	1	3
Spivak, John L.	1		1	1	3
Cezarec, Auguste		1	1	1	3
Milburn, George	3				3
Pasternak, Boris			1	2	3
Guéhenno, Jean	1	1	1		3
Paustovsky, Konstantin			1	2	3
Maltz, Albert	1		1	1	3
Pereda Valdés, Ildefonso	2			1	3
Abramov, Aleksandr	2			1	3
Fried, Jakov		1		2	3
Tikhonov, Nikolay		1		2	3

Kim, Roman		1	1	1	3
Kahana	1		2		3
Anderson, Sherwood	3				3
Gabor, Andor	1			2	3
Ellis, Fred		2	1		3
Zarudin, Nikolai			1	2	3
Buck, Pearl	3				3
Clay, Eugene	1	2			3
Harri			1	2	3
Bakushinskii, Anatolii		1	1	1	3
Spear, Leonard	1	2			3
Dikgof-Derental', Aleksandr	2			1	3
Arconada, César Muñoz	1			2	3
Balk, Theodor	1	1		1	3
Zugazagoitia, Julián	1		1	1	3
Brown, Bob		3			3
Terrace, Paul	2			1	3
Leacock, Stephen	3				3
Anisimov, Ivan	3				3
Lenin, Vladimir		2		1	3
Minlos, Bruno	2			1	3
Rubinstein, Lev		1	2		3
Vogeler, Heinrich		2	1		3
Gordon, Eugene	2	1			3
Weiskopf, Franz Carl		1	2		3
Dos Passos, John Randolph	3				3
Orozco, José Clemente		3			3
Bruck, Jacob		1	2		3
Zinoviev, Grigory		1	1	1	3
Andersen Nexø, Martin	1		1	1	3
Krieger, Esther		1	1	1	3
Khu Lan–Tchi	1	1		1	3

Fig. 2. Contributors (three and more entries) to *International Literature* in 1934–1935.

The top of the table (Fig. 2) contains the names of the most regular contributors to the project during 1934–35, the authors of three or more texts

International Literature | 159

(133 persons). Apparently, this list should be considered a set of permanent contributors to the project–much shorter than and different from the one on the cover. The authors of more than four contributions could potentially appear in all four versions of the journal: this latter list consists of just eighty-six names.

The core of the contributors corpus was rather suggestive as the most frequently published author was the editor-in-chief Sergei Dinamov, whose texts come signed either by his full name or initials SD. Most of his contributions were published in the Russian (nine) and English (eight) versions. It also comes as no surprise that while he had the leading position in the English version he headed, the leaders for the other versions were rather different: Theodore Dreiser, Johannes Becher, and Anatoly Lunacharsky for the Russian, German, and French versions respectively. Out of the three figures, only Becher was functionally similar to Dinamov. Apparently, Lunacharsky took the place one would reserve for the French editor-in-chief Vaillant-Couturier, while the Russian version showed an unexpected inclination towards fiction over the Marxist-Leninist theory and literary criticism: Dreiser's publications (fourteen) were twice as frequent as those of Feuchtwanger (seven) and even of the leaders of the other versions.

Switching to network analysis, we visualized the data from the list of all the contributors in the form of a network graph (Fig. 3) with four language versions of the journal as central nodes. The position of the contributor in the network depends on the number of entries in each version: those who appeared in only one edition are placed on the edges of the model; authors with publications in different versions are much closer to the center; the most central position is taken by those who were published most often and whose publications are distributed equally throughout all the versions. A distant reading of this model makes separate names unreadable,[34] but enables us to see its periphery clearly, i.e. the authors of texts participating only in bilateral exchange between languages (fan-shaped lines spreading from each language edition).

---

34   The coloured version of this graph can be found on the *Interlit* Project site.

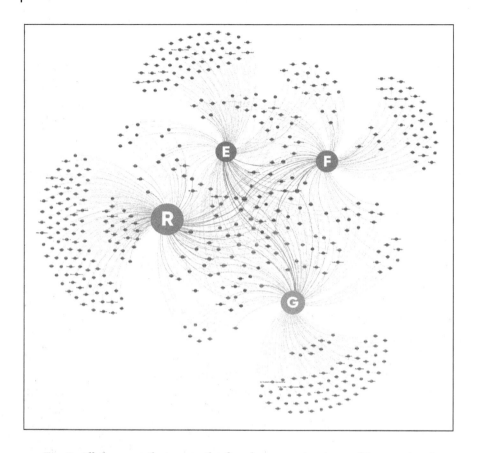

Fig. 3. All the contributors to the four language versions of *International Literature* in 1934–1935.

Less distant reading of the center of this model shows the intensity of connections within it: the most central positions are taken by the authors who were published in at least three of the four journals. Active contributors to one of the editions (such as Dreiser or Hemingway) turn out to be left far outside the center. This feature is extremely important for the journal's model of the world literature as a network: in the center of the graph appear not the most popular names, but the names of those more actively involved in the editorial network, and the editors themselves as authors. Next come the authors closest to the editorial office, among them a number of Germans and somewhat fewer French and English ones. A rather central position is taken by contributors whose texts are present in all the four versions, for example, in the case of political appeals, close to the center appear Stalin and the head of the Comintern Dimitrov, whose speeches were translated for all the versions.

Researchers approach the networking nature of periodicals in at least two perspectives defined by the objects, or subjects, becoming units and then nodes of networks. First, a periodical can be understood as a network of entries inside one issue or in the whole corpus, "bound together by conceptual, political, and personal ties frozen in a historical moment,"[35] in which case, a network graph shows connections between the texts implied by editors or perceived by readers. Second, periodicals could be considered as "objects and actors in a living intellectual environment,"[36] and then the interconnections between the authors and the editors of the journals become a visual representation of this environment. For instance, to represent some archival editorial correspondence as a network "may help in the process of recovery and discovery and extending the social network beyond the immediate links of writer and editor."[37]

The graph we have produced (Fig. 3) primarily works in the first perspective: it visualizes the correlation of texts, which are indicated by the authors' names, within the whole journal's project for 1934–1935. However, placing different authors closer to the center or at the periphery, the graph implies the hierarchy not only of the texts but also of people and in this way reflects the editorial policy of the different language versions. In other words, this graph visualizes the model of world literature as a set of texts, and also introduces a network of interrelations of editors and authors that makes a model of the world literature as a constant communication of agents and institutions.

Unfortunately, at the present stage of the project we do not have a full-text digital corpus of the journals. The data extracted from such a source would be highly valuable for a more precise understanding of the structure of this network. All the "letters from writers", "anniversary greetings" and other similar contributions on the pages of the journals functioned as tools for the permanent representation of the "imagined community" of the new world literature; analyzing this corpus would allow us to describe the connectivity within the writer's network. Furthermore, it is essential to analyze the huge body of archival documents, produced by the editorial staff of the journal, in particular, correspondence with actual and potential authors, as well as with other agents

---

35 Jeffrey Drouin, "Close- and Distant-Reading Modernism: Network Analysis, Text Mining, and Teaching the *Little Review* Author(s)," in "Visualizing Periodical Networks," ed. J. Stephen Murphy, Special issue, *The Journal of Modern Periodical Studies* 5, no. 1 (2014): 115.

36 Gleissner, "Soviet Union on the Seine: Kontinent, Sintaksis, and the Social Life of Émigré Journals," 448.

37 Chatham Ewing, "Perspective: Social Networks and Historical Contexts Author(s)," in "Visualizing Periodical Networks," ed. J. Stephen Murphy, Special issue, *The Journal of Modern Periodical Studies* 5, no. 1 (2014): 12.

of the literary and the power fields. Unfortunately, the latter sources are incomplete (there are few letters from 1934–35 left), and dispersed among different collections of several archives, and of course, they have not been digitalized, except for the Comintern fonds. To explore these sources and discover a network of different relationships between people, from friendly to hierarchical to patron-client, lying deep beneath the surface of the relationships between texts within a utopian project of world literature would be no less a utopian task for our research group.

Conclusion

Thus, *International Literature* became an ideal showcase of the Soviet literary utopia in construction. While the Marxist utopian model implied a masterpiece uniformly reproduced in, or translated into a number of languages, the real journal project brought about a network of texts meant to create a corpus of communist world literature, a communist "commons"[38] and a global network of authors from Europe, North and South America, the Far East, Middle and Central Asia. 1934–35 saw the construction at its peak with Moscow bustling with cosmopolites and German and Hungarian exiles, many of whom took part in the production of the journals, and Radek addressing the Congress and promoting a doctrine of world literature. By the end of the decade, against the backdrop of great historical events, such as the Spanish War, the Great Terror, the Hitler-Stalin Pact and the outbreak of World War II, some nodes of this network had been destroyed, the cosmopolites had had to leave Moscow, many of the German and Hungarian immigrants who had stayed were prosecuted and executed, and so were the journal's editors Sergei Tretyakov and Sergei Dinamov. All this changed the project in different ways, destroying the existing networks and preventing appearance of new ones. As some of the editors and contributors were physically destroyed by the state, their texts and pictures had to be cut out from the old issues. The resulting voids were both physical and symbolic. The contributors' list and the content were changing, and the "foreign" versions gradually became journals of translations from Russian and in 1946 renamed into "Soviet Literature." The culture of late Stalinism was incompatible with the utopia of literary internationalism of the 1920–1930s.

---

38 Katerina Clark, "Translation and Transnationalism: Non-European Writers and Soviet Power in the 1920s and 1930s," in *Translation in Russian Contexts: Culture, Politics, Identity*, ed. Baer Brian James and Susanna Witt (London, New York: Routledge, 2018), 142.

The scope of *International Literature*'s projection of world literature seems unique; however, it accentuates the role and specific features of a literary periodical at this stage of modernity. Addressing the transnational, trans-European and transatlantic character of many modernist and avant-garde periodicals, especially, little magazines (*Poetry, Little Review, transition, etc.*), modernist scholars regard little magazines as an expression of the very essence of modernism as networking[39] and a worldwide phenomenon: "together they worked within and against an emerging literary network that was truly global in scope and scale."[40] The added dimension of the communist utopian construction and the Soviet state's ambition to "share modernity" with the rest of the world[41] seemed to have provided the machinery for construction of world literature– the machinery modernism and avant-garde on their own lacked. However, a utopia in construction turned out to be still that, a utopia, a Tower of Babel that may seem to come close to completion only to fall down in the nearest future.

---

39 Murphy, "Visualizing Periodical Networks," iii-xv.
40 Eric Bulson, *Little Magazine, World Form* (New York: Columbia University Press, 2016).
41 Michael David-Fox, *Crossing Borders: Modernity, Ideology, and Culture in Russia and the Soviet Union* (Pittsburgh, PA: University of Pittsburgh Press, 2015).

CHAPTER 8

Translating China into *International Literature*: Stalin-Era World Literature Beyond the West

Edward Tyerman

The career of the journal *International Literature* offers a succinct history of the attempt by Soviet literary institutions in the Stalinist period to create a restructured world literature, centred in Moscow and mediated through the prestigious form of the literary journal.[1] The journal's first incarnation was the *Herald of Foreign Literature* (*Vestnik inostrannoi literatury*), founded by its chief editor Anatoly Lunacharsky in 1928. Officially the organ of the Comintern's International Bureau of Revolutionary Literature (*Mezhdunarodnoe biuro revoliutsionnoi literatury*—MBRL), the *Herald* published a broad range of authors, from proletarian writers to socialist sympathizers to more neutral figures. At the 1930 Second Conference of Revolutionary and Proletarian Writers in Kharkiv, an event dominated by the Russian Association of Proletarian Writers (RAPP) and its particular vision of a global proletarian literature, MBRL was reorganized as the International Organization of Revolutionary Writers

---

1 On the Soviet investment in world literature as a project see Maria Khotimsky, "World Literature, Soviet Style: A Forgotten Episode in the History of the Idea," *Ab Imperio* 3 (2013): 119–54; Katerina Clark, *Moscow, The Fourth Rome: Stalinism, Cosmopolitanism, and the Evolution of Soviet Culture, 1931–1941* (Cambridge, MA: Harvard University Press, 2011), 169–209. For a classic account of the Soviet cultural bureaucracy's investment in maintaining the medium of the literary journal inherited from the nineteenth century, see Robert A. Maguire, *Red Virgin Soil: Soviet Literature in the 1920s* (Princeton: Princeton University Press, 1968).

(*Mezhdunarodnaia organizatsiia revoluitsionnykh pisatelei*—MORP). The *Herald* became *Literature of the World Revolution* (*Literatura mirovoi revoluitsii*), a multi-lingual journal issued in Russian, French, English and German that focused more strictly on proletarian literature. *Literature of the World Revolution* lasted only two years, under the chief editorship of the Polish writer Bruno Jasieński. After RAPP's disbanding in 1932, the journal changed names again, appearing from 1933 as *International Literature* (*Internatsional'naia literatura*). Sergei Dinamov became chief editor; Sergei Tretyakov served as editor of the Russian edition from 1933 to 1936. *International Literature* appeared in Russian, French, English, German, Spanish (from 1942), and briefly Chinese. From 1935, with the disbanding of MORP and the creation of the United Front, *International Literature* became an organ of the Union of Soviet Writers. It ceased publication in 1943, the same year that the Comintern was dissolved.[2]

Discussions of the Russian edition of *International Literature* tend to emphasize its role as a conduit for Western literature into the USSR, including a significant number of modernist writers. In the mid-1930s, at a time when the establishment of Socialist Realism as state-approved literary doctrine coincided with increasing attacks on modernist experimentation, *International Literature* under the editorship of Dinamov and Tretyakov published Ernest Hemingway, Aldous Huxley, Louis-Ferdinand Céline, Alfred Döblin and, most notoriously, James Joyce's *Ulysses*.[3] (These catholic tendencies found themselves curtailed in the late 1930s, when the Purges claimed the lives of Dinamov, Tretyakov, and Jasieński.) Less attention has been paid, however, to the journal's coverage of literatures outside the West. This chapter focuses on the example of China, a country that during the 1920s and 1930s remained constantly at the centre of what we might call the Soviet state-sponsored internationalist imagination. Beginning in the late 1920s, *International Literature* and its predecessors hosted the first large-scale translation of modern Chinese literature into Russian. Close attention to this corpus can illuminate how *International Literature* situated a

---

2 For the journal's history, see E. E. Zemskova, "Istoriia zhurnala 'Internatsional'naia literatura': perspektivy issledovatel'skogo proekta," *Novye rossiiskie gumanitarnye issledovaniia* 9 (2014), accessed online on April 22, 2021, DOI: http://www.nrgumis.ru/articles/239/; Nailya Safiullina and Rachel Platonov, "Literary Translation and Soviet Cultural Politics in the 1930s: The Role of the Journal Internacional'naja Literatura," *Russian Literature* 72, no. 2 (2012): 248–53. For a remarkable digital project to map the contexts of the journal across its multiple languages of publication, organized by Elena Ostrovskaya and Elena Zemskova at Moscow's Higher School of Economics, see http://www.interlit.online/index.php.

3 Safiullina and Platonov, "Literary Translation and Soviet Cultural Politics," 253–55; Samantha Sherry, *Discourses of Regulation and Resistance: Censoring Translation in the Stalin and Khrushchev Era Soviet Union*, 67–101.

major non-Western country and its contemporary literary production within the map of world literature that the journal produced for its readers.

This chapter begins by tracing the historical conditions that led to the appearance of contemporary Chinese literature on the pages of *International Literature*. Next, I focus on two case studies that illuminate the translation strategies employed by the journal. Early Soviet debates on translation, in line with the broader history of European translation theory, oscillated between the two poles of "literalist" fidelity to the original and a "free" or "artistic" practice that privileged the smoothness of the translated text in the target language. By the end of the thirties, the latter approach had established itself as orthodoxy.[4] My two case studies offer different resolutions of this basic tension: the Russian poems of the Chinese poet Xiao San (known in Russian as Emi Siao), and Nikolai Fedorenko's translations of Lu Xun, the most iconic of twentieth-century Chinese writers. Though the translation strategies deployed in both cases differ radically, they both serve to affirm the fundamental principle of *translatability* on which rested the journal's model of a Soviet-centric world literature. Texts produced in diverse global spaces entered the pages of the journal as commensurable specimens of "international literature," rendered legible through translation and accompanying paratexual materials (introductions, critical essays, photographs, etc.).[5] Modern Chinese literature emerged from a literary tradition and a cultural context that remained less familiar, even exotic, for Russophone readers. At the same time, Soviet state media sought to present contemporary China as a crucial and recognizable site of revolutionary struggle. Tracking the translation of modern Chinese literature into *International Literature* thus offers an important case study for understanding how the Soviet world literature project negotiated the tensions between difference and commensurability within its literary map of the globe.

---

4 Maurice Friedberg, *Literary Translation in Russia: A Cultural History* (University Park: Pennsylvania State University Press, 1997), 69–108; Susanna Witt, "Arts of Accommodation: The First All-Union Conference of Translators, Moscow, 1936," in *The Art of Accommodation: Literary Translation in Russia*, ed. Leon Burnett and Emily Lygo (London: Peter Lang, 2013), 141–84.

5 My discussion here moves in the shadow of Emily Apter's polemical critique, made in a different historical context, of a model of world literature grounded in notions of translatability and commensurability. See Apter, *Against World Literature: On the Politics of Untranslatability* (London: Verso, 2013).

China in Early Soviet Culture and *International Literature*

The period immediately before the founding of the *Herald of World Literature* witnessed an intense moment of Soviet political and cultural engagement with China. During the 1920s, the Soviet-dominated Comintern formed an alliance with China's Nationalist Party (Guomindang), in line with the Leninist strategy of supporting nationalist parties in order to stoke anti-imperial revolutions in colonized and semi-colonized countries. China's last imperial dynasty, the Qing, had fallen in 1911, but the Chinese Republic founded in its place soon descended into civil war between rival military factions. Meanwhile, foreign powers including Britain, France, the USA and Japan retained the sizeable economic, legal and territorial concessions they had won from China since the First Opium War (1839–42), a process of "semi-colonization" that found its most visible expressions in the treaty ports of Shanghai and Tianjin.[6] Seeking to foster a national revolution in China that would overthrow the influence of the capitalist powers and pave the way for a socialist revolution, the Comintern sponsored a united front between the Nationalists and the recently formed Chinese Communist Party (CCP). This strategy ended in disaster: in April 1927, after capturing Shanghai, the Nationalists under Chiang Kai-shek turned violently against their erstwhile allies, executed and imprisoned large numbers of workers and Communists, and expelled all Comintern advisers from the country. The Comintern's "loss" of China became a central point of dispute in the struggle for power between Stalin and the Left Opposition, which led by late 1927 to Lev Trotsky's expulsion from the Party and Joseph Stalin's elevation to unquestioned primacy.[7]

While Comintern advisers led by Mikhail Borodin were working with the Guomindang in Guangzhou, the USSR also dispatched a steady stream of cultural emissaries to China in the mid-1920s. Most prominent among them was the avant-garde writer and theorist Sergei Tretyakov, the future editor of

---

6   The term "semi-colony" was coined by Lenin to describe China, Turkey and Persia; see V. I. Lenin, *Imperialism: The Highest Stage of Capitalism* (London: Pluto Press, 1996), 81. From the late 1920s, Mao Zedong and other Chinese Marxists adopted the term to describe China's economic and political status. See Tani Barlow, "Semifeudalism, Semicolonialism," in *Afterlives of Chinese Communism: Political Concepts from Mao to Xi*, ed. Christian Sorace, Ivan Franceschini, Nicholas Loubere (Acton: ANU Press, 2019), 237–41.

7   For the history of Soviet and Comintern engagement with China in the 1920s see C. Martin Wilbur and Julie Lien-ying How, *Missionaries of Revolution: Soviet Advisers and Nationalist China, 1920–1927* (Cambridge, MA: Harvard University Press, 1989); Alexander Pantsov, *The Bolsheviks and the Chinese Revolution, 1919–1927* (Richmond: Curzon Press, 2000).

International Literature, who spent 18 months teaching Russian at Beijing University in 1924–25. During his time in Beijing, Tretyakov served as a correspondent for *Pravda* and a host of other Soviet periodicals, dispatching a steady stream of articles on contemporary China that combined anti-imperialist political sentiment with a sustained attack on the aesthetics of exoticism. After his return to Moscow, Tretyakov continued to write about China: his most famous piece was the hit play *Roar, China!* (*Rychi, Kitai!*), first performed at the Meyerhold Theatre in January 1926 and subsequently staged across the world, including in Germany, Britain, New York, Japan and China.[8] Other cultural visitors to China in this period included the writer Boris Pilnyak, who visited Shanghai in the summer of 1926; the director Vladimir Shneiderov, one of the pioneers of the Soviet expedition film, whose debut film, *The Great Flight* (*Velikii perelet*, 1926) tracked the progress of an aviation expedition from Moscow to Beijing; and the director Iakov Bliokh, who shot the documentary *Shanghai Document* (*Shankhaiskii document*, 1928), a remarkable application of Soviet parallel montage to China's most important semi-colonial city, in the summer of 1927. Taken together, these exercises in cultural mediation represented a sustained attempt to inscribe China into the Soviet internationalist imaginary as the site of the next major revolution.[9]

In the wake of the Comintern's defeat in 1927, the Sino-Soviet relationship shifted. Soviet emissaries political and cultural were no longer welcome in a Republican China dominated by the Nationalists (though this would alter a little in the later 1930s, as the rising Japanese encroachment on Chinese territory led to a form of rapprochement under the umbrella of the anti-fascist United Front). The 1930s saw no major Soviet-authored works on China that achieved the social impact of *Roar, China!*, or the experiment in Soviet-internationalist *chinoiserie* that was the 1927 hit ballet *The Red Poppy*.[10] Instead, China's position in the Soviet state-sponsored internationalist imaginary migrated into the field of translated literature.

Translations of Chinese literature into Russian had hitherto focused on texts written prior to the twentieth century, before the vernacularization campaigns, critical reassessment of traditional culture, and intense engagement

---

8   Mark Gamsa, "Sergei Tret'iakov's *Roar, China!* between Moscow and China," *Itinerario* 36, no. 2 (August 2012): 91–108.

9   For an extensive discussion see Edward Tyerman, *Internationalist Aesthetics: China and Early Soviet Culture* (New York: Columbia University Press, 2021).

10 See Edward Tyerman, "Resignifying *The Red Poppy*: Internationalism and Symbolic Power in the Sino-Soviet Encounter," *Slavic and East European Journal* 61, No. 3 (Autumn 2017): 445–66.

with foreign literary models that shaped China's New Culture and May Fourth movements in the 1910s and 1920s.[11] By the 1920s, these early translations from the Chinese literary canon would find themselves drawn into ongoing debates over literalist versus artistic translation. Russia's modernists shared in a broader European fascination with classical Chinese poetry at the turn of the twentieth century. In 1914, two members of the *Soiuz molodezhi* art group, V. Egor'ev and Vladimir Markov (Voldemars Matveis), published *Svirel' Kitaia* (*The Chinese Flute*), the first anthology in Russian devoted entirely to Chinese poetry. (Euro-American modernism's most famous engagement with Chinese poetry, Ezra Pound's *Cathay*, appeared a year later.) Egor'ev and Markov did not work directly with the Chinese texts of their poems, which ranged from the *Shijing* (*Classic of Poetry*, eleventh to seventh centuries BC) to the nineteenth century. Instead, they drew mainly on the German poet Hans Bethge's anthology *Die Chinesische Flöte* (1907), itself based on an earlier German translation from Judith Gautier's popular 1867 volume *Le livre de jade*.[12] A few years later, Nikolai Gumilev's renderings of Chinese verse in *Farforovyi pavil'on* (*The Porcelain Pavilion*, 1918) would also draw their source material from Gautier, a non-Sinologist who composed her highly liberal translations in collaboration with her Chinese tutor.[13] In the early Soviet period, the short-lived *Vsemirnaia literatura* (World Literature) publishing house—founded by Maksim Gorky in 1918, and the first experiment in a Soviet world literature—included pre-twentieth century Chinese texts within its ambitious project to make the literary heritage of the world available to Soviet readers through translation.[14] Vasilii Mikhailovich Alekseev, the pre-eminent Russian Sinologist of the period, published his own literalist translations from the Tang poet Li Bai (along with copious explanatory footnotes) in the *Vsemirnaia literatura* journal *Vostok* (*The*

---

11 For an overview see Kirk Denton, ed., *Modern Chinese Literary Thought: Writings on Literature, 1893–1945* (Stanford University Press, 1996), 1–61. For the origins of New Culture and May Fourth cosmopolitanism in late Qing literature, see Theodor Huters, *Bringing the World Home: Appropriating the West in Late Qing and Early Republican China* (Honolulu: University of Hawai'i Press, 2005).

12 V. Egor'ev and V. Markov, eds., *Svirel' Kitaia* (Saint Petersburg: Soiuz molodezhi, 1914); E. A. Os'minina, "Kul'tura Kitaia v predstavlenii russkogo futurizma (na primere antologii 'Svirel' Kitaia')," *Vestnik Moskovskogo gosudarstvennogo lingvisticheskogo universiteta* 6 (2020): 234–44.

13 Jinyi Chu, "Patterns of the World: Chinese Fashion and Cosmopolitan Ideas in Late Imperial Russia" (Ph.D. dissertation, Stanford University, 2019), 156–58; Pauline Yu, "Your Alabaster in This Porcelain": Judith Gautier's *Le livre de jade*," *PMLA* 122., no. 2 (2007): 467–69.

14 For the history of the *Vsemirnaia literatura* publishing house, see Khotimsky, "World Literature, Soviet Style."

East) in 1923 and 1925.[15] Alekseev attacked the creative license of Gautier and her epigones in the foreword to his pupil Iulian Shchutskii's *Anthology of Chinese Poetry from the Seventh to Ninth Centuries AD*, a *Vsemirnaia literatura* volume from 1923 that sought a balance between accuracy and poetic form.[16] In the realm of prose, Alekseev's translations from Pu Songling's seventeenth-century story collection *Liaozhai zhiyi* (*Strange Tales from a Chinese Studio*) also appeared under the *Vsemirnaia literatura* imprint from 1922.[17] Alekseev's renderings of Pu's tales of the fantastic exerted a significant impact on contemporary readers, from Aleksei Remizov to Vasilii Tikhomirov, choreographer of *The Red Poppy*.[18]

Between the closing of *Vsemirnaia literatura* in 1924 and the appearance of the *Herald of World Literature* from 1928, the heightened contact between Soviet and Chinese intellectuals generated by the Comintern's engagement in China created the conditions for contemporary Chinese literature to appear in the Soviet literary system.[19] Beginning in 1928, the *Herald of World Literature, Literature of the World Revolution* and *International Literature* introduced their readers to an impressive cross-section of the contemporary Chinese literary scene, publishing works by Lu Xun, Mao Dun, Ding Ling, Ye Shengtao, Xiao Jun, Rou Shi, Hu Lanqi, Tai Jingnong, and Zhang Yiping.[20] Operating broadly

---

15 Li Bo, "Drevnee," trans. V. M. Alekseev, *Vostok* 2 (1923): 35–41; Li Bo, "Iz chetverostishii," trans. V. M. Alekseev, *Vostok* 5 (1925): 87–102.

16 *Antologiia kitaiskoi liriki VII-IX v. v. po R. Khr.*, trans. Iu. K. Shutskii, ed. V. M. Alekseev (Moscow: Gosudarstvennoe izdatel'stvo, Vsemirnaia literatura, 1923).

17 Pu Songling, *Lis'i chary: iz sbornika strannykh rasskazov Pu Sunlina* (*Liao chzhai chzhi i*), trans. V. M. Alekseev (Petrograd: Gosudarstvennoe izdatel'stvo, 1922). Alekseev's translations from *Liaozhai zhiyi* also appeared in *Vostok*: see Liao Chzhai, "Talanty kitaiskogo sud'i," trans. V. M. Alekseev, *Vostok* 5, 1925, 103–26.

18 Chu, "Patterns of the World," 207–14; Tyerman, "Resignifying *The Red Poppy*," 451.

19 Book-length literary translations of modern Chinese literature also began to appear at around the same time: see for example the collected volume *Pravdivoe zhizneopisanie: povesti i rasskazy Li-Tszi-Min, Lu-Siun', Chzhan-Tszy-Pin [i dr.]*, translated and edited by A. Kharkhatov (Moscow: Molodaia gvardiia, 1929). The Sinologist Vsevolod Kolokolov wrote an afterword for this volume.

20 In chronological order: Chzhan I-Pin [Zhang Yiping 章衣萍], "A-Lian," trans. S. Polevoi, *Vestnik inostrannoi literatury* 11 (1928): 66–74; Ye Shao-tsziun' [Ye Shaojun, a.k.a Ye Shengtao 葉聖陶], "Zolotaia ser'ga," trans. Zoia Kazakevich, ed. B. Vasil'ev, *Vestnik inostrannoi literatury* 4 (1930): 99–107; Tai Tszin-nun [Tai Jingnong 臺靜農], "My stroim" and "Vchera noch'iu," trans. A. Ivin, *Literatura mirovoi revoliutsii* 7 (1931): 70–76; Mao Dun [茅盾], "Vesennii shelk," trans. N. Nekrasov, *Internatsional'naia literatura* 3–4 (1934): 310–20; Khu Lan-chi [Hu Lanqi 胡蘭畦], "Konets Van Bo-pi," trans. Ia. Neiman, *Internatsional'naia literatura* 10 (1935): 74–84; Chzhou Shi [Rou Shi 柔石], "Mat'," tr. E. Kalashnikova, *Internatsional'naia literatura* 5 (1937): 96–106; Lu Sin' [Lu Xun 魯迅], "Blagoslovenie," trans. E. K., *Internatsional'naia literatura* 10 (1937): Tin Lin [Ding Ling 丁

172 | Edward Tyerman

on the left of the political spectrum, these writers all participated in a post-May Fourth turn towards literary realism, developed in close dialogue with European (and especially Russian) models. At a time shaped by a semi-colonial entry into modernity and the radical re-evaluation of traditional culture, realism offered a literary mode that promised to represent and potentially resolve China's political and cultural crises.[21] The social concerns of the Chinese realist texts translated for *International Literature* and its predecessors, with their focus on inequality and the pernicious nature of traditional gender and class relations, fitted neatly into these journals' broader project of materializing a transnational leftist realist literature.[22] These literary texts were supplemented by a steady stream of articles on contemporary Chinese culture, the history of Chinese literature, and cultural politics in contemporary China. In 1937, with Japan's invasion of China underway, *International Literature* published Mao Zedong's autobiography as recounted to the American journalist Edgar Snow, and a series of pieces on Mao's close ally Zhu De.[23]

The appearance of Chinese literature in *International Literature* was, in an important sense, the reverse ripple effect of the much larger and more transformative impact made by the reception of Russian and Soviet literature in the Chinese literary world. As Mark Gamsa has shown, Russian and Soviet literature in translation, often mediated through Japanese or another third language, exerted an enormous influence on the post-May Fourth generation of Chinese writers and their search for modern forms of vernacular writing.[24] By the late 1920s, as members of this generation turned increasingly towards Marxism in the wake of the Nationalist coup in 1927, translations of Soviet literature began to increase. A vigorous debate in the late 1920s over the question of "revolutionary

---

玲], "Podarok," trans. A. Ivin, *Internatsional'naia literatura* 11 (1937): 112–17; Tian' Tsziun' [Tian Jun, a.k.a Xiao Jun 蕭軍], "Derevnia v avguste," trans. M. Ukhanskii, *Internatsional'naia literatura* 6 (1938): 3–40; Lu Sin' [Lu Xun], "Lekarstvo," "Neznachitel'nyi sluchai," trans. N. Fedorenko, *Internatsional'naia literatura* 11 (1939): 80–85.

21 See, e.g., Roy Bing Chan, *The Edge of Knowing: Dreams, History, and Realism in Modern Chinese Literature* (Seattle: University of Washington Press, 2017), 25–34.

22 Few of these stories focused on proletarian experience; an exception is Yan Tsin-zhen [Yang Qingren], "Slepoi Li" [Blind Li], trans. Emi Siao, *Internatsional'naia literatura* 11–12 (1931): 84–88.

23 Mao Tsze-dun [Mao Zedong], "Moia zhizn'," trans. N. Sh., *Internatsional'naia literatura* 11 (1937): 101–111; idem, "Moia zhizn' (prodolzhenie)," *Internatsional'naia literatura* 12 (1937): 95–101; Emi Siao, "Chzhu De," Anna Louise Strong, "V gostiakh u Chzhu De," *Internatsional'naia literatura* 11 (1938): 140–51.

24 Mark Gamsa, *The Chinese Translation of Russian Literature: Three Studies* (Boston, MA: Brill, 2008); idem, *The Reading of Russian Literature in China: A Moral Example and Manual of Practice* (New York: Palgrave Macmillan, 2010).

literature" (*geming wenxue*) led in the early 1930s to the formation of the League of Left-Wing Writers (*Zhongguo zuoyi zuojia lianmeng*), an organization that actively sought to ally itself with Soviet-controlled bodies such as MORP. (Several of the Chinese writers published in *International Literature*, including Lu Xun, Mao Dun, Ding Ling, and Rou Shi, were affiliated with the League.) The debates and polemics of the Shanghai literary left absorbed the influence of the literary theories of Trotsky, Georgii Plekhanov, and Lunarcharsky, often mediated through the proletarian literature movement in Japan.[25] Chinese and Russian literatures thus found themselves already intertwined through a certain East Asian experience of world literature, one that Heekyoung Cho reads as a challenge to the Eurocentric models of world literature put forward by Franco Moretti and Pascale Casanova. In place of a center-periphery relationship where forms of aesthetic innovation compete for the validation of the center, Cho finds a relationship between two semi-peripheries in which Russian realist texts modelled for East Asian intellectuals a literature of social commitment.[26]

Returnees from Soviet educational institutions in Moscow—specifically the Communist University for the Workers of the East (KUTV, f. 1921) and the Sun Yat-sen University for the Workers of China (f. 1925)—played a key role in mediating Russian literature for Chinese leftist intellectual circles.[27] Figures such as the journalist, philosopher and briefly CCP leader Qu Qiubai, the writer Jiang Guangi, and the translator and scholar Cao Jinghua all drew on their time in the USSR to become important mediators of Soviet literature for a Chinese audience.[28] *International Literature*, in turn, enlisted a different set of intermediaries: Russian and Soviet Sinologists who combined literary specialization with some kind of

---

25 Wang-chi Wong, *Politics and Literature in Shanghai: the Chinese League of Left-Wing Writers, 1930–1936* (Manchester University Press, 1991); Leo Ou-Fan Lee, "Literature on the Eve of Revolution: Reflections on Lu Xun's Leftist Years, 1927–1936," *Modern China*, vol. 2, no. 3 (1976): 295, 300–308. Soviet films and film theory also exerted an important influence on a developing Chinese left-wing cinema in the early 1930s: see Pang Laikwan, *Building a New China in Cinema: The Chinese Left-Wing Cinema Movement, 1932–1937* (Lanham: Rowman & Littlefield Publishers, 2002), 41, 144–48; Weihong Bao, *Fiery Cinema: The Emergence of an Affective Medium in China, 1915–1945* (Minneapolis: University of Minnesota Press, 2015), 242–50.

26 Heekyoung Cho, "Rethinking World Literature through the Relations between Russian and East Asian Literatures," *Cross-Currents: East Asian History and Culture Review* 28 (2018): 7–26.

27 On the history of Chinese students at these institutions see Elizabeth McGuire, *Red at Heart: How Chinese Communists Fell in Love with the Russian Revolution* (Oxford University Press, 2018); L. Yu Min-ling, "Sun Yat-sen University in Moscow, 1925–1930," Ph.D. diss., New York University, 1995.

28 Gamsa, *Reading of Russian Literature*, 70–71, 76–78.

political work in contemporary China. For example, the February 1929 issue of the *Herald of World Literature* included an article by the Russian Sinologist Sergei Aleksandrovich Polevoi on recent Chinese translations of Russian books. A classical scholar and cultural liaison for the Third International who assisted Chinese students travelling in secret to Russia, Polevoi was involved in the establishment of Beijing University's Russian Department after 1918 (where Tretyakov was briefly his colleague).[29] Polevoi had already translated the first Chinese literary text to appear in the *Herald:* a short story by Zhang Yiping titled "A Liang," which told of the abusive treatment of a slave girl by the narrator's uncle.[30] In his article, Polevoi offered an overview of recent debates in the Chinese literary world on the theme of "literature and revolution," citing the influence of Li Jiye's translation of Trotsky's *Literature and Revolution,* a volume Polevoi had edited. Polevoi praised Jiang Guangci's recent volume on Russian literature after 1917, calling Jiang the "first Chinese revolutionary poet." He went on to list a broad range of Russian writers recently translated into Chinese, including Pilnyak, Vsevolod Ivanov, Ehrenburg, Zoshchenko, Andreev, Gorky, Turgenev, Artsybashev, Chekhov, and Tolstoy. Polevoi's article offered Soviet readers a clear picture of Chinese revolutionary literature developing under the tutelage of Russian and Soviet example.[31]

Polevoi was just one of several Soviet Sinologists who played this role of a mediating figure between the Chinese and Russian literary worlds on the pages of the journal. In 1930, the *Herald* published an article on "Chinese Literature" by Boris Aleksandrovich Vasiliev, a student of Alekseev who had served as a Comintern translator in China and published the first Russian translation of Lu Xun's *True Story of Ah Q (A Q zheng zhuan)* in 1929.[32] Vasiliev offered a nine-stage history of Chinese literature through the prism of class relations from its origins to the present. His account of contemporary literature as shaped by an opposition between pure aestheticism and a realism responsive to "social command" (*sotsial'nyi zakaz*) would not have sounded too unfamiliar to Soviet readers.[33]

---

29 Polevoi eventually fled the Japanese occupation in 1939 for the USA and Harvard University. For a hostile account of Polevoi by a former colleague at Beijing University, see Zhang Ximan 張西曼, "Bei dai Ewen xi eyun," in *Huiyi Zhang Ximan* (Beijing: Zhongguo wenshi chuban-she, 2017), 305; cf. Gao Xingya 高興亞, "Wusi qianhou de Beijing daxue eyu xi," in *Wenshi ziliao xuanji* 135 (1999): 181–85.

30 See note 20 above.

31 Sergei Polevoi, "Kitai: 'Rossica' v 1928 g.," in *Vestnik inostrannoi literatury* 2 (1929): 234–37.

32 Lu Sin' (Lu Xun), *Pravdivaia istoriia Ah–Keia,* trans. and ed. Boris Vasil'ev (Leningrad: Priboi, 1929).

33 B. Vasil'ev, "Kitaiskaia literatura," *Vestnik inostrannoi literatury* 1 (1930): 149–64.

Translating China into *International Literature* | 175

Among the social realists Vasiliev named Ye Shaojun (Ye Shengtao), whose story "The Gold Earring" (Zolotaia ser'ga) appeared in the *Herald's* April 1930 issue. This tale of a poor peasant turned soldier who dies clutching his fetishized object of desire, a gold earring, fitted the script for China as the site of an emerging social realism.[34] Other Sinologists involved in the journal included Aleksei Ivin, who had studied classical Chinese in Paris before moving to China to teach in Beijing University's Russian Department, and Nikolai Fedorenko, another student of Alekseev (whose translations of Lu Xun will be discussed below).[35] These men had been trained as Sinologists focused on the classical language: Vasiliev only became interested in modern, vernacular Chinese literature after an encounter with the translator Cao Jinghua in Kaifeng led him to the work of Lu Xun. Cao, in turn, had learned his Russian both in Moscow and with Tretyakov, Polevoi and Ivin in Beijing.[36] Thus the networks established by Comintern internationalism, which drew Chinese students to Moscow and dispatched Soviet Sinologists to China, made possible the emergence of modern Chinese literature in the Soviet literary system, most prominently on the pages of *International Literature*.

Xiao San (Emi Siao) in Translation

The most important mediator for Chinese literature's position in *International Literature*, however, was the poet Xiao San, known in the pages of the journal by his Europeanized name of Emi Siao (1896–1983). Born in Xiangxiang, Hunan province, Xiao shared a classroom as a child with Mao Zedong. He adopted the name Emi, in tribute to Émile Zola, while a student in Paris in the early twenties. Recent accounts of Xiao's life by Katerina Clark and Elizabeth McGuire emphasize his profound enmeshment in Soviet cultural institutions and his remarkably active career as a mediator between those institutions and the Chinese leftist literary world. After studying at Moscow's Communist

---

34 See note 20 above.

35 For Ivin's translations of Tai Jingnong and Ding Ling, see note 20 above. See also Liu-chzhi-tsin (Chao-iu-shi), "Na 1-oi konferentsii kitaiskikh sovetov," trans. Ivin, *Literatura mirovoi revoliutsii* 5–6 (1931): 157–60. Ivin, whose real name was Aleksei Alekseevich Ivanov, studied in Paris with the prominent French Sinologist Édouard Chavannes. For biographical details see A. Saran, "Livny–Parizh–Pekin. Zhizn' Alekseia Ivanova," *Na beregakh bystroi Sosny*, Almanac of the Livenskii kraevedchesvkii muzei, no. 9 (2001): 75–85.

36 Ge Baoquan, "Tan 'A Q zheng zhuan' de e wen yi ben," *Nankai daxue xuebao: zhexue shehui kexue ban* 2 (1978): 78–82; Charles J. Alber, "Soviet Criticism of Lu Xun," Ph.D. dissertation, Indiana University, 1971, 26–32; Gamsa, *Reading of Russian Literature*, 76–78. Vasiliev was executed in November 1937, during the Purges; see Gamsa, *Reading of Russian Literature*, 88.

University for the Workers of the East from 1922–24, Xiao found his way back to the USSR after the Nationalist coup against the Chinese Communists in 1927. In 1930 Xiao, though not at that time a practising writer, attended the Conference of Revolutionary and Proletarian Writers in Kharkiv as a representative of the Chinese League of Left-Wing Writers.[37] This initiation into the Soviet literary system would position Xiao to become the key intermediary for contemporary Chinese literature and cultural politics in this period.

Xiao served on the editorial board for the Russian edition of *International Literature*, and briefly edited a Chinese edition of the journal, which only appeared for two issues.[38] As well as offering the journal a direct connection to the Chinese literary world through his links to the League of Left-Wing Writers, Xiao also translated texts, wrote prefaces, and produced a steady stream of articles on leftist literature in China and the oppressive cultural policies of the Nationalist government.[39] Beginning in 1931, Xiao started to publish his own poems in *Literature of the World Revolution* and later *International Literature*, meeting the journals' demand for a Chinese revolutionary literature with pieces such as "A Letter in Blood," "Hoist Higher the Banner of the Comintern," "Song of the Manchurian Partisans," and "Red Square."[40] Xiao's poetic career prior to joining the journal extended no further than a few pieces of juvenilia.[41] This, then, was not simply contemporary Chinese literature translated into Russian; rather, this was a form of "international literature" that emerged directly from the experience of a Chinese writer working with a Soviet journal in Moscow.

---

37 For biographical information on Xiao see McGuire, *Red at Heart*, 19–30, 82–88, 184–87; Katerina Clark, "Translation and Transnationalism: Non-European Writers and Soviet Power in the 1920s and 1930s," in Brian James Baer and Susanna Witt, eds., *Translation in Russian Contexts: Culture, Politics, Identity* London: Routledge, 2018), 146–48.

38 Clark, "Translation and Transnationalism," 147; Gao Tao, *Xiao San yi shi yi pin* (Beijing: Wenhua yishu chubanshe, 2010), 3.

39 Clark, "Translation and Transnationalism," 147. For translations see Yan, "Slepoi Li"; Se-Bin-Iue, "Vstuplenie v otriad (iz avtobiografii soldata)," trans. Emi Siao and M. Borisova, *Internatsional'naia literatura* 10 (1937), 137–39; Khe Din, "Vozvrashchenie (rasskaz)," trans. Emi Siao, *Internatsional'naia literatura* 11 (1937): 117–24. For articles, see, e.g., E. Siao, "Dvizhenie proletliteratury v Kitae," *Vestnik inostrannoi literatury* 6 (1930): 162–68; idem, "Kitai: godovshchina rasstrela kitaiskikh revoliutsionnykh rabochikh," *Literatura mirovoi revoliutsii* 5 (1932): 93–94; idem, "Literatura kitaiskoi revoliutsii," *Internatsional'naia litera-tura* 3–4 (1934), 323–33.

40 E. Siao, "Krovavoe pis'mo," *Literatura mirovoi revoliutsii* 1 (1932): 29–30; idem, "Vyshe znamia Kominterna," *Internatsional'naia literatura* 3–4 (1934): 309; idem, "Pesnia man-chzhurskikh partizan," *Internatsional'naia literatura* 11 (1937): 125–26; idem, "Krasnaia ploshchad'," *Internatsional'naia literatura* 3–4 (1940): 17.

41 Xiao's collected works include three early poems from 1919, 1920, and 1923. Xiao San, *Shi wen ji*, vol. 1 (Beijing: Beijing tushuguan chubanshe, 1996), 1–3.

Translating China into *International Literature* | 177

The process that produced Xiao's Russian poems offers a compelling microcosm of the ways in which individual agency combined with the forces exerted by Soviet literary institutions to produce a transparent, *translatable* form of international literature. By the time Xiao made his poetic debut, Joseph Stalin had issued his definitive response to the question of how to handle the diversity of national cultures within the USSR: Soviet culture should be "national in form, socialist in content."[42] Stalin's maxim relies on a certain understanding of translatability: socialist *content* serves here as a stable, fixed meaning that can transfer between national *forms* without distortion or remainder. Xiao's Russian poems offer a variation on this formula, showcasing a dynamic blend of national form, revolutionary form, and socialist content. They also emerged through a process of collaborative translation that complicated questions of agency and authority. Xiao collaborated on these poems with Aleksandr Il'ich Romm, a poet and philologist whose extensive translation credits include the first Russian translation of Ferdinand de Saussure's *Cours de linguistique generale*.[43] Romm knew no Chinese, whereas Xiao's Russian was strong enough for him to produce his own translations of Chinese literature for the journal. Thus the poet came to play a central role in the translation of his own texts. Sometimes, according to Xiao's own memoirs, he would recite a poem aloud to Romm and provide a rough translation into Russian on the spot. Xiao and Romm also used interlinear cribs or *podstrochniki*, a device used frequently for literary translation between the languages of the Soviet Union that enabled writers to translate from languages they did not know.[44] Unusually, however, Xiao provided interlinear translations for his own poems.[45]

---

42 Stalin's original formulation, made in a speech at KUTV in 1925, stressed *proletarian* content: "Proletarian in content, national in form—such is the common human culture towards which socialism is heading." See I. V. Stalin, "O politicheskikh zadachakh universiteta narodov Vostoka: Rech' na sobranii studentov KUTV 18 maia 1925 g.," accessed online on September 2, 2019. The switch to "socialist in content and national in form" was made at the Sixteenth Party Congress in 1930. See *XVI s"ezd VKP(b). Stenograficheskii otchet* (Moscow: Ogiz, 1930), 55–56.

43 McGuire, *Red at Heart*, 188; A. L. Beglov and N. L. Vasil'ev, "Nenapisannaia retsenziia A. I. Romma na knigu M. M. Bakhtina i V. N. Voloshinova 'Marksizm i filosofiia iazyka'," *Philologica* 2 (1995): 199.

44 Clark, "Translation and Transnationalism," 147, 156n16. On the practice of *podstrochniki*, see Susanna Witt, "Between the Lines: Totalitarianism and Translation in the USSR," *Contexts, Subtexts and Pretexts: Literary Translation in Eastern Europe and Russia*, ed. Brian James Baer (Amsterdam: John Benjamins, 2011), 149–70.

45 Xiao was in this respect unusual but not unique: for example, the Georgian poet Titsian Tabidze supplied his own cribs for Boris Pasternak's translations. See Harsha Ram, "Towards a Cross-Cultural Poetics of the Contact Zone: Romantic, Modernist, and Soviet

The series of Russian-language poems published under the name of "E. Siao" in *International Literature* thus emerged from a complex process of interlinguistic exchange and institutional negotiation. Nonetheless, their most striking quality is their legibility. Themes of violent self-sacrifice ("Nanjing Road," "A Letter in Blood") and female liberation ("Auntie Chzhan-u-sao's Decision") certainly fitted the established Soviet repertoire. More strikingly, the translation strategies deployed by Romm shuttle dynamically between the poles of "literalist" and "free" approaches, guided above all by the imperative of clarity. Sometimes he domesticates: thus while Xiao, like many modern Chinese poets, alternates between rhyme and free verse, Romm, in line with Russian poetic conventions, consistently imposes his own rhyme schemes. Yet Romm's translations also attempt to register the effect of the greater concision of Chinese poetry, in which a line of five or seven syllables is common. In this attempt to capture in Russian some echo of the form of the original, however, Romm inevitably sacrifices some of its content.

Let us look briefly at a representative example. In "Nanjing Road," published in *Literature of the World Revolution* in 1931, Xiao describes the beating of activists by police for pasting revolutionary posters on colonial Shanghai's main drag. For the poem's opening sextain, Xiao uses a line structure inherited from classical Chinese poetry: seven syllables that divide into semantic clusters of two-plus-two and three syllables apiece, with a caesura before the final cluster of three syllables. The rhyme scheme is a neat AABBCC. Romm's translation is structurally looser, alternating a six-syllable line (dactyl, trochee, trochee) with an eight-syllable line (amphibrach, amphibrach, iamb), held together by a rhyme scheme of ABABCC. Each Russian line contains only three or four words, giving a strong sense of compression:

Nanjing lushang lengqingqing,	Tikho na Nankin Rod,
Wuli jiedeng ban an ming.	V tumane goriat fonari.
Xiyu feifei bei feng jin,	Kholodno, dozhd' idet,
Leng tou chefu gu he jin.	Do kostei probiraia riksh.
Simian shi qiang zhi faliang.	Mokrye steny blestiat.
Taitai laoye hao meng chang.	Dzhentl'meny i ledi spiat.[46]

Intertextualities in Boris Pasternak's Translations of T'itsian T'abidze," *Comparative Literature* 59, no. 1 (2007): 75–77.

46 Xiao, "Nanjing lushang," *Shi wen ji*, vol. 1, 18. Original text: "南京路上冷清清，雾里街灯半暗明。细雨霏霏北风紧，冷透车夫骨和筋。四面湿墙只发亮。太太老爷好

[Nanjing Road is deserted, / Streetlamps shine half dark in the fog. / A light rain falls, the north wind presses, / The cold pierces the bone and muscle of the rickshaw driver. / On all sides the damp walls glisten. / Mistress and master are dreaming soundly.]

Several elements of Xiao's scene fall away in the process of transferral into Romm's Russian form, sacrificed to the attempt to keep the line short in a language with a higher per-word syllable count. The phrase "xiyu feifei," with its sonic repetition and its invocation of a light, misty drizzle, becomes the more meteorologically direct "dozhd' idet" (it is raining). Xiao's north wind disappears, replaced by the less dynamic "kholodno"—"it is cold"—and Romm's rickshaw man has bones but not muscles. The effect is to remove some of the poetic qualities of the original, replaced in the Russian poem with a sparse, almost blunt clarity.

At other moments, however, original and translation suddenly click into seamless alignment. Notably, these are the moments when Xiao's original switches into a more modern idiom, with irregular line lengths and rhymes.[47] Here Romm deploys greater literalism, producing a translation that matches the original almost word for word. Towards the end of "Nanjing Road," Xiao describes the beating of the agitators by colonial police:

"Da!"		"Bei!"	
Qiang bazi...		Priklad...	
	Cidao...		Shtyk...
"Zhao ba,		"— Nu, govori,	
	zhe ni xiaozi!"		ty!"[48]

["Beat!" / Rifle butt... / Bayonet... / "OK, talk, / kid!"]

Instead of the classical Chinese canon, Xiao draws here on the formal resources of Soviet literature, borrowing from Vladimir Mayakovsky the device of "step construction" to fragment the moment of attack into a sequence of

---

梦长。" For Romm's translation, see E. Siao, "Nankin-rod," *Literatura mirovoi revoliutsii* 4 (1931): 67. My literal English translation of the Chinese text follows below.

47 On the formal innovations of modern Chinese poetry see Bonnie S. McDougall, "Modern Chinese Poetry (1900–1937)," *Modern Chinese Literature* 8, no. 1/2 (Spring/Fall 1994), 127–70; Michelle Yeh, "Modern Poetry in Chinese: Challenges and Contingencies," in *A Companion to Modern Chinese Literature*, ed. Yingjin Zhang (Chichester: Wiley Blackwell, 2016), 151–66.

48 Xiao, "Nanjing lushang," 20; Siao, "Nankin-rod," 69. Original text: "打！枪坝子... 刺刀... '召吧，这你小子！'"

blows and shouts. Romm commits even more than Xiao to the Mayakovskian form, which became a transnational visual signifier for revolutionary poetry in this period.[49] The Russian version even achieves greater compression than the original, reducing Xiao's two six-syllable lines to four and five syllables respectively. In this moment of sharp violence and barked colloquial language, the equivalents are precise: the modal particles "nu" and "ba" perform similar functions, while the second-person singular "ty" captures the condescension of *xiaozi* (boy, kid).

"Nanjing Road" dynamizes the rigid formula of "national in form, socialist in content," just as it complicates the opposition of "literalist" and "free" tendencies in Soviet translation practice. Xiao's original is already both "national" and "socialist" in form, and Romm's translations dilute the national form while doubling down on the echoes of existing Soviet poetic idioms. The language of "domesticating" and "foreignizing" deployed in contemporary translation studies, which depends on the assumption of two discrete linguistic and cultural contexts, does not fully capture this situation.[50] Instead, in its textual form and its collaborative history, "Nanjing Road" performs in miniature the claim of *International Literature* as a whole to mediate a world literature in which the specificities of local contexts merge within a shared context of international socialist revolution. Yet at the same time, Xiao's poems offered a vision of China itself as a space of incomplete revolution and ongoing violent struggle. At the level of both translational form and historical content, these poems positioned China within *International Literature* through a dynamic interplay of commensurability and difference, mapping a revolutionary world literature that reflected a single yet uneven world revolution.

Translating Lu Xun: Between Realism and Symbolism

For a different example of the translation of Chinese literature in *International Literature*, we might turn to Lu Xun (pen name of Zhou Shuren), the most celebrated Chinese writer of the period. A dedicated reader and translator of Russian literature, Lu Xun turned increasingly to Marxism in the wake of the

---

49 See for example the discussion of Langston Hughes' adoption of Mayakovsky's broken line in Steven S. Lee, *The Ethnic Avant-Garde: Minority Cultures and World Revolution* (New York: Columbia University Press, 2015), 78–80.

50 One influential formulation of these terms can be found in Lawrence Venuti, *The Scandals of Translation: Towards an Ethics of Difference* (London: Routledge, 1998).

Nationalist triumph in 1927. He was closely involved in the founding of the League of Left-Wing Writers and the debates around revolutionary literature, and also translated key works of Soviet literature into Chinese (most notably Aleksandr Fadeev's *The Rout/Razgrom*).[51] He was also one of the first modern Chinese writers to be translated into Russian, with the appearance in 1929 of Vasiliev's translation of *The True Story of Ah Q*, perhaps Lu Xun's most famous text. However, it took a while for *International Literature* to get round to actually publishing any of Lu Xun's fiction. Lu Xun's name featured prominently in Xiao's articles on the Left League for *Literature of the World Revolution*.[52] When *Literature of the World Revolution* became *International Literature* in 1933, Lu Xun's name appeared on the back cover, listed alongside the poet Guo Moruo as a member of the journal's "International Revolutionary Council" (*Mezhdunarodnyi revoliutsionnyi sovet*).[53] From the third issue for that year, *International Literature* began to include Lu Xun within an extended list of Chinese writers (including Ding Ling, Mao Dun, and Tian Han) as one of the "Permanent Collaborators of Our Journal."[54] That same issue also included a lengthy quote from Lu Xun's 1932 essay "Celebrating the Ties between Russian and Chinese Literatures" ("Zhu Zhong E wenzi zhi jiao"), advocating for ever greater engagement with Soviet literature in China.[55] Lu Xun could not attend the 1934 First Congress of Soviet Writers (where Xiao spoke), but *International Literature* published his message to the Congress in its bumper issue to celebrate the event. An explanatory note described Lu Xun as "one of the most important Chinese revolutionary writers."[56]

However, despite the journal's acknowledgement of Lu Xun as a central figure for its map of Chinese revolutionary literature, *International Literature* only published his fiction after his death. The journal marked his death in 1936 with great solemnity. Issue Eleven for that year began with full-page image of Lu Xun, framed within a mournful black border, accompanied by a eulogistic text that praised the writer in classically Stalinist language, as an "ardent friend of the Soviet Union". The next issue featured an extensive tribute from Xiao, "In Memory of the Great Chinese Writer Lu Xun," including photographs of

---

51 Wong, *Politics and Literature in Shanghai*; Gamsa, *Reading Russian Literature in China*, 76–78.
52 Siao, "Dvizhenie proletliteratury v Kitae," 164.
53 *Internatsional'naia literatura* 1 (1933): back cover.
54 *Internatsional'naia literatura* 3 (1933): back cover, inside.
55 "O Sovetskom Soiuze: Kitai," *Internatsional'naia literatura* 3 (1933): 151.
56 Lu Sin', "Kitai i Oktiabr'," *Internatsional'naia literatura* 3–4 (1934): 322. (Mao Dun's message is printed on the same page.) Lu Xun's message was also printed on the front page of *Pravda*, July 5, 1934.

Lu Xun's funeral in Shanghai. Lu Xun's central role in the search for a vernacular literary language—a key goal of China's New Culture Movement in the 1910s—enabled Xiao to produce a tribute that emphasized such key elements of the Stalinist paradigm of the Socialist Realist writer as mass accessibility and commitment to realism. "Lu Xun's language is simple, clear and strong" (*prostoi, iarkii i sil'nyi*), Xiao writes, a "language close to the people" (*iazyk, blizkii narodu*). Xiao's Lu Xun is both a "realist artist" and a "deeply national writer, with an excellent knowledge of the life of China and the Chinese people." At the close of his article, Xiao draws what would become a standard comparison between Lu Xun and Gorky.[57] Xiao's article frames Lu Xun for a Soviet reader within what had by 1936 become the standardized attributes of a Socialist Realist writer.

This drive to frame Lu Xun as a Chinese exemplar of a Soviet-style realism also shaped the translations of his short fiction that appeared in the journal after 1936. *International Literature* published three stories by Lu Xun. In 1937, a translation appeared of "New Year's Sacrifice" ("Zhufu," 1924),[58] followed in 1939 by "Medicine" ("Yao," 1919) and "An Incident" ("Yi jian xiaoshi," 1920).[59] I will focus my comments here on "Medicine," which, like "An Incident," was translated by the Sinologist, translator and diplomat Nikolai Fedorenko.[60] "Medicine" is one of Lu Xun's most famous stories: concise, dark, ambiguous and richly symbolic, it tells the story of two closely connected deaths. The Hua family run a tea shop, and have a single son who has contracted tuberculosis. Old Shuan, his father, arranges to buy a mantou (steamed bun) dipped in human blood, a folk remedy that an unpleasant acquaintance named Kang (the name means "health") has suggested will cure the boy's condition. The human blood comes from an executed prisoner, a young man from the Xia family who seems to have been sentenced to death for advocating the overthrow of the

---

57 E. Siao, "Pamiati velikogo pisatelia Lu Siunia," *Internatsional'naia literatura* 12 (1936): 184–89. The comparison with Gorky appears frequently, for example, in *Lu Sin', 1881–1936: Sbornik statei i perevodov posviashchennyi pamiati velikogo pisatelia sovremennogo Kitaia*, ed. K. I. Muratov (Moscow: Izd-vo akademii nauk SSSR, 1938).

58 Lu Sin', "Blagoslovenie," trans. E. K. [Kalashnikova?], *Internatsional'naia literatura* 10 (1937): 127–36.

59 Lu Sin', "Lekarstvo," "Neznachitel'nyi sluchai," trans. N. Fedorenko, *Internatsional'naia literature* 11 (1939): 80–85.

60 Fedorenko's career included extensive diplomatic work in China, a spell as deputy Minister of Foreign Affairs, and almost two decades as chief editor of the late-Soviet journal *Inostrannaia literatura* (*Foreign Literature*), a successor of sorts to *International Literature*. In 1949–1950 he served as an interpreter for the talks between Mao Zedong and Joseph Stalin that led to the Sino-Soviet Treaty of Friendship in February 1950. See N. T. Fedorenko, "Stalin i Mao Tsedun," pt 1, *Novaia i noveishaia istoriia* 5 (1992): 197–211; pt 2, *Novaia i noveishaia istoriia* 6 (1992): 83–95.

Qing dynasty. Lu Xun shows us the execution from the masterfully estranged perspective of Old Shuan in the first of the story's four sections. (Certain details allude to the execution of the feminist and revolutionary Qiu Jin, a native of Lu Xun's hometown of Xiamen, who was executed in 1907 for attempting to organize an uprising.) The remedy fails, and the story's final section brings together two mothers, Hua and Xia, at the graves of their dead sons. As the mother of the executed revolutionary receives comfort from the mother of the child who ate his blood, they notice a circle of red and white flowers has appeared on the revolutionary's grave. Xia calls out to her dead son, asking him to show he is listening by compelling a crow perched on a desolate tree to fly onto his grave. Nothing happens, and the mothers trudge away together. As they leave, they hear a loud caw, and turn to see the crow fly off into the sky.

Even before its translation in *International Literature*, "Medicine" itself emerged from a particular experience of world literature. Crucially for our purposes, the story shows Lu Xun's debt to the Russian writers whom he read and translated in the earlier stage of his career, *before* his turn to Marxism and Soviet literature in the late 1920s. Specifically, "Medicine" displays the influence of the Russian decadent modernist Leonid Andreev, whose story "Silence" ("Molchanie") Lu Xun translated in 1909.[61] "Silence" begins, like "Medicine," with two parents anxiously discussing their child's health in the dead of night. After their daughter commits suicide, the father, a priest, pays an emotionally charged visit to a desolate graveyard in a futile attempt to commune with his lost child's spirit. Lu Xun himself commented that the ending to "Medicine" "clearly retains the somber chill one associates with Andreev."[62] In other words, "Medicine" points towards the debts that Lu Xun, a writer canonized as a paradigm of Chinese social realism in both the USSR and the PRC, owed to modernist writers less admissible to the Socialist Realist canon. The story shows the early Lu Xun balanced ambivalently between realism and symbolism, a combination that he himself found exemplified in the work of Andreev.[63] This taut

---

61 Lu Xun's translation of "Silence" (默 Mo) appeared in the volume *Collected Stories from Abroad* (*Yuwai xiaoshuo ji*), which Lu Xun published with his brother Zhou Zuoren in Tokyo in 1909. For parallels between the stories see, e.g., Patrick Hanan, *Chinese Fiction of the Nineteenth and Early Twentieth Centuries: Essays* (New York: Columbia University Press, 2004), 222–26.

62 Quoted in Gamsa, *The Chinese Translation of Russian Literature*, 236–37.

63 "Andreev's works contain sober realism as well as depth and subtlety, creating a mutual harmony between symbolic impressionism and realism. <...> Although his writing has a symbolic flavor, it never loses its reality." Lu Xun, "'Andan de yan'ai li' yizhe fuji," in *Lu Xun quanji* (Beijing: Renmin wenxue chubanshe, 2005), vol. 10, 201.

and realistically narrated story teems with enigmatic symbols: the mantou dripping with blood; the red and white flowers whose provenance and significance is unclear; the black crow that obeys the order to fly, but not to the grave. What's more, as Zhang Lihua convincingly demonstrates, the specific relation between "Medicine" and "Silence" reveals how divergent translation practices shaped literary production in early twentieth-century China. Besides Lu Xun's fairly literalist translation of Andreev, Zhang also traces the influence of another, far more liberal Chinese translation by Liu Bannong, which inserted into Andreev's graveyard some red and white flowers and a symbolic bird. These images recur as ambivalent symbols at the close of "Medicine," a story whose genesis cannot be separated from the translation practices that rendered Russian literature available for modern Chinese writers.[64]

Fedorenko's translation of "Medicine" (back) into Russian distinguishes itself above all by the number of times its choices serve to downplay the richly suggestive figurative language of Lu Xun's story, and especially its ghoulish, Andreevian overtones. For example, when Old Shuan sees a crowd of people arriving to observe the execution, Lu Xun's text describes the face of one man as having a greedy look in his eyes, "like a person who hasn't eaten for a long time at the sight of food" (hen xiang jiu'e de ren jianle shiwu yiban).[65] Fedorenko simply omits this whole image, thus losing its premonition of the cannibalistic act of consuming the bloody mantou.[66] When the execution occurs, in an extraordinary image, Lu Xun has the crowd craning their necks "like many ducks pinched and lifted upwards by an invisible hand" (fangfu xuduo ya, bei wuxing de shou nie zhule, xiang shang tizhe).[67] Fedorenko keeps the invisible hand but drops the ducks (slovno ch'ia-to nezrimaia ruka dergala ikh kverkhu).[68] The organic metaphors connected with the mantou, which Shuan intends to "transplant" (yizhi) to his home in order to "reap" (shouhuo) much happiness, also disappear in Fedorenko, thereby sacrificing the connection with the rootless wreath of flowers at the story's end.[69]

Other omissions cut details directly related to the story's core symbolism. For example, when Lu Xun's Little Shuan picks up the mantou and prepares to eat it, he looks at it for a moment, "as if he were holding his own life" (sihu

---

64 Zhang Lihua, " 'Cuoyi' yu chuangzao: Lu Xun 'Yao' zhong 'hongbai de hua' yu 'wuya' de yulai," *Zhongguo xiandai wenxue yanjiu congkan* 1 (2016): 64–78.
65 Lu Xun, "Yao," *Lu Xun quanji*, vol. 1, 464. "很像久饿的人见了食物一般。"
66 Lu Sin', "Lekarstvo," 80.
67 Lu Xun, "Yao," 465.
68 Lu Sin', "Lekarstvo," 80. "仿佛许多鸭，被无形的手捏住了的，向上提着。"
69 Lu Xun, "Yao," 465; Lu Sin', "Lekarstvo," 81.

nazhe ziji de xingming yiban).[70] Fedorenko's Little Shuan has no such moment of reflection on the loaded symbolism of the blood-dipped roll. While Little Shuan eats, the Chinese text has his mother and father standing over him, "their eyes as if trying to pour something into him and draw something out of him" (liang ren de yanguang, dou fangfu yao zai ta shenshang zhu jin shenme you yao quchu shenme side).[71] Fedorenko erases this image, which succinctly expresses the combination of boundless parental love and superstitious attitude towards illness that drives the parent characters. Most strikingly of all, Fedorenko omits the colors of the flowers that appear unexpectedly on the revolutionary's grave: a major omission since their red and white color, beyond any revolutionary associations they may invoke, also combine with the black crow on the branch to parallel the color scheme of the story's central symbol of the mantou (white flour, red blood, blackened when cooked in the oven). Taken together, Fedorenko's omissions and alterations systematically downplay the original story's ambivalence over the presence or absence of supernatural forces, an ambivalence it shares with Andreev's "Silence." Both stories stage the impossibility of communication with the dead alongside an intense desire for such communication, charting the loss of a transcendent world in a literary style still pregnant with its possibility. Such epistemological ambiguities proved too risky for a Soviet realist paradigm suspicious of double meanings. "Medicine" perches its narrative between a world in which social suffering has material, immanent, political explanations, and a world in which coincidences of color and event (the flowers and the bun; the prayer and the sudden departure of the crow) point towards forms of pattern and order that exceed the material. Fedorenko's edits erase this ambivalence, and the corresponding ambiguity of the story's message, leaving a more smoothly realist tale of poverty and political injustice.

Conclusion

One question perhaps remains: the question of readership. Did anyone actually read the Chinese texts in *International Literature*? A recent survey of letters to the editors of *International Literature* finds readers responding in the main to texts by Western authors. One letter writer from 1938, a Bolshevik party

---

70 Lu Xun, "Yao," 466. "似乎拿着自己的性命一般."
71 Ibid. "两人的眼光，都仿佛要在他身上注进什么又要取出什么似的."

186 | Edward Tyerman

member, reports reading "with interest" Xiao Jun's *Village in August*, a classic account of the Japanese occupation of Manchuria published in *International Literature* that year. This correspondent insists that "the war in China, and the national rebirth of the Chinese people, elicit great interest in its literature."[72] At the same time, the letter calls for more translations of the American author Pearl Buck, whose best-selling novel about China, *The Good Earth*, had been excerpted in 1934. *The Good Earth* was ambivalently framed in *International Literature*: an accompanying article by the editor, Tretyakov, praised Buck's realism for escaping the strictures of romantic exoticism, but critiqued her lack of historical specificity and identified the novel's hero, Wang Lung, as a kulak.[73] Nonetheless, Buck's next two novels, *Sons* and *The Mother*, and her 1942 novel *Dragon Seed* were all excerpted in *International Literature*, far exceeding in sheer page numbers any Chinese writer besides Xiao.[74] Reviews and articles about Buck penned by Soviet critics (including Tretyakov and Karl Radek) made the case for the value of her realist writing as a source of knowledge about China despite the limitations of her political perspective.[75] The high level of attention given to Buck's work on the pages of *International Literature* may indicate that many Soviet readers were still receiving their knowledge of China as filtered through Western eyes.

Despite this abiding West-centrism in *International Literature* and among its readers, this chapter contends that the translation of non-Western literatures can shed useful light on our developing understanding of the Soviet project of world literature. From the time of *Vsemirnaia literatura* on, Chinese literature played a central role in debates about how the literatures of the "East" (i.e. the non-West) should be translated in order to introduce them into the common

---

72 Nailya Safiullina, "Window to the West: From the Collection of Readers' Letters to the Journal *Internatsional'naia literature*," *Slavonica* 15, no. 2 (2009): 159.

73 Pearl Buck, "Zemlia (Otryvki iz romana)," *Internatsional'naia literatura* 2 (1934): 34–57; Sergei Tret'iakov, "O 'Zemle' Perl' Bak," *Internatsional'naia literatura* 2 (1934): 99–102. Buck's novel was published in full the same year, with Tretyakov's article as foreword: Pearl Buck, *Zemlia*, trans. N. L. Daruzes (Moscow: Khudozhestvennaia literatura, 1934). On Buck's reception in China see So, *Transpacific Community: America, China, and the Rise and Fall of a Cultural Network* (New York: Columbia University Press, 2016), 41–82.

74 Pearl Buck, "Synov'ia (otryvki iz romana)" trans. N. L. Daruzes, *Internatsional'naia literatura* 5 (1935): 9–52; Pearl Buck, "Mat' (otryvki iz romana)" trans. N. L. Daruzes, *Internatsional'naia literatura* 9 (1935): 3–34; idem, "Dragonovo plemia," trans. N. Daruzes and T. Ozerskaia, *Internatsional'naia literatura* 1 (1943): 27–60.

75 Karl Radek, "Pro Kitai, Iaponiiu i sotsialisticheskii realizm," *Internatsional'naia literatura* 5 (1934): 166–69; Galina Kolesnikova, "Propoved' vozvrashcheniia," *Internatsional'naia literatura* 1 (1936): 120–127; A. Elistratova, "Perl' Bak. Mat'," *Internatsional'naia literatura* 9 (1936): 158–60.

store of world literature available to Soviet readers. By the time of the *Herald of World Literature* and its successors, Alekseev's precisely literal translations of classic poetry had given way to an emphasis on the translatability of modern Chinese literature, overcoming any potential sense of foreignness by producing smooth and legible texts in Russian. Yet the examples of Xiao San and Lu Xun also show that any easy binary of "foreign" and "domestic" had already become unstable. Just as Xiao San's poems betray the influence of Mayakovsky even before his translational collaboration with Romm, so Lu Xun's writing developed in dialogue with Andreev and other Russian modernists. Other Chinese writers published in *International Literature*, such as Mao Dun and Ding Ling, shaped their models of literary realism through close engagement with Russian and Soviet realism.[76] Modern Chinese literature, in other words, already emerged from a particular configuration of world literature, shaped by the cosmopolitan cultural flows that structured Chinese modernity in the early twentieth century. *International Literature's* attempts to position this literature within its own mapping of the literary globe proved both generative and restrictive. The journal revealed to its readers the existing links between Russian/Soviet literature and the Chinese leftist literary world, and even created the revolutionary poet Emi Siao at the point of their intersection. At the same time, it downplayed those aspects of the relationship that could not be aligned with a stylistically smooth and ideologically legible mode of social realism. What we see here, then, is the "translation" of one experience of world literature into the framework of another, a process in which meaning is both lost and created.

---

76 For a reading of the Russian influence in Mao Dun's fiction see Mau-sang Ng, *The Russian Hero in Modern Chinese Fiction* (Hong Kong: Chinese University Press, 1988), 130–79. Keru Cai notes Ding Ling's engagement with Dostoevsky in Cai, "Looking, Reading, and Intertextuality in Ding Ling's "Shafei nüshi de riji" 莎菲女士的日記 (Miss Sophia's Diary)," *Prism: Theory and Modern Chinese Literature* 17, no. 2 (2020): 298–325.

CHAPTER 9

World Literature and Ideology: The Case of Socialist Realism
Schamma Schahadat

Introduction: World Literature in the Soviet Union in 1934

On October 17 in 1934, Maxim Gorky presents a paper at the First All-Union Congress of Soviet Writers in Moscow; the title of the paper is *Sovetskaia literatura*, Soviet Literature. He argues that Soviet literature not only means literature written in Russian, since Soviet literature is an all-Union literature, but that this "Soviet-proletarian literature" also has an international (internatsional'nyi) character.[1] In his article Gorky traces Soviet-proletarian literature back to its roots in antiquity up into the future; its distinctive quality, he argues, lies in the fact that it has always been about material objects and work, in Greek mythology as well as in folklore. In this paper, Gorky rewrites literary history from the perspective of an ideologically correct perspective.

---

1   Maksim Gor'kii, *Sobranie sochinenii v tridtsati tomakh*, t. 27: *Stat'i, doklady, rechi, privetstviia: 1933–1936* (Moskva: Gosudarstvennoe izdatel'stvo khudozhestvennoi literatury, 1953), 324, 325: "советская литература не является только литературой русского языка, это— всесоюзная литература"; "советско-пролетарская художественная литература [. . .] постепенно приобретает интернациональный характер и по своей форме." By using the foreign word "internatsional'nyi" (international) instead of the Russian "mezhdunarodnyi" (literally meaning: between the peoples) that is normally used, Gorky evokes the Communist International. – A larger version of my paper has been published in German in the book *Weltliteratur in der longue durée*, ed. Schamma Schahadat & Annette Werberger Munich: Fink, 2021.

These arguments imply a specific understanding of literature. Gorky in his speech differentiates between bourgeois literature on the one hand and "proletarian Soviet literature" on the other, which means that he looks at literature through an ideological lens. The "international character" evokes not only the Communist International, the Comintern, but also wants literature to mirror the multinational Soviet Union, transgressing cultural and linguistic borders. The official term for literature produced in this multinational Soviet Union was "multinational Soviet literature," "mnogonatsional'naia sovetskaia literatura."[2]

Gorky is not the only one at the Writers' Congress who rescripts the literary history from a perspective of a correct socialist / proletarian / Soviet point of view in order to define a Soviet centered world literature. The papers presented at the Congress define what literature has to look like in the future, but they also recapitulate the past in order to establish a literary canon that leads up to 'correct' literature. Similarly to Gorky, Karl Radek, a politician and writer born in Galicia who lived between Germany and the Soviet Union, rewrites literary history. However, while Gorky chooses the concept of "Soviet literature" as a starting point, Radek broadens the literary space by moving from "proletarian" or "socialist" literature (two terms that he uses interchangeably) to the idea of "world literature." His paper is on "modern world literature and the tasks of proletarian art ("Современная мировая литература и задачи пролетарского искусства"). The aim of both papers, Gorky's and Radek's, is similar, however, they choose different paths: Gorky focuses on (proletarian) Soviet literature and follows its development from antiquity into the present, while Karl Radek's literary history of a "proletarian world literature" begins with World War I and is the reaction to and the opposite of a "bourgeois world literature." Radek connects the development of world literature with the fight against capitalism; for him the decline of "bourgeois world literature" and of capitalism are parallel processes where history and literature mirror each other.[3] Both, however, Gorky

---

2   See Georgii Lomidze's works on multinational literature "Metodologicheskie voprosy izucheniia vzaimosviazei i vzaimoobogashcheniia sovetskikh literatur," in *Puti razvitiia sovetskoi mnogonatsional'noi literatury*, ed. Georgii Lomidze (Moscow: Nauka, 1967), 5–41. Starting with a formulaic beginning that the October Revolution woke "productive national powers" and the "gigantic power of the peoples" ("Октябрьская революция разбудила все плодотворные национальные силы. Пришла в движение гигантская творческая энергия народов," 5), Lomidze describes his work on the history of multinational Soviet literature (Istoriia sovetskoi mnogonatsional'noi literatury, 6 vols. [Moscow: Nauka, 1971–1974]).

3   Karl Radek, "Doklad Karla Radeka 'sovremennaia mirovaia literatura i zadachi proletarskogo iskusstva', in *Pervyi vsesoiuznyi s"ezd sovetskikh pisatelei, 1934: Stenograficheskii otchet*, ed. Ivan K. Luppol (Moskva: Sovetskii pisatel', 1990), 291–318.

and Radek, perceive literary history from a new angle in order to tell a success story, a story of progress that mirrors the advancement of the proletariat.

The notion of "world literature" in this politicized context in 1934 acquires a completely different dimension from its original meaning when Goethe coined the term at the beginning of the 19th century. Still, one could argue that Karl Marx is the link between Goethe on the one side and Gorky and Radek on the other side: while Goethe substituted the concept of national literatures with the idea of world literature,[4] focusing on the interaction between various (national) literatures,[5] Karl Marx further develops Goethe's idea of the literary market as a market of goods,[6] redefining, as Marx writes in *Wage-Labour and Capital* (*Lohnarbeit und Kapital*) "so called 'higher' forms of labour—intellectual, artistic etc.—as 'commodities.'"[7] In the *Communist Manifesto* Marx understands literary texts as "products of the bourgeois state of production and ownership" ("Erzeugnisse der bürgerlichen Produktions- und Eigentumsverhältnisse")[8]— to these "products" Gorky later refers to as "bourgeois literature." For Gorky proletarian literature is the positive alternative to bourgeois literature, a literature that exists only in the Soviet Union.

However, Gorky's idea of an international Soviet proletarian literature, or alternatively of an all-Union literature (vsesoiuznaia literatura), shows striking parallels to Goethe's remarks on world literature. For both of them, literature transcends the concept of a nation, it is international, and for both of them literature has a political function: in *On Art and Antiquity* (*Über Kunst und Altertum*), Goethe writes that world literature will make nations pay attention to their neighbours; even if they do not love one another, they can accept one

---

4   "National literature does not mean much today, we are now in the era of world literature" ("Nationalliteratur will jetzt nicht viel sagen, die Epoche der Weltliteratur ist an der Zeit"), Eckermann records Goethe: J. W. von Goethe, "Goethes wichtigste Äußerungen zur Weltliteratur," in *Goethes Werke Bd. XXII* (Hamburg: Christian Wegner Verlag, 1953), 362.

5   See also Hendrik Birus, "Goethes Idee der Weltliteratur. Eine historische Vergegenwärtigung," in *Weltliteratur heute. Konzepte und Perspektiven*, ed. Manfred Schmeling (Würzburg: Königshausen & Neumann, 1995), 11; Goethe speaks about a "general free reciprocal interaction" ("allgemeine freie Wechselwirkung," Johann Wolfgang von Goethe, "Schriften zur Kunst 1800–1816. Kunstausstellungen und Preisausgaben," in *Werke* [Weimarer Ausgabe], vol. 1 (München: Böhlau, 1897), 48, 23.

6   Goethe, "Goethes wichtigste Äußerungen," 362.

7   Siegbert Salomon Prawer, *Karl Marx and World Literature*. Oxford: Clarendon Press, 197,6 here quotes Karl Marx' "Arbeitslohn. Aus dem handschriftlichen Nachlaß," in *Marx Engels Werke*, vol. 6 (Berlin: Karl Dietz Verlag, 1961), 555–56.

8   Karl Marx and Friedrich Engels, "Das Manifest der Kommunistischen Partei," in *Marx Engels Werke*, vol. 4 (Berlin: Karl Dietz Verlag, 1959), 477; Prawer, "Karl Marx und die Weltliteratur," 121.

another.[9] The knowledge of the literature of the other will, so Goethe argues, bring peace. Gorky's perspective, on the other hand, is an educational one: in 1919 he initiated the founding of the publishing house Vsemirnaia literatura, World Literature, that planned to publish important literary works from the 18th century up to the present in order to teach the reader about various literary schools, about the influence of literatures of different nations on each other and about the "literary evolution in its historical development."[10] An educational purpose can also be observed in Goethe's scattered remarks about world literature; his aim is to present the literatures of the world to a cultural elite, hoping that peace among the peoples will be a welcome side effect. Gorky's projected audience for his educational project via literature are the Soviet masses. Gorky as well as Radek emphasize that literature must educate, but their understanding of education via literature is less focused on the intellect than on emotions. In their papers both authors use a rhetoric of emotions, they speak about love and passion: "We will breathe the soul of the proletariat into this literature, its passion and its love, and it will be a literature of big images, big comforts [...] a literature of the victory of international socialism," Radek writes.[11] This bird's eye perspective on world literature *á la longue durée*, ranging from Goethe in classicist Weimar of the 1820s and 30s to Gorky in Stalinist Moscow in 1934, sheds light on a much neglected period and space of the debate on world literature which is usually not taken into account: the historical and geographically limited discussion about world literature in the Soviet Union in the 1930s. Gorky's and Radek's conceptions of world literature—*vsemirnaia literatura* or *mirovaia literatura*—in the Soviet context are part of a project of unification of literature in regard to the aesthetics of Socialist Realism, providing the literature of the future with a history in the past. Their invention of Soviet World Literature aims at a political goal, to Sovieticize the reader and to create the new Soviet man (and woman). The current debate on world literature from the Western point of view (also called "world's literature" [Dorothee Kimmich], "New World Literature" [Elke Sturm-Trigonakis] or "Global Literature" [Evi Zemanek/Alexander Nebrig]) has so far neglected the Eastern European perspective and focuses only on the globalized West, including the Angloamerican,

---

9 Goethe, "Goethes wichtigste Äußerungen zur Weltliteratur," 363.
10 See "Vsemirnaia literatura," *Literaturnaia entsiklopediia*, accessed March 23rd, 2020, http://www.endic.ru/enc_lit/Vsemirnaja-literatura-1167.html.
11 Radek, "Doklad Karla Radeka," 318: "В эту литературу мы вложим душу пролетариата–его страсть и его любовь, и это будет литература великих картин, великих утешений [. . .] литература победы межнародного социализма."

French, Spanish and German literatures as well as the postimperial literatures from the peripheries, which migrate in this global space, dislocating languages and cultures. When we shift the focus from those Western concepts to the Soviet debate of the 1930s, we can observe a globalization *á la soviétique*, a *république mondiale des lettres* (Pascale Casanova), whose center is not Paris, but Moscow as a political center that prescribes how to write (world) literature from a Soviet, proletarian, socialist perspective. World literature in its Soviet version was explicitly and decidedly political. The market, which is a central mechanism in Goethe's and Marx's concept, as well as the value are not literary in the case of the socialist-Soviet-proletarian concept of world literature, but normative. The literary text acquires its value not in regard to its aesthetic relevance or its market values, but because of its political and its educational impact, transforming literature into a product for the masses and educating these masses. The Soviet literary market functioned according to a "hierarchy of education":[12] the party educated the critics, the critics educated the writers, and the writers educated the readers.

In my article, I will, first, delineate the context of the speeches in which Gorky and Radek envisage a new, proletarian-socialist-Soviet world literature: the first all-union congress of Soviet writers as well as Soviet national politics, which was closely intertwined with this huge literary event. I will then go into the speeches in more detail, focusing on the question how they rewrite the literary history of the past in order to design a world literature of the future.

The Context: The First All-Union Congress of Soviet Writers and Soviet National Politics

The first all-union congress of Soviet writers took place in Moscow from August 7 to September 1, 1934. The congress can be discussed from—at least—two points of view. On the one hand, it was a kind of laboratory which allows us to observe the genesis of a cultural program governed by ideological and political ideas. At this congress the aesthetics of Socialist Realism was proclaimed as the only valid art form. On the other hand, the congress mirrored Soviet national politics; it was an event that not only invited writers from all republics and from abroad, but the discourse on Soviet multinational literature was opened. Speeches proclaimed the

---

12 Khans Giunter (Hans Günther), "Zhiznennye fazy sotsrealisticheskogo kanona," in *Sotsrealisticheskii kanon* ed. Khans Giunter and Evgenii Dobrenko (Moscow: Akademicheskii proekt, 2000), 285.

194 | Schamma Schahadat

multinational character of the Soviet Union which was to be realized in a Soviet multinational literature, or even better: a socialist/proletarian world literature. Also, the formation of a multinational program of reading was closely connected with the formation of the Soviet reader who was supposed to represent the new Soviet man.[13] Since the mid-1920s, official efforts had tried to unify the cultures in the Soviet Union, and the congress had been planned since 1932 as the final unifying act. There, the different, often inimical literary groups were to be unified under the leadership of the party.[14] These plans were in accordance with the party decree "On the restructuring of the literary-artistic organizations" ("O perestroike literaturno-khudozhestvennykh organizatsii") of April 23rd, 1932, which demanded that "all writers who support the platform of the Soviet power and want to take part in the building of socialism shall be united in a single union of writers."[15]

While the Writers' Congress was planned, first ideas about Socialist Realism were being developed,[16] based on statements by Lenin about a "process of canonization" in the field of literature.[17] The normative aesthetics of Socialist Realism was attached to several ideological premises: *partiinost'* (party-mindedness), *otrazhenie* (imitation), *tipichnost'* (the typical), *revoliucionnyi romantizm* (revolutionary romanticism that would change reality) and *narodnost'* (written for the people, as opposed to a complicated aesthetic "formalism"). The first Congress of Writers declared Socialist Realism as obligatory in all fields of art in order to provide an "authentic, historic correct presentation of reality in its revolutionary development."[18] Socialist Realism defines itself in opposition to

---

13 Evgenii Dobrenko, *Formovka sovetskogo chitatelia. Sotsial'nye i ésteticheskie predposylki retseptsii sovetskoi literatury* (Sankt-Peterburg: Akademicheskii proekt, 1997), 11. However, Dobrenko is interested in the formation of the Soviet reader as the new man, not in multinational literature.

14 Aleksandr Beliaev, "Liricheskii porokh reshili derzhat' sukhim Pervomu s"ezdu pisatelei 70 let," *Rossiiskaia gazeta*, August 17, 2004, accessed March 23, 2020, https://rg.ru/2004/08/17/a35614.html. Beliaev sees first ideas for an ideologically controlled, unified Writers' Union already in Evgenii Zamiatin's *My* (*We*), since in the "Single State" in the novel is already an "Institute for State Poets and Writers."

15 "Soiuz pisatelei SSSR (SP SSSR)," *Kratkaia literaturnaia entsiklopediia* (KLE), accessed March 23, 2020, http://feb-web.ru/feb/kle/kle-abc/ke7/ke7-1101.htm: „объединить всех писателей, поддерживающих платформу Советской власти и стремящихся участвовать в социалистическом строительстве, в единый союз советских писателей."

16 In my description of Socialist Realism I follow Hans Günther, *Die Verstaatlichung der Literatur. Entstehung und Funktionsweise des sozialistisch-realistischen Kanons in der sowjetischen Literatur der 30er Jahre* (Stuttgart: Metzler 1984), 1–54.

17 Günther, *Die Verstaatlichung der Literatur*, 6.

18 Definition of the first statutes of the Soviet Writers' Union, citing Wolfgang Kasack, "Sozialistischer Realismus," in *Lexikon der russischen Literatur ab 1917*, ed. Wolfgang Kasack (Stuttgart: Kröner, 1976), 380.

bourgeois literature. In his speech on "Soviet Literature, the most original und progressive literature in the world" ("Sovetskaia literatura—samaia ideinaia, samaia peredovaia literatura v mire"), Andrei Zhdanov says:

> Contemporary bourgeois literature today can no longer produce great works. [...] Bourgeois literature is characterized by its decline and corrosion which is the effect of the decline and the rot of the capitalist system.[19]

Zhdanov draws a direct connection between literature and society, assigning literature the function to revive the new society.

At the writers' congress, the speakers talk about bourgeois Western and Russian literature, about proletarian literature and also about the literatures of the non-Russian peoples, which are covered by the term "Soviet literature." The explicit project of the congress was to create a multinational (Soviet) literature; the approach to multinational literature was in accordance with the approach to the nationalities in the Soviet Union. Terry Martin calls the Soviet Union "the world's first Affirmative Action Empire;"[20] very soon after the revolution, in various decrees, Lenin had propagated the care of national cultures ("nasazhdat' natsional'nuiu kul'turu") in order to heighten the "backward" peoples to the level of an "all-human culture" ("obshchechelovecheskaia kul'tura").[21]

Soviet management of national politics was directed against the imperial politics of the Russian Empire right from the start.[22] Fifteen republics and smaller national territorial entities were established, national elites were educated and the according national language was declared to be the official

---

19 „Современное состояние буржуазной литературы таково, что она уже не может создать великих произведений [...] Упадок и разложение буржуазной литературы, вытекающие из упадка и загнивания капиталистического строя, представляют собой характерную черту." Andrei A. Zhdanov, "Rech' sekretaria TsK VKP(b) A. A. Zhdanova," in *Pervyi vsesoiuznyi s'ezd sovetskikh pisatelei, 1934: Stenograficheskii otchet* (Moskva: Sovetskii pisatel', 1990), 3.

20 Terry Martin, *The Affirmative Action Empire. Nations and Nationalism in the Soviet Union, 1923–1939* (Ithaca/London: Cornell University Press, 2001), 1.

21 Semen Dimanshtein, "Sovetskaia vlast' i melkie natsional'nosti," *Zhizn' natsional'nostei* 21, no. 29 (June 8, 1919); quoted in: Yuri Slezkine, "The USSR as a Communal Apartment, or How a Socialist State Promoted Ethnic Particularism," *Slavic Review* 53, no. 2 (Summer 1994), 420. Slezkine quotes (in English): "We are going to help you develop your Buriat, Votiak, etc. language and culture, because in this way you will join the universal culture [*obshchechelovecheskaia kul'tura*], revolution and communism sooner."

22 Martin, *Affirmative Action Empire*, 6–8.

language.[23] At the same time, national politics was based on a paradox since it was considered to be a relic of bourgeois societies on the one hand, on the other, the various peoples were to be strengthened in their autonomy. The idea was to grant national independence in the beginning, believing that in the course of history nationalism would abolish itself.[24] In 1923 two decrees were published that "affirmed that the Soviet state would maximally support these 'forms' of nationhood that did not conflict with a unitary central state."[25] Indigenization ("korenizatsiia") was the most urgent problem in national politics.[26]

Sovietness as a supranational concept encompassed all nationalities, which is important for Gorky's concept of "Soviet literature." In the 1930s, at the time of the writers' congress, the process of indigenization was retracted and the status of Russianness and Russian as an ethnic concept was advanced.[27] These processes did not only lead to the nation building of the Russian Soviet Federative Socialist Republic (RSFSR), but also to the special roles of Russian and Russianness as a unifying force of the Soviet Union.[28] In 1935 Stalin pronounced the slogan of the "friendship of the peoples" ("druzhba narodov"), which became part of the rhetoric of Soviet national politics and was enforced at festivals of friendship and other cultural events.[29]

So much for the context of the Writers' Congress in 1934. While official national politics supported the strengthening of the different languages and cultures—even if the predominance of Russianness became more and more

---

23 Martin, *Affirmative Action Empire*, 1.

24 Martin, *Affirmative Action Empire*, 3.

25 Martin, *Affirmative Action Empire*, 9–10.

26 Martin, *Affirmative Action Empire*, 12. The official politics of nationalization was accompanied by ethnography, not only in the form of ethnographic excursions, but also through the presentation of indigenous peoples. However, between 1923 and the 1930s this presentation in talks and expositions changed; Francine Hiersch describes a shift from the exotization to modernization of the peoples. This means that in 1923 an exhibition would focus on the exotic bodies, clothes and customs of the indigenous peoples, while in the 1930s they were perceived as cultures on their way to modernization, but still in need of help in order to overcome their traditional customs and habits. Francine Hirsch, *Empire of Nations. Ethnographic Knowledge and the Making of the Soviet Union* (Ithaca/London: Cornell University Press, 2005), 187–188.

27 Compared to other nationalities, in the first decade of the Soviet Union, Russian was not considered a nationality; being Russian, like being Soviet, was without national content. In the 1930s, however, at the time of the Writers' Congress, Russian would become a nationality and, at the same time, understood as a unifying force for Sovietness. Slezkine writes: "The USSR was like Russia insofar as both represented pure 'socialist content' completely devoid of 'national form," Yuri Slezkine, "The USSR as Communal Apartment," 435.

28 Martin, *Affirmative Action Empire*, 394.

29 Martin, *Affirmative Action Empire*, 439–40.

obvious, —the Writers' Congress presented itself as a show of the multinational Soviet Union with its various nationalities. 597 delegates were present at the congress, only 3.7 % of which were women. Of those delegates, 201 were Russians, 113 Jews, 28 Georgians, 25 Ukrainians, 19 Armenians and so on.[30] About 40 participants came from abroad, e.g., Louis Aragon, Johannes R. Becher and Martin Andersen Nexø.[31] In the context of so many different nationalities, Maxim Gorky's already mentioned speech on "Soviet Literature" played a central role. In a short opening statement, Gorky stressed the fact that the Soviet writers of various cultural and ethnic origin and with their different languages nonetheless presented a homogeneous whole.[32]

The Speeches: (World) Literature of the Future and of the Past

While designing the rules for future Soviet literature, the speakers at the congress also recapitulated the past and conceptualized the literature of the past as already being a proletarian and / or socialist world literature. Especially the two speeches by Gorky and Radek rewrote literary history from a Soviet point of view. While Gorky gave a broad overview of literary history from the Greek classics to the beginning of Soviet literature, disregarding national contexts, Radek focused on post-revolutionary times.

In order to understand what the Soviet concept of world literature means, one should look into its different semantic dimensions. Thomas Geider, a specialist for African studies, subdivided the concept of world literature into three possible semantic fields: first, world literature as an "accumulation" of all the literature produced in the world,[33] second, world literature as a "selection"

---

30 Beliaev, "Liricheskii porokh."
31 "S"ezdy pisatelei SSSR, vsesoiuznye," *Kratkaia literaturnaia entsiklopediia* (KLE), accessed March 23, 2020, http://feb-web.ru/feb/kle/kle-abc/ke7/ke7-2882.htm.
32 Maksim Gor'kii, "Vstupitel'naia rech' na otkrytii pervogo vsesoiuznogo s"ezda sovetskikh pisatelei 17 avgusta 1934 goda," in *Sobranie sochinenii v tridtsati tomakh*, vol. 27: *Stat'i, doklady, rechi, privetstviia 1933–1936* (Moskva: Gosudarstvennoe izdatel'stvo khudozhestvennoi literatury, 1953), 296. Already before the congress the *Pravda, Izvestiia* and the *Literaturnaia gazeta* reported about the congress; during the congress there were daily reports. See Diether Götz, *Analyse und Bewertung des I. Allunions-Kongresses der Sowjetschriftsteller in Literaturwissenschaft und Publizistik sozialistischer und westlicher Länder (von 1934 bis zum Ende der 60er Jahre)* (München: Sagner, 1989), 48–88.
33 Thomas Geider, "Weltliteratur in einer Perspektive der Longue durée II: Die Ökumene des Swahili-sprachigen Ostafrika," in *Wider den Kulturzwang. Migration, Kulturalisierung und Weltliteratur*, ed. Özkan Ezli et al. (Bielefeld: transcript Verlag, 2009), 365.

of literary masterpieces[34] and third, world literature as the "communication" between different national literatures. To begin with, Gorky and Radek speak of world literature as an accumulation of texts, meaning that it encompasses literature(s) from all over the world. In the course of their speeches, however, they increasingly focus on the selection of a certain literature: a literature that is ideologically fitting to be Soviet world literature.

Cultural history (including literature) should be written by Marxists, Gorky states, since the bourgeoisie has always overestimated its role in culture, especially in literature and painting—the bourgeoisie, it seems, has an ideologically distorted point of view.[35] This implies that a correct reading of literature is necessarily an ideological, Soviet reading. In his rerun of 2000 years of literary history, Gorky sees the process of labour as the central force of culture: the working man in Gorky's cultural history inspired the poets of antiquity, which means that labour has always been the basis of culture.[36] In order to prove his point, Gorky reinterprets Greek mythology as a series of class struggles. The Greek gods, Gorky states, were not abstract concepts but social heroes, each of them equipped with a working tool.[37]

Literary history—and this is Gorky's second insight—shows the increasing power of the "malen'kii chelovek" (little man) in history, who for Gorky is a hero born out of folklore, of a literature that has its origin in the people. "The fools were cleverer than their masters," or as Gorky puts it: "the 'fools' of folklore were transformed into Sancho Panza, Simplicissimus and Ulenspiegel and became cleverer than the feudal class."[38] The people's oral creations teach us the true history of the working class; this oral literature in turn influenced high literature such as for example Goethe, Rabelais or Shelley.[39] Real literature, i.e., Soviet literature, has its origin in people's folklore.

Gorky's third point touches upon the aesthetics of socialist literature: literature, he argues, is not mimesis but creation. This argument contains the core of Socialist Realism, the oxymoron which forces together two concepts that exclude each other: socialism and realism. Gorky defines realism as "extracting

---

34 Geider, "Weltliteratur," 366.

35 Gor'kii, "Sovetskaia literatura," 302–303.

36 Ibid., 301.

37 Ibid.

38 Gor'kii, "Sovetskaia literatura," 311: "Наступил момент, когда 'дураки' фольклора, превратясь в Санчо Пансу, Симплициссимуса, Уленшпигеля, стали умнее феодалов."

39 Ibid.: "Подлинную историю трудового народа нельзя знать, не зная устного народного творчества."

from the whole of facts the central idea and embodying it in a figure."[40] The opposite of realism for Gorky is romanticism, where a wish is added to the facts.[41] This, actually, very well describes the functioning of Socialist Realism: it presents what you wish. This oxymoron is already present in Gorky's concept of "revolutionary romanticism" which he developed in the 1920s.[42]

Gorky does not use the word "world literature," since for him "Soviet literature" is a supranational literature, similar to what could be world literature.[43] In accordance with the party line, he demands that the national minorities ("natsmen'shinstva") should not be ignored:

> If in our past we had the giant Pushkin, that does not mean that the Armenians, the Georgians, the Tatars, the Ukrainians and the other tribes are not able to have their great masters of literature, of music, painting or architecture.[44]

Radek, on the other hand, places the notion of "world literature" at the center of his speech that encompasses more than 70 pages. Radek repeats the same arguments and ideas over and over again, making his talk sound like a kind of incantation, words conjuring up a reality that is not yet there. In his approach to world literature, Radek measures it according to its reaction to world history. He subdivides world literature into two sections, differentiating between bourgeois and proletarian/revolutionary world literature. Bourgeois literature, he argues, showed (from a proletarian point of view) a wrong reaction to the events of world history: for instance, literature should have been the voice of protest in a fight against world imperialism. This, however, has not happened, instead, it turned into a voice of imperialism in favour of war, weakening the powers of the proletarians.[45] In eight chapters, from WWI up to "James Joyce or

---

40 Gor'kii, "Sovetskaia literatura," 312: "извлечь из суммы реально данного основной его смысл и воплотить в образ."

41 Ibid.

42 On Gorky's "revolutionary romanticism" see Günther, *Verstaatlichung*, 37.

43 Gor'kii, "Sovetskaia literatura," 324: "Далее, я считаю необходимым указать, что советская литература не является только литературой русского языка, этовсесоюзная литература" ("Further, I see it as necessary to show that Soviet literature is not only literature in the Russian language, it is an all-Union literature.").

44 Gor'kii, "Sovetskaia literatura," 324: "Если у нас в прошлом–гигант Пушкин, отсюда еще не значит, что армяне, грузины, татары, украинцы и прочие племена не способны дать величайших мастеров литературы, музыки, живописи, зодчества."

45 Radek, "Doklad Karla Radeka," 294: "Она не стала голосом протеста и голосом борьбы против мирового империализма,–она стала средством восхваления войны или

Socialist Realism,"[46] Radek describes the "wrong" reactions of bourgeois world literature to history and contrasts it to the "correct" reactions of proletarian world literature:

> Bourgeois literature worships the juggernaut of the war. The literature of the proletariat must present the masses with the picture of the very difficult machinery of murders and destruction that made modern capitalism possible [...] Proletarian literature finds itself before the task to show the people's mass protest, their desire for fighting and it also has to show these masses a way out of the war that the Soviet proletariat already found, overthrowing the bourgeoisie and founding the proletarian republic.[47]

Radek thus de-aestheticizes literature and takes up a tendency that was already typical for early Russian realism,[48] which also understood mimesis to be the basic principle of art. Radek's speech is a good example for the educational impetus of literature and its proponents: the politician/journalist Karl Radek explains to the writers how to educate the masses. A literature that depicts the heroic actions of the Soviet proletariat is at the same time "proletarian" and "Soviet." Both adjectives imply a supranational but class-oriented (proletarian) idea of world history and world literature. And if world revolution has to wait, world literature is already prepared to spread all over the world.

While bourgeois world literature is in decline due to its lost connection to history and reality, Radek argues, proletarian world literature is in the process of producing a new world literature, collecting the ruins of the old world literature and reshaping it. For Radek, the development of literary history follows "the

---

усыпления боевой готовности пролетариата." ([Bourgeois literature] did not become the voice of protest and the voice of the fight against world imperialism,—it became a means of praising the war or soothing the proletariat's will to fight.)

46 Radek, "Doklad Karla Radeka," 315 ff.

47 Radek, "Doklad Karla Radeka," 295: "Литература буржуазии стала на колени перед молохом войны. Литература пролетариата должна дать народным массам картину сложнейшего механизма убийств, разрушения, который создал современный капитализм . . . Перед пролетарской литературой стоит задача отобразить протест народных масс, их стремление к борьбе и показать им тот выход из войны, который советский пролетариат нашел, опрокинув власть буржуазии и создав пролетарскую республику."

48 See Renate Lachmann, *Die Zerstörung der schönen Rede* (München: Fink, 1994), 284–305.

logic of an inner law" (vnutrenniaia zakonomernost'),[49] a seemingly 'scientific' development of literature, that on the one hand aims to reproduce reality and on the other follows didactic goals. As an example for didactic literature Radek mentions Mikhail Sholokhov, the author of *Quiet Flows the Don (Tikhii Don)*, a novel that from 1928 on was published in the journal *October (Oktiabr')* serially, telling the history of the Cossacks during WWI, the Bolshevik Revolution and the civil war. It was the reading of this novel, Radek argues, that made unsatisfied people understand that the "serious, hard, drastic measures [...] were absolutely necessary for the building of socialism"—meaning the forceful dekulakization at the end of the 1920s.[50]

Drawing on writers from the whole world (from Russia, Europe, America and Japan), one could, following Radek, design a family tree of proletarian and Soviet literature, similar to the tree that Franco Moretti devised for writing literary history. With the help of family trees, Moretti shows how literature has developed from a homogeneous origin to heterogeneous texts and genres. In his literary trees Moretti goes back to Darwin:

> For Darwin, 'divergence of character' interacts throughout history with 'natural selection and extinction': as variations grow apart from each other, selection intervenes, allowing only a few to survive.[51]

Radek describes the development from the other end: many different literatures in different parts of the world show enough similarities to be called proletarian literature, thus moving from heterogeneity to homogeneity. While these proletarian literatures treat the same topics (e.g., class struggles), they have not yet found a convincing artistic method.[52] This method is Socialist Realism that will bring together the various proletarian literatures of the world.[53] A graphic depiction of Radek's argument would look like this:

---

49 Radek, "Doklad Karla Radeka," 306.

50 Radek, "Doklad Karla Radeka," 307: "Через такое сочинение, они поняли необходимость тех крутых, твердых, жестоких мер, которые нужно было проводить для строительства социализма."

51 Franco Moretti, *Graphs, Maps, Trees. Abstract Models for Literary History* (London/New York: Verso 2005), 70–72.

52 Radek, "Doklad Karla Radeka," 310: "[пролетарская литература] не овладела еще полностью формой" ([proletarian literature] has not yet completely mastered form).

53 Radek, "Doklad Karla Radeka," 316.

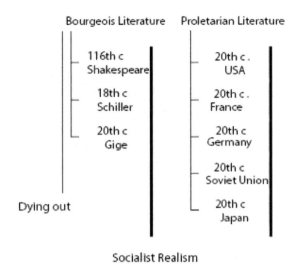

Fig. 1. Graph of World Literature, as Radek sees it–inspired by Franco Moretti

The writers' congress was a politically important event, because here the Soviet management of national politics was exhibited: The (proletarian, revolutionary, Soviet) writers from Europe and from the Soviet republics, who participated in the congress, together created the (world) literature of the future. At the same time this congress continued in the tradition of the logo- and grammatocentrism of Russian culture; literature played a major role in the building of the new socialist society and the new man. The idea that the word is dangerous because it creates the world leads, consequently, to a restrictive control of the word. Establishing Socialist Realism as the only form of literary or even artistic creation in general is based on the belief that the correct literature (the correct word) will create a correct society. Boris Groys defines Socialist Realist mimesis as a mimesis that concentrates on that which is to be created, not that which already exists;[54] it devises an ideologically saturated reality where one sees what one should see, not that what is; it is a poetics of "nonbeing,"[55] thus transforming the word into a substitute for a radiant future.

Only within the context of a logocentric culture it becomes clear why the burden to bring about world revolution can be carried by the writers, as Zhdanov states:

---

54 Boris Groys, *Gesamtkunstwerk Stalin. Die gespaltene Kultur in der Sowjetunion* (München: Hanser, 1988), 58.
55 Groys, *Gesamtkunstwerk Stalin*, 57–64.

We firmly believe that the few foreign comrades who are here with us are the core and the cell of a powerful army of proletarian writers who will create the proletarian world revolution abroad.[56]

Gorky's and Radek's retelling of literary history as a history of the (bourgeois and socialist/proletarian) literatures of the world are foundation narratives of Socialist Realism, narratives that create and legitimize the formation of a new, ideological literature—while proletarian literature has always existed, it finally finds its form in Socialist Realism. Already the Greek gods, Gorky argues, have been laborers, and already Shakespeare and Schiller have written about class struggles. The Russian revolution was the last impulse in the course of this development, awakening "huge masses for a new cultural life."[57]

Yet, what does this awakening look like? How can a country be culturally awakened in which sixty percent of the population before WWI was not able to read?[58] Literature must educate, Gorky and Radek state, but this education is more an emotional than an intellectual one. The speeches at the first Soviet Writers Congress are emotionally filled, they speak of love, passion and the "deepness of the souls" to be reached. The aestheticism of Socialist Realism is based on affects, its goal is to educate, as Radek says, "not only a small circle of writers, but millions of people, that means all readers of Soviet literature"[59]— and that means: millions of people all over the world. The reader plays an important role in this scenario, since the formation of the Soviet (or, if you take

---

56 Zhdanov, "Rech' sekretariia," 4: *"Мы твердо верим в то, что те несколько иностранных товарищей, которые присутствуют здесь, являются ядром и зачатком могучей армии пролетарских писателей, которую создаст мировая пролетарская революция в зарубежных странах"* [italics in the original].

57 Radek, "Doklad Karla Radeka," 308: "Революция поднимает громадные массы к новой культурной жизни."

58 "Literacy rates rose from 21 percent of the population of the Russian Empire in 1897, according to the census of that year, to an estimated 40 percent on the eve of World War I.," Jeffrey Brooks writes: *When Russia learned to read* (Princeton: Northwestern University Press, 1985), 4. The dates provided by the all-Russian census in 1897 show that at this point 21.1 percent of the population were taught to read and write. However, the measures to fight against analphabetism started only later, and the big change in alphabetization started after 1905. In 1920 already 61 percent of the population that was 14 years old could read and write. See Manfred Hildermeier, *Geschichte Russlands vom Mittelalter bis zur Oktoberrevolution* (München: C.H. Beck, 2013), 1259–1260.

59 Radek, "Doklad Karla Radeka," 309: "дело идет о поднятии до уровня лучших образцов старой культуры не маленькой группы писателей, а миллионов масс, которые являются читателями советской литературы" ("We are not talking about a small group of writers that we want to lift up to the level of the best examples of the old culture, but about millions of the masses who are the readers of Soviet literature").

the whole world: the socialist) reader goes hand in hand with the formation of the new man. Writers are seen as "engineers of the human soul" and have to act as builders of these readers, of the new man.[60] Emotion was the way to get to these readers. Radek writes:

> Hundreds of great writers in the world find this way. They find it by making a number of mistakes [...] under one condition: [...] if those writers are connected to the masses of the people, if the great tragedy which mankind is experiencing at the moment, the tragedy of the demise of a social order and the joy about the genesis of another order, if it finds its way to their brains through their hearts [...].[61]

World literature and international socialism go hand in hand in the Socialist Realistic aesthetics as its founders imagine it, and the literature as well as the ideology need an emotional commitment: of love, of passion, of the heart. The idea of an emotional infection[62] has its origin in Leo Tolstoy's treatise *What is Art?* (*Chto takoe iskusstvo?*), where Tolstoy describes the effect of art as an "emotional infection." In Tolstoy's model art creates an emotional community of readers.[63]

In order to reach this goal, several institutions were founded in the Soviet Union, for example Gorky's already mentioned publishing house World

---

60 Dobrenko, *Formovka sovetskogo chitatelia*; Frank Westermann, *Ingenieure der Seele. Schriftsteller unter Stalin—eine Erkundungsreise* (Berlin: C.H. Links Verlag, 2003). The beginnings of this emotional rhetoric lie in an early text by Maxim Gorky, in his essay *About how I learned to write* (*O tom, kak ia uchilsia pisat'*) from 1928. Here Gorky describes how he first turned into a reader and, in a next step, into a writer. This essay is interesting in the context of world literature, since Gorky here anticipates the charged emotionality of Socialist Realism; however, he himself learned how to write with the help of French (bourgeois) literature, not Russian literature.

61 Radek, "Doklad Karla Radeka," 313: "Его [путь] найдут сотни крупных мировых писателей. Они найдут его, пройдя через ряд ошибок [...] при одном основном условии: [...] если эти писатели связаны с народными массами, если большая трагедия, которую сейчас переживает человечество, трагедия гибели одного строя и радость рождения другого строя, доходит до их мозгов через сердце."

62 Infection is not mentioned here, but it is a central concept in Socialist Realism, see Schamma Schahadat, "Stars–Personen–Kult. Der Filmstar als Band zwischen Masse und Macht," in *Morphologie–Mündlichkeit–Medien: Festschrift für Jochen Raecke,* ed. Tilman Berger et al. (Hamburg: Verlag Dr. Kovač, 2008), 241–253.

63 About infection in Tolstoy's work see Sylvia Sasse, "Moralische Infektion. Lev Tolstojs Theorie der Ansteckung und die Symptome der Leser, " in *Ansteckung. Zur Körperlichkeit eines ästhetischen Prinzips*, ed. Erika Fischer-Lichte et al. (München: Fink, 2005), 275–93.

Literature (*Vsemirnaia literatura*), the Institute for World Literature (*Institut mirovoi literatury*, IMLI) that with full name is called Gorky's Institute for World Literature,[64] and the Gorky's Literary Institute (*Literaturnyi institut im. Gor'kogo*) as an elite school for Soviet writers, which was founded in 1933 as an evening school for workers and, once again, on Gorky's initiative.[65] However, Gorky went a long way from his first educational project, the publishing house *Vsemirnaia Literatura*, founded in 1918, to Socialist realism and Soviet world literature. *Vsemirnaia Literatura* was found in order to publish important literary works from the 18th century up to the present, so that the reader gets to know literature in its historical development.[66] Gorky's approach to literature in the early postrevolutionary years was not yet political; his „vision of world literature has its precedents in Russian prerevolutionary culture", Maria Khotimsky writes in her very interesting history of the publishing house where she gives an insight into a discussion about world literature that was going on in Russia long before Western European debates (again) turned to the topic. And: "The very title of the World Literature Publishing House embodied the humanistic dream of its founders. The idea of ‚vsemirnaia' ("whole-world" or universal) literature alluded to Gorky's vision of literature as a path to universal humanism."[67] Gorkii's early concept of world literature was eurocentric,[68] but it was not yet ideologically motivated.

But let us return to 1934, to the Soviet idea of world literature that both Gorky and Radek designed in the context of Socialist realism. If we try to find a place for this very specific case in the context of the current (Western)

---

64 About the history of the Institute see "Istoriia IMLI," Institut mirovoi literatury im. A.M. Gor'kogo Rossiiskoi akademii nauk (IMLI RAN), accessed March 24, 2020, http://imli.ru/index.php/institut/istoriya-imli: The Institute was founded in 1932 on the 40th anniversary of Gorky's literary activities. The first directors became victims of the Stalinist purges; since 1938 the IMLI is part of the Academy of Science. Gradually the Institute loosened its ties to Gorky's work; since various literatures are being worked on (Soviet, Russian, foreign literatures, classical literatures and so on), various departments have been installed.

65 About the history of the Gorky's Institute for Literature see "Istoriia Literaturnogo instituta imeni A. M. Gor'kogo," Litinstitut, accessed March 24, 2020, http://www.litinstitut.ru/info_history. The Institute was founded in 1933. Some writers who were educated in the Gorky's Institute for Literature wrote novels about it, see, for example Iurii Andrukhovych's *Moskoviada*, 1993, or Ismail Kadare's *Twilight of the Eastern Gods*, 1978. Andrukhovych and Kadare were amongst hundreds of writers educated in the Gorky's Institute for Literature in order to become 'socialist' writers, an experience they describe in their novels.

66 See *Literaturnaia entsiklopediia: online* (accessed March 16th, 2021). About the history of the publishing house „Vsemirnaia Literatura" see Maria Khotimsky: "World Literature, Soviet Style: A Forgotten Episode in the History of Ideas," *Ab Imperio* 3 (2013), 119–154.

67 Khotimsky, "World Literature, Soviet Style," 137.

68 Ibid.

debate on world literature, Pascale Casanova's model of the "world republic of letters"[69] would be quite intriguing, since by 1934 Moscow has become the center of the socialist *république mondiale des lettres*, or, more precisely: the capital of Socialist world literature for the Soviet republics as well as for the socialist world. Paris, Casanova writes, was at the same time the capital of the revolution and the capital of the arts,[70] which made it possible to become the "universal capital of the literary World."[71] Even though the fact that Paris as well as Moscow were literary centers makes them comparable, in Moscow–compared to Paris in the 19th and 20th century–the literary and the political field had to converge completely; aesthetic deviations could only take place in the underground or they were excluded (murdered, executed or sent into the GULAG) from the literary and political system. The political and the aesthetic and/or literary system were homogeneous; the economic factor which even then was so important for the Western literary system and which finds itself in a dynamic relationship to the literary field was not relevant in the case of Moscow. Instead, literature rigidly dependent on the political, and it could only function as a signifier for the one signified: the bright future of socialism embracing the countries and the literatures of the world.

---

69 Pascale Casanova, Pascale: *The World Republic of Letters*, translated by M.B. Bebevoise, Cambridge, Mass/London: Harvard Univ. Press, 2004.
70 Casanova: *World Republic of Letters*, 25.
71 Casanova: *World Republic of Letters* 34.

CHAPTER 10

Premature Postcolonialists: The Afro-Asian Writers Association (1958–1991) and Its Literary Field

Rossen Djagalov

In October 1958, over a hundred writers from Asia and the emerging African nations descended onto Tashkent, the capital of the Soviet Republic of Uzbekistan. Among the list of participants we find the nonagenarian W.E.B. Du Bois, who had just flown from Moscow, having persuaded Nikita Khrushchev to found the Institute for the Study of Africa. In Tashkent, he was joined by the major figures of the 1930s literary left outside of Europe or the Americas: the modernist Turkish poet Nâzım Hikmet, the Chinese polymath Mao Dun, as well as the founding figures of the Popular-Front-era All-Indian Progressive Writers Association–Mulk Raj Anand and Sajjad Zaheer. Though poorly known at the time, some of the younger delegates at that meeting would go on to become the leading literary figures of their countries: the Indonesian Pramoedya Toer, the Senegalese novelist soon-to-become filmmaker Sembène Ousmane, the poet and one of the founders of Angola's Communist Party Mario Pinto de Andrade, his Mozambican counterpart–the poet and FRELIMO politician Marcelino dos Santos. Also in attendance were some leading Russian, Central Asian, and Caucasian writers and Writers Union officials, the formal hosts of the event: the Russians Konstantin Simonov, Nikolai Tikhonov, and Boris Polevoi, the Dagestani Rasul Gamzatov, the Georgian Iraklii Abashidze, the Kazakh Mukhtar Auezov, the Tajik Mirzo Tursun-Zade, and the Uzbek Kamil Yashen.

The Soviet state documented the event exhaustively: in addition to the 523-page publication of the conference proceedings and Orest Mal'tsev's

Tashkent Encounters (1959), a stylized book of interviews with several Afro-Asian writers, the archives of the Foreign Section of the Soviet Writers Union contain multiple clippings from foreign newspapers with articles about the Tashkent Congress that participants published upon returning to their home countries accompanied by their Russian translations.[1] And while the vast majority of those articles represent little more than expressions of gratitude to the Soviet hosts, a few more critical ones, penned by authors less favourably disposed to the USSR, predictably concern themselves with the hosts' efforts to impose their political agenda on the Congress.

One of the latter was written by the Indian poet, playwright, and journalist Krishnalal Shridharani (1911–60).[2] His contacts with Uzbek reality, on the one hand, and the other Afro-Asian writers, on the other, form the core of his account. Both were somewhat limited and mediated by linguistic barriers and the rigid conduct of the Soviet guides and interpreters. The latter did not share Shridharani's sightseeing priorities and only unwillingly took the foreign visitors to spaces that might have contradicted the official narrative of a modernizing Soviet Central Asia. Nevertheless, Shridharani is thankful for the chance to talk to writers from other Afro-Asian countries. Like himself, he observes in the newspaper article he wrote upon his return from Tashkent, they knew all the nuances of Western European literatures, but had never spoken to each other. Echoing most participants' fascination with Tashkent, Shridharani also keeps returning to the city's mixture of familiar Easternness and Western modernity:

> Ask very insistently of your omni-present interpreter to take you to the old town and even to the side streets off the side of the asphalted alleys and you will see clay shacks covered with hay, mosques, and even burkas. Despite the world's biggest textile factory and straight asphalt roads ... this still remains a colourful Eastern city. ... The people! Smiling and hospitable, warm and unofficial and unforced, as any Eastern peoples. Here you can see the faces, beards, and suits that will remind you of Kashmir, Darjeeling and even Bombay.[3]

---

1   Orest Mal'tsev, *Tashkentskie vstrechi; literaturnye portrety uchastnikov Tashkentskoi konferentii—pisatelei stran Azii i Afriki* (Tashkent: Gosizd-vo khudozhlit-ry UzSSR, 1960). All in all, in the archive of the Soviet Union of Writers, there are over eighty folders devoted to the Afro-Asian Writers Association. RGALI f. 631, op. 2, ex. 6100–80.

2   Shridharani, "Pisateli stran Azii i Afriki v Tashkente." RGALI f. 631, op. 2, ex. 6100, l. 1–8. Translations of archival passages, here and elsewhere, are mine.

3   Ibid., l. 1–2.

Tashkent's effect on such visitors was hardly unforeseen or unintended by the Soviet hosts. In fact, the Afro-Asian Writers' Congress helped inaugurate the Uzbek capital's role as a showcase city, where the Soviet state would seek to impress its Afro-Asian guests with displays of Central Asian modernity.[4] From the late 1950s until the collapse of the Soviet Union, Tashkent and Alma-Ata, Samarkand and Bukhara, and to a lesser extent, Yerevan, Baku, and Tbilisi disproportionately figured on many itineraries of African, Asian, and Latin American cultural delegations to the Soviet Union.

Indeed, Tashkent synthesized the dual, if contradictory, role the Soviet state sought to play, "a superpower offering a successful model of development and also the greatest Third-World country of all time," in Christine Evans's apt formulation.[5] Like few other Soviet cities, Tashkent captured both roles. On the one hand, the Afro-Asian visitors were hosted in the giant and ultramodern Hotel Tashkent, completed a few months before their arrival. In the opening speeches, the Uzbek hosts sought to emphasize their republic's success in overcoming the problems familiar to their African and Asian guests: poverty, mass illiteracy, the difficulties of creating a multinational state. They also extolled Soviet achievements in the cultural realm: the creation of modern Central Asian literatures and the elevation of the figure of the writer under Soviet rule. On the other hand, the cultural program the Soviet hosts ran specifically highlighted traditional Central Asian performance. In this spirit, a number of visitors would be taken to the ancient cities of Samarkand or Bukhara (each several hours away from Tashkent).

Shridharani's interest in the Central Asian culture on display and praise for Soviet achievements did not keep him from complaining about the monotony of the speeches, not all of which had much to do with literature, or the hosts' insistence on passing political resolutions written well before the arrival of the delegates. Thus, for him and for many others, the conference's real achievement lay not in the resolutions and planned organizational growth of the emerging writers' movement but in the person-to-person contacts it enabled between Asian and African writers, who had so far lacked basic familiarity with each other

---

4   A more extended treatment of Tashkent as a showcase Soviet city for the Third World was offered in Paul Stronski, "Exporting Modernity: Tashkent as a Cold War Model of Decolonization in Asia" (paper presented at the Association for the Study of Slavic, East European and Eurasian Studies, Washington, DC, November 2006).

5   Rossen Djagalov and Christine Evans, "Moskau, 1960: Wie man sich eine sowjetische Freundschaft mit der Dritten Welt vorstellte." In *Die Sowjetunion und die Dritte Welt: UdSSR, Staatssozialismus und Antikolonialismus im Kalten Krieg 1945–1991*, ed. Andreas Hilger, (Munich: Oldenbourg, 2009), 90.

despite their common schooling in the nuances of European literature. These encounters, he goes on to assert, "took place on the periphery rather than the main conference auditorium."[6] While we should not take Shridharani's report as representative of the experience of the Afro-Asian writers at the Tashkent conference–for every critical newspaper article like his the archival folder contains a dozen glowing accounts by other participants,–it sheds light on one of the most enduring and paradigmatic conflicts in the history of the Afro-Asian Writers Association: between those writers who favoured strong connections between literature and politics and a minority who sought to maintain literature's independence; between the top-down official program, drawn by the Soviet hosts, and the unplanned encounters in the corridors, the streets, and other spaces.

The Afro-Asian Writers movement (formally, the Afro-Asian Writers Association would be inaugurated not in Tashkent, but three years later, at its second, Cairo Congress) presents a unique opportunity for a conversation between (post-)Soviet and post-colonial scholars. To be sure, there has already been some traffic between the two, but rather one-sided: some of the more exciting scholarship in Slavic literary studies in the last two decades has been the result of applying postcolonial methods and perspectives to Russian, East European, and Eurasian material. The reverse side of the (post)colonial-(post)socialist relationship–a systematic study of the implications of the October Revolution, of Russian and Soviet culture, for postcolonial culture and thought–however, has until recently been missing from contemporary scholarship.[7]

One would have thought that this blind spot would be resolved in the wealth of "world literature" scholarship, which in the last few years has been claimed to replace postcolonial studies as the main approach to transnationalism in literature. Unlike postcolonial scholarship, which have primarily concerned itself with the power asymmetry in the relationship between East and West (as a result, leaving out not only entities such as Russia but also the engagements among the very diverse Easts), world literature promised a greater openness to new geographical scenarios of textual circulation. And yet even in the more critical and materialist models for world literary circulation such as those developed by Franco Moretti and Pascale Casanova have insisted on the centrality of London and Paris as the point of origin of literary modes

---

6   Shridharani, "Pisateli stran Azii i Afriki v Tashkente," RGALI f. 631, op. 2, ex. 6100, l. 8.
7   The main exceptions would be Robert Young, *Postcolonialism: An Historical Introduction* (London: Wiley-Blackwell, 2001).

and aesthetic criteria.[8] It is telling that out of the fifty chapters comprising the authoritative *Routledge Companion to World Literature* (2012), many of them devoted to the geographical dimensions of world literature, Russia and the Soviet Union are decidedly absent, despite the former's paradigmatic example of moving from the literary periphery to the literary core or the latter's ambitious projects for world literature.[9] The issue at stake here is not so much filling in another blind spot on the geographical and historical map of world literature–there are plenty of these and it is uncharitable to hold any book or its author(s) responsible for failing to provide comprehensive coverage of the whole world,–but the alternative textual circulation logics of which Russian and Soviet literature have been paradigmatic. Had, for example, Moretti and Casanova considered the reception of the proletarian novel in the early twentieth century (or even of Tolstoy's and Dostoevsky's works), they would have been forced to acknowledge, respectively, that modern literary models can travel in multiple directions, not only West to East, and that competition among national literatures and individual writers is hardly the sole force that keeps the World Republic of Letters running.

Arguably, the most significant phenomenon to emerge out of this territory was the Soviet project for world literature (or as I shall call it here, the Soviet Republic of Letters), perhaps the most concerted and best-resourced effort in history to transform the workings of literary production, circulation, and consumption worldwide and fundamentally rework literature's valences with respect to politics and society. The first generation of works to examine its impact on the world literary system has just reached its readers. Katerina Clark, Susanne Frank, Edward Tyerman, the members of the Moscow-based InterLit group--Elena Zemskova and Elena Ostrovskaya,—and scholars of Maxim Gorky's World Literature project such as Masha Khotimsky and Sergey Tyulenev have identified the contours of the interwar Writers International.[10]

---

8   See, for example, Pascale Casanova, *The World Republic of Letters* (Cambridge, MA: Harvard University Press, 2004). Franco Moretti, *Atlas of the European Novel, 1800–1900* (London: Verso, 1999), and Franco Moretti, *Distant Reading* (London: Verso, 2013).

9   Theo d'Haen, David Damrosch, and Djelal Kadir, eds. *The Routledge Companion to World Literature* (New York, NY: Routledge, 2012).

10 Katerina Clark, *Moscow, the Fourth Rome: Stalinism, Cosmopolitanism, and the Evolution of Soviet Culture, 1931–1941* (Cambridge, MA: Harvard University Press, 2011) and *Eurasia without Borders: the Dream of a Leftist Literary Commons, 1919–1943* (Cambridge, MA: Harvard UP, 2021); Maria Khotimsky, "World Literature, Soviet Style: a Forgotten Episode in The History of the Idea." *Ab Imperio* 3, no. 13(2013), 119–154; Elena Ostrovskaya and Elena Zemskova, "From *International Literature* to world literature: English translators in 1930s Moscow, "*Translation and Interpreting Studies* 14, no. 3(2019), 351–371; Edward

Another contributor to this volume—Galin Tihanov—has polemicized against Anglo-American models of world literature to establish space for alternatives such as the Soviet Republic of Letters.[11] Most of this work, however, has focused on the Soviet-Western literary engagements has yet to cross the post-Second World War divide, after which the previously unitary Soviet Republic of Letters breaks up into three distinct sub-republics, reflecting the Cold-War division of the world into three geopolitical entities.

Relying on the archives of Soviet literary internationalism and the biographies of numerous Third-World authors who entered its orbit, this essay reconstructs the literary space connecting the USSR and the Third World, or more specifically, the way the Afro-Asian Writers Association sought to organize it. The Association aspired to be the literary equivalent of the newly founded Non-Aligned Movement, except that it was aligned: the presence of Soviet Central Asian writers allowed Soviet literary bureaucracies a place on the Afro-Asian table. This dual role—as a segment Soviet Republic of Letters oriented to these two continents and a vehicle for South-to-South literary traffic—was both its condition of possibility and the source of the multiple fissures it experienced during its existence. It also placed the Association in competition with other literary internationalisms of the decolonizing era: the postcolonial initiatives of the CIA-sponsored Congress for Cultural Freedom (CCF), *negritude*, pan-Arabism, Maoism, and Guevarism. In designing the Association's structures such as its international congresses, permanent bureau, literary prize, and multi-lingual literary magazine (*Lotus*), the Soviet cultural bureaucracies drew heavily on their experience of earlier interwar literary internationalism though they decidedly lacked the authority they enjoyed previously. While it never succeeded in its stated aim of breaking off from Western-dominated world literature, the Association did forge "links that bind us," as one of its participants, Ngũgĩ wa Thiong'o, called the living connections between Afro-Asian literatures at the 1973 Alma-Ata Congress. Thus, when it dissolved with the disappearance of the Second and the Third World ca. 1990, those links became severely attenuated. These disappearances have cleared

---

Tyerman, The *Internationalist Aesthetic: China and Early Soviet Culture* (New York: Columbia University Press, 2021); Susanne Frank, "Multinationale Sowjetliteratur' und ihre Agenten auf dem Buchmarkt zwischen Ost und West: Der Fall Ajtmatov," in *Berliner WeltLiteraturen: Internationale Literarische Beziehungen in Ost und West nach dem Mauerbau*, ed Jutta Müller-Tamm. (Berlin: De Gruyter, 2021), 285–312.

11 Galin Tihanov, "The Location of World Literature," *Canadian Review of Comparative Literature* 44, no. 3 (2017), 468–81.

the way for post-colonial studies in Anglo-American universities to assume the role of the main champion of Afro-Asian (now called postcolonial) literature.

The Interwar-era Soviet Republic of Letters

The 1958 Afro-Asian Writers Congress in Tashkent did not inaugurate Soviet literary engagement with the (post-/semi-)colonial world. Such outreach had already begun in the interwar era although on the margins of the largely Western-centric Soviet Republic of Letters.

Soviet literary internationalism was announced in the midst of the civil war. In August 1920, during the Second Congress of the Comintern, the Temporary International Proletkult Bureau was announced, counting Comintern delegates such as the writers Anatoly Lunacharsky, John Reed, and Raymond Lefevbre among its members. To be sure, almost all participants of this Literary International hailed from Russia, Europe and North America, yet already at the Fourth Comintern Congress in 1922, it counted among its members Claude McKay, the Jamaica-born pioneer of the Harlem Renaissance, who famously delivered "The Report on the Negro Question." He was the first of a whole procession of African-American writers to make his pilgrimage to the land of the Bolsheviks, attracted by their promise for a worldwide struggle against class and race oppression.[12]

With the country's resources still absorbed by the civil war and its aftermath and given the state of international isolation, visionary initiatives such as the Literary International were initially bound to remain on paper. The early efforts of the Comintern-affiliated International Bureau of Revolutionary Literature (MBRL) to unite national proletarian writers' organizations worldwide were, however, doomed because such organizations did not exist at the time. For a time, the Bureau–best thought of as an organizing committee for a future proletarian writers' organization–claimed an international status thanks to a few minor foreign communist writers living in or visiting Moscow, including the Turk Nâzım Hikmet, the Chinese Emi Siao, the Arab Hamdi Selam, the

---

12 For a study of his pilgrimage to the USSR, see Katherine Anne Baldwin, *Beyond the Color Line and the Iron Curtain: Reading Encounters Between Black and Red, 1922–1963* (Durham: Duke University Press, 2002), 25–85.

Iranian Abolqasem Lahouti and M. N. Roy, who all studied or taught at the Communist University for Toilers of the East (KUTV).[13]

MBRL thus continued to exist, mostly as an unpronounceable acronym until 1927, when it announced itself to the broader literary world. The event (an improvised gathering of visiting foreign writers only retrospectively called the First International Conference of Proletarian and Revolutionary Writers) apparently convinced the assembled delegates that they were witnessing the birth of an international movement. The thirty or so participants, coming from eleven countries, had only happened to be in Moscow for the tenth anniversary of the October Revolution and represented no one in particular.[14]

Yet the Second Conference of Proletarian Writers held in November 1930 in Kharkiv was already a much more ambitious and better organized affair, bringing to the Ukrainian city of Kharkiv 120 writers from 22 countries. More importantly, however, these writers were already representing genuine proletarian writers' organizations, a number of which had been established between the two conferences. This time Asian, African, and Latin American literatures were represented by actual writers: Emi Siao, from China; the Egyptian Hamdi Selam (both KUTV alumni); Katsumoto Seitiro and Fudzimori Seikiti from Japan; and the Brazilian Salvador Borges (born Betsalel Borodinny, he had emigrated to Brazil from his Ukrainian shtetl on the eve of the First World War). It was in Kharkiv that MBRL's mission–uniting national proletarian organizations–was formally fulfilled with the inauguration of the International Union of Revolutionary Writers (MORP).[15]

The place of the Asian delegates, of course, was marginal in comparison to that of the more illustrious participants of that conference such as Louis Aragon, Johannes Becher, Ludwig Renn, Harold Heslop, or Michael Gold. Nevertheless, some lasting East-West connections were forged at Kharkiv such as the decades-long friendship between Emi Siao and Anna Seghers.[16] But what is more important was that they were speaking on behalf of organized groups of proletarian/ left-wing/ revolutionary writers. While the literary and political

---

13 For more on this unique university, see Masha Kirasirova, "The 'East' as a Category of Bolshevik Ideology and Comintern Administration: The Arab Section of the Communist University of the Toilers of the East," *Kritika: Explorations in Russian and Eurasian History* 18, no. 1 (2017): 7–34.

14 RGALI, f. 2876 (the papers of M. Ia. Apletin), op. 1, ex. 2, l. 2.

15 *Vtoraia mezhdunarodnaia konferentsiia revoliutsionnykh pisatelei. Spetsial'nyi vypusk zhurnala Literatura mirovoi revoliutsii* (Moscow, 1931).

16 Weijia Li, *China und China-Erfahrung in Leben und Werk von Anna Seghers* (Oxford: Peter Lang, 2011), 71–2.

powerhouses of Germany, France, and the United States had the biggest proletarian writers' organizations, others were founded in China, Japan, and Korea, which played a significant role in the literary histories of their countries.[17] The Soviet example was infectious, but it was an internal Chinese dynamic and initiative that led the major politically engaged writers of Shanghai–China's literary capital of the time–to establish the League of Left-Wing Writers in March 1930. Of its founding members, only "the youngsters" Emi Siao and Jiang Guangi had spent time in the USSR, as KUTV students, and knew Russian. Even without knowing any Russian, however, the League's heavyweights, from Lu Xun, arguably the foremost figure in modern Chinese letters, to Guo Moruo, the future president of the Chinese Academy of Sciences, and Mao Dun, the PRC's future Minister of Culture, were translating both pre-Revolutionary Russian and Soviet literature, via Japanese, English, or French.[18] Similar proletarian writers associations emerged in Japan and Korea.

Indeed, as a feature of the Third Period, MORP came to an end with it. After Comintern's abandonment of that policy in favour of the Popular Front, all of MORP's national sections were dissolved or rebranded. In the Soviet case, that process coincided with the closure of RAPP in 1932 and the formation of the Writers Union in 1934. The anti-fascist Association of Writers for the Defence of Culture, the international literary organization that replaced MORP, may have lasted only four years, but represented the high point of the Soviet Republic of Letters and its de facto convergence with the Paris-based Republic of Letters of Pascale Casanova. Indeed, looking at the composition of the Association's presidium at its inaugural congress in Paris in 1935, the list of writers who agreed to lend their name to the cause of Popular-Front literary anti-fascism reads like a Who's Who of contemporary world literature: Romain Rolland, Louis Aragon, Ernest Hemingway, Langston Hughes, Thomas Mann, Bertolt Brecht, Anna Seghers, Bernard Show, E. M. Foster, Virginia Woolf, W. H. Auden, Mikhail Sholokhov.

And while the story of the Association for the Defence of Culture is indeed a mostly Euro-American story, on its margins and much less visibly, there was a growing number of writers from the colonial and semi-colonial world. The Spanish Civil War, for example, brought a number of Latin American authors, most famously Pablo Neruda, to the Second Barcelona-Valencia-Madrid-Paris

---

17   A.N. Dubovikov and L.R. Lanskii, eds. *Iz Istorii Mezhdunarodnogo Ob"edinenia Proletarskikh Pisatelei (MORP)* (Moscow: Nauka, 196), 487–542.

18   Wang-chi Wong, *Politics and Literature in Shanghai: The Chinese League of Left-Wing Writers, 1930–1936* (Manchester: Manchester University Press, 1991).

Congress of the Association of Writers for the Defence of Culture (1937) and thus into the orbit of the Soviet Republic of Letters.[19] And though the Popular-Front period is rightly thought of as marking a decline in Soviet and Western leftist anti-colonialism (after all, geopolitically, the USSR entered into an anti-German coalition with the main colonial powers, England and France), the new ecumenism of national communist parties enhanced the appeal of their literary initiatives. Thus, for example, if the Urdu poet Sajjad Zaheer and fellow CP members had been trying to call into existence a proletarian writers' organization in India ever since 1930, it was only in the 1935 that the All-Indian Progressive Writers' Association (AIPWA) could be founded. Under the loose self-descriptor "progressive," the Association brought together an ideologically broader multilingual constellation of Indian letters that included the Nobel Prize laureate and modernizer of Bengali literature Rabindranath Tagore, Munshi Premchand ("The Emperor among Novelists"), writing in Hindi, and most importantly for our story, the Urdu poet Faiz Ahmad Faiz and the above-mentioned Mulk Raj Anand. Twenty years later, after the 1955 Bandung Afro-Asian Congress, Anand would propose to Prime-Minister Jawaharlal Nehru to follow up the politicians' meeting with an Asian Writers conference in 1956. It was towards the latter's conclusion that the Soviet delegates proposed that their next meeting should take place in Tashkent.

Competing Literary Internationalisms in the Age of Three Worlds

What had spurred the Soviet literary bureaucracies into relaunching their engagement with (semi-/post-)colonial world was both the new international-ism of the post-Stalin Soviet leadership and the emergence of that world, after Bandung, as a distinct political force, which historian Vijay Prashad has termed "The Third World project."[20] Taken by surprise, the Soviet authorities joined the fierce competition for influence over (sections of this) newly announced project. In the realm of literature, competing internationalisms—*negritude* and

---

19 Manuel Aznar Soler, *Segundo Congreso Internacional de Escritores para la Defensa de la Cultura (Valencia-Madrid-Barcelona-París, 1937): actas, discursos, memorias, testimonios, textos marginales y apéndices* (Valencia: Institució Alfons el Magnànim, Centre Valencià d'Estudis i d'Investigació, 2018).

20 Vijay Prashad, *The Darker Nations: People's History of the Third World* (New York: New Press, 2007), 1.

pan-Arabism, *francophonie*, Commonwealth literature and US literary outreach, and a little later, Maoism and Guevarism—sought to give this project the shape and definition best suited to their geopolitical vision. The competitive dynamic among these internationalisms opened up a multitude of venues for Cold-War-era African, Asian, and Latin American writers in ways unimaginable before. Indeed, for all the exhausting national liberation struggles and bloody proxy wars, the Cold War was a golden age for the literatures of the three continents. The competition among the above-mentioned literary internationalisms not only expanded the room for manoeuvre available to individual writers and national literatures but vastly increased the symbolic and material resources available to cultural producers from the three continents: international royalties, invitations, and audiences. That one of the main protagonists of the Cold War—the Soviet state—down to its very bureaucracy believed in literature's capacity to win hearts and minds and fantastically applied this belief to societies vastly different from its own, meant, by the reciprocal nature of the Cold War, that its investments had to be matched by its main and best funded antagonist, the US, and in particular the CIA-sponsored Congress for Cultural Freedom (CCF).[21]

Founded in 1950 to combat what many at Langley saw as global Soviet cultural hegemony, CCF elicited much attention among Soviet cultural bureaucracies.[22] Whether genuinely alarmed or–as often happened–seeking to justify their requests for resources, countless reports generated by Soviet embassies, Soviet writers' delegations sent abroad, or pro-Soviet visitors describe Western efforts to "manipulate" Afro-Asian writers, such as the long-term visits Nigeria's major writer Cyprian Ekwensi paid to the US and Canada,[23]

> where almost all of his works have come out. The same could be said of the Nigerian writers [Onuora] Nzekvu, [Chinua] Achebe, and [J. P.] Clarke. Over the course of a number of years Englishmen and Americans have been courting the leading Sri Lankan writer Martin Wickramasinghe, offering him money to organize a literary journal and a publishing house. By contrast,

---

21 Monica Popescu's *At Penpoint: African Literary History, Postcolonial Studies, and the Cold War* (Durham: Duke University Press, 2020) offers a persuasive account of post-colonial African literature as an object of intense competition between Soviet and US literary internationalisms.

22 For the classical history of CCF, see Frances Saunders, *The Cultural Cold War: The CIA and the World of Arts and Letters* (New York: New Press, 1999).

23 RGANI f. 5, op. 55, ex. 103, l. 169.

in many cases, Soviet publishing houses and journals do not pay foreign authors royalties, which causes them serious offense and inflicts us serious political damage. (It is typical, for example, that no royalties have been paid to the above-mentioned Nigerian writers Ekwensi, Nzekvu, and Achebe.)[24]

Over the course of this competition, between the mid-1950s and mid-1960s, the CCF built a veritable literary empire of magazines, many of them situated in Africa, Asia, and Latin America: *Quest* (India), *Hiwar* (Lebanon), *Black Orpheus* (Nigeria), *Transition* (Uganda), *Horison* (Indonesia), *Cuardenoros* (Latin America).[25] While the CCF's goals were constant everywhere–using the keywords of "freedom" and "democracy" to unite intellectuals worldwide against communism–in practice, the funding came with few strings attached because CCF feared being seen as overly ideological and many of the fiercely independent non-Western writers and literary venues would simply not have agreed to collaborate if the material help came with greater requirements. Thus, modernism, neutrality, and separation of politics from literature became more realistic criteria to maintain than an explicitly pro-Western, "anti-totalitarian" stance.

In addition to such magazines, the CCF's network organized numerous gatherings–from more universal ones, such as its Second Congress for Cultural Freedom in Bombay (1951), to more regional and specifically literary ones, such as the Makerere African Writers Conference, in June 1962, probably the seminal gathering of anglophone African writers.[26] Whether through the CCF or other vehicles, the US government also funded much translation, publication, and book distribution activity throughout Africa, Asia, and Latin America. The cumulative effect of these efforts was not only a massive amount of pro-Western and anti-Soviet propaganda to readers of the three continents but also a massive subsidy for local literary institutions.

Much more complex, if hardly more amiable, was the Soviet position vis-à-vis the different Third-Worldisms. Over the course of the 1960s, Maoism posed the most direct challenge to Soviet literary internationalism, splitting or

---

24 Ibid., l. 170–1.
25 A full-fledged account of these journals could be found in Giles Scott-Smith and Charlotte Lerg's edited volume *Campaigning Culture and the Global Cold War: The Journals of the Congress for Cultural Freedom* (London: Palgrave Macmillan, 2017).
26 See Popescu, *At Penpoint* and Peter Kalliney, *The Aesthetic Cold War: Decolonization and Global Literature* (Princeton: Princeton University Press, 2022).

duplicating Soviet-aligned platforms.[27] Third-Worldist movements particularly concerned with racial justice were much more inconvenient to post-Second World War Soviet cultural bureaucracies than they had been to their predecessors in the interwar era, when, of all the great powers, the Soviet state enjoyed a near-monopoly on determined anti-racist and anti-colonial rhetoric and policies. The first time the Soviet literary bureaucracies were forced to clarify their relationship with *negritude* was the decision as to whether to invite Alioune Diop, the editor of *Présence Africaine* and the main organizer of the 1956 Congress of Black Writers and Artists, to the upcoming 1958 Tashkent Congress. On the one hand, they reasoned, his presence would help legitimize the event in the eyes of a number of African writers; on the other hand, it would introduce an agenda and an interest group that they were keen to avoid. As the question regarding his invitation was deemed broadly political and thus beyond the competence of the Writers Union, it was addressed to CPSU's Central Committee's Foreign and Cultural sections, where it was decided in the negative.[28] At the same time, another of *negritude*'s leading figures, Leopold Senghor, was widely published and translated in Russian. (It helped that he was a head of state, that is, a serious person.)

The Soviet bureaucracies' mixture of intense interest and alarm about such Third-Worldist movements is easy to explain. On the one hand, the latter seemed progressive, if not always socialist, and shared the same opponent: Western hegemony. On the other hand, even (or especially) the more Marxist-inflected movements refused to acknowledge the leading role of the Soviet state and the Party, and their radicalism and espousal of revolution went against the more conservative orientation of the Soviet state and its commitment to peaceful co-existence with the West. The question of race—or more precisely, the struggle for racial justice at the core of movements such as pan-Africanism—also alarmed Soviet cultural bureaucracies. While Cold War Soviet propaganda lambasted institutionalized US racism, thus facilitating the success of the civil rights movement, it rarely evoked the category of race domestically or in its African, Asian, or Latin American outreach, thus erecting a major barrier to its interactions with Third-Worldist forces.[29] Despite the fact that Soviet literature would

---

27 See Duncan Yoon, "'Our Forces Have Redoubled': World Literature, Postcolonialism, and the Afro-Asian Writers' Bureau."

28 For Soviet reports monitoring with apprehension the growth of the *negritude* movement in the mid-1950s, see RGALI f. 631, op. 26, ex. 4806. For the resolution not to invite Diop to Tashkent, see RGANI f. 5, op. 36, ex. 63, l. 1.

29 Mary Dudziak, *Cold War Civil Rights: Race and the Image of American Democracy* (Princeton: Princeton University Press, 2002).

be largely represented in these interactions by writers from Central Asia and the Caucasus, Russian cultural bureaucrats would take a West African critic's comment that "[i]n white countries they do not know or publish the literatures of Africa and Asia" as a reference to themselves.[30]

Indeed, these multiple fissures extended to the Soviet-aligned Afro-Asian Writers Association itself. That many countries' writers (and especially those of the main constituent powers of the Association, Egypt, China, and to a lesser extent, India) acted as state representatives tied the Association's fortunes to the vicissitudes of interstate relations. As a result, every political tension or crisis in Third-Word geopolitics was replicated in the history of the Association. Thus, for example, in the first years of the Association, the Sino-Soviet split of the 1960s provide near-fatal, resulting as it did in the near-cessation of any activity and the eventual formation of two competing formations: a short-lived pro-Chinese Afro-Asian Writers Bureau and a pro-Soviet Afro-Asian Writers' Association. Beyond fiery denunciatory speeches and conspiratorial committee meetings, the struggle between them took multiple forms such as the Chinese writers' furtively waiting in the corridors of the 1967 Beirut Afro-Asian Writers Congress, handing out their anti-Soviet leaflets and inviting for a conversation a bemused Ngũgĩ wa Thiong'o.[31] After the Association overcame the Chinese challenge, it was the centrality of the Cairo between the late 1960s and late 1970s that occasionally concerned Soviet cultural bureaucrats and eventually proved a crucial setback when Egyptian President Sadat practically switched his country's allegiance from the USSR to its Cold-War adversary and made peace with Israel, angering many Arab intellectuals and writers.[32]

The Structures of the Afro-Asian Literary Field

Fully pervious to the geopolitics of the Global Cold War though it was, the Association cannot be reduced to it. It sought to forge an Afro-Asian literary field that would ensure not only the widest possible circulation of African and

---

30 "Stenogramma podgotovitel'nogo komiteta kongressa Afro-aziatskikh pisatelei, Alma-Ata (12.06.1973), Moscow." RGALI f. 631, op. 27, ex. 1365, l. 50.
31 Ngũgĩ wa Thiong'o, Videoconference at the Jordan Center, New York University (May 19, 2017).
32 The circumstances surrounding the fall of the Cairo base are best recounted by Nida Ghouse, "'Lotus Notes': A Series on the Afro-Asian Writers Association, Part A, B, C." *Mada Masr* (blog), August 2014, accessed May 6, 2023, https://madamasr.com/en/topic/afro-asian-writers-association/.

Asian texts among the peoples of the two continents and beyond but also the independence of this circulation and the aesthetic criteria by which it is judged from the colonial metropoles of Paris, London, and New York. That field was also meant to amplify the writers' voices in the common struggle against (neo-) colonialism and the processes of nation-building. In designing that field, Soviet literary bureaucracies relied on structures they developed in their efforts to construct a Soviet Republic of Letters during the interwar era: writers' congresses, a permanent bureau, a multilingual literary magazine, and an international literary prize.

The most visible of these structures were the Afro-Asian Writers congresses at which writers from the two continents would descend upon a city for a week, providing what we would nowadays call a media event as well as an opportunity for them to announce themselves as a movement and determine its direction. In practice, congresses would be divided into official proceedings, a cultural program organized by the hosts in the city and beyond, and a less structured time for informal get-togethers with other writers or sight-seeing, which of course could always be expanded at the expense of the official proceedings. As a whole, the congresses gave visibility to what were largely two imagined communities of Afro-Asian writers, on the one hand, and their readerships, on the other. Indeed, the local organizers of those congresses emphasized their guests' relations with reading publics from their country by facilitating formal and informal meetings between the two and showcasing local translations of the visitors' works. Illustrating the writers' commitment to progressive causes, at the end of each Congress, resolutions were passed on political issues such as ongoing independence struggles, military invasions, and disarmament. Indeed, there was little to separate the literary from the political in the Association's agenda.

Not unlike the gatherings of previous, Soviet-affiliated international writers' formations–MORP's Moscow (1927) and Kharkiv (1930) conferences, the Association of Writers for the Defence of Culture Paris (1935) and Valencia-Madrid-Barcelona-Paris (1937) congresses–writers' congresses became the main feature of the Afro-Asian Writers Association. Starting with the 1958 Tashkent Congress, Afro-Asian writers would similarly come together at seven other congresses: Cairo (1962), Beirut (1967), Delhi (1970), Alma-Ata (1973), Luanda (1979), again in Tashkent (1983), and finally in Tunis (1988). In between the larger congresses, the Association would hold regular meetings of the *Lotus* editorial board, and conferences, such as a poets' symposium in September 1973 in Yerevan, a young writers' meeting in Tashkent in the fall of 1976, and smaller anniversary conferences, also in Tashkent, held in 1968 and 1978.

The Soviet organizers published (in Russian) the transcripts of the first five congresses. It is difficult to evaluate the overall significance of the official proceedings, between the excerpting of the speeches, which smoothed conflicts or rough edges, and the nature of such formal events. For many participants, as Shridharani's coverage of the Tashkent Congress makes abundantly clear, it was not the formal resolutions passed by the congress or the individual speeches that left the most powerful impressions but rather the encounters and conversations outside of the conference hall, with locals or fellow visiting writers, some of which, as Shridharani's, were recorded in articles or other autobiographical writing.[33] Each of these tells us as much about its author's perspective as it does about the congress. Nevertheless, many of the motifs of Shridharani's article recur twenty years later, in the travel notes of the radical feminist Afro-American poet Audre Lorde, an invited American observer to the 1976 Young Afro-Asian Writers Conference in Tashkent.[34] A not unsympathetic commentator, she is less taken by Soviet modernity (unlike the other delegates, she is, after all, visiting from New York) but does admire the bread, the free education and healthcare, which the Soviet state–unlike the United States–guaranteed for its citizens. Reading her notes, one can sense the difference between her more distanced interactions with Russians in Moscow and the warmth and engagement she feels for the people of Uzbekistan:

> As we descended the plane in Tashkent, it was deliciously hot and smelled like Accra, Ghana. ... I felt genuinely welcomed. ... I had the distinct feeling here, that for the first time in Russia, I was meeting warm-blooded people; in the sense of contact unavoided, desires and emotions possible, the sense that there was something hauntingly, personally familiar–not in the way

---

33 See, for example, W.E.B. Du Bois's recollections of the inaugural Tashkent conference in his posthumous memoir (*The Autobiography of W.E.B DuBois* (New York: International Publishers, 1968), 36–37 and the Japanese writer Kato Shuichi's account of the same event in his memoir *A Sheep's Song: A Writers' Reminiscences of Japan and the World* (Berkeley: University of California Press, 1999), 379–388. Both are more focused on their admiration of Tashkent's modernity (and the developmentalist model the USSR offered to the Third World) than on meeting other writers.

34 Audre Lorde, "Notes from a Trip to Russia." Sister Outsider: Essays and Speeches (Berkeley: Crossing Press, 1984), 13–35. I am grateful to Jennifer Wilson for pointing out this travelogue to me.

the town looks because it looked like nothing I'd ever seen before, night and the minarets—but the tempo of life felt quicker than Moscow; and in place of Moscow's determined pleasantness, the people displayed a kind of warmth that was very engaging. They are an Asian people in Tashkent. Uzbeki. ...

If Moscow is New York, Tashkent is Accra. It is African in so many ways—the stalls, the mix of the old and the new, the corrugated tin roofs on top of adobe houses. The corn smell in the plaza, although plazas were more modern than in West Africa. ...

And it's not that there are no individuals who are nationalists or racists, but that the taking of a state position against nationalism, against racism is what makes possible for a society like this to function. I remember the Moslem woman who came up to me in the market place, asking Fikre [a Patrice Lumumba University student from Ethiopia accompanying Lorde–RLD] if I had a boy also. She said that she had never seen a Black woman before, that she had seen black men, but she had never seen a Black woman, and that she so much liked the way I looked that she wanted to bring her little boy and find out if I had a little boy, too. Then we blessed each other and spoke good words and then she passed on.[35]

The actual Afro-Asian conference takes much less space in Lorde's travel notes. She is disappointed to find "only four sisters in this whole conference," unclear about her "observer" status as an African-American, and unhappy about the absence of a meeting for the oppressed peoples of Black America given the abundance of "meeting[s] of solidarity for the oppressed people of Somewhere."[36] The strict geographical demarcations of Afro-Asian solidarity left little space for her.

In between congresses—periods that could last a long time because of the Afro-Asian Writers Association's multiple crises and the inertia of its last decade—day-to-day decisions about the Association's running were made by a headquarters, an international Bureau not unlike those previously coordinating the national sections of MORP and the Association of Writers for the Defence of Culture. Initially located in Colombo, Sri Lanka, as a neutral location

---

35 Ibid., 22–25.
36 Ibid., 22, 26–7.

equidistant between the great powers of the Association, it was presided over by the chairman of the Sri Lankan Union of Writers, Ratna D. Senanayake. The latter's decision to side with China during the Sino-Soviet split caused the first and nearly fatal crisis in the life of the Association.[37] That period of internal strife was reflected in the five-year gap between the 1962 Cairo and the 1967 Beirut Congresses during which much of the Association's activity was paralyzed. As the Bureau was the main decision-making organ of the Association between congresses and those were not taking place, the Soviet side even contemplated abandoning the Afro-Asian format and devoting their energies to a new, African Writers Association, which would be free of Chinese influence.[38] Eventually, the Soviet and the Egyptian sides organized an emergency meeting in 1965 at which it was decided to move the Permanent Bureau to Cairo and replace Senanayake with the Egyptian novelist Yusuf al-Sibai (1917–78), the general secretary of the Afro-Asian Solidarity Organization.[39]

In the face of this decision, the Colombo-based Afro-Asian Writers Bureau did not back down and fold but continued to function as the focal point of Maoist literary internationalism, publishing a number of volumes of Afro-Asian poetry, model Peking operas, Maoist propaganda, and even a short-lived and nearly unfindable English-language literary journal, *The Call*. This effort to compete internationally with the pro-Soviet Association came to an end with the purges of the Cultural Revolution and the general solipsism into which the Chinese cultural policy of the late 1960s collapsed. While this phenomenon did command the sympathies of radical Afro-Asian writers, it was relatively short-lived and a poor match for the cultural capital and material investments of the Soviet-Egyptian-Indian literary alliance.[40]

The decade during which Cairo hosted the Permanent Bureau of Afro-Asian Writers was the period of its greatest stability and growth. It ended abruptly in 1978 with the Camp David Accords, and the assassination of the Association's General Secretary, Yusuf al-Sibai, earlier that year by Palestinian militants upset with his personal support of a peace treaty with Israel. This dual loss–both of a

---

37 A. Surkov, "O perspektivakh pisatel'skogo dvizheniia stran Azii i Afriki," RGANI f. 5, op. 36, ex. 149, l. 161–4.

38 RGALI 631, op. 26, ex. 6186, l. 1–4.

39 There is only one English-language study of the writings of this figure of the Afro-Asian Writers Association: Gail Ramsay, *The Novels of an Egyptian Romanticist: Yusuf al Sibai (Stockholm 1996)*.

40 The fate of the pro-Chinese Colombo-based bureau is the subject of Duncan Yoon, "'Our Forces Have Redoubled': World Literature, Postcolonialism, and the Afro-Asian Writers' Bureau." *The Cambridge Journal of Postcolonial Literary Inquiry* 2, no. 2 (2015), 233–252.

founding member-state of the Association (Egypt) and of somebody who had been by all accounts a capable and well-connected organizer (al-Sibai)–initiated a period of uncertainty and itineracy, which was never fully resolved until the very end of the Association ca. 1991.[41] At the same time, al-Sibai's successor as the Association's general secretary for most of this period, the South African writer Alex La Guma (1925–1985), lived in Cuba, hardly a location conducive to the day-to-day running of the Afro-Asian Association.

The Bureau (at least during its Cairo phase) hosted the Association's literary quarterly, *Lotus* (1967–91), which offered the most tangible proof of the existence of an Afro-Asian literary field.[42] While the idea of a journal was broached as early as the 1958 Tashkent Congress, a detailed plan for a magazine with a circulation of about 5,000 copies and length of about 150 pages (*Lotus's* eventual parameters) had to wait until 1963, when Faiz Ahmad Faiz submitted his proposal to the Soviet Writers Union.[43] It was based on multiple conversations with writers, editors, and politicians in Beirut, Cairo, Paris, and Geneva, and was made weightier by Faiz's recent receipt of a Lenin Peace Prize. In a lengthy preamble illustrative of Cold War dynamics, he explains the need to counter several already existing hostile publications: on the one hand, the jewel in the crown of the CIA-sponsored Congress for Cultural Freedom, the Anglo-American *Encounter*, which, over the course of the 1960s, under the editorship of Stephen Spender and Melvin Lasky, had increasingly turned its sights to (formerly) colonial literatures; on the other, against two English-language Maoist magazines, the Hong-Kong-based *Eastern Horizons* and the Geneva-based *Revolutions in Africa, Asia, and Latin America*.[44] As the ideal location for such a magazine, Faiz proposes Beirut: in his view, the city combines an excellent geographical location with an abundance of local writers and politicians supporting the cause, good publishing and distribution facilities, and a relative paucity of censorship restrictions, which he feared might cripple the magazine if it were to be founded in Cairo.[45] Faiz's initial project was not realized until 1967, when *Afro-Asian Writings* began publishing prose and poetry, literary criticism, and

---

41 RGANI f. 5, op. 55, ex. 46, l. 129.

42 See Tariq Mehmood's "The Lotus Project" based at the American University in Beirut.

43 RGALI f. 631, op. 27, ex. 627, l. 20.

44 Faiz's proposal and the preliminary labour on which it is based, could be found here: RGALI f. 631, op. 26, ex. 6164.

45 Ironically, sixteen years after this proposal, in 1979, Faiz would become Lotus's editor after its offices were forced to migrate from Cairo to Beirut. See Kassamali, "'You Had no Address': Faiz Ahmed Faiz in Beirut." *The Caravan*, May 31, 2016, accessed May 6, 2023, https://caravanmagazine.in/reviews-essays/you-had-no-address-faiz-beirut.

book reviews by writers from all over the two continents. (At Mulk Raj Anand's instigation, the title was changed to *Lotus* after the first issues had come out, during a 1969 meeting of its international editorial board in Moscow.)[46]

Faiz, however, had proposed an English-language magazine explicitly modelled after *Encounter*. Just like *Encounter*, he insisted, it should be prepared to publish major writers without "clear political views" and even material hostile to its agenda (as long as it is effectively countered).[47] His efforts to broaden the ideological parameters of the magazine ran against the model Soviet cultural bureaucracies had in mind: *International Literature*, the Moscow-based literary organ of the worldwide Popular Front. Indeed, as Faiz would discover, somewhat to his frustration, during his own four years at the helm of *Lotus* (1979–1982), it resembled *International Literature* in its unswerving loyalty to its hosts and sponsors–the USSR and the PLO.[48] Another–more striking–commonality between the two magazines was that they simultaneously published issues in several languages: French, English, Arabic in the case of *Lotus*; Russian, German, French, English, and, occasionally, Italian, Spanish, and Chinese in the case of *International Literature*.[49] Through translation, they sought to overcome the national and regional boundaries dividing their intended readership and to forge a truly international reading public, spanning Africa and Asia.

With only 5,000 of each issue printed in each language, *Lotus* could hardly reach numerically significant readerships in Africa or Asia, but a consistent effort was made to send it to libraries and writers' organizations in the two continents and beyond. For its distribution, it relied on the Association's transnational network as well as on foreign publishing companies such as the French Maspero or the British London Publishers.[50] Practically, every aspect of the journal was international: not only the contributors and the readers but also its peripatetic editorial offices (Cairo, and after the Egyptian "defection," Beirut and then Tunis) and the location of its printing press (Egypt, for the Arab version; East Berlin for the English and French ones). The international editorial committee

---

46 RGALI F. 631, op. 27, d. 628, l. 9 (June 27, 1969).

47 RGALI F. 631, op. 26, ex. 6164, l. 24.

48 Liudmila Vasilieva, Faiz's personal Russian translator during his regular visits to Moscow, describes his conflicts with Soviet cultural bureaucracies, who sought a clearer alignment between the magazine and the Association's geopolitical goals. Vasilieva, interview (June 18, 2018)

49 Anatoly Sofronov would periodically propose to the leadership of the Writers Union to publish the magazine in Russian, but apparently unsuccessfully. RGALI f. 631, op. 30, ex. 2337, l. 51.

50 RGALI F. 631, op. 27, d. 628, l. 10 (27 June 1969).

was spread among Algeria (Malek Haddad), Angola (Fernando da Costa Andrade), Iraq (Fouad al-Takerly), Japan (Hiroshi Noma), Lebanon (Michel Suleiman), Mongolia (Sonomyn Udval), the USSR (Anatoly Sofronov), India (Mulk Raj Anand), Pakistan (Faiz Ahmad Faiz) and Senegal (Doudou Gueye). After al-Sibai's assassination, *Lotus*'s helm passed on to Faiz, who edited it out of Beirut until 1982, when Israel invaded Lebanon, rendering the work of *Lotus* impossible. In the last and probably least documented part of its history, when publication and distribution grew increasingly irregular, *Lotus* was first briefly run by Faiz's deputy, the Palestinian poet Muin Bseiso, and later, after his death, by the PLO's chief press officer, Ziad Abdel Fattah.

Lotus's pages also reflected this imperative to cover as many national literatures in as many different genres as possible. The limited number of pages available meant that, unlike *International Literature*, it could not easily lend them to novels, so the main genres represented were short stories and selections of poetry. The magazine did not limit itself to literature but included neighbouring arts as well. In addition to the occasional play or folklore, most issues included several pages of images, whether of paintings or art objects, accompanied by a detailed explanation. The articles in the Studies section, prepared especially for the magazine, exhibited a certain regional or (bi-)continental focus: "The Role of Translation for Rapprochement between the Afro-Asian Peoples," "The Popular Hero in the Arabic Play," "Where does African Literature go from here?" Occasionally a single author or national literature would be showcased, for example, "Ghalib and Progressive Urdu Literature."[51] Rounding out each issue were book reviews as well as a chronicle of current events of Afro-Asian literature. Such chronicles helped foster a sense of simultaneity and coherence of the whole among the bi-continental readers. Not unlike Benedict Anderson's newspaper, which helped its readers imagine the nation by placing next to each other articles on a natural disaster in province X and on a major cultural event in the capital, such chronicles or book reviews constructed the category of an Afro-Asian literature by placing its geographically dispersed manifestations alongside each other.[52] On the basis of *Lotus*'s contents, Hala Halim has offered a more detailed account of that Afro-Asian imagining.[53]

---

51 All article titles are drawn from *Lotus*'s fifth issue published in April 1970.
52 Benedict Anderson, *Imagined Communities: Reflections on the Origin and Spread of Nationalism* (London: Verso, 1983), 33.
53 See Halim's "Lotus, the Afro-Asian Nexus, and Global South Comparatism," *Comparative Studies of South Asia, Africa and the Middle East* 32 (2012), 563–83.

The fourth and last structure through which the Afro-Asian Writers Association sought to consolidate Afro-Asian literature as a coherent field was the Lotus Prize. Awarded between 1969 to 1988 to leading Afro-Asian writers, it was modelled after the World Peace Council's Stalin Peace Prize given to writers, artists, and scientists who had contributed to the cause of world peace. The World Peace Council established its award in the hottest moment of the Cold War, as a more political and less Western alternative to the Nobel Prizes for Literature and Peace. By the same token, the Lotus Prize acquired the reputation of an Afro-Asian Nobel for literature, at a time when very few African and Asian writers were awarded an actual Nobel. In the process, it contributed to the production of an Afro-Asian literary canon. The success of this prize is reflected in the continued fame of its recipients: the Palestinian poet Mahmoud Darwish and the South African prose writer Alex La Guma (the 1969 awards); the Angolan poet-president Augostinho Neto (1970) and the Senegalese novelist Sembène Ousmane; the Algerian Kateb Yasin and Ngũgĩ wa Thiong'o (both in 1972); Chinua Achebe and Faiz Ahmad Faiz (the 1975 awards) are still among the best known Afro-Asian writers. Some of them, like Mahmoud Darwish and Alex La Guma, received the award well before they reached the peak of their fame in the West.[54] There is no uniform aesthetic unifying the diverse writings of its recipients: the modernism of the older Egyptian novelist Taha Husien, the militant anti-colonial verse of the Mozambican militant poet-independence-fighter Marcelino dos Santos, Aziz Nesin's biting satire of Turkish state and society, and Chinghiz Aitmatov's unique synthesis of socialist and magical realism.

Judging by the transcript of the discussion of the first batch of Lotus awards, its principles were not particularly well codified, giving the prize committee a good deal of flexibility.[55] The award could be given not only for individual work but also for overall contributions to the Afro-Asian Writers Association; it would be desirable if at least one award (out of the six awarded for 1969–70) would go to a writer from a country fighting for independence. Palestinian literature was the major beneficiary of this last principle: in the first ten years of the award's existence, Palestinian writers won five Lotuses, making them, for some time at

---

54 Of course, tribute was paid to the cultural bureaucrats running the Association: its head Yusuf al-Sibai and the head of the Soviet Committee for Solidarity with Africa and Asia Anatoly Sofronov received the two 1974 awards.

55 "Stenogramma zasedaniia Postoiannogo Biuro APSAA o prisuzhdenii premii Lotos afroaziatskim pisateliam (22.06.1970)." RGALI f. 631, op. 27, ex. 767.

least, the absolute leader in this regard.[56] (By the time the last Lotus award was made in 1988, Soviet prize-winners had overtaken them.) By the same token, as literatures fighting a foreign occupation, Vietnam and Lusophone Africa (Angola and Mozambique) were given four prizes each, making them a joint third. Otherwise, the Lotus Prize committees sought the widest geographical representation of its awards. The non-inclusion of a francophone African writer among the first six recipients became the main source of contention during the inaugural meeting of the Lotus Prize Committee in 1970, when the Senegalese representative Doudou Gueye asked that his protest be officially registered in the proceedings.[57]

While geography seems to have been a major consideration in selecting Lotus Prize winners, gender balance does not seem to have been a factor. In fact, of the fifty-nine awards that were given, only two went to women: the Uzbek poet Zulfiya and the Mongolian prose writer Sonomyn Udval. This poor representation of women was hardly limited to Lotus Prizes but extended to all other aspects of the Afro-Asian Writers Association: the awards were made by the nearly all-male *Lotus* editorial board, which in turn published mostly male writers.

Gradually, the award experienced a Brezhnevization of sorts. In a discussion of its workings in the Soviet Writers Union following the Association's last conference in Tunis (December 1988), one perestroika-minded Writers Union official, Evgeny Sidorov, revealed what the main criterion for the Lotus awards over the previous decade had become: if you were a literary official heading your national section of the Afro-Asian Writers Association, sooner or later you would receive your Lotus.[58]

The congresses, the permanent bureau, the literary quarterly, and the Lotus Prize were only the most visible structures of the Afro-Asian literary. Underneath them lay a whole network of national committees, publishing houses, magazines, and translators located within different African and Asian countries, who were performing the much less visible work of bringing foreign literature produced within the two continents to their national readerships and thus establishing literary connections unmediated by British or French

---

56 The Lotus Prize was only one of the ways through which the Association facilitated the Palestinian and other anti-colonial struggles for international cultural recognition. Even before the PLO came to host the *Lotus* magazine in the late 1970s, Palestine was a cause célèbre for the Association.

57 Ibid., 79–85.

58 RGALI f. 631, op. 30, ex. 2337, l. 45.

publishing houses. Lydia Liu has called this engagement Great Translation Movement.[59]

The Birth of Postcolonial Studies out of the Ashes of the Second and Third World

The Afro-Asian Writers Association's life was very uneven: a spectacular birth in 1958, paralysis for the first half of the 1960s occasioned by the Sino-Soviet split, followed by a decade of organizational growth. Then it became a dual casualty of Brezhnev-era stagnation and what Vijay Prashad has called "the pitfalls" and "assassinations" of the Third World.[60] After the loss of its Cairo base in 1978, the Association entered a period of homelessness from which it never fully recovered. Over the course of the 1980s, *Lotus* was becoming a largely Arabic and increasingly irregular publication, compiled and edited within PLO, using this underground organization's meagre resources, and supported by a Soviet subsidy and free printing in East Germany rather than subscriptions, as was the original hope. But what worried the Soviet delegation at the last, Eighth, Congress of the Association held in Tunis in December 1988 was the disappearance of major and/or young writers from the movement. Bemoaning the recent death of Alex La Guma, Faiz Ahmad Faiz, and Mirzo Tursun-Zade, the non-attendance of others, their report described the measures taken by the Congress to bring fresh blood into the Association's bloodstream.[61] Heralded as "a perestroika," these included stabilizing its headquarters (a return to Cairo), electing a new general secretary (the Egyptian novelist Lutfi al-Khuli), entering into partnerships with other international organizations (UNESCO, PEN International), and even yet another proposal to publish *Lotus* in Russian, thus helping the magazine break even. (Thanks to Soviet efforts to showcase the enormous quantities of Afro-Asian literature published in the USSR in various languages, many Afro-Asian writers must have placed their hopes in the Soviet reader as the most reliable supporter of the movement.) There were plans to expand the Association to Latin America and to re-invite Chinese writers,

---

59 Lydia Liu, "After Tashkent," accessed May 5, 2023, https://www.youtube.com/watch?v=r5FZzKzSxwM.

60 Vijay Prashad, *The Darker Nations*, 119–276.

61 Such an account of the organization's gradual decline could be found in the report the leader of the Soviet delegation to the Tunis Congress, Evgeny Sidorov, had to deliver to the Soviet Writers Union. RGALI f. 631, op. 30, ex. 2337, l. 42–56.

absent since the 1962 Cairo Congress.[62] According to the last written trace I found of the Association's life in the Soviet archives, some of these proposals were followed up on. Despite its economic difficulties, the Egyptian government had given the Association a villa, and agreements were reached with PEN. But such plans, whether realistic or not, were running up against time and geopolitical tides. Already at the Tunis Congress, the East German Afro-Asian Solidarity Committee served notice that it was giving up publishing *Lotus* in German and English, as it had been doing for free since the very beginning of the journal. The Arabic version lasted two more years. Over these years the Soviet Writers Union's budget was being cut, and finally, in 1991, the Soviet Union itself, the state most invested–symbolically and materially–in the Afro-Asian Writers Association, ceased to exist.

Since then, the Soviet Union's imperial ambition to map the whole world and its belief in the power of culture, and especially literature, to reach out to other societies, has given way to contemporary Russia's shrunken geopolitical priorities. The famous Progress publishing house, the biggest Soviet publisher of African and Asian literature, which ensured that Soviet readers had almost as much access to that literature as their English and French counterparts, is no more. The once rich ecology of non-Western literature in Soviet print culture, imbricated with ideology though it may have been, has been reduced to a tiny number of representative contemporary writers who can be found in Russian bookstores today: on the contemporary Russian publishing map, J. M. Coetzee stands for the whole of African literature, Orhan Pamuk for West Asia, Salman Rushdie for India, Haruki Murakami and Kazuo Ishiguro for Japan. Most non-Western national literatures are, however, left without a single representative. The overall impression has been well-captured by the translator Elena Malykhina, who complained that "if you enter a [Russian] bookstore, you'd think that literature is being written only in English and German."[63]

Similarly, the once formidable Soviet area-studies apparatus, which fully competed with and, in certain areas, bested that of the United States, is no more. Thus, when the author of these lines was invited to give a talk at the Institute of Oriental Studies–an institution with a glorious 150-year-old history, his hosts from the department of the Literatures of the East found it necessary to apologize for the low attendance. If in 1990, they explained, the department

---

62 All these plans are recorded in the Arabic section of the internal Bulletin of the Soviet Writers Union, *Literaturnaia zhizn' za rubezhom* (1990), 20–22.

63 Elena Kalashnikova, *Po-russki s liubov'iu: besedy s perevodchikami* (Moscow: Novoe literaturnoe obozrenie, 2008), 256.

had employed over forty researchers, that number was now fewer than ten, with the majority of them well into retirement age. Indeed, if this and other such institutes continue to function at all, it is because of these people's commitment to the languages, literatures, and cultures they study. But it is not the kind of employment that pays the bills.

Also gone, in any meaningful sense, is the Soviet Writers Union, with its Foreign Commission, which employed dozens of consultants in the 1980s, who served as Soviet experts and liaisons with national literatures worldwide.[64] While work there–being so close to Soviet foreign policy–was often more political than work at the research institutes, the Foreign Commission boasted many remarkable translators, scholars, and people genuinely committed to the cultures in which they specialized.

In African, Asian, and Latin American societies, too, the once vibrant Soviet–Third-World cultural engagements have become a fading generational phenomenon. The end of the Soviet Union was experienced as a heavy blow, often figured as betrayal or abandonment, by many politically engaged intellectual and cultural producers in the three continents. The title of the Chilean Communist Luis Guostavino's memoir, *The Fall of the Cathedrals* (1990), written as the Soviet centre was crumbling, is telling.[65] As many Cubans would testify, the sentiment extended well beyond communist party members.[66] In addition, outside of certain leftist communities in the non-Western world and their function as "classics," Russian and Soviet literature has ceased to be a major point of reference or source of inspiration for politically engaged artists and audiences from these continents. The cheap Progress Publishers volumes once widely available in over 70 languages have since become objects of nostalgia.[67]

---

64 At the break-up of the USSR, it too broke up into numerous writers' associations in the post-Soviet space with none of them possessing the symbolic or financial power of its Soviet predecessor. In Russia alone, there are at least three such associations. Tellingly, it is the nationalist Union of Writers of Russia (UWR), which maintains the most active engagement with respect to non-Western literatures beyond the former Soviet space. In fact, UWR has become a founding member of a renewed Afro-Asian Writers Association, which has had its revival congress in Cairo in 2012 and has re-established *Lotus* (in Arabic only).

65 Luis Guostavino, *Caen las Catedrales* (Santiago: Hachette, 1990).

66 See, for example, Jorge Ferrer, "Around the Sun: the Adventures of a Wayward Satellite." in *Caviar with Rum: Cuba-USSR and the post-Soviet Experience*, ed. by Jacqueline Loss et al. (London: Palgrave McMillan, 2012), 99.

67 In addition to translating foreign literature in Russian, Progress was charged with translating Russian literature, scholarship, and Marxist classics in foreign languages. For a brief history, see Rossen Djagalov, "Progress Publishers: a Short History," in *The East Was Read*, ed. Vijay Prashad (New Delhi: LeftWord Books, 2019), 78–86. For a much more elaborate one, see

With the disappearance of the Soviet bloc, the political fields available to politicians, writers, and audiences from the three continents have become profoundly reconfigured. For one, the available room for manoeuvre has vastly shrunk: no longer is a prominent African writer simultaneously courted by two sets of cultural outreach bureaucracies, Soviet and Western, willing to outbid each other to secure that writer's manuscript, presence, and goodwill.

In this hollowed-out One World, in the absence of a cultural Second and Third Worlds, the work of championing non-Western literary production, introducing it to foreign audiences, and, more generally, fighting for its place on the world literature canon, has shifted to postcolonial scholars on Western campuses. Initially located in (English) literature departments, they–and their concerns–have made themselves felt in most humanities fields. Though Said's *Orientalism* announced the emergence of the field in 1978, it was not until the first post-Cold-War decade that postcolonial studies began to experience explosive institutional growth in positions, publication outlets, conferences, and grants. The relationship between the geopolitical context and this new field did not escape one of its pioneers, Robert J. C. Young, who stated in the inaugural issue of the flagship journal *Interventions: International Journal of Postcolonial Studies* (1998):

> Does "postcolonialism" mark the end of the "Third World"? … With the collapse of the Soviet bloc, and the conversion of China to a form of controlled capitalist economy, today there is effectively no longer any choice: de facto there is now only a single world economic system. One implication of this is that with the demise of the second world, a Third World no longer exists. Indeed, the emergence of postcolonial theory could be viewed as marking the moment in which the Third World moved from an affiliation with the second to the first. The rise of postcolonial studies coincided with the end of Marxism as the defining political, cultural, and economic objective of much of the third world."[68]

In many ways, postcolonial scholars have continued the work of earlier Third-Worldist and Soviet critics and scholars. What has changed, however,

---

Jessica Bachman's forthcoming dissertation, "Reading Soviet Books in Postcolonial India, 1951–1991."

68 Robert Young, "Ideologies of the Postcolonial." *Interventions* 1, no. 1 (October 1998): 4–8.

was not only the location where that cultural and intellectual labour is performed (from the capitals of Africa, Asia, and Latin America or Moscow to Anglo-American literature departments) but also its substance. Partly in reflecting of the historical period in which it was born (the retreat of the left globally, the rise of neoliberalism, the hegemony of poststructuralism in the humanities), partly as a critique of the limitations of earlier emancipatory projects (Soviet-aligned or not), mainstream postcolonial scholarship has struggled to take progressive political aspirations beyond its writings and the classroom; and even there, revolutionary Third-Worldist rhetoric has given way to subtle French poststructuralism; the harsh (neo)colonized-colonizer binaries with which Third-Worldists and Soviets operated have been sidelined in favour of a deconstructionist celebration of hybridity; the embrace of progressive nationalisms, discursively compatible with Soviet internationalism, replaced by postcolonial interest in diasporas and transnationality. Following Homi Bhabha, mainstream postcolonial theorists have been suspicious of the nation, which had constituted one of the main political horizons of earlier national liberation struggles.[69] They have been even more critical of the (postcolonial) state, in which earlier Third-Worldist intellectuals and Soviet bureaucracies had placed so much hope: to reduce inequality, to industrialize the country, to raise national culture. In the theory of social change underlying the writings of the Subaltern Studies historians, one of the main intellectual streams within postcolonial studies, there has been a remarkable suspicion of, if not active hostility to, organizations, parties, and other representative political structures as vehicles of advancing the interests of "the subalterns." Whether implicitly or explicitly, this view represents a major challenge to the very nature of the Afro-Asian Writers Association and other such anti-colonialist formations. Instead, the subaltern scholars' main focus has lain on the spontaneous and unorganized resistance of "the subalterns" to impositions or representations from above.[70]

These differences reflect the differences between an earlier, Afro-Asian (Latin American) anti-colonial moment and the present-day, post-colonial one. Understanding them and the transition between them is imperative if we are to understand the present-day state of postcolonial studies, a field that has excelled in theorizing vast swaths of the humanities and social sciences but

---

69 Homi Bhabha, "A Question of Survival: Nations and Psychic States," in *Psychoanalysis and Cultural Theory: Thresholds*, ed. James Donald (New York: St. Martin Press, 1991), 102.

70 See the ten volumes of the Subaltern Studies collective printed between 1982 and 1999 by the New Delhi branch of Oxford University Press.

until recently at least and with such exceptions as Robert Young's, Timothy Brennan's and the Warwick school's work, not necessarily good at historicizing itself. Operating with a foreshortened, post-*Orientalism,* canon of itself has not only made it difficult to account for postcolonialism's debts to earlier intellectual and cultural formations (Marxist, pro-Soviet, Third-Worldist) but has also shrunk its political horizons, when compared to those earlier formations. In this sense, the Afro-Asian Writers Association, whose transnational field this article has reconstructed, offers an unsurpassed moment of reflection on postcolonialism's history.

CHAPTER 11

Can "Worldliness" Be Inscribed into the Literary Text?: Russian Diasporic Writing in the Context of World Literature

Maria Rubins

Sometimes it seems that the World Literature discourse is sustained mainly by the polemic that sets out to deconstruct it. The foundational models of World Literature have repeatedly come under attack for their Western/Eurocentric bias (despite the professed commitment to "peripheral" voices, with their potential to change the system from within); constructing the "world" from the majoritarian viewpoint;[1] their failure "to integrate the study of literature with urgent matters of global significance";[2] their tendency to endorse cultural equivalency and substitutability;[3] the risk of World Literature becoming World Literature in English,[4] etc. More radical critics even cast doubt as to whether World Literature, as it has evolved over the last few decades, has done much more than provide a kind of psychotherapy for readers and literary scholars alike, inviting them to embrace their natural and professional limitations.

---

1   Cf. Lital Levy and Allison Schachter, "A Non-Universal Global: on Jewish Writing and World Literature," *Prooftexts* 36, no. 1 (2017): 1–26.
2   Karen L. Thornber, "Why (Not) World Literature: Challenges and Opportunities for the Twenty-First Century," *Journal of World Literature* 1, no. 1 (2016): 107–118.
3   Emily Apter, *Against World Literature? On the Politics of Untranslatability* (New York: Verso, 2013) and "Philosophizing World Literature," *Contemporary French and Francophone Studies* 16, no. 2 (2012): 171–186.
4   Mads Rosendahl Thomsen, *Mapping World Literature: International Canonization and Transnational Literatures* (New York: Continuum, 2008), 10.

Indeed, most mere mortals cannot master more than a handful of languages and become experts in multiple cultural contexts and literary traditions. We are compelled to read most texts in translation and rather superficially, unable to tap fully into their distinctive cultural, historical, and linguistic contexts. Never mind, World Literature theoreticians tell us. It is better to practice "distant reading" and "detached engagement" with narratives that are beyond our immediate expertise. Our habitual reading practice is thereby elevated into a sophisticated "mode of reading."

Such skepticism aside, the recent expansion of World Literature is symptomatic. With the current departure from essentialism evident in many disciplines, World Literature indirectly prompts us to reconsider important questions. Is a literary text an essential(ized) object invested with an intrinsic meaning, or is the meaning continuously produced in the process of its circulation? Does each new interpretation, each new (mis)reading and (mis)translation transform the text itself, or does it just reflect the sensibilities and intellectual experiences of the receiving culture, leaving the text intact? While just a few decades ago such questions would have appeared ill-conceived, now they feed into broader cross-disciplinary debates. Today, cognitive scientists often recall the visionary formula of the Russian physiologist Alexei Ukhtomsky: "There is no object without a subject, and no subject without an object."[5] The relevance of this perspective for the literary domain consists in further empowerment of the reader. In some cultures, Russian in particular, this leads to a radical reversal of the canonical roles of the writer, once worshiped as a prophet, and the reader, once a passive receiver of the wisdom imparted in literary texts and now a co-creator. Of course, reception theory has already engaged with the evolution of the writer/reader relationship, arguably in a more persuasive manner. Where World Literature knows no competition is the sociology of the book market, the calibration of the work's value based on economic aspects, the number of translations, the proximity to or remoteness from "prestige-bestowing centers," and strategies of success defined by how a specific author emphasizes or downplays this distance.

With so much attention given to circulation and macro/micro literary structures, the dominant World Literature discourses have so far done precious little to engage with the text itself. This poses no problem for Franco Moretti who, explaining his concept of distant reading, says bluntly: "If in process text

---

5 Tat'ana Chernigovskaia, "Raznoiazychie i kibernetika mozga," accessed August 5, 2020, https://m.polit.ru/article/2009/11/24/brain/.

disappears, well, less is more."[6] Not everyone, even in the World Literature circles, is ready to subscribe to this view. Close reading still remains for many a form of connecting to the philosophy, style, and forms of human experience encoded in the literary narrative before extra layers of meaning are added through the efforts of critics, translators, and diverse readerships. Can we bring the text back while retaining global cross-cultural parameters? Is there a way to appreciate the work as part of World Literature by re-focusing on the narrative itself? In her article "Writing World Literature: Approaches from the Maghreb," Jane Hiddleston makes a compelling argument, observing that the standard models of World Literature leave out the question of what constitutes the worldliness of the text. She suggests that "[t]he worldliness of World Literature may be intrinsic to the form of the work." A text, she continues, is "enmeshed" in the world not because "it circulates after completion but because it comes to life through the dialogues it maintains with the place of its creation––with the broader, multiple cultural histories that its language draws on or taps into; and with itself."[7]

In this chapter, I will test the assumption that "worldliness" *can* be inscribed into the text by turning to diasporic, or extraterritorial, Russian literature. The internal diversity of this corpus calls for multiple methodological optics, and the conceptual foundations of World Literature will inevitably come into conversation with other sub-disciplines, including diaspora studies, translation theory, and scholarship on bi- and translingualism. Created over the last century beyond the geographical, ideological, or aesthetic purview of the Soviet and post-Soviet literary establishments, yet indirectly linked to the metropolitan culture in a number of ways, Russian diasporic writing is likely to offer a distinct variation on the World Literature paradigms examined in this volume. To reflect on this specificity, I will engage with the following questions. Has diasporic literature, positioned as it is in a contact zone between national and transnational, predicated on hybridity and standing for culturally pluralistic aesthetic practices, developed distinctive features that mark it as potential World Literature? How does it negotiate its origins, language(s), and the concept of the "national literary space"? What distinguishes its patterns of circulation? Finally, how does this corpus problematize the basic tenets of World Literature? Various sociocultural formations of diasporic literary culture, which have emerged over a century of massive Russian dispersion, are likely to yield different answers to the above questions. I will therefore draw on a range of contexts, including the

---

6   Franco Moretti, "Conjectures on World Literature," *New Left Review*, no. 1 (2000): 54–68, 57.

7   Jane Hiddleston, "Writing World Literature: Approaches from the Maghreb," *PMLA* 131, no. 5 (2016): 1386–95, 1388.

cultural policies of interwar Russian Paris; contemporary Russian Israeli writing and cultural polemics, with a detailed case study focused on Gali-Dana Singer's poetry; the problematic reception of Andreï Makine's francophone novels in Russia; and the russophone poetry of the Fergana school.

It is a basic premise in World Literature theory that the text "begins" in its original language and ceases to be the exclusive product of its culture of origin once it is translated.[8] The concept "culture of origin" is problematic in itself since, as Thornber correctly points out, "many works of literature ... have 'origins' in multiple cultural spaces"[9] This multiplicity of roots is certainly a marker of diaspora writing created in the "contact zone" between different cultures. And what is the "original language" of diasporic texts written, for the most part, in-between languages and consciously responding to global cultural and linguistic diversity? Over time, Russian writers who found themselves beyond the metropolitan borders have made different linguistic choices, roughly classified as:

(1) loyalty to the metropolitan linguistic idiom;
(2) complete or partial language shift;
(3) creolization.

For example, stubborn loyalty to the prerevolutionary linguistic norm (and even orthography) was the preferred option of first-wave émigré writers, whose mission was ostensibly to preserve Russian culture for future generations. This was the case of the émigré literary elite represented by the likes of Bunin, Merezhkovsky, Khodasevich, Gippius, Zaitsev, Shmelev, Kuprin, and many others. Occasionally even this cohort paid lip service to the "worldliness" (*vsemirnost'*) of Russian émigré literature. In the words of Gippius:

> ... contemporary Russian literature (personified by its main authors) has been thrown out of Russia into Europe. This is where one should look for it. [...]. They threw literature out the window and slammed the window shut. Not to worry. One day the doors to Russia will reopen and literature will return there,

---

8   David Damrosch, *What Is World Literature?* (Princeton: Princeton University Press, 2003), 22.
9   Karen Thornber, "Why (Not) World Literature? Challenges and Opportunities for the Twenty-First Century," *Journal of World Literature*, no. 1 (2016): 107–118, 108.

God willing, with a greater consciousness of worldliness than before.[10]

But in reality, this "worldliness" was just rhetorical. The émigré establishment, absorbed by the national agenda, showed very little interest in adopting contemporary Western literary trends and aesthetic languages.

The second option, complete or partial switching to adopted languages, has been practiced by émigrés at various times, including Nabokov, Pozner, Nemirovsky, Brodsky, Zinik, Makine, Shteyngart, and Zaidman. In fact, gradually more writers living outside of Russia began to experiment with writing in foreign tongues. In this way, they foreshadowed the global cultural reality of the early twenty-first century, when universal diasporization transformed what used to be specific (trans)cultural practices of displaced people into "a mode of everyday existence."[11]

The third type of practice consists in using a creolized idiom (writing between and across Russian and the host language, creating translingual texts within ostensibly Russian narratives). Such works present the most interesting case, because they implicitly interrogate the very concept of language, rewriting Russian from within, and destabilizing the Russian literary "center." This kind of practice is reminiscent of immigrant writing, the traditional object of diaspora studies, except the process is reversed. The Russian émigré author estranges not the adopted tongue of the former colonial metropolis (as per the postcolonialist paradigm) and Eurocentric master narratives but his own native language, by creatively manipulating, weirding, and foreignizing it, fusing it with foreign words and concepts, altering it using unconventional syntax, word-play and translingual puns.

While such experimental texts have appeared more frequently in the contemporary period, they were also produced during the earlier stages of the Russian dispersion. For example, alongside the "purists" in interwar Paris was a large group of authors (such as Poplavsky, Felzen, Bakunina, Yanovsky, Shteiger, Odoevtseva, Berberova, and Gazdanov) who peppered their texts with foreign words, concepts, and cultural references—to such an extent that

---

10 Anton Krainii [Zinaida Gippius], "'Polet v Evropu'," in *Kritika russkogo zarubezh'ia*, ed. O. A. Korostelev and N. G. Mel'nikov, vol. 1 (Moscow: Olimp, 2002), 60.

11 Igor Maver, "Introduction: Positioning Diasporic Literary Cultures," in *Diasporic Subjectivity and Cultural Brokering in Contemporary Post-Colonial Literatures* (Lanham: Lexington Books, 2009), ix–xiv, xi.

critics complained that their books read as poor translations into Russian from Western European languages.

Most of the time, this odd linguistic usage served as an ironic reflection of the Russian-French cross-pollination characteristic of the speech of many émigrés, who had no refined linguistic consciousness. These Russian texts ply calques, transliterated French words and hybrid expressions, conveying the flavor of this peculiar Russian-Parisian "dialect," as in the following examples:

> *шомаж, карт д'идантитэ, вакансы, маршан, мезон де кутюр,* concierge, croissant, "bande de châtrés," *консомации, жимназ, лавабо, ажан, апаш, куаферша;* «Подходит ко мне *жином. Садится у вуатюру. О ла-ла!-* думаю» (Poplavsky); « *карт-постальный* залив », « группа дам предавалась *интегральному нюдизму* »; « Он плыл *brasse-омъ coulée* » ; «мулат [. . .] прекрасным *indienne-ном* понесся вперед» (Yanovsky);
>
> «Да можно прямо сказать, что мы, мол, не ручаемся, что она очень странно *пейе* за свой *плясъ,* и что ее *персонъ* не *коне*» (Teffi);
>
> «взять ванну»; «Вы крутите с понедельника» (крутить— снимать фильм (tourner un film)); «Я онетт» (Odoevtseva); "тайна, которой нельзя профанировать никакими словами" (Bakunina); «экзаминировать билан»; «будем вместе ходить по моим туалетным делам» (as the heroine of Felzen's novel *Obman* suggests to her suitor implying shopping for her new outfits) etc.

As the later development of diasporic literature demonstrates, this last strategy of breaking out not only of the "monolingual paradigm" but also of the monolingual/multilingual dichotomy has proven to be the most generative.[12] Since the turn of the century, extraterritorial writers have more dramatically emphasized their postnational and postmonolingual condition through idiosyncratic use of the Russian language. The parodic intent is no longer a dominant motivation underlying this practice. Rather, authors seek more or less consciously to assert their distinctness from the metropolitan idiom, to

---

12 For a detailed discussion of the "monolingual" and "postmonolingual" paradigms, see: Yasemin Yildiz, *Beyond the Mother Tongue: The Postmonolingual Condition* (New York: Fordham University Press, 2011).

destabilize the "original language," and to flesh out their multiple linguistic affiliations. This may also reflect the markedly different political context compared to the postrevolutionary period. First-wave émigrés were eager to emphasize their connection to the culture of their homeland from which they were banned, hence their conservationist pathos, insistence on the purity of the language, and travesty of substandard usage. But since *perestroika*, the place of former émigrés' residence and, more importantly, their cultural and linguistic affinity, became a matter of personal preference—and some choose to highlight their extraterritorial hybridity through unconventional linguistic gestures.[13]

As the editors of the 2003 anthology *Simvol "My"* (featuring russophone Jewish literature created in North America, Europe, and Israel) state in their preface, many decades of emigration and dispersion transformed Russian language and literature into diasporic phenomena. In their opinion, the hierarchy of "dominance and subordination," determined by the geographical location of the text and the author, was replaced by a relationship of "complementary distribution" between metropolis and diaspora. Diaspora writers are therefore encouraged to cultivate their "foreignness," in particular by means of linguistic distancing from the metropole.[14]

It is important to keep in mind that the majority of writers who reject a straightforward national identity and position themselves in a broader, imprecisely defined "world," greatly depend on the metropolitan book market. Published in Russia and read by Russian readers often unaware of the cultural, political, and social parameters specific to these authors' locality, their texts inevitably acquire different significations, losing some of the meanings relevant in the places where they were created. This deterritorialization of meanings and concepts (and acquisition of new interpretations) is similar to what happens to any translated text as it crosses the national boundary and enters World Literature. Far from being viewed as an obstacle, this tint of foreignness is often seen by today's publishers and critics as a marketable feature.[15]

---

13 This chapter was written in 2019 and reflects the post-Soviet situation through the first two decades of the twenty-first century. Since 2022, the new wave of massive and sometimes forced emigration of Russian intellectuals has considerably changed the relations between the metropolitan and diasporic cultures, as they are presented in this study.

14 Irina Vrubel'-Golubkina, ed., *Simvol "My." Evreiskaia khrestomatiia novoi russkoi literatury* (Mosow: NLO, 2003), 6–7.

15 Cf. Kevin M.F. Platt, "The Benefits of Distance: Extraterritoriality as Cultural Capital in the Literary Marketplace," in *Redefining Russian Literature Diaspora, 1920–2020*, ed. Maria Rubins (London: UCL Press, 2021), 214–43.

Over the last decades, postmonolingual practices found strong conceptual reinforcement and practical application in the writing of russophone authors in Israel. The Tel Aviv-based avant-garde journal *Zerkalo* organized a series of discussions about the *sui generis* quality of Russian Israeli writing and its conscious and strategic opposition to metropolitan master narratives and normative language. Critic Yakov Shaus articulated this position unambiguously: "We are fundamentally different from Russian literary emigration. Our texts are not Russian in spirit! . . . 'But the TV brings us the Noise of perestroika and its call' ['Зато доносит телевизия Шум перестройки и призыв']—this is not Russia contemplated from afar by a native, this is not Russian poetry and already not quite the Russian language!"[16] The reference in the last part of the quotation is to avant-garde artist Mikhail Grobman, defined by Alexander Goldstein, another participant in the *Zerkalo* polemic, as "a good poet, but with a psychic essence alien to Russians—and for this reason interesting."[17] Goldstein's own imaginative essays have been interpreted by Shaus as a radical departure from the Russian cultural code: "And Goldstein's new texts about Israel, about the eclipse of Ashkenazi culture—these are not Russian preoccupations! This is not the Russian cultural code. All of it can provoke interest in Russia—but as non-Russian literature written in Russian."[18]

One of the most radical steps towards estranging Russian from its original territory has been taken by Gali-Dana and Nekod Singer, writers, poets, and editors of bilingual Hebrew-Russian journals, particularly *Dvoetochie/Nikudotaim* (the title of the journal, meaning "colon" (:) in both languages, in itself asserts linguistic duality). The Singers seem to have abandoned any commitment to a single language, favoring linguistic polyphony instead. Here, I will focus on Gali-Dana Singer's poetry as a representative case study that illustrates some important tendencies of contemporary diasporic writing. Reflecting on her creative evolution, she says:

---

16   "Ostrov liubvi ili poluostrov otchuzhdeniia? Problemy evreiskoi identifikatsii. Kruglyi stol zhurnala *Zerkalo*," in *Razgovory v "Zerkale,"* ed. Irina-Vrubel'-Golubkina (Moscow: NLO, 216), 448–68, 464.

17   Ibid., 466.

18   Ibid., 464.

Признание власти языка всегда было важнейшим побудительным фактором для меня. То, что вместо единственного тотального языка я обрела два, каждый из которых, казалось бы, потерял своё право претендовать на единственность и тотальность, не пошатнуло моих верноподданнических сантиментов. Да, я получила относительно редкую для поэта возможность взглянуть с тыла на свой язык (свои языки). С той стороны, где обнажены потаённые слабости и немочи всевластных владык. Но только оттуда можно разглядеть и постичь простейшую и насущную в кажущейся своей простоте истину: тотальный и единственный язык, которому присягают на верность некоторые поэты, по-прежнему существует, и это-язык поэзии. И здесь я безусловно не имею в виду этакий всемирный свод метафор и гипербол, рифм и аллитераций, но праязык, осознающий себя и диктующий свои законы сотворения мира через поэтов и посредством современных языков, располагающих грамматиками и словарями.[19]	Recognition of the power of language has always been for me an essential motivating factor. That instead of a single total language I acquired two, each of which would seem to have lost any claim to uniqueness and totality, did not shake my feeling of loyalty. Yes, I gained an opportunity, quite rare for a poet, to look at my language (languages) from the rear. A point of view from which the hidden weaknesses and ailments of omnipotent rulers are exposed. But only from there can one perceive and understand the simplest truth, essential in its apparent simplicity: the total and sole language to which some poets swear allegiance persists—and this is the language of poetry. And I certainly do not mean by this some global repository of metaphors and hyperboles, rhymes and alliterations, but the self-conscious proto-language that dictates its laws of world creation through the medium of poets and modern tongues equipped with grammars and dictionaries.

---

19 Gali-Dana Zinger, "Oshchushchenie zemli, uhodiashchei iz-pod nog (s Marinoi Astinoi)," Kontkest, November 13, 2003, accessed August 5, 2020, https://peregrinasimilitudo. blogspot.fr/2010/07/blog-post.html.

I propose to view the poetics of Gali-Dana Singer, who claims dual allegiance to Russian and Hebrew (and who has also composed poems in English) as a productive model for creating World Literature in the current situation of universal diasporization. It is ultimately irrelevant how many readers her elitist and complex poems actually attract, or whether she even aspires to write herself into World Literature. Her very method illustrates the worldliness that, in Hiddleston's words, "may be intrinsic to the form of the work." The multiplicity of meanings so characteristic of her texts results from the superimposition of different associations. This is of course typical of poetry in general. But the "worldliness" is produced when different sets of associations engage respective cultures, languages, literary canons, and historical traditions on equal footing, forcing a dialogue between them.

To illustrate this point, let us consider the poem "Gorodu i miru" (To the City and the World) from Singer's poetic collection *Osazhdennyi Iarusarim* (2002). From the outset, the poem's title indicates several vectors pointing to diverse cultural contexts. It is a translation from Latin of *Urbi et orbi*, a message of blessing delivered by the Pope on important Christian holidays and addressed to the city of Rome and to the world (traditionally to the entire Catholic community). Singer just changes the stylistic register in Russian substituting the colloquial "gorodu" for the Old Church Slavonic form "gradu" usually used in the translation of this expression. Jerusalem is thereby linked to Rome.

The title also recalls Valerii Briusov's 1903 cycle *Urbi et orbi*, and in this way Singer plugs into the Russian literary tradition of representing Rome. Maria Virolainen traces Briusov's Rome to its portrayal by Gogol as an old, rundown city of faded glory, but which still retains sacred meaning and a capacity for renewal and transformation:

> We see a persistent set of characteristics which shape the reputation of Italy and Rome: the former lost glory and decay on the one hand, and magical or sacral opportunities for revival, for acquiring renewed power and a new story on the other . . . the Russian perception of Rome, recorded both by Gogol and Briusov, is informed by this logic that construes paucity, decay and even death as a pledge of future mobility, renaissance and even transfiguration.[20]

---

20 M. Virolainen, "Rim i mir Valeriia Briusova," *Toronto Slavic Quarterly*, accessed July 20, 2020, http://sites.utoronto.ca/tsq/21/virolajnen21.shtml.

Building a parallel between Jerusalem and Rome of the Russian tradition, Singer shows the city as decrepit, dilapidated, and dusty:

Идейской матери дырявые чертоги [...]	Shabby palaces of Mater Ideae [...]
А дервиша в пыли лежит старуха	and the dervish's old wife is lying in the dust
и пыльной пресмыкается дорогой. [...] Ее змеиной судорогой сводит.²¹	And slithering along the dusty road [...] wracked with serpentine convulsions.

Singer reinforces the Jerusalem/Rome association by weaving classical antiquity into her complex portrait of the unnamed city. *Ideiskaia Mat'* (*Mater Idaea*) is a reference to the cult of the mother of gods, in some ancient sources also identified as Rhea (likewise mentioned in Singer's poem). While Idaea was derived from Mount Ida in Troy, the near-homonymy in Russian between *ideiskaia* and *iudeiskaia* (Judean) transposes this myth into the Jewish context, with Jerusalem becoming the matrix for all cities of the world. The image of the serpent, meanwhile, recalls Briusov and offers a faint hint at the possibility of renewal through shedding the old skin.

Singer uses the spelling of мір according to the prerevolutionary orthography, which is a more precise rendition of "orbi" (as opposed to мир—peace, мір signified world, people, community). This spelling also recalls the confusion about the title of Tolstoy's novel *War and Peace*. It has often been speculated that the original title contemplated by the author was *Война и мір* (War and the World) and only through typographical error or editorial misunderstanding was the alternative spelling adopted and subsequently approved by Tolstoy. Be this as it may, the reference carries special significance in a poem addressing Jerusalem. Its name in Hebrew incorporates two roots: one meaning "city" and the second derived either from שלום (peace) or שלם (entire, whole). Thus, Jerusalem signifies either "the city of peace" or a "whole/indivisible city." The opening lines of the poem may refer to the etymological proximity of the Latin *urbi* and *orbi* (implied in the title), or between שלום and שלם :

---

21 Gali-Dana Zinger, *Khozhdenie za naznachennuiu chertu* (Moscow: NLO, 2009), 53.

Отрадно сознавать, что оба слова, из одного быв извлечены корня, двумя стволами разветвили крону.[22]	How pleasant to know that both words, extracted from the single root, split the tree's crown into two trunks.

Singer plays with the duality of the word *koren'*: the root of a tree and a linguistic root. Her main trope for Jerusalem is that of a "world tree," growing from one root but split into two trunks, presumably Judaism and Islam, Jews and Arabs. Each tree trunk is crowned with a book. Because celestial Jerusalem is very distant, it is unclear whether the books contain an identical religious message, or whether there are multiple conflicting messages:

Один ствол в белом небе держит книгу, другой ствол в черном небе, белоглазый, [...]	One trunk holds a book in a white sky, the other, white-eyed, in a black sky. [...]
Держатель книги держит книгу в небе так высоко, что ничего не видно—она одна, а может, ее много?	The book holder is holding the book in heaven so high that nothing can be seen— is it one, or perhaps many?

The tree is so heavily weighted down with legends, myths, and narratives, that it is on the brink of collapse:

Гроссбухи на вершине накренились, Вот-вот и рухнет груда счетовода	Grossbücher at the top leaned over, The accountant's pile will collapse any moment

Towards the end of the poem, Singer incorporates vague references to Jerusalem's internal conflict into a thick network of folk and mythological allusions and even early Sovietisms:

---

22 Ibid., 53.

Вершки и корешки не поделивши грядущего, мужик и черт на грядках сидят и судят, черт-те что городят, рядят о смычке города с деревней	The peasant and the devil contesting the tops and roots of the future Are sitting in the vegetable patch arguing, devil knows what they are saying About the union of city and country

The formula смычка города с деревней (union/alliance between the city and the country) in the 1930s designated the Soviet social policy directed at bridging the gap between urban dwellers and peasants. In Singer's poem, it may ironically hint at the ill-defined boundaries of East Jerusalem, incorporating Arab villages, some of which are under either Israeli or Palestinian Authority control, and some under Jordanian jurisdiction or with no legal status at all. A city of unique and endless contention, in reality Jerusalem in large part is but an endless amorphous sprawl of barren or chaotically built-up hills with no visible boundary. The immediately following lines refer to the "siege" of the city, rendered in language reminiscent of Russian medieval epic songs describing the military campaigns of legendary Slavic princes:

Они стоят под городом осадой, они сидят под городом дружиной, Рух-птица во древлянах новых княжит и Гарудой с червем земным Нидхеггом бухгалтерскому подлежит учету. (54)	They are laying siege to the city, Legions beneath the walls, The Rukh bird reigns over a new *drevliane* And Garuda, with the earth-worm Nidhogg Will subject it to an account-ing audit.

Suggesting two conflictual perceptions of the geopolitical situation, the "legions beneath the walls" may refer to the Arab villages associated with a potential terrorist threat or with Jewish settlements around Jerusalem, considered illegal by the Arab authorities. The text thus comes alive through constantly shifting interlocking perspectives much more complex than mere self-identification with one or the other "trunk" of the split city.

The destructive potential of the Rukh bird (a giant bird from Arab folklore and *1001 Nights*) is amplified by its appearance in the immediate proximity to the ancient East Slavic tribe (*drevliane*) who murdered Prince Igor and whose city was subsequently destroyed by his vengeful widow, Princess Olga.

Pretending that she wanted to make peace with the rebellious vassals, she asked for a modest donation instead of the usual onerous levy—just one pigeon from each household. But she sent the birds back, each with a flaming branch tied to its leg. Returning to their nests, the birds burned down the entire city. This bird series is continued with Garuda—a mount of god Vishnu. Significantly, the last fantastic creature featured at the end of the poem is Nidhogg of Norse legends, a dragon or giant worm who gnaws at the root of the world tree.

A hostage to its own universal significance, Jerusalem is portrayed as under siege from all the mythological claims to the city. Various imaginative histories, clashing cultural vocabularies, and competing religious and national master narratives are metaphorically gnawing at its roots, and together with the voluminous texts accumulated in the branches of this "world tree" they threaten to send the entire structure crashing down. Despite its association with eternal Rome, the message of Jerusalem's ultimate survival is marked by ambivalence in Singer's poem. Compressing wide-ranging historical, mythological, poetic, and geopolitical subtexts, this poem, to use Hiddleston's words, indeed "comes to life through the dialogues it maintains with the place of its creation––with the broader, multiple cultural histories that its language draws on or taps into; and with itself."

In almost all of her works, Singer creates an original blend between her present *chronotope*, distant memories, and broader historical and mythological narratives. In "Pis'ma k One" (from the cycle "Informatsiia vremenno nedostupna"), the experience of the 1991 Iraq-Israel military confrontation (suggested by gas masks and windows sealed with plastic in anticipation of gas attacks on Tel Aviv) is superimposed onto recollections of childhood visits to her grandmother's house. The image of the grandmother activates the post-memory of the war and pogroms ("крыльцо/куда выходила бабушка Ами и Тами/встречать автоматы цветами" [25]; "как тополь в погромном пухе и перьях" [26]). Insulation against poisonous gases recalls a gas water heater, a feature of Soviet life, and also the Gaza Strip (when filtered through Russian linguistic consciousness, a false etymology is created (*gaz*—gas), absent from other languages):[23]

---

23 Pronounced as *aza* in Hebrew, and *ghaza* in Arabic, Gaza is most likely linked to the Semitic root for "fortress" or "stronghold."

абсолютно ничейный разум не объемлет ничейные земли между стеклом и полиэтиленовой пленкой не говоря уж о секторе газа и поэтому разом вспоминаются газовая колонка и развешанные нестиранные пеленки (26)	absolutely no one's mind embraces no-man's land between glass and plastic film not to mention the gaza strip and this is why one recalls at once the gas heater and unwashed nappies hung out to dry.

The Middle-Eastern geopolitical context creeps into an almost pastoral setting in the poem "At the Dacha" (title in English) subtitled "Utopia." The poem's main topic is making jam in a big basin at the *dacha*, but the summery imagery is woven from many sources, including Karl Briullov's "Italian Midday," a small-scale portrait of a lovely young woman contemplating a bunch of ripe grapes. In the low-tech setting of Russian dachas, basins filled with freshly picked berries and sugar were often placed on a gas primus in the middle of a crowded courtyard:

В тазу с вареньем полдень италийский В глазу конфорки полдень италийский Огонь поводит плечиком брюлловским Медного таза	Italian midday in the basin with jam In the eye of a gas burner Italian midday The flame shrugs the Briullovian shoulder Of the copper basin
В грозу ряд примусов стоит как обелиски В лазури римской медной обелиски Огонь пускается на модные уловки Цыганки Азы (68)	A line of primuses stand in the storm like obelisks Obelisks in Roman copper lapis The flame does the latest tricks of the Gypsy girl Aza

There is something unsettling in this idyllic-nostalgic recollection. In the context of post-Holocaust Jewish literature, "gas" inevitably recalls the gas chambers. The Holocaust and its ancient and contemporary variations constitute one of the core themes of Israeli literature, and Singer's poetry in particular.[24] The gas burner and flame of this poem are subtly associated with Gaza through innocent mention of "Gypsy Aza" (a more direct association is with the heroine of an eponymous late-Soviet film)—by virtue of a phonetic homology between the Gypsy girl's name and the Hebrew pronunciation of the Gaza Strip, as noted above. If the reader is aware of these multiple additional translingual and transcultural allusions, his expectations of a countryside utopia announced in the poem's title are frustrated at once.[25]

A light touch, walking a fine line between and across many diverse meanings, is a hallmark of Gali-Dana Singer's poetic style. The title of her cycle "Osazhdennyi Iarusarim" (Besieged Iarusarim) furnishes a dense exemplary formula of the fusion of cross-cultural references: the title immediately recalls Torquato Tasso's epic poem *Liberated Jerusalem*, except Singer reverses the gaze and switches sides, viewing the conflict from the perspective of the besieged city and not that of the victorious Christian knights. The corrupted name of the city (*Iarusarim* instead of Russian *Ierusalim*), can be broken into sub-modules: *ia* (I), *rus* (Russian), *Rim* (Russian pronunciation for Rome), *arim* (Hebrew for "cities"), and *iarus* (tier in a theater). The last element spells the poet's strategy of building successive "tiers," or layers of meaning. Commenting on this title in his article in Hebrew, Nekod Singer focuses on the connection between Jerusalem and Rome: in his view, by placing the city in this Roman, Western, and imperial context Gali-Dana Singer deemphasizes its Babylonian, Eastern profile.[26] In addition, a visual image on the book cover featuring Saint Petersburg adds yet another dimension, estranging Jerusalem even more. With such a rich palette of connotations, built through the medium of Russian, this title (and Singer's poetry more generally) cannot be adequately rendered in a foreign language. Do words and texts that push the limits of translatability pose a problem for a poet whose ambition is to transcend her mother tongue? Quite to the contrary. Nekod Singer suggests that the sheer untranslatability gives the reader an extra opportunity to engage creatively with the text—by building a philological and

---

24 For example, Singer's poem "Ritual," describing the Passover *seder* in Jerusalem, suggests a reading of the Jewish exodus from Egypt as a foundational story of persecution and antisemitism culminating in the Holocaust and persisting in the present time in other forms, including suicide bombings and other forms of terrorism.

25 Cf. Mikhail Gendelev's poem "K arabskoi rechi," in which Gaza is linked to asthma, real and figurative suffocation induced by the firecrackers periodically launched into Israel by Hamas youth activists, heavy smoke from burning tires, and the Russian connotation of Gaza/*gaz*: "а взять горючую автопокрышку под язык таблетку к въезду в астму Газы негасимой."

26 Nekoda Singer, "Nekoda Zinger: arba ha-birot shel hashirah harusit beyisra'el," Nekudatayim:, December 19, 2014, https://nekudataim.wordpress.com/2014/12/19/nekoda-singer-4cities/.

philosophical discussion around the untranslatable concept: (״לתרגם את המלה
ואת המושג אי־אפשר, אבל אפשר לערוך סביבם דיון פילולוגי ופילוסופי.״)[27]

But if this kind of reflection on the proximity and distance between languages, histories, cultures, memories, and mythologies is engendered in the mind of the reader, do we not approach the ideal of World Literature?

The most direct way to stimulate such a transcultural dialogue is when the author recreates his or her own text in another language, modifying it according to the logic of that language. The reader, provided he shares the author's linguistic competence, has simultaneous access to both versions and can examine the relationship between them. This kind of creative self-translation, resulting in the production of complementary non-identical variants of the work, was previously a rare eccentric practice: its best achievements can be illustrated by Nabokov. But gradually, with the rise of diasporic literatures and readerships over the last decades, it has become more common.

For Gali-Dana Singer, non-equivalent self-translation becomes a conscious exploration of additional dimensions and meanings of her poetic project, and of her own poetic persona. As Adrian Wanner remarks, "a self-translator is forced to grapple with his or her own multiple identities, which may not always be reducible to a common denominator."[28]

Asked whether there is any connection between two versions of her book that came out in Russian and Hebrew, she explains:

Конечно, связь есть. Всё же это один и тот же голос одного и того же поэта, исповедующего одно и то же отношение к двум разным языкам. Новый язык, в свою очередь, диктует различия, иначе, на мой взгляд, не имело бы смысла выходить за рамки русского. И если бы я была способна объяснить, в чем эти различия заключаются, я не писала бы стихи. Стихи—это мой способ постижения мира.[29]	Of course there is a connection. This is still the same voice of the same poet, professing the same attitude to two different languages. The new language, in turn, dictates the differences, otherwise, I think, it would not have made any sense to transcend the Russian. And if I had been able to explain the nature of these differences I would not be writing poems. Poetry is my way of understanding the world.

---

27 Ibid.
28 Adrian Wanner, *The Bilingual Muse. Self-Translation among Russian Poets* (Evanston: Northwestern University Press, 2020), 175.
29 Zinger, "Oshchushchenie zemli."

Poetically, Gali-Dana Singer expresses this idea through the trope of a split tongue:[30]

Непонимание мое, ты тут? Мое чужое, непойманное, ты не оставляй меня. Ужо тебе, негоже мне одной, сменяя двух языков ободранную кожу на жалящий себя ж раздвоенный язык. («Тут» 62)	Are you here, my non-under-standing? My foreign, my uncaptured, do not leave me. Don't you dare! It is not appropriate for me alone, changing the scratched skin of two tongues for a self-biting split language.

Singer lays bare her strategy in "Sonet, perevod s chuzhogo iazyka" (Sonnet, translation from a foreign language). The poem consists of two parts, one entitled "Podstrochnik" (Interlinear translation) and the other "Perevod" (Translation). The first part exemplifies a rough attempt to convey the meaning of the "original" by placing awkward synonymous constructions side by side. It is deprived of any elegance, poeticity, style, and in many respects remains imprecise (it is unclear whether the lyric voice is male or female, etc.). The multiple variants fuse into a robust sonnet in the second part, but the last line is given in transliterated Hebrew:

как розовая жвачка растянулась изо рта Рут из мисрад-а-тайярут.	like pink chewing gum stretched from the mouth of Ruth from misrad-ha-taiarut.

In the "interlinear translation" this corresponds to:

как розовая жевательная резинка изо рта Рути из министерства [конторы] туризма.	like pink chewing gum from the mouth of Ruth from the Tourism ministry [bureau]

---

30 Split tongue (Safa seshua), incidentally, is the title of the novel of another Israeli writer from the Russian aliah—Boris Zaidman. As opposed to Singer, he works in Hebrew only, but his Hebrew is saturated with cross-references to the Russian language and experience.

Frustrating the reader's expectations, this ending raises a number of questions: What is the language of the "original?" Into which language is the "original" translated? No answers are provided, and the "Sonnet" becomes a performance of a multiplicity of tongues, or indeed, the multiplicity of the poetic Self highlighted in Singer's poem by the unlikely a-grammatical declension of the Russian pronoun "I" ("склоняя я—о яе, яей, яю" (57)).

The practice of writing in two languages—and between them—can be approached through Mikhail Epstein's concepts of interlation and stereotextuality. As Epstein argues, in the contemporary globalized cultural reality, with a marked increase of multilingual competence among both writers and readers, the role of translation changes considerably—instead of creating a double or a simulacrum of the original, it produces a variation, "a dialogical counterpart to the original text." Such contrastive juxtaposition of two apparently identical but in fact non-equivalent texts suspends the binary between "source" and "target" languages, making them interchangeable, and each variant allows the bilingual reader to perceive what the other language "misses or conceals."[31] Interlation effectively cancels the idea that something can be lost in translation. It creates the effect of stereotextuality, discrepancies between languages come to the foreground, and a reader conversant in all of them can savor additional shades of meaning and layers of imagery. The "same" text unfolds in alternative incarnations, providing a "surplus of poetic value" but also pointing to more fundamental questions: "Can an idea be adequately presented in a single language? Or do we need a minimum of two languages (as with two eyes or two ears) to convey the volume of a thought or symbol? Will we, at some future time, accustom ourselves to new genres of stereo poetry and stereo philosophy as we have become accustomed to stereo music and stereo cinema? Will the development of translingual discourses . . . become a hallmark of globalization?"[32] And, we might add, a trajectory of World Literature?

The recent poetic experiments and philosophical speculations discussed so far seem to render irrelevant David Damrosch's point that literature stays within its national or regional tradition when it loses in translation and becomes World Literature when it gains in translation.[33] Such rigid definitions cannot account for diverse patterns of writing in and out of the "originary language" and the "national tradition" demonstrated by extraterritorial Russian writers.

---

31 Mikhail Epstein, "The Unasked Question: What Would Bakhtin Say?," *Common Knowledge* 10, no. 1 (2004): 42–60.

32 Ibid., 51.

33 Damrosch, *What Is World Literature?*, 289.

Let us now turn to a different model, exemplified by the francophone Russian author Andreï Makine. As opposed to Singer or bilingual émigré writers of the earlier period, Makine works only in French, his adopted tongue. In 1995, he was awarded the prestigious Prix Goncourt for his French novel *Le Testament français* (translated into English as *Dreams of My Russian Summers*). At the time, Makine's strategy seemed quite innovative. Written in French heavily marked by interference from the Russian language, the novel tapped into French and Russian cultural traditions. Most importantly, its plot revolved around the protagonist's linguistic and cultural hybridity, and a significant part of the narrative was consecrated to the negotiation of a complex relationship between two of his tongues. The pseudo-autobiographical narrator contemplates alternative sets of cultural and historical associations (for example, *derevnia/village*), the phonetic discrepancies recalling very different realities (for example, Russian and French pronunciation of the word *tsar*), etc. Makine effectively engaged with translingualism and cross-cultural translation, which would soon become key concepts in the emerging disciplines of translation studies and World Literature. Translated into dozens of languages, his novel became part of World Literature on any view. Yet, the reception of this author in his homeland was problematic. When the Russian translation appeared Makine was ridiculed, perhaps unfairly, as most of the criticism should have been directed at the translators. Indeed, rendering the French word "enfilade" with the Russian cognate *anfilada,* normally used to describe a grand palatial setting, in the context of the all-too familiar Soviet communal apartment could not but provoke laughter. And there were many blunders of the sort. As a result, neither this nor any other of Makine's works achieved popularity, interest, or wide circulation in Russia. Russian reality, culture and—vitally—language, which were so gracefully transposed by the author into French prose, turned into flat clichés when translated "back" into Russian. This failure in one of the novel's "originary contexts" did not prevent it from participating in World Literature. Why did this text lose so much in translation into the author's native tongue? How could this have been prevented?

For Emily Apter, the Untranslatable is a linguistic form of creative failure with homeopathic uses.[34] Like many other works of bilingual authors whose writing is in fact a form of reflection on their experiences in their homeland, Makine's novel should not have been translated by professionals who had no

---

34 Emily Apter, "Philosophizing World Literature," *Contemporary French and Francophone Studies* 16, no. 2 (2012): 171–86, 178.

choice but to be faithful to the original, but should rather have been rewritten, recreated by the writer himself. Only a non-equivalent translation, an alternative narrative, could have any chance of success with a Russian readership. Makine's example serves as a foil to the creative practices of those authors who not only work across cultures and languages but create parallel non-identical variants of the same literary text.

Finally, let us consider another, arguably a more self-conscious way of writing World Literature by authors from the post-Soviet states. One of the most interesting examples is the Fergana school of poetry, which was active in the 1990s. Its central figures were Shamshad Abdullaev, Khamdam Zakirov, and Hamid Ismailov. They articulated the utopian project of a "new Uzbek poetry" that would draw on Western modernism, Italian neorealist cinema, and Mediterranean literature (Constantin Cavafis' verse was among their key references). The Fergana valley and Uzbekistan more generally were construed as an intermediary cultural space facilitating the interface between East and West. The most paradoxical part of this project was that they wrote exclusively in Russian but elided the Russian literary tradition. Had they embraced Russian literature, they reasoned, they would have been regarded as mere peripheral adepts of the metropolitan cultural lexicons. Aspiring to set their own independent intellectual and artistic agenda, the Fergana poets used Russian as a neutral verbal code for their experimental cosmopolitan verse and also promoted it as a language of creativity that could be shared by russophone writers across the post-Soviet space. This elevated Russian from a national idiom or imperial *lingua franca* to a language of international artistic communication—a far cry from the hierarchical approach of the Soviet language policy makers, who envisaged a dominant role for Russian language and ethnicity in the "union of free nations."

The Fergana practice is reminiscent of that of globe-trotting authors who select English in order to access broader audiences without tapping into any specific Anglophone literary tradition. Their narratives are often characterized by a certain sterility. Released from its deep-rooted connection to a specific cultural territory, with its ethnic, historical, and national discourses, Russian can be positioned alongside "international" English, Spanish, Modern Standard Arabic, or French (especially when it was used as a pan-European literary language in the eighteenth and nineteenth centuries).[35]

---

35 This "international Russian" has recently become more visible, as some émigrés who left Russia as teenagers decide to recover their linguistic heritage through writing. For example, this is the case of Alexander Stesin, a writer, traveler, and doctor who grew up in the United

258 | Maria Rubins

The verse of the Fergana poets can also be defined as "non-Russian literature written in Russian," to use Yakov Shaus' formula quoted above. But in contrast to Russian-Israeli writing, it is not informed by a polemic or ironic subversion of the metropolitan canon. Despite (and possibly because of) this Otherness of the Fergana school, these poets have mostly circulated in Russia, and Shamshad Abdullaev has been awarded prestigious Russian literary awards (including the Andrei Bely prize and Russkaia premiia [Russian Prize]). In his speech at the Andrei Bely awards ceremony, his fellow poet Arkady Dragomoshchenko praised Abdullaev for his characteristic "worldliness":

> I have been most amazed at how he can weave together the finest threads of various cultures into a particular pattern, understanding that he is present in a conversation with great European culture from the shores of Algeria, and at the possibility of a response from Europe by whatever roundabout paths it returns there, at how mighty these invisible linkages can be. I think that precisely this second part, the co-articulation, the creation of these linkages, of these separate cultures (of course they are separate, or they wouldn't be other) is the most important task of the poet.[36]

By co-articulating diverse and ostensibly unconnected works within the medium of his own poetic text, Abdullaev effectively builds constellations, or patterns, that combine authors as broad-ranging as Rousseau, Rimbaud, and Italian avant-garde poets. The concept of constellation was discussed by M. R. Thomsen as a way of drawing less canonized works into the scene of World Literature.[37] Abdullaev's poems that stimulate a parallel reading of texts separated in time and space position themselves in this global literary landscape.

Regarding the Fergana poetry in the optic of the postcolonial theory, Kirill Korchagin finds its rejection of the Russian ("colonial") tradition typical

---

States but made a conscious decision to write books in Russian. In *Afrikanskaia kniga*, for example, Stesin describes his medical work and adventures in Africa, providing fascinating details on the diverse modes of life, social structures, cultures and literatures found across the continent. Given the American cultural and linguistic background that shaped Stesin's profile and the exotic topics of his narratives, his neutral Russian is hard to pin down to any specific location.

36 "Premiia Andreia Belogo za 1993 god (stenogramma tseremonii vrucheniia)," *Mitin zhurnal* 51 (1994): 277–286.

37 Cf. Rosendahl, *Mapping World Literature.*

of the sensibilities of the postcolonial subject.[38] But at the same time, these poets engage in a paradoxical practice of self-colonization, by adopting a view of themselves shaped by a different, non-Russian, type of colonial imagination. They often construct the Uzbek locality in the language of Western Orientalism, long critiqued by Edward Said. Since Uzbekistan rarely figured on the map of European Orientalist literature, among some stand-ins for Fergana we find Damascus, Cordova, or India. Korchagin points out recurrent references to "expansiveness," "monotony," "repetitiveness," unbearable heat, and dead-end dusty streets, which together form the visual image of Fergana, however, "this image does not emerge independently, but is invented, constructed out of the visual elements, associated with the ideas about the magic East."[39]

Among Western visual references through which this "East forgotten in its formlessness" ("Восток, забытый в бесформии") is filtered in Abdullaev's verse, allusions to Italian locales predominate, transposed from books and cinema. The poet openly acknowledges his sources:

Местность, где я открывался открытому и соответствовал себе,—Фергана как повод для снов и отрешенности, Фергана, перекликавшаяся с напластованиями будоражащих аллюзий, с моей внутренней землей, которую я нашел в Италии, воспринятой мной через литературу (фрагментаристы, герметики) и кино постромантического плана.[40]	The territory where I was opening up to the open and was true to myself—Fergana, as a reason for dreams and detachment, Fergana echoing the layers of disturbing allusions, my internal land that I found in Italy and incorporated though the medium of literature (Fragmentarists, Hermetics) and postromantic cinema.

---

38 Kirill Korchagin, "'Kogda my zamenim svoi mir . . .': ferganskaia poeticheskaia shkola v poiskakh postkolonial'nogo sub"ekta," *Novoe literaturnoe obozrenie*, no. 2 (2017), accessed July 31, 2020, https://magazines.gorky.media/nlo/2017/2/kogda-my-zame nim-svoj-mir-ferganskaya-poeticheskaya-shkola-v-poiskah-postkolonialnogo-subekta.html.

39 Ibid.

40 "Shamshad Abdullaev," Ferganskii Al'manakh, accessed July 30, 2020, http://library.fer ghana.ru/almanac/pers/shamshad.htm.

260 | Maria Rubins

What lurks behind this crafted exoticism, however, is a rather apocalyptic vision of a run-down, sleepy city at the southern periphery of the Soviet empire, as in the following examples:

Ни дерева, ни дощатого навеса: только белая стена, залитая огнем,—под нею дуреет желтый, худосочный кот. . . ("Забытый фильм двадцатых годов")	Not a single tree, no wooden awning: only a whitewashed wall splashed with fire— Beneath it a yellow, emaciated cat Is going crazy. . . ("Forgotten Film from the 1920s")
Сломанный стул в тени обгоревшей когда-то двери;	A broken chair in the shadow of a once-burnt door;
оса, парящая по глухому периметру над полуденной свалкой.	a wasp gliding along the solid perimeter above a midday garbage pile.
За городом– холм и пустырь, навлекшие на грудь морскую горечь. ("Тоска по Средиземноморью")[41]	Beyond the town— a hill and wasteland, burdening the chest with sea bitterness. ("Yearning for the Mediterranean")

The palimpsest of East and West in this poetry results from an endless process of cultural transmission. There is an unresolved ambivalence here between self-exotization in the language of the Other and reinvention of the self in terms of world culture. Potentially, the Fergana school embodies a decentered model of World Literature, bypassing the majoritarian Russian tradition and establishing lateral exchanges with a widely understood European legacy.

Coming back to the original question in the title of this chapter, we can answer it affirmatively. "Worldliness" can indeed be built into the text, and Russian diasporic literature, already embedded in the world by virtue of its geographical situation, offers multiple ways of doing so. As we have

---

41 Ibid.

seen, extraterritorial authors deploy diverse linguistic strategies to dissociate language, territory, and national identity. They range from translingual discourses, non-equivalent self-translation, decoupling the language and the corresponding literary tradition, and generating a dialogue between different cultures, histories, and mythologies. Diasporic texts, poised in interstitial locations between counties and languages and informed by migration, spell mobility that stimulates reflection on untranslatable concepts, alternative memories, and hybrid identities. The literary practices described in this chapter interrogate not only the "original language" but also such attendant concepts as "original context," "source culture," "linguistic and cultural point of origin," "home," as well as "target" and "non-target audience." As they negotiate the fundamentals of World Literature, they propose new models of inscribing the "world," thereby shaping this theoretical discourse in many innovative ways. While my examples here were drawn from the Russian context, they illustrate a broader recent phenomenon: global writing created by translingual authors with hybrid identities.

Contributors

Evgeniia Belskaia is a PhD student in history and the social sciences at Paris Cité University, working on a dissertation titled "The French Edition of the Journal *International Literature*: Institutional and Political History of a Journal between World Literature and Communist Literature (1933-1945)." She received her MA in Russian and comparative literature from HSE University, Moscow (2018). She is a member of the online Interlit Project. Her primary research interests are Russian and Soviet literature and politics and Russian-French relations in the early and mid-20th century.

Katerina Clark is the B. E. Bensinger Professor of Comparative Literature and of Slavic Languages and Literatures at Yale University. Amongst her books are *The Soviet Novel: History as Ritual* (1981), *Petersburg: Crucible of Cultural Revolution* (1995), *Moscow, the Fourth Rome: Stalinism, Cosmopolitanism and the Evolution of Soviet Culture, 1931–1941* (2011), and her most recent monograph, *Eurasia without Borders: The Dream of a Leftist Literary Commons, 1919–1943* (2022). Her research interests include Russian culture of the twentieth century (literature, theatre, film, art and architecture, opera, linguistics and scientific thought).

Rossen Djagalov is an associate professor of Russian at New York University; he is a scholar of Soviet literary and cinematic internationalism, Eastern European cultures, and the history of the Left. He is the author of *From Internationalism to Postcolonialism: Literature and Cinema between the Second and the Third Worlds* (2020). Currently he is working on two book manuscripts: *Friendship of the Peoples: the Uneven and Combined Development of Multinational Soviet Literature*, and *The People's Republic of Letters: Towards a Media History of Twentieth-Century Socialist Internationalism* which examines the Left's relationship with various media that connected its audiences around the world.

Susanne Frank is a professor of East Slavic literatures and cultures at Humboldt University, Berlin. She is a principal investigator at the EXC 2020 "Temporal Communities: Doing Literature in a Global Perspective" (FU Berlin) and in the

GK 2190 „Literatur- und Wissensgeschichte kleiner Formen" (HU Berlin). She is on the boards of the Friedrich Schlegel Graduate School for Literary Studies, the publication series „Weltliteraturen" (de Gruyter), and the journal *Welt der Slaven*. The author or (co)editor of several books, her research interests include East Slavic literatures; Russian and (post)Soviet Literatures in (post)imperial contexts; modes of translingual writing; cultural theory; geopoetics and geo-politics.

Maria Khotimsky is a senior lecturer in Russian in the Global Languages Department at MIT. She is the co-editor of *The Poetry and Poetics of Olga Sedakova: Origins, Philosophies, Points of Contention* (2019) and *Olga Sedakova: stikhi, smysly, prochteniia* (2017). She has published several research articles on the institutional history of literary translation and on the aesthetics of translation and translingual poetry. Her research interests include literary translation in Russia, content-based language pedagogy, and translingual poetry.

Georgii Korotkov is a PhD student in Slavic languages and literatures at Stanford University. He received his MA in Russian and comparative literature from HSE University, Moscow (2015). He is core programmer at the online Interlit Project. His primary research interests are Soviet periodicals, digital humanities, and network analysis.

Anne Lounsbery is a professor of Russian literature at New York University. She has published widely on nineteenth-century Russian prose in comparative context; her particular interests include symbolic geography, the aesthetic history of the bourgeois, and ideologies of taste. Her most recent book is *Life is Elsewhere: Symbolic Geography in the Russian Provinces, 1800–1917* (Cornell University Press, 2020).

Elena Ostrovskaya (Ostrovskaia), PhD, is a Pause researcher at the University of Strasbourg, France, and, until recently, an associate professor in the School of Philology at HSE University, Moscow. Her research areas are comparative literature, literary translation, and digital humanities. She co-directs, with Elena Zemskova, the online Interlit Project. Recent publications include "W. H. Auden and Translation in the USSR of the 1930s: From the Soviet Press to An Anthology of New English Poetry," *Slavic and East European Journal* 66, no. 1 and "Perevod i kanon: «Antologiia novoi angliiskoi poezii» (1937)," *NLO* 176, no. 4 (2022).

Contributors | 265

Maria Rubins is a professor of Russian and comparative literature at University College London. She has published widely on modernism, diaspora, Russian literature, cultural relations between France and Russia; Art deco and Jazz Age in European literature and culture; and Hebrew, Arabic, and Russian writing in the Middle East. Her authored and edited books include *Crossroad of Arts, Crossroad of Cultures: Ecphrasis in Russian and French poetry* (2000), *Russian Montparnasse: Transnational writing in interwar Paris* (2015), and *Redefining Russian Literary Diaspora, 1920–2020* (2021). She is also a translator of fiction from English and French into Russian. For more information visit: mariarubins.com.

Schamma Schahadat is a professor of Slavic literatures at Eberhard Karls University Tübingen, Germany. She works mainly on Russian and Polish literatures with a focus on literary theory, translation studies, gender studies, and film history. Her latest publications are: *"Alles ist teurer als ukrainisches Leben." Texte über Westsplaining und den Krieg*, ed. with Aleksandra Konarzewska and Nina Weller (2023); *Central and Eastern European Literary Theory and the West*, ed. with Michał Mrugalski and Irina Wutsdorff (2022); *Weltliteratur in der longue durée*, ed. with Annette Werberger (Paderborn, 2021). She is a member of the Heidelberg Academy of Science.

Galin Tihanov is the George Steiner Professor of Comparative Literature at Queen Mary University of London. The author of six books, he has held visiting professorships in Europe, North and South America, and Asia. His most recent book, *The Birth and Death of Literary Theory: Regimes of Relevance in Russia and Beyond* (Stanford University Press, 2019), won the 2020 AATSEEL prize for "best book in literary studies." He serves on the executive board of the Institute for World Literature at Harvard and as honorary scientific advisor to the Institute of Foreign Literatures, CASS, Beijing.

Edward Tyerman is an associate professor in the Department of Slavic Languages and Literatures at the University of California, Berkeley. His research focuses on cultural connections and exchanges between Russia and China from the early 20th century to the present. His first book, *Internationalist Aesthetics: China and Early Soviet Culture* (Columbia University Press, 2021), rediscovers the intensive engagement with China in 1920s Soviet culture. Current research projects explore Sino-Soviet cultural collaboration in the 1950s and the social imaginary of the Russia-China relationship in the post-socialist period.

Sergey Tyulenev is a professor of translation studies at the School of Modern Languages and Cultures, Durham University, the editor of *Routledge Introductions to Translation and Interpreting*, and a member of the advisory boards of the journals *Translation and Interpreting Studies* and *Translation in Society*. He has published widely in leading translation and interpretion studies journals, and among his major publications are *Theory of Translation* (2004); *Applying Luhmann to Translation Studies* (2011); *Translation and the Westernization of Eighteenth-Century Russia* (2012); *Translation and Society: An Introduction* (2014); and *Translation in the Public Sphere* (2018). His personal website is tyulenev.org.

Elena Zemskova, PhD, is an independent scholar from Israel. Until August 2022 she was an associate professor at HSE University, Moscow. She works on literary translation in the Soviet Union, international literary contacts and periodicals, and Digital Humanities. She co-directs, with Elena Ostrovskaya, the online Interlit Project. Recent publications include an article in Russian on poetic translation in the biography of Tarkovsky (*NLO* 4 [2022]) and "Soviet 'Folklore' as Tanslation Project: The Case of *Tvorchestvo narodov SSSR*, 1937 1,", in *Translation in Russian Contexts: Transcultural and Transdisciplinary Points of Departure,* ed. Brian J. Bear and Susanna Witt (Routledge, 2018.)

Index

A

Abashidze, Iraklii, 207
Abdullaev, Shamshad, 257–59
Abovian, Khachatur, 41
Abramov, Aleksandr, 157
Accra, 222–23
Achaemenid, dynasty, 58n50
Achebe, Chinua, 217–18, 228
Africa, 11, 13, 103, 105, 207, 218, 220, 223, 226, 228n54, 229, 234, 258n35
Ahmad, Aijaz, 25
Aitmatov, Chinghiz, 228
Akhtamartsi, 50
Aksionov, Ivan, 156
Alberti, Rafael, 156
Alekseev, Vasilii, 107–8, 112–13, 133, 170–71, 174–75, 187
Algeria, 227, 258
al-Khuli, Lutfi. See Khuli, Lutfi al-
al-Sibai, Yusuf. See Sibai, Yusuf al-
al-Takerly, Fouad. See Takerly, Fouad al-
Alma-Ata, 209, 212, 221
Aloian, Sirakan (pseud. Grkez/Hrkez), 62
Alpatov, Vladimir, 18n19
Alter, Robert, 81
Ata (pseud), folk singer. See Sailian, Ata
Anand, Mulk Raj, 207, 216, 226–27
Ananun, Davit, 45, 46n26
Andersen Nexø, Martin, 147, 149, 158, 197
Anderson, Benedict, 227
Anderson, Sherwood, 157
Andreev, Leonid, 174, 183–85, 187
Andronikashvili, Zaal, 54n39
Andrukhovych, Iurii, 205n65
Angola, 207, 227, 229
Anisimov, Ivan, 147, 150, 158
Anisimov, Yulian, 157
Apter, Emily, 25, 89, 167n5, 237n3, 256
Appadurai, Arjun, 29
Arabia, 101
Aragon, Louis, 147, 150, 157, 197, 214–15
Arconada, César Muñoz, 158
Arcos, René, 156

Armenia, 36–37, 41, 45, 50, 52–53, 56, 58–60, 62n58, 63–64, 106, 134, 149
Arnold, Matthew, 9
Arouet, François-Marie. See Voltaire
Artsybashev, Mikhail, 174
Ashkhuzh (pseud), folk singer. See Grigorian, Khachatur
Ashkenazi culture, 244
Asia, xiii, 11, 13, 17n18, 67, 97–98, 105, 162, 207–8, 218, 220, 226, 228n54, 231, 234
Assyria, 105
Atkarsk, 73
Auden, Wystan Hugh, 215
Auezov, Mukhtar, 207
Australia, 87n48, 103
Austria, 147, 149
Avdeeva, Ol'ga, 43, 44n22

B

Babel, Isaac, 7, 140, 155
Babylon, 105
Badaev, Evgenii, 17n18
Baer, Brian James, 101, 122n3, 134n45, 162n38, 176n37
Bagdasarian, Robert, 39n11, 40n12, 42n18, 51n36, 56n44, 58n49
Bagritsky, Eduard, 155
Bakhtin, Mikhail, 14–15, 18, 34, 68
Baku, 51, 55n40, 209
Bakunina, Ekaterina, 241–42
Bakushinskii, Anatolii, 158
Balk, Theodor, 158
Bal'mont, Konstantin, 46, 49
Balzac, Honoré de, 127, 134, 136
Bandung, 216
Bannong, Liu, 184
Barbusse, Henri, 7, 147, 149
Barcelona, 215, 221
Bartold, Vasily, 104
Batchelor, Kathryn, 108
Batiushkov, Fyodor, 103, 115
Baudelaire, Charles, 41

268   Index

Baudouin de Courtenay, Ivan A., 44n24
Bauer, Otto, 54n39
Becher, Johannes R., 146–47, 149–50, 155, 159, 197, 214
Bednyi, Dem'ian (pseud), 125
Beijing, 169, 174–75
Beirut, 220–21, 224–27
Belarus, 149
Belgrade, 11
Beliaev, Aleksandr, 194n14, 197n30
Belskaia, Evgeniia, xii, 137
Bely, Andrei, 258
Benavides, Manuel Dominguez, 156
Berberova, Nina, 241
Berdnikov, Georgii, 20n22
Berlin, 10, 77–78, 226
Bertels, Evgenii, 104
Bethge, Hans, 170
Beyle, Marie-Henri. See Stendhal
Bhabha, Homi, 234
Bjornson, Richard, 80
Blackburn, Alexander, 81n38
Blium, Arlen, 11n10
Bliokh, Iakov (Yakov), 169
Bloch, Jean-Richard, 146, 155
Blok, Aleksandr, 46, 103, 110–11, 133–34
Boccaccio, Giovanni, 75n22, 131
Bombay, 208, 218
Bogoraz, Vladimir, 104
Borges, Salvador, 214
Borodin, Mikhail, 168
Borodinny, Betsalel. See Borges, Salvador
Borozdin, Il'ia, 13n12
Bourdeaux, 28n15
Braun, Fyodor, 103
Brazil, 17, 103, 149, 214
Brecht, Bertolt, 140, 215
Bredel, Willi, 155
Brennan, Timothy, 235
Brik, Osip, 70, 74
Briullov, Karl, 251
Briusov, Valerii, 36–38, 40, 42–43, 44n22, 46–47, 49–58, 61–66, 246–47
Brodsky, Joseph, 27n9, 241
Brooks, Jeffrey, 203n58
Brown, Bob, 158
Bruck, Jacob, 158
Bseiso, Muin, 227
Buck, Pearl, 158, 186
Budapest, 20n22
Bukhara, 209
Bukharin, Nikolai, 64, 131–32, 156
Bulgaria, 149
Bunin, Ivan, 46, 48–49, 240

Bunsen, Robert, 31
Burgundy, 28n15
Byron, George Gordon, 98, 111–12, 127

C

Cai, Keru, 187n76
Cairo, 210, 220–21, 224–26, 230–31, 232n64
Caldwell, Erskine, 156
Calmer, Alan, 157
Camp David, 224
Canada, 103, 217
Cao Jinghua, 173, 175
Carmon, Walt, 146, 150, 155
Casanova, Pascale, x, 25–30, 32, 138n4, 153, 173, 193, 206, 210–11, 215
Caucasus, the, xiii, 17n18, 37, 102, 105–6, 220
Cavafis, Constantin, 257
Čavčavadze, Ilya, 54n39
Céline, Louis-Ferdinand, 166
Cellini, Benvenuto, 131
Cervantes, Miguel de, 14, 73, 75, 77
Cezarec, Auguste, 157
Chaadaev, Pyotr, 29, 32
Charents, Yeghishe, 56n44, 58, 63–66
Chavannes, Édouard, 175n35
Chekhov, Anton, 30–31, 115, 174
Chernyshevsky, Nikolay, 155
Chiang Kai-shek, 168
China, 11, 16, 92n1, 101–2, 105–6, 147, 149, 165–76, 180–82, 184, 186, 214–15, 220, 224, 233. See also PRC
Chinese Civil War, 168, 186
Cho, Heekyoung, 173
Chu, Jinyi, 170n13, 171n18
Chudakov, Aleksandr, 69n4
Chukovskii, Kornei, 6, 95n17, 103, 116, 122–23, 126, 128–29, 132–35
Chzhan I-Pin (Zhang Yiping), 171, 174
Chzhu De (Zhu De), 172
Chzhou Shi (Rou Shi), 171, 173
Civil War in Russia, xi, 5, 69, 79, 83–85, 201, 213
Clark, Katerina, xi, 5n4, 7n8, 67, 117n86, 123nn6–7, 139n8, 162n38, 165n1, 175, 176nn37–39, 177n44, 211
Clarke, Johnson Pepper, 217
Clay, Eugene, 158
Clemens, Samuel Langhorne. See Twain, Mark
Coetzee, John Maxwell, 231
Colombo, 223–24
Cold War, xiii, 212, 217, 219–20, 225, 228, 233
Congo, 11
Cordoba, 259
Cuba, 225

Čxenkeli, Akaki, 54n39
Czechoslovakia, 149

D

da Costa Andrade, Fernando, 227
Damascus, 259
Damrosch, David, 3–4, 6, 25, 89, 92n1, 93, 211n9, 240n8, 255
D'Annunzio, Gabriele, 101
Darjeeling, 208
Darwin, Charles, 201
Darwish, Mahmoud, 228
David, Jérôme, 5n4, 96–97, 108
David-Fox, Michael, 7n8, 139n7, 163n41
Defoe, Daniel, 79
Delhi, 221
Dehmel, Richard, 100
Deleuze, Gilles, 55
Demirchian, Derenik, 49, 52n38
Denmark, 149
Dent, Joseph M., 98
Denton, Kirk, 170n11
D'haen, Theo, 92nn1–2
Dickens, Charles, 104
Dikgof-Derental', Aleksandr, 158
Dimitrov, Georgi, 160
Dinamov, Sergei, 146, 150, 153, 155, 158–60, 166
Ding Ling (Tin Lin), 171, 173, 175n35, 181, 187
Diop, Alioune, 219
Djagalov, Rossen, xiii, 5n4, 207, 209n5, 232n67
Dmitrievskii, Vladimir, 146, 155
Döblin, Alfred, 143, 145, 166
Dobrenko, Evgeny, 113, 123n7, 194n13, 204n60
Dos Santos, Marcelino, 207, 228
Dos Passos, John Randolph, 149, 158
Dostoevsky, Fyodor, 25, 30, 187n76, 211
Dragomoshchenko, Arkady, 258
Dreiser, Theodore, 8, 146–47, 155, 159–60
Drieu la Rochelle, Pierre Eugène, 155
Du Bois, William Edward Burghardt, 207, 222n33
Dublin, 116
Durus, Alfred, 155
Dzhavakhishvili, Mikhail, 136
Dzhansugurov, Ilias, 134

E

Eckermann, Johann Peter, 4, 191n4
Eglītis, Viktors, 44
Egor'ev, Viacheslav, 170

Egypt, 11, 102, 105–6, 214, 220, 224–26, 228, 230–31, 252n24
Ehrenburg, Ilya, 7, 79, 174
Eisenstein, Sergei, 155
Eikhenbaum, Boris, 72
Ekwensi, Cyprian, 217–18
Eliot, Thomas Stearns, 27n9, 34
Eliseev, Sergei, 107
Elistratova, Anna, 157
Ellis, Fred, 158
El-Sadat, Anvar, 220
Emerson, Ralph Waldo, 31
Emi Siao (pseud), xii, 150, 156, 167, 172nn22–23, 175–82, 186–87, 213–15
Emin-Terian, Gevorg, 41n16
Engels, Friedrich, 5, 21, 125–26, 137–38, 191n8
England, 100, 149, 216. See also Great Britain
Epelboin, Annie, 5n4
Epstein, Mikhail, 255
Essmann, Helga, 39n10
Europe, 2–3, 12–13, 15, 17, 19–21, 27, 41, 58, 92, 97, 100, 102–3, 105, 162, 201–2, 207, 213, 240, 243, 258
Evans, Christine, 209
Even-Zohar, Itamar, 126–28

F

Fadeich, Ivan, 48–49
Fadeev, Aleksandr, 150, 181
Faiz Ahmad Faiz, 216, 225–28, 230
Fallada, Hans, 155
Fanger, Donald, 32n23
Far East, the, 11, 17, 105, 107, 151, 162
Far North, the, 38
Fattah, Ziad Abdel, 227
Faulkner, William, 28
Fedin, Konstantin, 157
Fedorenko, Nikolai, 167, 175, 182, 184–85
Felzen, Yuri, 241–42
Fergana, 240, 257–60
Feuchtwanger, Lion, 7, 155, 159
Fielding, Henry, 73, 77
Finer, Emily, 72n13, 89n58
Finland, 78, 103, 149
Fitzpatrick, Sheila, 93, 95
Florence, 101
Fonvizin, Denis, 28n15
Forster, Edward Morgan, 215
Foucault, Michel, 3
France, 11, 26, 27n9, 28, 100, 104, 147, 149, 168, 202, 215–16
France, Anatole, 100, 134
Frank, Susanne, xi, 35, 211, 212n10

Freidenberg, Olga, 15
Freinet, Célestin, 147
Fried, Yakov, 157
Fudzimori Seikiti, 214
Fussell, Paul, 84

G

Gabor, Andor, 158
Galicia, 190
Gálik, Marián, 14n14
Galperina, Eugenia, 157
Galsworthy, John, 155
Galushkin, Aleksandr, 69n4, 73, 77, 78n28
Gamsa, Mark, 172
Gamzatov, Rasul, 207
Garuda, mythical figure, 249–50
Gastev, Aleksei, 120–21
Gautier, Judith, 170–71
Gaza Strip, 250, 252
Gazdanov, Gaito, 241
Geider, Thomas, 197
Genette, Gérard, 94, 109
Geneva, 225
Georgia, 40, 54n39, 149
Gergely, Sándor, 156
Germanetto, Giovanni, 150
Germany, 40, 54n39, 100, 104, 144n24, 147, 149–50, 169, 190, 202, 215, 230
Gershenzon, Mikhail, 43
Ghana, 222
Gide, André, 7, 147, 155, 202
Giono, Jean, 145, 156
Gippius, Zinaida, 240–41
Gladkov, Fedor, 156
Glaser, Amelia M., 5n4
Glinka, Mikhail, 28n15
Goethe, Johann Wolfgang von, 4–5, 92, 96, 99–100, 104, 127, 132, 137, 191–93, 198
Go Ma-Jo, 149
Gogol, Nikolai, 30–32, 33n24, 34, 246
Gold, Michael, 149, 214
Goldstein, Alexander, 244
Gollerbakh, Evgenii, 98, 115n80
Gorbachev, Mikhail, 124n11
Gordon, Eugene, 158
Gorky, Maxim, xi–xii, 5–7, 9–10, 12–13, 21, 36–38, 42–45, 46n27, 47–50, 53–54, 56, 58, 65–66, 91, 94, 95n17, 96–103, 107, 111, 113n72, 114, 120, 122–23, 125–26, 129, 131–32, 134, 149–50, 156, 170, 174, 182, 189–93, 196–99, 203–5, 211
Göttingen, 2
Great Britain, 10–11, 168–69. *See also* England
Great War. *See* World War I

Gredeskul, Nikolai, 44n24
Greece, 17
Greenleaf, Monika, 32n22
Grimmelshausen, Johann, 79
Grigor (pseud), folk singer. *See* Paghtasar, Grigori
Grigorian, Khachatur (pseud. Ashkhuzh), 62
Grkez (pseud), folk singer. *See* Aloian, Sirakan
Grobman, Mikhail, 244
Groys, Boris, 202
Gruzinskii, Aleksei, 51
Grzhebin, Zinovii, 97
Gsell, Paul, 156
Guangzhou, 168
Guattari, Félix, 55
Gueguen-Dreyfus, Georgette, 155
Guéhenno, Jean, 157
Gueye, Doudou, 227, 229
Gumilev, Nikolai, 103, 133–34, 170
Günther, Hans (1899-1938), 150, 156
Günther, Hans (b. 1941), 193n12, 194nn16–17, 199n42
Guo Moruo, 181, 215
Guostavino, Luis, 232
Gürçağlar, Şehnaz Tahir, 109n58
Gurevich, Boris, 44n24

H

Haddad, Malek, 227
Haleta, Olena, 39
Halim, Hala, 227
Hamid, sultan, 60
Harri, Aleksei, 158
Harutiunian, S.S., 58
Heekyoung Cho, 173
Heine, Heinrich, 104, 110–11
Hemingway, Ernest, 156, 160, 166, 215
Herder, Johann Gottfried von, 2, 4
Herzen, Alexander, 31
Heslop, Harold, 214
Hickey, Martha Weitzel, 95n17
Hidas, Antal, 150
Hiddleston, Jane, 239, 246, 250
Hiersch, Francine, 196n26
Hikmet, Nâzım, 207
Hitler, Adolf, 162
Homer, 131
Holland, 149
Holland, Kate, 34n28
Holocaust, the, 251, 252n24
Holquist, Michael, 33, 68
Holquist, Peter, 86n47
Hong Kong, 225
Hovhanisian, T., 54–55

Hovhannisian, Ashot, 64n60
Hovhannisyan, Hovhannes, 50
Hrkez (pseud), folk singer. *See* Aloian, Sirakan
Hu Lanqi (Khu Lan–Tchi), 158, 171
Hughes, Langston, 155, 180n49, 215
Hugo, Victor, 104, 111, 129, 134
Hunan, province, 175
Hungary, 149
Husien, Taha, 228
Huss-Michel, Angela, 140
Huxley, Aldous, 143, 145, 166

I

Iaffe, Leib, 43–44
Iceland, 147
Ida, mountain, 247
Igor, prince, 249
Illés, Béla, 150
Inber, Vera, 157
India, 11, 101–3, 105–6, 108, 133, 207–8, 216, 218, 220, 224, 227, 231, 259
Indonesia, 11, 106, 149, 207, 218
Ioannisian, Ioannes, 49
Ionov, Ilya, 101, 129
Iran, 16, 106, 213
Iraq, 227, 250
Isahakian, Avetik, 49–50
Ishiguro, Kazuo, 231
Ismailov, Hamid, 257
Israel, 220, 224, 227, 243–44, 249–50, 252n25
Italy, 16–17, 20, 100, 246, 259
Ivanov, Aleksei. *See* Ivin, Aleksei
Ivanov, Vyacheslav, 97n26
Ivanov, Vsevolod, 174
Ivin, Aleksei (pseud), 175
Izmalkova, Varvara, 114

J

Jakobson, Roman, 122n4
Jamaica, 213
James, Henry, 84
Jameson, Fredric, 25
Japan, 101–2, 105, 107, 149, 168–69, 172–73, 201–2, 214–15, 227, 231
Jasieński, Bruno, 166
Jena, 42
Jerusalem, 246–50, 252
Jiang Guangi, 173–74, 215
Job, biblical figure, 112
Joyce, James, 143, 145, 156, 166, 199

K

Kahana, Mozes, 157
Kadare, Ismail, 205n65

Kafka, Franz, 55
Kaifeng, 175
Kalar, Joseph, 157
Kananov, Georgii, 36n3
Kandinsky, Wassily, 74
Karamian, Melkon, 40
Kars, 62
Kashmir, 208
Kassil, Lev, 156
Kataev, Ivan, 157
Katsumoto Seitiro, 214
Kazakhstan, 134
Kel'in, Fedor, 155
Kensaku, Shimaki (Simagi), 157
Keru Cai, 187n76
Kerzhentsev, Platon (pseud). *See* Lebedev, Platon
Kerzhentsev, V., (pseud). *See* Lebedev, Platon
Khalatiants, Grigorii, 58
Khanzadian, Tsolak, 40
Kharkiv, 139, 165, 176, 214, 221
Khlebnikov, Velimir, 71, 74
Khodasevich, Vladislav, 43, 44n23, 46, 240
Kholodovich, Aleksandr, 18–19
Khotimsky, Maria, xi, 6n5, 72n11, 91, 92n3, 122n6, 128n24, 137n1, 165n1, 170n14, 205, 211
Khrushchev, Nikita, 207
Khu Lan–Tchi (Hu Lanqi), 158, 171
Khuli, Lutfi al-, 230
Kim, Roman, 157
Kimmich, Dorothee, 192
Kirpotin, Valerii, 58
Kiš, Danilo, 27–28
Kisch, Egon Erwin, 156
Klein, Wolfgang, 7n9
Kleist, Bernd Heinrich Wilhelm von, 104
Kliger, Ilya, 34n28
Kolokolov, Vsevolod, 171n19
Koltsov, Mikhail, 150, 157
Kom, Anton de, 149
Konan, Naito, 16n17
Konrad, Nikolai, 14–20, 22, 113
Korchagin, Kirill, 258–59
Korea, 215
Korotkov, Georgii, xii, 137
Kots, Arkadii, 119
Krachkovsky, Ignaty, 103–4, 108, 133
Krieger, Esther, 158
Kruchenykh, Aleksei, 71
Kuchak, Nahapet, 50
Kukushkina, Tatiana, 95n18
Kulik, Ivan, 127–28, 131–34
Kundera, Milan, 27

Index

Kuprin, Aleksandr, 240
Kurella, Alfred, 157

L

La Guma, Alex, 225, 228–30
Lahouti, Abolqasem (Lakhuti), 149, 214
Lamb, Charles, 131–32
Lamb, Mary, 132
Lamping, Dieter, 2n1, 4n3, 138n2
Langley, 217
Lao-Tze, 98
Larbaud, Valery, 27
Lardner, Ring., Jr., 157
Lasky, Melvin, 225
Last, Jef, 156
Latin America, 11–12, 67, 151, 209, 214–15, 217–19, 230, 232, 234. *See also* South America
Latvia, 149
Lazzarin, Francesca, 92n3, 96, 110nn59–60
Leacock, Stephen, 158
Lebanon, 218, 227
Lebedev, Platon, 75n20
Lee, Steven S., 180n49
Lefevbre, Raymond, 213
LEF, journal, 63, 150
Leipzig, 98
Lenin, Vladimir, 35n2, 124n13, 125n16, 130, 146, 158, 168n6, 194–95, 225
Leopardi, Giacomo, 98
Lesage, Alain-René, 79
Leschnitzer, Adolf, 155
Leskov, Nikolai, 33n24
Levidov, Mikhail, 157
Levinson, Andrei, 103, 133
Liao Chzhai (Liao Zhai), 171n17, 112n68
Li Jiye, 174
Li Bai (Li Bo), 170
Likhachev, Dmitry, 19–20
Lithuania, 149
Liu Bannong, 184
Liu, Lydia, 230
Livy, Titus, 131
Llosa, Vargas, 28
Loewberg, Maria E., 111
Lomidze, Georgii, 190n2
London, 27–28, 71, 210, 221, 226
Lorde, Audre, 222–23
Lozinsky, Georgii, 103
Lozinsky, Mikhail, 103, 134
Lotman, Yuri, 34
Lounsbery, Anne, x, 25
Luanda, 221
Ludkiewicz, Klemens (Fenigstein), 146, 150, 155

Lukács, Georg, 33, 140, 146, 156
Lumumba, Patrice, 11, 223
Lunacharsky, Anatoly, 129–30, 146, 150, 155, 159, 165, 173, 213
Lu Xun (pseud.), xii, 149, 167, 171, 172n20, 173–75, 180–84, 185n70, 187, 215

M

Macpherson, James, 38
Madagascar, 2
Madrid, 215, 221
Magil, Abraham, 149
Makine, Andrei, xiii, 240–41, 256–57
Makintsian, Poghos (Pavel Nikitich), 39–40, 46–47, 49, 51
Malevich, Kazimir, 74
Malraux, Georges André, 156
Mal'tsev, Orest, 207
Maltz, Albert, 157
Malykhina, Elena, 231
Manchuria, 186
Mani, Venkat, 93, 99
Mann, Heinrich, 145, 156
Mann, Thomas, 215
Mao Dun, 156, 171, 173, 181, 187, 207, 215
Mao Zedong (Tse-Tung), 168n6, 172, 175, 182n60
Margueritte, Victor, 156
Markov, Vladimir, 170
Marr, Nikolai, 15, 18, 40, 53, 103–4
Marshak, Samuil, 131–32
Martin, Terry, 195
Martinez-Sierra, Gregorio, 115n79
Marx, Karl, 5, 21, 125–26, 137–38, 141n16, 191, 193
Masereel, Frans, 156
Matveis, Voldemars. *See* Markov, Vladimir
Mayakovsky, Vladimir, 63, 70, 155, 179–80, 187
Mayilian Brothers, 51
McGuire, Elizabeth, 173n27, 175
McKay, Claude, 213
Meissen, Thomas, 16n17
Melnikov-Pechersky, Pavel, 31
Merezhkovsky, Dmitry, 240
Metallov, Yakov, 156
Metsarents, Misak, 60
Mexico, 27
Meyerhold, Vsevolod, 169
Middle East, the, 17, 102, 251
Mikayelian, Karen, 38–42, 46–47, 50, 52, 54, 56–58, 63, 65–66
Mikitenko, Ivan, 150
Milburn, George, 157
Miller, Stuart, 82

Minlos, Bruno, 158
Mittler, Barbara, 16n17
Mnatsakanyan, Eva, 50n34, 51n35
Molière, 127, 134
Møller, Peter Ulf, 12n11
Mongolia, 227, 229
Moretti, Franco, xi, 16–17, 25, 67–68, 89–90, 138n4, 141, 173, 201–2, 210–11, 238, 239n6
Moscow, xiii, 11, 28, 30, 36–43, 49, 51, 63, 65, 74, 123, 129, 138–39, 142, 146, 148–51, 153–54, 162, 165, 166n2, 169, 173, 175–76, 189, 192–93, 206–7, 211, 213–14, 221–23, 226, 234
Moussinac, Louis, 147, 150
Mozambique, 229
Murakami, Haruki, 231
Musta Miaki, 42n18
Myasnikian, Aleksandr, 64n60

N

Nabokov, Vladimir, 25, 27n9, 241, 253
Nadezhdin, Nikolai, 32
Nairi, 53, 61
Namur, 84
Narekatsi, Grigor, 50
Nebrig, Alexander, 192
Nechkina, Militsa, 155
Nehru, Jawaharlal, 216
Nekhotin, Vladimir, 78n28
Nemirovsky, Irène, 241
Neruda, Pablo, 215
Nesin, Aziz, 228
Neto, Augustinho, 228
Neupokoeva, Irina, 20–21
New York, 27–28, 169, 221–23
Ngũgĩ wa Thiong'o, 212, 220, 228
Nidhogg, mythical figure, 249–50
Nigeria, 217–18
Nikulin, Lev, 156
Nizan, Paul, 146–47, 150, 155
Noma, Hiroshi, 227
Nuriev, Vitaly, 135nn47–48
Nzekvu, Onuora, 217–18

O

Odoevtseva, Irina, 241–42
Ognev, Vladimir, 150
Ohanjanian, Onik, 40
Ol'denburg, Sergei, 13, 103–4, 108, 116, 133
Olesha, Yury, 156
Olga, Princess, 249–50
Opium War, 168, 186
Orozco, Olga, 158

Ossian, 38
Ostrovskaya, Elena, xii, 123n6, 137, 140nn12–13, 145n26, 151n29, 166n2, 211
Ostrovsky, Nikolai, 157
Ottoman Empire, 45, 58–59, 86n47
Ottwald, Ernst, 155
Ousmane, Sembène, 207, 228

P

Paghtasar, Grigori (pseud. Grigor), 62
Pakistan, 227
Palestine, 229n56
Pamuk, Orhan, 231
Paris, 7, 26–28, 30, 64n60, 139, 142, 150, 153, 175, 193, 206, 210, 215, 221, 225, 240–41
Paroian, Aghajan (pseud. Sazai), 62
Pascal, Blaise, 112
Passover, 252
Pasternak, Boris, 7, 157, 177–78n45
Patakanian, Rafael, 49
Paustovsky, Konstantin, 157
Pavlov, N., 147
Pavlovich, Mikhail, 13
Paz, Octavio, 27–28
Peking opera, 224
Pereda Valdés, Ildefonso, 157
Persia, 58n50, 62n58, 69, 83, 85–87, 101, 149, 168n6
Persian Empire, 45, 58–59, 86n47
Peru, 2, 28
Pesis, Boris, 157
Petrarca, Francesco, 112
Petrograd, 6, 37, 42–43, 47–48, 51, 53, 70. *See also* St. Petersburg
Petrov, Mark, 16n17
Phrygia, 53
Piatnitskii, Konstantin, 43n19
Picasso, Pablo, 76
Pilnyak, Boris, 156, 169, 174
Pinto de Andrade, Mario, 207
Piscator, Erwin, 155
Pla y Beltrán, Pascual José, 157
Platonov, Andrei, 32, 33n24
Platonov, Rachel, 140n10, 143n22, 166nn2–3
Platt, Kevin M. F., 5n4, 243n15
Plekhanov, Georgii, 173
Plievier, Theodor, 156
Pogodin, Nikolai, 157
Poe, Edgar Allan, 28
Poland, 147, 149
Polevoi, Boris, 207
Polevoi, Sergei, 174–75
Poplavsky, Boris, 241–42

274 Index

Poquelin, Jean-Baptiste. *See* Molière
Pottier, Eugène, 119
Pound, Ezra, 170
Powers, Martin, 16n17
Pozner, Vladimir, 240
Prague, 55
Pramoedya, Ananta Toer, 207
Prashad, Vijay, 216, 230
Prawer, Siegbert, 191nn7–8
PRC, the, 183, 215. *See also* China
Premchand, Munshi (pseud), 216
Propp, Vladimir, 75–76
Prutkov, Koz'ma (pseud), 38
Pu Songling, 112, 171
Puchner, Martin, 141n16
Pudovkin, Vsevolod, 155
Punin, Nikolai, 75
Pushkin, Alexander, 65, 136, 199

Q
Qu Qiubai, 173
Queens, Peter, 157
Qing, dynasty, 168, 170n11, 183

R
Rabelais, François, 14–15, 198
Radek, Karl, xii, 138, 147–48, 156, 162, 186, 190–93, 197–205
Ram, Harsha, 117, 177n45
Razumovskaya, Sofia, 157
Reed, John, 150, 153, 213
Rein, Boris, 157
Remizov, Aleksei, 171
Renn, Ludwig, 214
Rhea, goddess, 247
Richter, Trude, 146, 155
Rimbaud, Arthur, 258
Rolland, Romain, 7, 129, 147, 155, 215
Romania, 149
Rome, 246–47, 250, 252
Romm, Aleksandr, 177–80, 187
Rose, Jonathan, 98n29–30
Rosenberg, Harold, 27
Rou Shi (Chzhou Shi), 171, 173
Rousseau, Jean-Jacques, 258
Roy, Manabendra Nath, 214
Rozanov, Vasily, 44n22
RSFSR, the, 149, 196
Rubins, Maria, xiii, 5n4, 237, 243n15
Rubinstein, Lev, 158
Rukh, mythical bird, 249
Rushdie, Salman, 25, 231
Russia, xiii–ix, 1–3, 6–8, 13, 18–19, 25–26, 28–31, 33, 36–37, 41, 43, 44n24, 45–46, 50–51, 54–55, 58–59, 61, 66, 83, 85,
91–93, 99–103, 100–11, 115, 121–22, 149, 174, 196n27, 201, 205, 210–11, 213, 222, 232n64, 240–41, 243–44, 256, 257n35, 258. *See also* USSR
Russian Empire, 36–37, 42–43, 53–54, 59, 135, 195, 203n58
Rustaveli, Shota, 136

S
Saadi, 116
Sabashnikov, Mikhail, 97
Sadat, Anvar El-, 220
Safiulina, Nailya, 140
Said, Edward, 33, 233, 259
Sailian, Ata (pseud. Ata), 60
Saltykov-Shchedrin, Mikhail, 33n24
Samarin, Roman, 20n22
Samarkand, 209
Saratov, 73
Sarian, Martiros, 41
Sartre, Jean-Paul, 28
Saussure, Ferdinand de, 177
Sayat Nova (pseud). *See* Sayatyan, Harutyun, 50, 62n58
Sazai (pseud), folk singer. *See* Paroian, Aghajan
Scandinavia, 100
Schahadat, Schamma, xii, 15n16, 189, 204n62
Scharrer, Adam, 156
Schiller, Friedrich, 44n22, 202–3
Schlözer, August Ludwig von, 2, 4
Schmidt, Michael, 39
Schmückle, Karl, 150, 156
Schnitzler, Arthur, 41
Scotland, 114
Scott, Walter, 114
Seghers, Anna, 145, 156, 214–15
Seifrid, Thomas, 32–33n24
Seifullina, Lidiya, 156
Selam, Hamdi, 213–14
Selivanovskii, Aleksei, 138
Semenov, Grigory (Vasiliev), 77
Semenovskii, Dmitry, 42n18
Senanayake, Ratna, 224
Sender, Ramón José, 155
Senegal, 227
Senghor, Leopold, 219
Serafimovich, Alexander, 149–50
Serveze, Gérard, 157
Sevak, Ruben, 60
Seven Years' War, 84
Shah-Aziz, Smbat, 37, 49
Shakespeare, William, 14, 75–76, 131, 135–36, 150, 202–3
Shanghai, 168–69, 173, 178, 182, 215

Shaniavskii, Alfons, 63
Shchutskii, Iulian, 171
Shaus, Yakov, 244, 258
Shaw, Bernard, 116
Sheldon, Richard, 88n52
Shelley, Percy Bysshe, 198
Sheram (pseud), folk singer. *See* Talian, Grigor
Sherry, Samantha, 140
Shklovsky, Viktor, xi, 6, 15, 67–90
Shneiderov, Vladimir, 169
Shmelev, Ivan, 240
Sholokhov, Mikhail, 201, 215
Show, Bernard, 215
Shridharani, Krishnalal, 208–10, 222
Shteiger, Anatoly, 241
Shteyngart, Gary, 241
Shuichi, Kato, 222n33
Shutskii, Iulian, 171
Siamanto (pseud). *See* Yarchanian, Atom
Siao, Emi. *See* Emi Siao
Sibai, Yusuf al-, 224–25, 227, 228n54
Siberia, 105–6
Sidorov, Evgeny, 229, 230n61
Signiac, Paul, 147
Simonov, Konstantin, 207
Sinclair, Upton, 149
Singer, Gali-Dana, 240, 244, 246, 252–54
Singer, Nekod, 244, 252
Sinyavsky, Andrei (pseud. Terts), 32
Slaveikov, Pencho, 38–39
Slezkine, Yuri, 195n21, 196n27
Smedley, Agnes, 156
Snow, Edgar, 172
Sofronov, Anatoly, 226n49, 227, 228n54
Sologub, Fyodor, 30, 115
South America, 13, 162. *See also* Latin America
Soviet Union, x–xi, 1, 6–8, 11, 14, 17n18, 22, 25, 58, 64, 77, 79, 91, 122n6, 129, 134–37, 143, 177, 181, 189–92, 194–97, 202, 204, 208n1, 209, 211, 231–32. *See also* Russia
Spain, 79, 82, 147, 149, 153
Spanish Civil War, 162, 215
Spear, Leonard, 158
Spender, Stephen, 225
Spengler, Oswald, 10
Spivak, John L., 157
Sri Lanka, 217, 223–24
Stalin, Joseph (Iosif), 7, 40, 44n24, 59, 63, 88, 124, 146, 157, 160, 162, 165, 168, 177, 182n60, 196, 216, 228
Stendhal (pseud), 134
Sterne, Laurence, 72–73, 75–79, 83–84, 85n45, 88, 89n53
Stesin, Alexander, 257–58n35

Stetskii, Aleksei, 132
St. Petersburg, 2, 28, 30, 40, 89n53, 91, 103, 117, 129, 133, 252. *See also* Petrograd
Strachey, John, 156
Sturm-Trigonakis, Elke, 192
Stuttgart, 54n39
Suleiman, Michel, 227
Sun Yat-sen, 173
Sundukian, Gabriel, 4
Surinam, 149
Svyatopolk-Mirsky, Dmitry, 156
Swift, Jonathan, 100

T

Tabidze, Titsian, 177n45
Tacitus, Publius Cornelius, 131
Tadeosian, Hovsep, 36n3
Tai Jingnong (Tai Tszin-nun), 171, 175n35
Tagore, Rabindranath, 92n1, 216
Takerly, Fouad al-, 227
Talian, Grigor (pseud. Sheram), 62
Tang, dynasty, 170
Tashkent, 207–10, 213, 216, 219, 221–23, 225
Tasso, Torquato, 252
Tatar Republic, the, 149
Tatlin, Vladimir, 74
Tbilisi, 41, 51–52, 55, 63, 209
Teffi, Nadezhda, 242
Tel Aviv, 244, 250
Terian, Vahan (pseud. Shvin/Volo), 39–42, 45–51, 53, 61, 63, 66
Teroni, Sandra, 7n9
Terrace, Paul, 158
Ter-Simonian, Drastamat, 134
Terterian, Arsen, 41
Terts, Abram (pseud). *See* Sinyanvsky, Andrei
Thackeray, William Makepeace, 129
Tian Han, 181
Tian Jun ('Tian' Tsziun'), *See* Xiao Jun
Tianjin, 168
Tihanov, Galin, x, 1, 2n1, 6n6, 15n16, 34n28, 39n9, 78, 83, 93, 124n12, 126n19, 138n2, 212
Tikhomirov, Vasilii, 171
Tikhonov, Aleksandr, 42n18, 43, 44n22, 45, 95, 100n34, 110n60, 123, 134, 157
Tikhonov, Nikolai, 207
Tin Lin (Ding Ling), 171, 173, 175n35, 181, 187
Tokunawa, Naoshi, 149
Tokyo, 183n61
Toller, Ernst, 156
Tolstoi, Aleksei, 38
Tolstoy, Leo, x, 26, 73, 136, 174, 204, 211, 247

Index

Tomashevsky, Boris, 68
Thomsen, Mads Rosendahl, 20n22, 138n4, 237n4, 258
Töpffer, Rodolphe, 26
Thornber, Karen, 240
Totomian (Totomiants), Vahan, 47
Toynbee, Arnold, 17n18
Tretyakov, Sergei, 146, 150, 155, 162, 166, 168–69, 174–75, 186
Trotsky, Lev, 31, 168, 173–74
Troy, 247
Tsaturian, Aleksandr, 46n27, 49–50
Tumanian, Hovhannes, 40–41, 46n27, 48n31, 49–51, 52n38, 55
Tumanian, Nvard (Nvart), 46n27, 48
Tunis, 221, 226, 229–31
Turaev, Boris, 104
Turgenev, Ivan, 30–31, 174
Turkey, 50, 60, 62n58, 168n6
Tursun-Zade, Mirzo, 207, 230
Twain, Mark (pseud), 155
Tyerman, Edward, xii, 165, 169nn9–10, 171n18, 211, 212n10
Tynianov, Yurii, 6, 34, 38n8
Tyulenev, Sergey, xii, 6n5, 92n4, 95n14, 119, 130n28, 135nn47–48, 211

U
Udval, Sonomyn, 227, 229
Uganda, 218
Ukhtomsky, Alexei, 238
Ukraine, 23, 149
Urartia, 53
USA, the, 8, 11, 13, 64n60, 100, 147, 149, 168, 174n29, 202, 215, 222, 231, 257–58n35
Uzbekistan, 207, 222, 257, 259
USSR, the, 7, 12, 20, 58, 124, 127, 133, 135, 137–38, 150–51, 153, 166, 168, 173, 176–77, 183, 196n27, 208, 212, 213n12, 215–16, 220, 222n33, 226–27, 230, 232n64. *See also* Soviet Union

V
Vaillant-Couturier, Paul, 147, 150, 159
Valencia, 147, 215, 221
Varuzhan, Daniel, 60
Vasiliev, Boris A., 174–75, 181
Vasiliev, Grigory. *See* Semenov, Grigory
Vasilieva, Liudmila, 226n48
Veniče, 37
Venuti, Lawrence, 180n50
Veselovskii, Alexander, 34, 37
Veselovskii, Aleksei, 37
Veselovskii, Yurii, 37, 47, 58

Vienna, 64n60
Vietnam, 229
Vildrac, Charles, 157
Vipper, Yuri, 20n22
Virolainen, Maria, 246
Vishnu, god, 250
Vitt, Susanna. *See* Witt, Susanna
Vladimirtsov, Boris, 133
Vogeler, Heinrich, 158
Voloshinov, Valentin, 18
Voltaire, 14, 31, 100, 104, 115, 134
Volynskii, Akim, 103, 133
Voroshilov, Kliment, 124
Vorovsky, Vatslav, 100

W
Walzel, Oskar, 22
Wanner, Adrian, 253
Weimar, 192
Weinert, Erich, 149, 156
Weiskopf, Franz Carl, 158
Wells, Herbert George, 71, 100
Whitman, Walt, 28
Wickramasinghe, Martin, 217
Wieland, Christoph Martin, 3–4, 9
Wilde, Oscar, 116
Witt, Susanna, 57n46, 124n10, 167n4, 177n44
Wolf, Friedrich, 145, 156
Woolf, Virginia, 215
World War I, 15, 50, 69, 79, 83–85, 190, 199–201, 203, 214
World War II, xiii, 10, 162, 212, 219

X
Xiamen, 18
Xiangxiang, 175
Xiao San. *See* Emi Siao
Xiao Jun (pseud), 171–72, 186

Y
Yanovsky, Vasily, 241–42
Yarchanian, Atom (pseud. Siamanto), 60
Yasin, Kateb, 228
Yashen, Kamil, 207
Ye Shaojun (Ye Shengtao), 171, 175
Yerevan, 37–38, 51, 63, 65, 209, 221
Yesaian, Zabel, 62
Young, Robert J. C., 210n7, 233, 235
Yugoslavia, 11

Z
Zaheer, Sajjad, 207, 216
Zaidman, Boris, 241, 254n30

Zaitsev, Boris, 240
Zakarian, Anushavan, 51n37
Zakirov, Khamdam, 257
Zamiatin, Evgenii, 103, 133–34, 194n14
Zarudin, Nikolai, 158
Zech, Paul, 157
Zemanek, Evi, 192
Zemskova, Elena, xii, 123n6, 137, 140nn12–13, 145n26, 151n29, 166n2, 211
Zhang Lihua, 184
Zhang Yiping (Chzhan I-Pin), 171, 174
Zhdanov, Andrei, 123, 130–31, 195, 202, 203n56

Zhemchuzhnikov brothers, 38
Zhirmunsky, Viktor, 111–12
Zhou Shuren. *See* Lu Xun
Zhou Zuoren, 183n61
Zhu De (Chzhu De), 172
Zinik, Zinovii, 241
Zinoviev, Grigory, 158
Zola, Émile, 129, 175
Zorgenfrei, Vladimir, 111
Zorian, Stepan, 40n14
Zoshchenko, Mikhail, 157, 174
Zugazagoitia, Julián, 158
Zulfiya, 229

Printed in the USA
CPSIA information can be obtained
at www.ICGtesting.com
JSHW050226180424
61201JS00020B/67